Praise for Rana Dasgupta's *Capital*

"[An] unsparing portrait of moneyed Delhi, no telling detail seems to escape Dasgupta's notice. His novelistic talents are matched by his skill at eliciting astonishing cand passages are incisive summaries of costs of the elite's wealth and privi tions of crises yet to come. Dasgu conventional wisdom about Delhi, money, and the roots of its periodic outbursts of violence, making this one of the most worthwhile in a strong field of recent books about India's free-market revolution and its unintended consequences."
                                                                    —*The New Yorker*

"[Dasgupta] mostly lets his subjects speak for themselves. . . . The interviews at the core of the book are a cleverly tangential way to investigate a city that is among the world's largest—about twenty-two million people live in and around Delhi—and has been made a microcosm of India by the hundreds of thousands who arrive each year as migrants. As we read of Delhi's frantic modernization—from, among others, an outsourcing entrepreneur, a gay fashion designer, a property speculator, assorted tycoons, and the victims of medical scams that extract cash from the relatives of the dying—we trace Dasgupta's personal journey from excited arrival in 2000 to disillusionment."
                                                                    —*Financial Times*

"[Dasgupta] offers a rich and troubling nonfiction examination of Delhi, his adoptive home and the site of some of globalization's most dramatic transformations. . . . Yet what may be most interesting about contemporary Delhi, suggests Dasgupta, is that this packed and broken city represents the eventual future of much of the world."
                                                                    —*Booklist* (starred review)

"A grim picture of a city run by oligarchs and the 'new black-money elite,' where success depends on 'influence, assets, and connections.' This book is highly recommended for anyone looking

"Compelling, often terrifying . . . [Dasgupta's] lyrical encounters with a wide range of modern Delhiites reveal a novelist's ear and are beautifully sketched."   —*The Telegraph* (UK)

"Lyrical and haunting."   —*The International New York Times*

"*Capital* is constructed around a series of mesmerising interviews. . . . Among many lively episodes in Dasgupta's appropriately large, sprawling, and populous book is one describing the experience of driving in Delhi."   —*The Spectator* (London)

"*Capital* is a beautifully written study of a corrupt, violent, and traumatized city growing so fast it is almost unrecognizable to its own inhabitants. An astonishing tour de force by a major writer at the peak of his powers, it will do for Delhi what Suketu Mehta so memorably did for Bombay with *Maximum City*."
    —William Dalrymple, author of *City of Djinns: A Year in Delhi*

ABOUT THE AUTHOR

Rana Dasgupta won the 2010 Commonwealth Writers' Prize for Best Book for his debut novel, *Solo*. He is also the author of a collection of urban folktales, *Tokyo Cancelled*, which was shortlisted for the 2005 John Llewllyn Rhys Prize. *Capital* is his first work of nonfiction. Born in Canterbury, England, in 1971, he now lives in Delhi.

Capital

The Eruption of Delhi

RANA DASGUPTA

PENGUIN BOOKS

PENGUIN BOOKS

Published by the Penguin Group
Penguin Group (USA) LLC
375 Hudson Street
New York, New York 10014

USA | Canada | UK | Ireland | Australia
New Zealand | India | South Africa | China
penguin.com
A Penguin Random House Company

First published in Great Britain by Canongate Books Ltd 2014
First published in the United States of America by The Penguin Press,
a member of Penguin Group (USA) LLC, 2014
Published in Penguin Books 2015

Map illustrations by Jamie Whyte

Page 455 constitutes an extension of this copyright page.

THE LIBRARY OF CONGRESS HAS CATALOGED THE HARDCOVER EDITION AS FOLLOWS:
Dasgupta, Rana.
Capital : the eruption of Delhi / Rana Dasgupta.
pages cm
ISBN 978-1-59420-447-0 (hc.)
ISBN 978-0-14-312699-7 (pbk.)
1. Delhi (India)—Economic conditions.   2. Delhi (India)—Social conditions.
3. Capitalism—India—Delhi.   4. Elite (Social sciences)—India—Delhi.
5. Wealth—India—Delhi.   I. Title.
HC438.D4D37 2014
330.954'56—dc23
2014005338

Printed in the United States of America
1   3   5   7   9   10   8   6   4   2

for the unborn

Oh, Moon of Alabama
We now must say goodbye
We've lost our good ol' mama
And must have dollars, oh, you know why.

From *The Rise & Fall of the City of Mahagonny (1930)* by
Kurt Weill and Bertolt Brecht

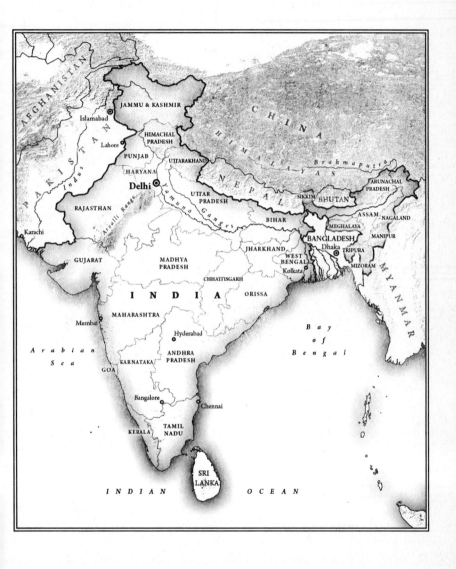

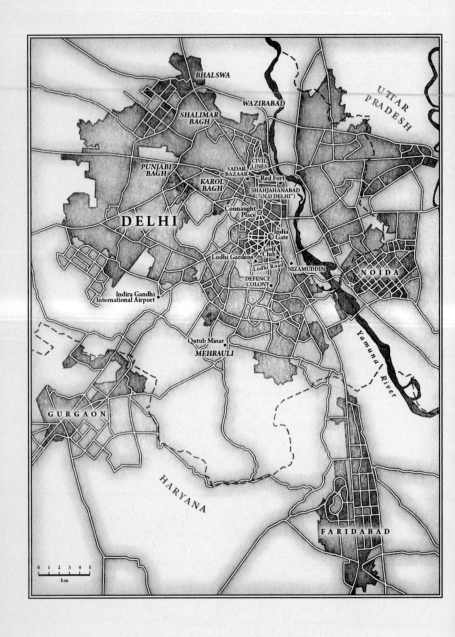

Note to the Reader

This book would not exist were it not for the generosity of several Delhi residents who agreed to discuss with me their lives, thoughts and experiences. These were often intimate discussions, which is why I have changed all names (except of public figures), and, in some cases, other identifying details. I request readers to respect the candour of these people – who sometimes took personal risks to speak to me – and not to attempt either to identify them or, where it is known, to reveal their identity.

In a place – and a world – where a person's intellectual power is judged so much on the basis of their facility with the English language, I have chosen to make all characters in this book speak the same, standard, English so that their widely differing relationships to this language do not themselves become the issue. In reality, English was the second or third language for many of these individuals, and they did not speak it in this standard way; others did not speak English at all, and our interviews were carried out in Hindi. (In these latter cases I had the assistance of an interpreter.)

In Indian parlance, large amounts of money are measured in 'lakhs' and 'crores'. A lakh is 100,000 rupees (Rs), or approximately US$2,000. A crore is 100 lakhs, or 10 million rupees:

US$200,000. I have preserved these terms, which carry so much of the flavour of Indian financial discussion.

In certain places in the world, a 'bungalow' is a modest, even derisory, single-storey dwelling. In their colonial possessions, the British used this word to apply to the self-contained houses they built for their administrators, which were often, contrastingly, generous and grand. This is the usage that persists in modern Delhi – whose British-era centre is full of such houses – and in this book.

Capital is about the members of that rising, moneyed section of the Indian urban population who see themselves as the primary agents – and beneficiaries – of globalisation. It has become common to refer to these people as 'the new Indian middle class', and I, too, employ this phrase. But while their lifestyle has come to bear some resemblance to that of the 'middle classes' in Europe or America, the phrase sits uncomfortably with the Indian situation. At the time of writing, those Indians whose families earned more than Rs 500,000 [$10,000] per year represented less than 10 per cent of the population, which meant that 'middle-class' accoutrements and ideas belonged, in the Indian context, to the elite. Since the Indian economy was being restructured around the spending power of this emerging class, and since this entailed conflicts over land and resources which often punished the much greater number of the country's rural poor – many of whom earned closer to $500 per year – it is important to retain this sense that the interests of the Indian middle classes were not lowly or innocent. The phrase 'bourgeoisie', in fact, which I also sometimes use, more accurately described their condition. At the same time, however, many of those who thought of themselves as 'middle class' did so because they identified with the hard-working, socially constructive overtones of the phrase, and because they wished to differentiate themselves from another, even smaller, elite – far richer and more powerful than they: moguls from the political and business classes, many of whom they regarded as selfish, reckless and fundamentally destructive to society. This distinction is also significant, which is why I generally follow the conventional terminology of 'middle classes' and 'elites' – even though the 'middle classes' are not really in the 'middle' at all.

Landscape

March is the prettiest month, bringing flawless blooms to the dour frangipanis – which are placed artfully around the compound, in pleasing congruity with the posted security guards, who wave me on as I drive up to the house.

The day is done. Evening flowers have come into their own, and the air tides with scent. Ahead of me, under a velvet sky, the glass mansion glows like a giant yellow aquarium.

I park my car according to instructions, and walk out along the low-lit paths. At every corner a guard awaits, and directs me to the next. They pass me on, the guards, one to another, with walkie-talkie confirmations crackling back down the line. I arrive at the house.

The building is like two space stations, one glass and one stone, crossing over each other. One of them floats free of the earth, a shining bridge to nowhere, its underside glinting with landing beacons.

Everything is improbably pristine. The corners are straight and sharp. No gravel spills from the decorative channels that border the path.

The guards instruct me to walk through the house to the swimming pool at the back. They indicate a spot-lit passageway. The sliding doors are drawn half across, blocking one side of the entrance: I set off through the other, open side and – do I hear the guards' warning cries before or after? – walk straight into a sheet of plate glass, so clean and so non-reflective that even though I have just staggered back from it, even though I have just bent double, clutching my crumpled nose, I still cannot tell it is there.

The guards are laughing. One of them runs to assist the idiot visitor. He advises me to enter the passage not through the glass but through the door – a normal door, nothing sliding about it. He demonstrates to me a how a door works so that I do not injure myself again.

I pass through the house. A hall sweeps away from me, done up like a designer hotel. Velvet lampshades in high-frequency colours hang from the high ceiling. Designer couches are clustered here and there around crystal tables. On the walls hang enormous canvasses painted with the kind of energetic soft porn you see on posters for DJ dance nights. Lounge music plays from speakers hidden throughout the building.

I come out on the other side of the house, where everything is lit by that secret, erotic blue that rises from private pools at night. I am led to a poolside seat. A glass is placed in front of me with a sealed bottle of water.

"Sir will be with you in a minute."

In a city of euphemisms, this place is called a 'farmhouse'.

Nothing is farmed here, of course. But when, in the 1970s, the Delhi elite began seizing swathes of land to the south of the city to build private estates, the entire belt was reserved, according to the regulations, for agriculture – and, with a pang of propriety that touched the names of things even if it could not touch the things themselves, they called their new mansions 'farmhouses'. This was especially important since many of the first farmhouses were built by the very bureaucrats and politicians who had made the regulations, severely correct individuals for whom irregularities in the names of things were an offence to the dignity of their office.

In the decades since then, the farmhouses to the south of Delhi have not only increased in number, changed hands several times, and ultimately acquired the legitimacy that accrues to every land grab once enough time has passed. They have also come to epitomise the lives of the city's rich and well-connected, whose astonishing parties, car collections, sculpture gardens and loping Australian wildlife would be inconceivable except in the context of such fantastic estates. In no other Indian metropolis does the urban elite bask in such pastoral tranquillity: this is an idiosyncrasy of the capital. It is striking in fact how Delhi's rich, a quintessentially metropolitan set of people, who have made their money by tirelessly networking in the capital's many clubs and corridors, eschew the urbane. They do not, as the rich do in Mumbai or New York, dream of apartments with sparkling views of the city from which their fortune derives. They are not drawn to that energy of streets, sidewalks and bustle which was so heroic a part of great nineteenth- and twentieth-century cities. No: the Delhi rich like to wake up looking at empty, manicured lawns stretching away to walls topped with barbed wire.

Modern Delhi was born out of the catastrophe of India's partition, whose ravages turned its culture towards security and self-reliance. The compounds in which its richest citizens take refuge from society are only the most extravagant manifestations of a more widespread isolationist ethos. Delhi is the pioneer, after all, of India's private townships, where life is administered by corporations and surrounded by fences, and where one is cut away, therefore, from the broad currents of the country. Gurgaon, the Delhi suburb established by real estate giant DLF in the 1990s, is the largest such township in Asia, and now has imitators all over the country. An expanse of fields until thirty years ago, Gurgaon's looming apartment blocks and steely towers now look as if they have emerged from a computer game set in some super-saturated future. Gurgaon makes no pretence of being a 'public' space: the great numbers of the poor who clean and guard its houses and offices, for instance, cannot live there. To live in Gurgaon is to live in a housing complex protected from the outside by security cameras and armed guards, where residents pay corporations to service all their fundamental needs: garbage collection, water supply and even, in the frequent event that state-owned electricity fails, electricity generation. It therefore appeals to a group of people for whom the corporation has come to seem a far more fertile form of social organisation than the state, and who seek out enclaves of efficient, post-public living.

The place where I now sip my bottled water is venerable. For far in excess of a millennium, men and women have made their lives on the soil where my feet now rest. From my seat by the pool I can gaze up at the soaring trunk of the Qutab Minar, the triumphal tower built in the wake of an ancient conquest of Delhi by central Asian invaders: massive and serrated, it has punctured eight centuries of evenings like this, the only man-made thing, even now, to make any claim on these fallow skies.

In this landscaped compound, every attempt has been made to carpet over the land. But in the nearby woods and wastelands, by the sides of all the roads hereabout, ornate tombs, palaces and mosques press up from the obstinate past – and, waiting here in the gathering night, I sense, even through the hard crust of twenty-first century cement, ghosts rising from the earth, the spirits of those who, for hundreds of years, herded cattle, raised crops, worshipped gods, built settlements, made song, petitioned rulers, buried their dead. Just here, where these mute paths now run perfectly level, on this soil now sealed with emerald lawns.

From the chlorinated depths of the pool rises something else: the recollection of a dream. Eight centuries ago, a few paces away from here, the sultan Iltutmish lay sleeping. Suddenly the doors of his slumber burst open – and there before him was the Prophet Mohammad mounted on the winged steed of Heaven, Buraq. Buraq looked at the sultan with a face that was sometimes man, sometimes woman and sometimes horse; the quivering of its mighty wings produced an indomitable gale. The sultan felt he was being called and, as horse and rider withdrew, he followed them. When they reached a certain place, the horse struck the earth with its hoof, and from the ground spurted a jet of water.

And the chamber of the dream closed again.

In the morning, the sultan went to the place where he had been led in the dream. When he arrived, he saw on the ground a sign – the imprint of Buraq's mighty hoof – and he gave orders for the digging of a new reservoir. Before long there was built a magnificent lake with a mosque in the centre, accessible by boat; there were grand villas all around the waterside, and a vast encampment for all the musicians needed to entertain such an assembly – and the people gave thanks for their ruler's wise and glorious works.

Iltutmish also constructed a five-storey-deep step-well nearby, surrounded by colonnaded terraces where townsfolk could meet and chat by the water. A second step-well, conceived on an even more lavish scale, was sunk next to it a couple of centuries later, so that this place of blistering summers became famous among travellers for the abundance of its water.

The reason these tanks were so bountiful had to do with their position. They were situated at the end of the long and rocky slope that channelled water down from the Aravalli mountains, the ancient range which gnarls India from the state of Gujarat almost all the way to the city of Delhi. In this landscape of brush and dust, moreover, the wells were placed in a forest whose densely rooted soil did not blow away or silt up the system but held water like a sponge and even filtered it in the process. For such reasons, these community tanks were full of water for more than six centuries. As late as the 1960s, they provided sport to local boys who performed the startling feat of diving to the bottom to fish out coins.

Now they are just dry craters in the ground, littered at the bottom with plastic bags and dead pigeons.

It is not just that groundwater levels have plummeted in these decades of ever more intensive extraction, when the number of those packed together in this baked place edges towards the twenty millions. It is also that these wells depended on a delicate and extensive field of capillary action, which has since been carved up by the superstructure of modern life. The profusion of concrete surfaces prevents water from being absorbed into those capillaries, which anyway are greatly depleted by the disappearance of the forests. Industrial drainage systems carry water away from its ancient courses. Tarmac roads interrupt the age-old seep.

The crackle of such ruptures is barely audible to the modern ear. These recent impositions are so much a part of our being that it is difficult for us to appreciate the greatness of the other, alien, arrangements with which they have done away. We are programmed to consider pre-modern engineering infantile, and to treat with scepticism the phantasmagorical dreams of medieval emperors. But when you watch women in the contemporary city gathering water for their families from dripping pipelines or from flooded potholes, the majesty of the dream, and the great works performed in its name, can impress itself upon you again.

Is it because of this history that it feels so deeply *apt* to sit next to this swimming pool? Pools, after all, have been Delhi's salvation for centuries. And in our superstitious epoch when water is faith, not science, when the old tanks stand dry, their technology forgotten, when house dwellers have little clue where their water comes from, when everyone is desperately pumping from the earth whatever they can while they still can – there is something decadently exquisite about this calm and pregnant pool.

Rakesh comes out to meet me at a jog. We have not met before. He exudes immediate charm, which derives partly from the way he throws himself into our encounter, holding nothing back. He looks me straight in the eye as he talks and he frequently slips my first name into the conversation. He arranges wine for me, and makes sure I like it. Such manners are de rigueur for Delhi businessmen, masters of persuasion – but I enjoy them nonetheless.

"Frankly, I was trying to dodge you for some time," he smiles. "I never talk about myself or what I do. I don't do anything for the world to know about it. If I do something, I do it for myself, I do it for my family and I do it for my friends. For nobody else. I don't give a fuck what anyone else thinks."

Two plates of assorted hors d'oeuvres are brought. One each.

"But then I spoke to Mickey. We discussed you. He said you were okay. So I decided to tell you my story."

What surprises me about Delhi business families is how few levels of formality there are. Doors are securely closed until they are not – and then everything is open. If you have come with the approval of a friend, you are automatically a 'bro' – as the slang goes. This is the clannish ethos, by turns charming and infuriating, by which so much of the city functions.

In these inclusive times, it should be said, it is increasingly appropriate to address a woman as 'bro'.

"I've never liked America," says Rakesh. "I didn't finish my studies there. I finished them in England. Plus I had family in England; in America I was very far from home. But generally I've never liked the American culture. It's too opportunistic. Too lacking in *culture*.

"When I finished my Bachelor's in business, I was supposed to come back from England and join my dad. But I didn't want to come back. Luckily we had a close family friend from Delhi who ran a clothing company in Amsterdam. Very different to what my dad does and to what I'm doing now. He gave me a two-year internship over there."

He speaks fondly about his own past. In the distance, his wife walks hand-in-hand with their toddler son around the compound's marble paths.

"Then my dad came to Amsterdam to talk to me about

coming back. I was very happy in Amsterdam but he more or less convinced me to come back. Well, not *more or less*. So that's when I joined him in the automotive business. And I thought, '*I don't know anything about the automotive business.*' I told myself that the best way to learn is to actually make the product with my own hands. So I did that for exactly a year and four months. I worked as a fucking operator on the shop floor. My decision, completely my decision. Because that's the only way I was going to learn.

"Nine months I spent in Japan. In a place called Hamamatsu, about an hour and a half from Tokyo, which is the headquarters of Suzuki. I tell you, that was my – that kind of learning I could never fathom without – I mean today, sitting here, if I hadn't done that, I would be a different man. Unreal, man – I used to wake up at five, I had a room so small that you couldn't fit an ironing board in it – you know, the Japs are very strict on discipline.

"The company I was working for had just begun an alliance with my dad. We had this beautiful relationship because as soon as I got there – usually the Japs are very reserved and everything – the president adopted me as his own son. My desk stood right next to his. They worked open-plan: no cubicles. This was a 300-million-dollar company at that time – I'm talking 1990. But my desk was only for writing my reports in the evening. All day I spent in the workshop, the store and all that."

Rakesh's family has been in the north Indian jewellery business for the last century and a quarter. He emerges from a community of traders for whom business has been far more than a means of making a living: it is an ethos, a form of life, a social identity. His merchant forebears were involved in commercial networks that extended not only across the Indian sub-continent but also along the trade routes leading west to Arabia and Africa, and east to China. These networks were constituted of singular business practices, designed to transcend the gaps of trust arising both from the fact that they comprised many different communities, religions and languages, and from the nature of the jewellery trade itself. Because of the very high value of the goods involved, there was at every link in the jewellery supply chain an issue of credit: merchants could usually not pay up-front for the goods they received. The entire transnational system therefore depended on traders handing over extremely valuable goods in return for nothing except the promise of payment in the future. The problem was obvious: how could anyone be sure that the merchant to whom one had given such credit would ever show his face again?

There were of course penalties for defaulters: the entire trading community would cooperate to ensure that such people were made to pay for their violations – or at least that they never trade in that place again. Merchants also invested heavily in their own reputations, which translated directly into commercial opportunity. They lived magnificently, so that all would know they were financially sound. They gave money to mosques and temples and the poor, they employed poets to eulogise their wealth and integrity, and they made a big show of wounded pride in their negotiations – "Me? You would think this of *me*? You do me wrong."

Most of all, however, they found ways to broaden purely commercial relationships into other forms of interdependence in order to make double-crossing difficult or impossible. They would bind their partners to them with gifts, favours and hospitality – and even through the intermarriage of their families. They would extend to each other a kind of intimacy that was spoken about in the language of friendship or even brotherhood – and indeed it had precisely those depths and qualities unless something went wrong in business. There was not really an 'outside' to the life of business: the household and family were set up to support and enhance it – and to provide trusted partners and heirs – while the pursuit of friendship and social life was never entirely separate from the project of cementing the relationships necessary for commerce.

Such an ethos has been modified but not replaced among the business families of this part of the world. It is striking how many of them found their inspiration in the Japanese corporations that were so significant to the development of Indian industry in the 1980s and '90s – for, vast as these were, they worked according to small-scale principles of hospitality and loyalty that Delhi businessmen could understand and respect. American corporations, on the other hand, seemed, for all their evident dynamism, distastefully distant and ungenerous at the personal level. If contemporary Indian business can seem like a bewildering mesh of personal connections and nepotism, this is in part a legacy of once-august traditions of transnational commerce, which, though they have been overshadowed by the supposedly universal corporation, still give form to the business culture.

"My dad left the jewellery trade and ran a successful fabrics business with his brother until 1993, when they had an amicable separation: 'You have a son, I have a son: let us go our separate ways.' How decent is that? So my dad set up a new business manufacturing seating systems for cars. Later on he got into making automobile mirrors. Then we set up the plastics division in 1999 when I went to apprentice in Japan. He gave me full charge of setting up the plastics division and the headliner division."

"What's headliner?"

"It's what you have on the roof interior. It's like fabric but it's not fabric. It's a full thick composite – it's polyurethane, it's non-woven, it's a lot of things – they're sandwiched in a process, then they're pressed, they're cut by a water-jet cutting machine and then they're finally finished. It's not a simple thing.

"Our turning point was in 2005. Before that we had only one client – Maruti Suzuki – and we were strategising to see how we could expand. We got the opportunity to acquire a metal components company, one of Suzuki's joint ventures. You need to know that when Suzuki came into India, there was no supply chain and they had to develop it for themselves. To develop a supply chain they had to motivate people. To motivate people they did joint ventures. One of the joint ventures was my dad's. And this company we acquired, which made fuel tanks, exhaust systems, suspension, axles, was another. That acquisition expanded our client base. Now we supply five or six big car companies."

Darkness has fallen by now, and, through the panoramic windows of the house, the interior burns with light. Rakesh points out his father, a powerful man, still in his prime, as he walks through the lounge. Three generations live together in this house; business families are powerfully committed to such traditions.

"Currently we're a 2,600-crore company and I'm aiming to double that in the next four years. That's over a billion dollars. Do you realise what that means? It took us sixteen years to get to where we are, and I'm going to do the same again in four. Some of this will come from strategic acquisitions and the rest from organic growth – it's all laid out in my medium-term plan.

"Two years from now I'm looking at 30 per cent of revenues from outside India. Right now it's about 5 per cent. Because there's so much growth in this market you don't need to look outside. And we're still preparing to have the kind of solid base we need to go global. It's not so easy to go global. There are acquisition opportunities coming my way every day but, you know, the easiest thing to do is just take them and then later on you'll get fucked. We'll do it when we're ready for it – we're preparing to make acquisitions in the Middle East and Europe but only when we know it really makes sense."

"Who owns your company?"

"Over a period of time it's gone completely professionalised, we have a management board, supervisory board and all that. But ownership is very clear. The metals division, I own, 100 per cent. The interiors divisions, my dad owns. And the plan is that in two years the entire interiors division will come under my control. And I've made it very clear to my dad I don't want any ambiguity or confusion. No one comes into my business for sure. Apart from that he can do whatever he wants to do."

A man wanders out to the pool. Rakesh introduces his brother-in-law, who has pointed shoes on, a fresh shirt and a lot of gold. He is ready to hang out. His perfume outdoes the evening flowers. Through the window I can see uniformed waiters laying out dinner places for twelve at the long white table. Others have arrived and are drinking inside. It feels like a nightly ritual: I get the impression that a lot of people have the habit of ending their days here.

"In India, the good thing is, our fundamentals are strong. The only thing that will pull us down is the infrastructure and education. If it weren't for the people who run our country, we would actually have children educated and roads built. And the corruption! You know these pollution inspectors? They can hold you to ransom. I've got nineteen manufacturing divisions. Even if every one of them conforms 100 per cent to the environmental regulations – they will still fuck you up the ass. And it's serious. It's really serious. They can seal your company and then you're dead.

"Because I have to supply my customers every *hour*. No interruptions. I hold only three to four hours of inventory. And you know how many cars on an average I supply components for? Just have a guess. A wild guess. Daily. Okay, I'll tell you. Five and a half thousand cars a day. Can you imagine the supply chain, the profit floor, the material floor . . . ? The automotive segment teaches you to work with the highest levels of precision. You can't fuck around with bad components of a car because people can die. You've got to be so accurate. I can't tell my customers I met 99.9 per cent of their requirements. If bad components get to the field and there's a recall, my entire group will be wiped out."

"How did you learn to do all this?" I ask.

"Nearly everything I learned from Suzuki. That company for me is the best company in the world. Undoubtedly. Look at their systems, their processes, their people. The collaborative approach they have in managing their supply chain. It's not: 'You fucked up, so fuck off.' If you fucked up, if you're eager to learn, if you have that bent of mind where you accept that you've made a mistake but you're open to them, they say: 'We'll teach you and we'll be with you for life.' That's the kind of approach these guys have. That's the Japanese approach."

Rakesh has his eye on the friends arriving inside – some have wandered out to say "Wassup?" His staff come from time to time to consult him about logistics, and after each interruption he resumes his sentence where he left it. I imagine him efficient at work, moving rapidly and intently from task to task.

But he needs to join the party. We get up. The house is like a reality theatre: through the glass is an illuminated stage with characters in all sorts of costumes. At one end, friends recline in deep sofas, their Italian shoes twitching in the air, while at the other, a waiter in a white uniform floats fresh flowers in the marble fountain. Above his head are enormous chandeliers made of bright blue Murano glass.

"I have two lives," says Rakesh, contemplating the view. "I have an automotive business, but I also have a real estate business. During the day I'm in fucking uniform. I have an open-door policy: can you imagine what that means in a 2,600-crore concern? But what you see in front of you is the wealth generated from my real estate. Not from my automotive business. Real estate is something that we've been investing in for a long while. Some inherited wealth, some great investments my dad made over a period of time, which went through the roof. Two lives. I don't mix the two lives at all."

He is proud of his house and wants to show off some highlights before I leave. It is clearly inspired by travels in five-star hotels. There is a massage room and a *post-massage chill-out room*. A beauty parlour. A teppanyaki restaurant.

He walks around quickly, pointing out details: "I knew from the beginning I wanted a water body near my dining table, which is why we have this fountain." He is obsessed by small imperfections. He talks about the architect, with whom things ended acrimoniously – apparently because the architect presumed to have his own ideas: "Sometimes all you want from someone is to understand what's inside your head and to get it out." He is quick to explain, in case I should underestimate his vision, that what I see around me is not the final version. The ventilation system in the cigar room has still to be installed. They haven't finished the spa.

One of the men sitting around inside jumps up when he sees Rakesh. They shake hands.

"This is my artist," says Rakesh to me. "He troubles me a lot but he's all right."

The 'artist' has come to show Rakesh the proofs of a party invitation he has designed. Rakesh shows it to me: a large, cushiony card covered in silver tracery. "This is for my big party. I do one every year."

"Here?"

"In my house? No way. They would trash the place. The party is at another farmhouse we have across the road. We'll go fucking crazy."

Rakesh is aroused by the talk of parties, he has had a couple of glasses of wine, and as he walks me out, he is thinking about libidinal things. He looks for something on his phone and passes it to me. On the screen is a photograph.

"This is what I looked like when I was in London. Check out the blue contact lenses. Look how much hair I had."

It is a fiercely sensual picture, fifteen years old. When I hand his phone back, he muses wistfully over the screen.

"Now – you know, I'm fucking married, travelling, eating . . . And life is very stressful. There's a lot of pressure. I'm always thinking the worst of myself and my business. You might think we've achieved something but my ambition is far deeper. I can't relax, man – that's the fucking problem. Most of the time I work twelve or thirteen hours a day, six days a week. The only time

I relax is when I have a massage. I go on vacations some weekends but I can't relax, even on the beach."

We come to the front door. If my earlier collision with the glass left any smears, they have since been cleaned away.

"In the end, Rana, the only thing is values. These days, parents don't have any time for their kids so what they do is throw money at them. So the kids don't have any values. They spend loads of cash doing all this rubbish stuff and not getting anywhere. The only thing they know is money. But money doesn't make you a bigger person. It just means that God has been more kind to you.

"Everyone works hard. *Everybody* works hard – you know the guy who rides the bullock cart? – he works hard. So why is it that I'm here and he's there? It's all because of God. So you have to respect that. You're the chosen one. God has been kind to you – if you don't share that wealth, what good is it? I love my parents, I love my family. I'd do anything for them. I'd do anything for Mickey. If he came and said, 'Get out of this house, I want to move in' – I'd do that for him."

Mickey is the person who introduced us, a prominent real-estate tycoon, younger and richer than Rakesh. I ask how they met.

"You know, I'd come back from Japan and in addition to car seating we were also doing auditorium seating, entertainment seating – you know, with the multitextures and all that. He was building his first shopping mall at that time, and I was supplying seats for the cinema, so I went to his office to meet his guys. And as I went down the stairs to leave, he was walking up, and he asked me who I was and for thirty seconds on the stairs there was this amazing chemistry. And I sent him an invitation to my party that year and my asshole security guys forgot to clear his name and he was turned away at the gate. He didn't even say anything. His grace and humility were amazing, man. And the next year I invited him again. And that party was the real cement of our relationship. We got so close that night and it's been the same ever since."

I'm standing in the night outside. Rakesh says, "But the fact is in this bad-guy world you can be *too* nice to people. People take you for granted. I'm nice. I'm not ruthless, frankly I'm not ruthless. That's probably a drawback I have. I should be ruthless."

And he adds, by way of explanation,

"We come to this world naked, and we fucking go back naked."

I walk through the car park, which has filled up with the sports cars of Rakesh's friends. The moon is bright. I get in my car and set off down the drive, the security guards semaphoring. I pass the massive electricity generators that supply the compound. The guard house. Finally, the gate is opened and I pull out into the street. I drive through the desolate high-walled lanes that wind between the farmhouses, reach the roar of the main road, and head back towards the city.

In Delhi, the road is the place from which people derive their image of the *entire city*. It is a segregated city, a city of hierarchies and clannish allegiances, where very few people from any sector of society enjoy the idea of social distinctions being lost – and it has no truly democratic spaces. Delhi's bizarre vocabulary of residential addresses – much of it derived from the time when the city was a British administrative township, with all the attendant social and security paranoia – says much about what people in this city expect from home: they live in *housing societies* and *estates* which are contained in *blocks*, themselves sub-divisions of *sectors*, *enclaves* and *colonies*. In wealthy neighbourhoods, gates and security guards prevent unauthorised movement across the dividing lines. Social life is no different. Delhi is not like Mumbai, whose citizens readily strike up conversations with strangers in bars and restaurants; here, introductions are necessary. People want to know who you are before they will let you in, which is why name- and address-dropping are so much part of social conversation: people must advertise their connections and allegiances if they are to enjoy a proper social existence. At the top end, social spaces cater to the desire for segregation by allocating price tags, which is why otherwise unremarkable nightclubs can find people queuing up to pay a Rs 20,000 [$400] cover charge.

Not even the snaking Delhi Metro can bring everyone together: though it provides 2.3 million rides a day, it is neglected by both the poorest and richest slices of society. So it is on heaving, honking, smoking traffic arteries such as the one I now drive on – and on which pretty much everyone is forced to move with me – that Delhi residents may have their urban revelation: the entire city, arrayed.

The first thing one notices here, perhaps, is that little allowance is made for walking. Delhi is sometimes compared to Los Angeles because of the highway-like thoroughfares that have grown up over the last fifteen years, which disregard all movement save that of the automobile; and getting around on foot can be fantastically arduous. Middle-class newcomers from other cities sometimes try to walk here, but even before concerned Delhiites can rush to inform them how unseemly this is for people of their station, they discover for themselves that Delhi's sidewalks, where they exist, are a hoax. Setting out on one of these rickety things they have watched it come to an abrupt end; persisting nonetheless with their journey they have found themselves clambering over great piles of rubble, throwing bricks ahead of themselves on which to step through lakes of stagnant water, running madly across eight lanes of a highway – and they have quickly decided to buy themselves a car. This is why Delhi accounts for such a disproportionately large percentage of India's booming car sales – the sales that help to stoke Rakesh's ambitious growth plans. Cramped Mumbai, whose elongation is well served with trains, provides diminishing returns to car buyers; in Delhi, with its broad, radial avenues, nothing works as well as having your own vehicle, which is why the capital, whose cars could have been numbered with four digits in 1980, now sinks under their jammed-up weight.

For middle-class people, therefore, the spectacle of the city is seen through car windows. If a painter were to paint this middle-class view, as, for instance, so many nineteenth-century painters tried to paint Paris from the perspective of its new, cosmopolitan boulevards, it would not, accordingly, be smooth or intimate. There would be no dwelling, like the Impressionists, on details of costume and gesture, no slow rendition of café light falling on pedestrian faces, no capturing of the almost unnoticeable interactions that happen between strangers in a public place. No, it would be a strobe-lit succession of unrelated glimpses: the covers of *Vogue* and *Autocar* flashing in front of the window as a magazine seller rushes between vehicles stopped at a traffic light, the wind-rushed hair of a woman and her child on the back of a speeding motorbike, the one eye of a stray dog caught in the headlights, the glinting instruments of a wedding band – and the whirl of the dancing procession, and the improbable white of the groom's horse – the lipstick of a cluster of eunuchs pressing their faces to the window, the slump of a human form under a blanket on the highway's central divide, a face in another car momentarily stripe-lit as veering headlights dazzle the rear-view mirror – and a host of impressions of other, unformed characters, animal and human, whose identity it is difficult to discern.

This is my field of vision as I drive. Car lights weave in every direction, blinding high beams all, and in the retinal shadow dart unlit human bodies, almost indistinguishable from the night. Horns blare continually, for the traffic is not a stream that carries you with it, but a jungle through which you hack. People drive as if everyone is against them, and in fact it is true: any space or opportunity they do not seize with all the speed and bulk of their vehicle is immediately usurped by someone else. You can see it here, at a red light, where everyone is looking around to make sure no one else is scheming to take their advantage away.

Some cars out front, of course, simply make a dash across the junction, through the contrary traffic – those who wish to assert their freedom from plebeian constraints like traffic lights. The remaining cars inch forward intently, annexing what ground they can, trying to block their neighbours from leaping ahead of them when the lights change. The pack jostles onwards and gradually bleeds out into the junction.

Waiting at a traffic light is not empty time. On the contrary. It is in this ceasefire that the anxiety of the battlefield suddenly erupts. Drivers are racked with apprehension. They light cigarettes, curse, tap the steering wheel, honk impotently. The wait is intense and unbearable.

Finally, the lights turn to green. And at that point, the engines of the cars out front – rearing, straining, irrepressible – stall.

A furious wail of horns starts up behind them – *the light is green, the promise made us is denied, it is too awful, we always knew the world would turn out to be a swindle . . .* – until the dead engines are cranked into life once more, and the swarm moves off.

A strange kind of performance anxiety.

I once drove with an Israeli psychologist who was very disturbed by this spectacle. "*We* had the holocaust," he said. "But we don't behave like this. We've put that behind us. What I see here is slave behaviour. This is survival mode. Why are they so scared they won't get what they want?"

This is not how people drive in other Indian cities. But Delhi is a place where people generally assume – far more, say, than in Bangalore or Mumbai – that the world is programmed to deny them everything, and that making a proper life will there-fore require constant hustle – and manipulation of the rules. Everyone, myself included, uses bribes and connections to get the things they need – a visa, a driving license, a quick resolu-tion of a legal case, a place in a school, a place on a guest list – and if this city seems obsessed by status it is for good reason: power, wealth and networks deliver an immeasurably easier and better life. People who run schools and hospitals spend much of their time, not running schools and hospitals, but attending to the list of important people and their hangers-on who are haranguing them for preferential, queue-jumping treatment – which throws the systems of those places into a similar disarray as the one here on the roads. But no one wants to be just one of the anonymous mass for whom nothing ever happens. One might think that a place of inequalities as entrenched as Delhi's would breed democratic yearnings, but it is not the case: Delhi's fantasies are feudal. Even those who have rather little social power respect the privileges of those who have a lot – perhaps hoping that one day they will enjoy for themselves their same exemption from law and custom. Look at the advertising all around us, with its incoherent mash of mass-culture and aristocracy: this easily available consumer item will turn you into the person who never has to stop at the barriers that hold everyone else back.

Privilege dominates the roads, too. The scramble for driving opportunity is not equal. The status of people hidden behind tinted car windows may be difficult to discern accurately, but in this new era, which has overwritten previous, more indecipherable, forms of status with the single catch-all of *cost*, advantages accrue, quite simply, to the most expensive cars. Mercedes flash Marutis to let them through the throng, and Marutis obediently move aside. BMW limousines are so well insulated that passengers don't even hear the unflinching horn with which chauffeurs disperse everything in their path. Canary yellow Hummers lumber over the concrete barriers from the heaving jam into the empty bus lane and accelerate illegally past the masses – and traffic police look away, for which cop is going to risk his life challenging the entitlement of rich kids? Yes, the privileges of brand rank are enforced by violence if need be: a Hyundai driver gets out of his car to kick in the doors of a Maruti that kept him dawdling behind, while young men in a Mercedes chase after a Tata driver who dared abuse them out of the window, running him down and slapping him as if he were an insubordinate kid. It is easy to see why people do not generally drive a less expensive car than they can afford. Investing in the best possible conveyance yields tangible dividends.

One may imagine where all this leaves everyone else. Cars, though ferociously dominant, transport fewer than 20 per cent of road users. The majority travel by auto-rickshaws, buses and motorised scooters. A significant proportion of urban travellers, however, navigate these packed roads on bicycles or on foot. These are overwhelmingly from the lower rungs of the economic ladder, and motor vehicles give them scant consideration; it is they, therefore, who supply the majority of Delhi's impressive number of road deaths. For while vehicles bump into each other all the time, they are rarely travelling at speeds high enough for their passengers to sustain harm. The speeds are sufficient to do a lot of damage, however, to the ones who put their unarmoured flesh in the way of all this steel.

And for countless thousands of Delhi residents, these streets are not simply a passageway but a home, and their flesh is never far from moving vehicles.

At this hour I can already see them settling down into resting places for the night. There are the throngs of refugees from 'development' and 'real estate', the ones who lived relatively stable lives until they were displaced by the new factories and private townships of India's boom. There are the labourers and religious pilgrims who have come to the city to conduct their business and leave again, and the ones so destitute and uprooted that they have not even been able to assemble for themselves the components of a tent. Here they sleep, in the roving glare of headlights, their heads drawn in under their blankets.

The raised central division of this busy road – the width, perhaps, of two adults – might not look like a desirable bed. But the traffic on either side keeps dogs away, and other animal disturbances. It does not of course prevent heat, cold or mosquitoes – and for the sober, the night will bring only half-sleep.

The sleep that comes from never letting your attention flag. The poor can be robbed too, after all. Even the experienced pavement-sleeper can roll into the road. And if not she, then her children, who are so much more mobile when they dream.

Rickshaw drivers sleep with their vehicles. These provide some insulation, but they bring additional problems. The seat of a cycle rickshaw, while softer than a pavement, is only large enough for a torso; drivers must therefore twist their sleep around their vehicles in the most strange and gymnastic of ways. You can see them now, their feet and legs poked through railings or hoisted into ropes hanging from trees.

These itinerant masses store their personal effects in the furniture of the city. At this time of night you can see people climbing up to retrieve sacks of bedding from the roofs where they threw them in the morning. There is hardly a tree crook, hardly a concrete niche that is not stuffed with the clothes and plastic bottles of Delhi's street dwellers. Cloth bags hang from every protrusion on every wall. Tarpaulin and bamboo poles saved from dismantled lean-tos are lashed into the tops of trees, ready for another building.

The fact that the city's outer surfaces function as a giant bedroom, bathroom and closet for the hundreds of thousands who live in it unenclosed, helps to give the roads a run-down air. But these frayed edges – the cartoons etched on the walls by those who sleep against them, the saved-up string on nails, the blankets airing on a fence – are among the more picturesque aspects of this teeming road. For the constructions of those who run this city are just as ragged, and far more lugubrious. The road I drive on now, for instance, has recently been widened: rows of buildings on either side have had their fronts ripped off in the process, and for months this stretch has looked like a war zone. This impression is all the stronger for the fact that life does not stop in the severed rooms, as everyone driving up against them can see. Even in the upper levels, where it would be possible to fall off the floors' hacked edge to certain death, lights are on, desks stand against walls and clerks cover their ears against the traffic to hear telephone conversations. Calendars on the walls flap in the slipstream of trucks; ceiling fans whisk the exhaust fumes of the street.

Outside, blasted trees stick up like burnt matches from the rubble.

I pass under one of the blistered flyovers across which Delhi's orbital roads soar and dip like a rollercoaster. These scattered megaliths do not feel as if they constitute a system: each of them proclaims different traffic principles, and looks quite unlike the next. Several different construction firms have built them; each has used a different design, a different kind of brick and a different variety of street light, and each has finished things off with its own kind of ornamental flourish. Driving from one to the next is to find the road broadening and narrowing arbitrarily, which creates the crawl-surge rhythm that is so much a part of movement in this city. Two flyovers end in the same place, as if they were not informed about each other, thus feeding fast-moving traffic into a criss-cross swamp of cars from which it takes twenty minutes to emerge.

Like so much of the rest of the city's infrastructure, these gap-toothed flyovers look ancient even when they have only just been built. Delhi's recent multibillion-dollar makeover, completed just in time for the 2010 Commonwealth Games, is already difficult to remember: down the centre of main roads, great sections of the new dividing walls have broken off and fallen into the path of traffic, while the roofs are falling off the rusty Games stadiums, whose car parks lie cracked and empty. The thousands of trees planted to soften the edges of so much new concrete are long since withered, as if they were never intended to outlast the Games themselves. Time in Delhi is macabre: it is a fast-dissolving time that makes bus stops leak and apartment blocks crumble even before they are finished. A time that sinks potholes in month-old roads, built only just well enough to hold together for their inauguration. A time that instantly makes superfluous the avenues recently slashed through slums because the state-of-the-art sports facilities they led to have been padlocked and left to collapse. To be here is to exist in that kind of time in which everything is old even when it is new, in which everything is always already lost to decay and obsolescence.

Nothing endures: everything is passing away before one's eyes, and it is difficult to preserve the soul from the general tendency. Perhaps one can see why the pristine maintenance of Rakesh's private compound was so arresting. In the Delhi context, its force was almost existential, as if, with every piece of gravel his gardeners swept back into place, Rakesh attempted to immunise himself against the general impermanence.

I turn through the heart of British Delhi, still preserved as the city's administrative centre and therefore largely unaffected by the tearing-down and rebuilding that has taken over the rest of the city. The tree canopy is luxurious overhead and the traffic flows freely. I pass two elephants lumbering steadily along the road. Here and there they pause to pull down branches from the trees, which they chew on meditatively as they trudge home from their labours. Car headlights shine at the level of their knees and only their bandy-legs are illuminated: the great dome of their backs, where the sleepy rider sits, rises above it all, into the darkness.

The sight of these animals always fills me with a rush of love for Delhi. Even in the megapolis, they are still improbably vast – vast enough to be a kind of sink for the city's strife, removing, like a rainforest, the poisons from its air.

Just beyond the elephants lumbers something else: a massive water tanker. Large sections of Delhi, and not only the poor ones, have no piped water and must fill their household tanks, expensively and laboriously, from trucks like these. I have never seen one that is not leaking at a catastrophic rate. It seems to be part of the cold humour of this city, where water is so precious that the Water Board that controls it pours half of it away on the dusty roads.

Rusty and battered, this particular truck has the regulation deluge escaping from several places on its underside. For added comic effect the operators have also left the cap off the filling hole above, so that a great wave pours out every time it brakes.

It stops now at some traffic lights, and I stop with it.

The traffic lights are shining constant red and flashing amber together. At other times I have seen constant amber with flashing green, red and green together, or flashing amber in all directions. It would be possible to see this expanded traffic light vocabulary as festive, except that it arises from impotence and gloom – from the authorities' inability to stop nocturnal drivers shooting through intersections like this at high speed, whatever the colour of the lights, killing themselves and others. Traditional red lights were too static, too passé perhaps, to arrest the contemporary rush of life, money and drink. So it was decided to introduce something more spirited and fresh. Lights flashing in different colours might just stimulate people – if not into stopping, at least into a moment of hesitation.

In other cases, the waning power of the light symbols is propped up with text annotations: "Do not move on red light. Proceed only on green light."

Piled up on the pavements are the rusty corpses of the last generation of traffic lights.

A man with severed arms begs at the windows of stationary cars; he cannot take the money, obviously, but proffers his trouser pocket to anyone feeling generous. I wonder how a man with no arms eats. I wonder how he unbuttons his trousers.

The intersection is enormous and pummelled by neon light. The roads are divided by raised triangular islands which are covered with sleeping people. A large air-conditioned bus crosses in front of me, full of retired European tourists reading guide books – or sleeping, too.

All around the intersection are large advertising hoardings. One is for a new corporate housing development called Cape Town. It shows computer-generated images of sunny apartments, well-parked BMWs, cute flower beds and rich, happy, light-skinned people laughing around the swimming pool. Ten years ago such a development would have been named after an American locale. Delhi's consumers have become more worldly in that time, however, and they realise that the American suburb is too democratic and open for their tastes. For glamour they turn now to South Africa, Russia or Dubai, where things are more in control.

Another advertisement is for a shopping mall. It shows a man bursting with consumer glee because he has so many different kinds of outfit to try on. The slogan says, "Change Keeps Boring Away." It takes me a moment to realise what these words mean. Having just driven forty minutes through a much-punctured city, I am led immediately to thoughts of drills. Of the enormous perforations that have opened up in Delhi's consciousness during this period of transition. But then I realise that the advertisement is talking, neologistically, about *boredom*. In this churning metropolis of instant millionaires and imperial ambition, where people who fifteen years ago had not seen a microwave now drive Lamborghinis – the biggest threat, apparently, is ennui.

Next to the advertising hoardings is a big garbage heap. Pigs nuzzle among plastic bags and rotting food. I scan the scruffy sign above it, which says, "There Are No Bars To Excrement." Surprised, I look at it again. This time it says, "There Are No Bars To Excellence."

I must be tired.

The lights change. The water tanker heaves, and another tide washes over its back, drenching the road. I turn under another cavernous flyover where lines of washing hang, adults sleep and children play with sticks. I am on the last stretch before home.

Suddenly the cars around me are braking and swerving. In front of me, the traffic parts, and I see, standing in my path, a young man dressed in rags. I slow down, expecting him to get out of the way. But he stands his ground, stares at me haughtily and holds up his palm so I halt. My car stops a few inches from where he is standing. For a few moments we stare into each other's eyes. He is about sixteen and his hair is wild. Around his neck he wears a great number of tinsel garlands adorned with images of elemental divine power. Kali, Durga and Shiva. There are so many of them that the bundle of tinsel around his neck rises over his ears and covers half his face.

Over the top of these garlands he wears a similar number of corporate swipe cards on woven ribbons: those magnetic cards with digital photographs which so many corporate employees wear around their necks to access their offices. He wears thirty or forty of them, keys to the new global networks.

It is a technique that has long stood people in good stead in this much-pillaged part of the world. Hang on to your old gods, but don't ignore the new.

As I look at him, he grabs one of these magnetic cards and holds it up to me imperiously: "You will go when I say." He stares into my eyes, and his look is blazing and magnificent. We stare at each other for an indefinable moment: he holds my gaze until he is satisfied that I have accepted his authority. Then he wanders away into the racing lines of traffic. I watch him recede, take my foot off the brake, and set off again for home.

One

It is said of Indian cities that Calcutta, the former British
capital, owned the nineteenth century, Bombay, centre of
films and corporations, possessed the twentieth, while Delhi,
seat of politics, has the twenty-first.

Before 1911, when the British uprooted their administration and
moved it to Delhi, the capital of India was Calcutta, in the eastern
state of Bengal. Decades of interaction with imperial personnel
had created there an anglicised middle class, which supplied a
great number of bureaucrats and professionals to the Raj. One
of them was my father's father, an accountant who worked in
British companies all over northern India.

Until the Partition of 1947, which divided the British territory in the west and the east into the two new states of India
and (East and West) Pakistan, my grandfather was chief accountant
with Commercial Union Assurance in Lahore, and it is from
there that my father's earliest memories float back. They are
fond: the family was affluent, the city harmonious. My father
remembers affectionately the vibrant mix of Hindus, Muslims
and Sikhs in his school, his gracious Muslim headmaster. But
as his tenth year drew on, it became apparent that political
machinations would mutilate this tranquil existence. As Partition

approached, the Police Commissioner of Lahore, Allauddin Khan, who was my grandfather's bridge partner, became concerned for the safety of his Hindu friend: he sent his car to take the family to the railway station. He then deputed guards to accompany them on the train as far as Amritsar, on the other side of the imminent cleavage. Allauddin Khan probably saved their lives: in the ensuing violence, the building in which they had lived was burned down and the Hindu landlord and his family murdered.

My father's family returned to Bengal, where the other, eastern, Partition was in progress, and my father found himself on the other side of the game. He remembers the unreal sight of slaughtered Muslims lined up like trophies in the Calcutta streets.

Something seems to have snapped in my grandfather after those upheavals. He became moody and withdrawn. He secured another well-paid position, but walked out of it on a point of principle. Suddenly there was no income for his family of nine children. The electricity was cut off. They could not afford food or candles. My grandfather borrowed from moneylenders to pay his bills; when they sent thugs to reclaim the loans, it was my thirteen-year-old father who had to plead with them in the street, for my grandfather, who wanted to know nothing of all this, was shut up in a room smoking cigarettes and reading English spy novels.

Friends and relatives shunned them. My father got a job selling cooking oil door-to-door, and so kept the entire family from starvation.

He sold, first of all, to people he knew. One day he knocked on the door of an aunt who, seeing how gaunt he was, offered him lunch. From there he took his wares to the house of another aunt, and she too offered him food. Since he did not know when he would be able to eat again, he accepted and sat down to the meal. But he was still in the middle of it when the first aunt came to call and saw him stuffing himself for the second time. Telling the story sixty years later, my father still shakes with the humiliation of having been caught out in such desperation.

Things turned for the better. My grandfather got another job, as chief accountant of a British tractor company. The job was in Delhi: the whole family moved to the capital and took up residence in a district named Karol Bagh – a former Mughal garden, as the name ('bagh') implies, settled in the early twentieth century by communities evicted from villages levelled for the British city and, still later, and in much greater numbers, by refugees from Partition. But in the 1950s the place still had a leafy feel: my father remembers parks and lazy streets through which he walked to school. "Delhi was beautiful," my father says. "I used to borrow a bike and ride all over the city on those enormous, empty roads."

In an era when the ideal of every middle-class Indian family was a job for life, my grandfather held on to this one for a year. He begrudged his Scottish superior, a Mr McPherson, and decided he would complain about him to the managing director, who worked in Calcutta. Exploiting his position as senior accountant, he arm-twisted the treasurer into giving him money from petty cash to pay for a first-class rail ticket, and departed for Calcutta in search of satisfaction. He was immediately sacked.

My grandfather was an anglophile. His most prominent theory of child-rearing was: "They must speak English." He demanded English at the dinner table and, when away from home, wrote letters in English to his children in an elegant, fussy hand. But after he was uprooted from Lahore, his situation in British companies seems to have rankled in deep and private ways: certainly it drove him to erupt regularly over indignities, real or imagined, to the dismay of all around him. Plunged back into poverty, the family returned to Calcutta. More jobs came and went. An English boss requested my grandfather not to smoke in the office: he understood this as an anti-Indian slight and walked out of his employment.

My grandmother, who came from a wealthy family, was bent

close to insanity by those years of fear and hunger, of social humiliations, of children studying in the stairwell, where the lights were left on for just this purpose by a sympathetic Sikh caretaker. She reminisced endlessly about Lahore, now lost to Pakistan, where life had provided and they had been happy.

It was in this context that my father conceived his plan to redeem the family. Germany was offering cheap passage and guaranteed employment to those who would come there as Gastarbeiter. He decided he would use this as a bridge to studying in England; when he returned, he thought, there would never again be question of unemployment or hunger.

In the weeks before his departure, his anglophile father sat on the balcony calling out proudly to passers-by: "My son is going to England!"

My father embarked in Bombay and spent two of the most carefree weeks of his life sailing across the Arabian Sea, passing through the Suez Canal into the Mediterranean and docking, finally, in Genoa. He took a train to Stuttgart, where he worked for a year as an unskilled labourer in a paper factory. In 1962, he arrived in London. He began to study accountancy and to work for British Rail. With his first pay cheque he bought a Parker pen for his father, who wrote to thank him: "I can say with confidence that the pen you sent me is the most famous pen in India. In Calcutta, at least, there is not a man with eyes who has not seen it."

He went to look at a room in the house of a young Jewish couple in east London. The wife had arrived as a refugee from Hitler and was the only member of her family to have escaped the Nazi death camps. He liked them, they liked him. But another bedroom was already rented to a white South African, who was alarmed when he realised my father was looking to move in. He took the landlady aside in consternation: "I can't live with a Coloured man!"

"Then you can leave today," she replied, and evicted him. My father lived in that house for years.

London was supposed to be temporary. My father's home was in Calcutta, and that was where he would return. He missed his beloved Hindustani classical music, which was just then enjoying an amazing efflorescence in Calcutta: much of his teens he had spent listening, ticketless, at the windows of all-night concerts. And he had raised no protest against the engagement that was arranged for him before his departure – an attempt by his family to inoculate him, for the duration of his absence, against the pernicious attentions of Western girls.

But London in the early 1960s gave my father an ecstatic jolt. He had always wanted to be free of constraints, and now he found himself in a freewheeling world of people and experiences. He read about European history. He fell in love with jazz: he went to see Ella and Louis at the Albert Hall. He found himself in a professional system that was gratifying in its simplicity: you worked hard and you got promoted – and before long he could send money home. He was surrounded by other newcomers like him, free, suddenly, of all ties, and ready to live hard. He had girlfriends. He went to see movies and West End shows.

On 12 November 1965, he bought a newspaper in his lunch hour to read about the Rhodesian declaration of independence from the British empire, which had been telegrammed to London on the previous day. Having lived through the paroxysms of one British colony's independence, he was electrified to read of this audacious secession of another. He walked into a restaurant and was seated at the only remaining place, which was opposite a pretty young woman. He remained buried in his newspaper, however, until the waitress mistakenly served his dish to his neighbour and hers to him. Laughing, my father and the woman exchanged plates and began to talk. They arranged to meet again the next day.

The beginning of this relationship says something more extraordinary about my mother than about my father. He had seen something of the world, he was far from home, and he was twenty-seven years old. My mother was eighteen and working as a clerk in an insurance company. She still lived with her working-class parents in a small town in Essex, where life revolved around church fêtes, neighbourhood gossip and fish for tea on Fridays. She had met precisely one Indian before that day in 1965. There were many around her who were appalled at this new friendship. Her parents were unhappy; friends stopped speaking to her. And yet the romance endured. They went on holiday to Italy. My father sent photographs to show his family in Calcutta what European idylls he was now able to enjoy; he took scissors to them so they would not see the Western girl with whom he travelled.

He still entertained the idea that all this was temporary and he was eventually going back. But as time went by, he found himself drawn in. Before long, he was married, living in Kent, and playing on the village cricket team. Before long he had children and an excellent situation with a multinational corporation. Before long, he was staying.

My father, whose career was a great success, who sent his two children to Oxford, and who was made a Member of the Order of the British Empire in recognition of his services to his adopted country, is in many ways a paragon of immigrant achievement. But this is not the whole story. It does not explain the listlessness he has in retirement, the feeling of never having really arrived. It does not explain the inchoate grief that lingers behind his still-energetic exterior – a grief that even he cannot really articulate, and that flows freely only when he lies in the bath with the door shut and listens to Hindustani classical music. It is the grief of a kind of exile – unimposed, unintentional even, but real all the same. The exile of devoting one's life to a place where people understand nothing of the powerful and shattering experiences that formed him. The exile, simultaneously, of losing all means of return – because to his family members in Calcutta he gradually became an incomprehensible foreigner whose life did not translate into theirs: they became awkward and subdued around him. His parents died long ago. Some of his siblings have visited his home in Cambridge, but these visits have never quite brought the consummation he desires. The physical evidence of his life – a house, photographs, an accumulation of objects – somehow fails to disclose *life* itself, and even in his own front room there can be incomprehension. Meanwhile, his own trips to Calcutta – "home" as he still says – are even less satisfying, for the environment he grew up in has been completely obliterated in half a century, and he can find nothing of himself. These days, Kolkata, whose name has changed too, sees him perpetually on the brink of rage: that it is not what it should be, that people have moved on, that he cannot tell his siblings who he is, that even in the house where his parents' pictures ceremonially hang, there is no one to understand him.

Before all this, back in 1963, at the very beginning, before my mother, before his professional success, my father was travelling one day on the London Underground. He could see his own reflection in the black window opposite and, out of the corner of his eye, he saw there something else: a vision of his father being loaded, dead, into a hearse in Calcutta. It was as if it were happening inside the train compartment and it was so vivid that he could read the name of the firm of undertakers on the side of the car. When he arrived at his friends' house he told them what he had seen and began to weep so uncontrollably that they could not find it within themselves to tell him the news they had just received by telegram, which only leaked out late that night.

My father had only been away from Calcutta for eighteen months. It is another reason his successes feel so incomplete: the person for whom – in defiance of whom – he pushed himself with such zeal towards achievement never lived to see any part of it.

At the dawn of the present century I was working for a marketing consultancy firm in New York. The job was becoming a burden:

I was increasingly consumed by the novel I was trying to write in the evenings and, moreover, I was in love with a woman who lived on the other side of the world – in Delhi. And so, at the end of 2000, I emulated, contrariwise, my father's journey.

I arrived with one suitcase and a box of notes and articles I had collected for my writing. Everything else I owned I stored with an uncle in New Jersey. I didn't think it would be long before I was back. I didn't know how long it took to write a novel, but it surely couldn't take more than six months. I had no intention of staying in Delhi: I had passed through it a few times during childhood visits to Calcutta, and remembered it as a polluted, charmless sprawl. I had no doubt I could convince my beloved to forsake it for sparkling Manhattan.

But such attitudes quickly fell away when I arrived in Delhi. It would be too simple to say that I fell in love with the city – it is just as true that I fell in hate – but there was certainly an all-consuming plunge. A drawing-in, as if Delhi's attractive power exceeded mere like or dislike – for, in 2000, all that was comfortable and settled in the places I had lived before was here in turbulent preparation, and the city was a vortex of prophecy and possibility. I had fallen, by pure chance, into one of the great churns of the age and, without ever planning to do so, I stayed.

I am still there – here. Well over a decade later, my uncle in New Jersey still lugs my dusty possessions from basement to basement each time he moves house.

At the time I arrived, Delhi had gone through a decade of the changes resulting from the 'liberalisation' of 1991 – that is to say, the reforms which led to the dismantling of the closed and centrally planned economy that had been in place since India's independence, and which opened the country to global flows of products, media and capital.

As far as life in the city was concerned, that decade before my arrival had been devoted mainly to what you could call changes to its 'software', while its 'hardware' remained relatively untouched. Middle-class houses resounded with new commercial – and foreign – TV programming, and unfamiliar dreams unfurled in their whitewashed rooms, but their original architecture – balconies for the winter and darkened rooms for the summer – remained intact. Shops now stocked the imported jeans previously accessible only to those with contacts abroad, but they were still housed in the old cramped quarters of Connaught Place – the British-era commercial arcade – or in the ramshackle community markets built in the 1960s. The great tumult of destruction and creation that has dominated my acquaintance with Delhi, the furious tearing-down of all that hardware in the pursuit of globalism – "From Walled City to World City" as one leading newspaper sloganned it – still lay in the future.

That tearing-down would remove much of what was settled about Delhi. It removed, certainly, the homes of hundreds of thousands of the poor, in order that shopping malls and apartment complexes could be erected in their place: this enormous transfer of wealth and resources from the city's poorest to its richest citizens turned many of the former into refugees in their own city, and made working-class life in general more edgy and precarious. Many of the businesses run by poorer entrepreneurs were destroyed in the 2000s in the name of aesthetic order – such as the informal tea stalls where you could order a cup of hot, sugary tea for 2 rupees [$0.04], sit on a plastic chair and feel mysteriously insulated from the eddies of people and traffic all around. But the wave of destruction also felled enormous numbers of houses of the affluent who, in their case, were cashing in on the real-estate boom of that decade by knocking down their properties and building blocks of apartments for sale. Built to maximise floor area and therefore sale price, these stern new blocks eschewed the generous terraces and balconies of the former architecture. Life retreated to the air conditioning inside, and so undid the cat's cradle of inter-balcony conversations that had previously straddled the afternoons.

But in 2000 this was all still to come, and in much of the city, people continued to experience an older kind of time – a languorous breed of time imported from small towns and villages by Partition refugees, which still clung to the environs they had made for themselves all those years ago. The little apartment I found myself occupying that winter was in a neighbourhood originally allocated to such refugees, and looking out I could see them, aged now, wrapped in shawls and sitting out, unmoving, on roofs and balconies. The north Indian winter is cold, and the unheated, stone-floored houses, designed for summer heat, are the same temperature indoors as out; so my neighbours cherished the same winter comforts as their rural forbears: steaming ginger tea in their hands, and the pale afternoon sun on their faces. With their offspring out at work and their grandchildren at school, these venerable neighbours transmitted the serenity of another era to all around them: the men who purchased house-hold glass and paper waste rode their bikes among the houses in unhurried arcs; the cries of the vegetable sellers who wheeled their barrows through the sun-dappled streets seemed patient and placid. Sometimes an old woman would call down to such a man, order some vegetables and agree on a price. She would lower the money down from the roof of her house in a basket on a string; he would take out the money and put in the goods, and slowly, ever so slowly, she would pull the basket up.

That bygone Delhi also shut down early. It has become diffi-cult to remember, because the years after my arrival were occu-pied with the building of a glittering archipelago of cafés, restaurants, bars and clubs, and now one can scarcely move in the city on weekend evenings for the traffic jams of fervent bar-goers. But none of this existed in 2000, when an older conservatism ruled the city's nights, and when most areas were desolate after the shops shut around 9 p.m. My neighbours, certainly, who believed in the virtues of home and early rising, had little truck with nights on the town. Profoundly shaped by the terrors and losses of Partition, this generation of Delhi's middle classes was frugal and suspicious of the outside, and spending money in restaurants – and eating food cooked by unknown hands – was anathema to them. It was their Delhi I arrived in, a Delhi which – quite unlike the New York I had just left – made little attempt to seduce or entertain, and which sent you home when the day was done.

Even for the bohemians I now found myself amongst, the evening entertainment was, as it had been for such people for decades, domestic. We did not go out because there was nowhere to go. Instead we gathered in various apartments – small, bare and, in those days, cheap – and, in rooms foggy with cigarette smoke, we sat on cushions on the floor around a motley assemblage of rum and whisky bottles, and we talked.

All conversation is infused with its moment; and it is through those nights of conversation that I realised I had landed in an extraordinary place and time.

The Delhi artists and intellectuals among whom I now found myself spoke at a pitch I have never encountered in another place or, indeed, in the same place since that period. Certainly, they were people of striking brilliance and originality, but the furious energy of their debates came also from the city outside. The old was dying, the new was in preparation, and we were living in the in-between, when nothing was resolved, everything was potential. Everyone was trying to absorb, to imagine, what the city – and their own lives – might become. They lived with empty stomachs, filling themselves on books and conversation – for forms of thought that are deemed formal and remote in stable times become intimate and necessary when all boundaries are lifted away. People need philosophy because they are at a loss for how to understand the upheaval that is themselves. They need more than they already have, more ideas, more words, more language – and they throw themselves into discourse, not caring if they don't sleep.

Some of this energy was exquisitely local. The city was changing in startling ways and there was a sense that life in this place would become marvellous: that it would be liberated from the constraints of the past, and many unknown fruits would sprout in its ground. Another literary newcomer to the city wrote a poem entitled, 'In the Early Days of the Delhi Metro',[1] a title which captured both the epochal feel of those years and also the considerable idealism aroused by the new subway system, whose first line opened shortly after my arrival in the city. Not only did the hi-tech trains and stations seem to inaugurate a new era of high-quality public infrastructure, implemented – *Yes, India can do it too!* – without any of the incompetence or corruption normally associated with such projects, but its effortless glide under the city, bypassing the competitive ruckus of the Delhi roads and sweeping easily through rich and poor areas alike, seemed to herald a new kind of mobility – social and economic too – for this town so enamoured, traditionally, of boundaries and hierarchies.

But the anticipation of those years had a much larger scope than the city itself. It sprang from a universal sense: *What will happen here will change the entire world.*

The people I met were cosmopolitans, and they were delighted to see walls coming down around India. They disdained nationalism and loved the new riches that reached them via the internet. But true to their own scepticism – and to the history of anti-imperial thought in this part of the world – they were also critical of the economic and social bases of Western societies – and the last thing they wanted from this moment of India's opening-up was that a similar society be established here. Much of their intellectual inspiration came from Western capitalism's internal critics: from American free software theorists, from the squatter movement in the Netherlands, from artists in Britain who challenged corporate food and property cultures, from Harvard and Oxford legal scholars who imagined alternative possibilities for the ownership of seeds, images and ideas. These

areas of inquiry could not have been more relevant to post-
liberalisation India, where the big question, precisely, was *ownership*. There were so many areas of Indian life in which fundamental
resources – certain kinds of land, knowledge and culture, for
instance – had always been kept free of ownership, but as India
signed up to international trade agreements, things tended towards
the privatisation of these previously 'common' goods. Among my
Delhi peers, there was a sense that corporate culture, which
advertised itself as a recipe for plenty, would herald a new kind
of scarcity if it were not fundamentally adapted for this place.

And there was a feeling that through such adaptation it would
be possible to imagine new, hybrid forms of capitalism that
provide inspiration not just here but everywhere. It was during
this period, after all, that New York was struck by the devasta-
tion of 9/11 and, as Western societies began to feel the pressure
of anxieties about Islam, their multiculturalism – and indeed
their sense of superiority – seemed brittle. This multiculturalism
might have embraced people from many backgrounds and beliefs,
but it also expected them to adopt a deep level of homogeneity:
everyone was supposed to abide by a single legal system, for
instance, and to put away all practices inconsistent with the
state's ethos of efficiency and sobriety. Delhi, where all 15 million
people were accustomed to living alongside others whose lives
bore absolutely no points of contact with their own, offered a
spectacle of life immeasurably more varied and paradoxical than
this – and yet it felt fluid and functional. This ability of the
Third-World city to embrace utter unintelligibility within its
own population, to say not, "Let me understand you so I may
live alongside you," but "I will live alongside you without condition, for I will never understand you," seemed not only more
profoundly humane but also more promising as a general ethos
of globalisation, since it was clear, in these times of global inter-
connections, that we were all implicated in relationships with
people we would never know or understand. Perhaps the Third-
World city, long thought of as a place of desolation and despair,

might actually contain implicit forms of knowledge that all places could benefit from.

It was not all talk; for Delhi was erupting, too, with new culture. Even as I sat down to write my first book, realising that Delhi was a far more inspiring place than New York to do so, I was surrounded on every side by people doing similar things. One Delhi writer, Arundhati Roy, who was the first member of this scene to achieve international visibility, had recently won the Booker Prize; and suddenly it seemed that all over this unliterary city young people were writing books and movies. Other twenty- and thirty-somethings were starting publishing houses, magazines and newspapers. Cafés and bars decided they would attract more customers with poetry readings and film screenings.

Most dynamic of all was the nascent art scene, which brought together a motley collection of people attracted to Delhi by the quality of its universities or by the cheapness of its studio space – or simply by the city's whispered promise, so tangible in those days, that it could reveal to you your new self. I remember an experimental show in those early years in an abandoned house: there were pools of water on the floor, and the rigged-up lighting left one groping through the corridors. People were talking in the bathtub. Artworks were drawn on the walls of bathrooms or hidden in kitchen drawers. The show captured something of the city's disintegration in those days, and the new reality, uncanny and wonderful, that would emerge. The show was undeniably cool, and it did not seem outlandish to see Bianca Jagger there, picking her way through those damp rooms in a pristine white suit. People still talk about that evening, when we witnessed something of what was to come – for, within a few years, several of those artists had become darlings of the international art world. Art collectors everywhere wanted to own a piece of India's rise – something that would make tangible the rumours of eastern emergence, the soaring abstractions of the Bombay Stock Exchange – and they bought up steel and marble sculptures whose massive scale seemed to speak of the epic circumstances from which they sprang. Artists moved into studios like aircraft hangars, they became multinational in their own right – they began to manufacture, like all good twenty-first-century enterprises, in China – and they sold their works for $1 million a piece. Their rapid journey from marginal pranksters to wealthy powerhouses could not fail to impress even a society as artistically disinclined as this one, and artists were quickly welcomed into the pantheon of Indian celebrity. But people assumed, because they had become rich, that they had never thought of anything else. I had seen them before, however, when money was not yet on the horizon, when their only thought was how to give form to that great voice whose roar so many of us could hear, here, in the early days of the Delhi Metro.

A decade later, this utopian clamour was no more.

Those astonishing early years already seemed remote. The future had arrived and it was not very impressive. The city had been taken over by more dismal energies, and Delhi once again seemed peripheral and irrelevant. If we had ever thought that this city could teach the rest of the world something about twenty-first-century living, we were disappointed. The land grabs and corruption-as-usual that became so blatant in those later years, the extension of the power of elites at the cost of everyone else, the conversion of all that was slow, intimate and idiosyncratic into the fast, vast and generic – it made it difficult to dream of surprising futures any more. Money ruled this place as it did not even the 'materialistic' West, and the new lifestyle that we saw emerging around us was a spiritless, degraded copy of what Western societies had developed: office blocks, apartment blocks, shopping malls and, all around, the millions who never entered any of them except, perhaps, to sweep the floors.

An upsurge in urban violence, moreover, which displayed itself most sensationally in a depressingly repetitive series of ghoulish sexual crimes, led to widespread consternation about the kind of society that was taking shape in this rapidly changing metropolis. As thousands took to the streets to demonstrate both their sympathy for the victims and their indignation at the vulnerability that everyone now felt in the streets of their city, Delhi became a place of bewildered introspection. Some had hoped, in these days of India's economic rise, that it would be possible to lay to rest forever those attitudes, dating from colonial times and affecting Indian and foreigner alike, which held that India's was an inferior and atavistic culture; the brutal reports in the city page of Delhi's newspapers gave many of them profound doubts as to the legitimacy of this hope. No longer was the city building a paradise to inspire the world; now it was trying to pull itself back from the brink of hell.

At the end of that decade, I decided to write a book about my adopted city, in part to understand the nature of this transition, which I had lived through alongside so many million others. It felt to me that very wild human energies were at play – those of money, change and ambition, but those also of anxiety, asceticism, and historical trauma – and that the reality of the city could only be discovered by asking residents how they actually lived and felt. Statistics were the favoured language for discussing India's change, for how else could one represent the existence of such a disparate billion? – but the smooth upward graphs of boom-time India expressed nothing at all of the intensity with which every new day landed on the residents of this city. That intensity derived from the deep contortion of daily life, which pulled people between exhilaration and horror, between old value systems and new, between self-realisation and self-annihilation. There was no hieroglyph to sum up the wrench of a globalising society, and indeed the enthusiasm for statistics, and the accompanying neglect of paradox, dream-life and doubt, was a part of the problem. It was too often assumed that the inner life of an apparently prospering population should be as smooth as its external measures, but the accelerated changes of this emerging-world metropolis were often experienced as a violent and bewildering storm. Even as people made more money, things made less sense.

But the deficiency was not in things, necessarily, so much as in the imagination. It felt as though Delhi had somehow not been imagined yet, and unlike those who lived in much-imagined cities – Paris, New York, Mumbai – we in Delhi had very few codes with which to order the data-chaos around us. The 'city' did not yet exist: it remained for the present a mere force field of raw and raging stimuli – which was one of the reasons it left us all so petulant and exhausted. "Senseless!" cried the local newspapers with each new abomination, so reiterating one of Delhi's centuries-old ideas – that everything is ultimately without meaning. But I wondered if it was possible to turn this history on its head. Though we were caught in the vortex of change, there seemed to be meaning everywhere, and even the horror seemed to have something to say. Individuals, certainly, were ferociously convinced of their own significance, even as they despaired of the rest. I resolved to start with them, with the torrent of Delhi's inner life, and to seek there the rhythm, the history, the mesh, from which a city's lineaments might emerge. It did all mean something, I felt. There *was* a 'city' to be made.

But the book I began to write was only in part a book about Delhi. It was just as much a book about the global system itself. I did not feel that the scenes I witnessed around me were of concern only to this place. Nor did I feel that they were scenes of a 'primitive' part of the system, which was struggling to 'catch up' with the advanced West. They felt, rather, to be hypermodern scenes which were replicated, with some variations, elsewhere on the rockface of contemporary global capitalism. Indeed, the book I began to write felt like a report from the global future: for it seemed to be in those 'emerging' centres like this, which missed out on international capitalism's mid-twentieth-century

– its moment of greatest inclusiveness and hope – that one could best observe the most recent layer of global time. It was no longer in the West, I felt, but in places such as this, that people from all over the world could find their own destiny most clearly writ.

In this sense, I remained true to the universalism of my early years in Delhi. But it was a universalism of a darker kind, and one that had to work much harder to uncover the idealism within.

My father was anxious when I moved to Delhi. He had spent too much of his life escaping this country to watch his son migrate there with equanimity. But as time went on he began to see the possibilities in this unforeseen situation. I became a route back into his past, an emissary between his adult life and his youth. When he and my mother came to stay with me in Delhi, he was more animated than I had seen him in years. His teenage self emerged as he spoke Hindi again – a language he had hardly spoken since his Delhi days – and browsed the music stores for CDs of his beloved Hindustani classical music. In his enthusiasm he asked me to take him to see the house he had lived in during the time his family lived in Delhi in the 1950s.

We set out, he and my mother and I, for Karol Bagh. "15/64 Western Extension Area, Ajmal Khan Road," he chanted momentously in the back of the car. We drove through the wide, fluid streets of the bureaucratic area, turned off in the direction of Karol Bagh. The afternoon was drawing to a close and the streets were full of trucks loading and unloading at Karol Bagh's endless stores. The Punjabi traders who moved here in 1947 had prospered, and now the entire area was bursting at the seams: shops and warehouses extended out onto the streets, apartments had grown upwards and outwards into every possible gap, and parked cars filled in the rest. We missed our turn and had to do a U-turn, a mistake that cost us half an hour. Sitting in the traffic, we watched cycle rickshaws weaving ahead and dropping women off in front of sari shops. In the smoking force-field of the Delhi market, a car was the worst form of transport, and there was no market more smoking than Karol Bagh.

My father became increasingly upset as we penetrated deeper and deeper into the end-of-day clamour. "Karol Bagh used to be a *bagh*," he said, "a *garden*. I used to ride my bike on these streets. What happened?" We asked again and again for the address, "15/64 Western Extension Area?" No one could help. My mother read out numbers from the doors, which climbed promisingly close to our target, then skipped it and began a new series altogether. It didn't seem to exist anymore. Where the house must have been was now a row of steel-fronted warehouses. More U-turns were an exhausting prospect. "Let's go home," said my father, agitated. "You can't drive in this chaos. Let's go."

As we drove home, my father silent with the disappointment of another failed homecoming, I remember thinking that his sixty-year absence from this place was not necessary to the shock he was feeling. Even people who had never left Karol Bagh, even men and women who had watched every transformation of the past six decades, also had moments of incredulity when they thought back to the past. You could hear them often, in fact, those old people who tried to convey to those who had not been around then, *how things were*. But often they could not articulate it well. Words and memories jammed; for the human organism is superbly adaptive, and rewires itself with such uncanny efficiency for a changed environment that it becomes difficult to remember how things were – or how one was – before. This process, in early twenty-first century Delhi, was greatly accelerated. Change was happening at such a stupefying pace that people of every age were cut off even from their recent existence. They looked at vast shopping malls, malls whose construction had appalled and offended them, and now they could not even remember what had been there before, or why they had objected so strongly. My father's failure to revisit his Delhi home was only a particular example of a general condition: no one, not even the young, could revisit the Delhi they had come from because it no longer existed.

We tend to think of migration as movement in space; but in some ways this kind of migration is a sideways step within the far grander, onward exodus that everyone who lives amid the churn of capitalism is part of: the migration across the plains of time.

I find it interesting, therefore, that my father has in his old age displaced onto a collection of clocks – and not, say, maps – his attachments to lost places. Like many migrants, he has always been mesmerised by the idea of the *heirloom*. His corporate success swung him into the orbit of the British bourgeoisie, whose houses were full of inheritance: chests and ornaments, paintings and vases. He by contrast had not a single object to show from where or which lineage he had come. So in recent years my frugal father has begun to spend significant amounts of money on amassing a collection of nineteenth-century French carriage clocks. He is not a great Francophile, and it is not romantic to him, except in the terms of clock-making history, that these timepieces were made in Paris. What is important is that they have been ticking for the entirety of his life and long before: they are old enough to have chimed the quarter-hour not only for the entire history of independent India but throughout the British rule which went before. And so, with each pealing cacophony in his Cambridge home, they restore all the absences of time. Aged, stately things, they make time calm and complete, they gather up all history and store it so that it will never seep away.

Two

1991

I'm very proud to be an Indian. When I was a kid and people would ask me where I was from I would be embarrassed to say I was from India. But something changed in the nineties. Now I'm very proud to say I'm from here. In those days there was nothing, you know, and the place was so dirty. Now we have BMWs on the streets. By the time I'm fifty it will really have arrived. My kids' generation will really see it. Everything is happening, people have so much energy. It's all happening here.

– Indira, jewellery designer

On 24 July 1991, Manmohan Singh, India's new finance minister, announced in his budget speech that his nation would henceforth embrace the principles of open markets and free enterprise. Life changed immediately, even in its most basic elements. A new landscape appeared: as one person remarked to me, "Before that I had never seen the colour pink."

It could be said that India's departure from the centrally planned, closed-economy orthodoxy that had prevailed since Independence was slow in coming. After all, India's traditional exemplar, the Soviet Union, had already passed into history. A free-market doctrine – the 'Washington Consensus' – had gripped the world's power centres for the entire previous decade, leading to the – frequently forcible – conversion of much of Latin America and Africa. Even within India, free-market advocates – among them Manmohan Singh himself, who was a respected economist – had been pushing since the 1970s for state controls to be relaxed. But such appeals, seen as 'pro-business' and 'anti-populist', had always proved politically unviable, and even those pro-market concessions that were implemented before 1991 were usually rolled back in the approach to elections. The fact was that any politician who came out and said that the so-called 'Socialist' system did not work implied, thereby, that he or she was disloyal to the sacred legacy of the nation's founding father, Jawaharlal Nehru.

Like Manmohan Singh half a century later, Nehru had studied at Cambridge University – as, too, did his opposite numbers in the independence struggle: the king-emperor George VI and the viceroy, Lord Mountbatten (Nehru was the only one of these three to complete his degree). Having gone to Harrow before Cambridge, Nehru had lived in England from 1905 until the end of his undergraduate studies in 1912, and he was in nearly every respect more like the British rulers whose eviction he superintended than the 350 million people he then undertook to govern. But his vision for the society he would build in India was radically different from that of the departing British. What had inspired him at Cambridge was not the British empire's laissez-faireism but the social engineering of its Fabian Socialist intellectuals. He disliked the excessive luxury of Britain's landed aristocrats, industrialists and bankers, and felt they had no place in the modern republic. He wanted to rid India not only of British rule but also of the economic system with which, he felt, Britain had pauperised India, whose per capita income had not increased at all between 1757 and 1947.[2]

Nor was this Nehru's private view alone. The independence movement owed its origins in part to a 1901 book – *Poverty and Un-British Rule in India* – whose detailed analysis of India's economic flows found that the principle cause of its contemporary poverty was the enormous drain exerted on Indian wealth during the British era – wealth that had accounted as recently as the seventeenth century for a spectacular 25 per cent of global GDP. The book's author, Dadabhai Naoroji, was no hot-headed amateur. Writer, publisher and professor at both Bombay University and University College London, Naoroji was also a wealthy and successful cotton merchant who became the first Indian magnate to set up his own British subsidiary. Beyond all this, Naoroji set up one of the first associations devoted to the advancement of the status and interests of the Indian peoples. Drawn increasingly into politics, he served as prime minister of Baroda and, later, as Liberal member of parliament for Finsbury Central: as the first Indian to be elected to the British parliament, he was able to express in London's power establishment his analysis of the injustices of imperial rule both in India and Ireland. By the time Nehru returned from Cambridge, Naoroji too was back in India and serving for the third time as president of the Indian National Congress – the political vehicle for India's eventual independence campaign, and the foundation of the post-Independence Congress Party, which dominated the country's democracy until the 1970s – which Nehru would himself later head.

A decade after Nehru's return to India, as his political career began, he was enraptured by the news of the Bolshevik revolution – and within the independence movement he was the most vocal and articulate of those who argued for a centrally planned economy. Nehru was a modern, and he was filled with that modern dream of the total society, in which injustice, inequality and indeed all of human beings' baser drives would be defeated by the perfect nation system. His 1927 visit to the USSR, where he attended the tenth anniversary celebrations of the revolution, filled him with hope and excitement. The book he later wrote about this visit overflows with awe at the Soviet achievement: the industry, the art, the high-minded bureaucrats – the enterprise so majestic that even its failures were difficult to judge too harshly. In Russia, Nehru did not – or could not – see the luxurious few lording it over the miserable many. The image he brought away with him was that of Mikhail Kalinin, chairman of the Central Executive Committee – and head of state – wearing peasant clothes and receiving a salary that was barely more than that of a worker. "Russia thus interests us," he wrote, "because it may help us to find some solution for the great problems which face the world today. It interests us specially because conditions there have not been, and are not even now, very dissimilar to conditions in India. Both are vast agricultural countries with only the beginning of industrialisation, and both have to face poverty and illiteracy. If Russia finds a satisfactory solution for these, our work in India is made easier."[3]

As prime minister of India, then, Nehru embarked on a bold experiment – one whose incongruities would hold together only while he, with his unique aura, was around to ensure it. On the one hand, incredibly, he made this largely feudal country instantly and indiscriminately democratic. The constitution granted universal suffrage to adult citizens, despite the fact that only 12 per cent of them could read, and contrary to a widespread feeling that it was dangerous – and unnecessary – to give the country's fate away to people so ignorant of democracy that it would never occur to them even to ask for it. Nehru and his colleagues in the Constituent Assembly, which drafted the constitution, were in this respect liberals of affecting conviction who unhesitatingly gave guarantees to the justice, equality and liberty of all citizens and to the freedom of the press. The fact that this gamble – of democracy and stable liberal institutions – paid off and endured is deservedly seen as an extraordinary legacy of India's founding politicians, and it is has secured for Nehru himself a posthumous aura of quasi-divine rectitude and foresight.

On the other hand, Nehru felt, having studied the rapid

industrial development of Japan and the Soviet Union, that only the state would be able to drive economic expansion fast enough to realise his fledgling nation's epic dreams – and he instituted a centrally planned economy inspired by that of the USSR. India's growth and modernisation would be achieved through a series of Five-year Plans which would harness the nation's resources into coordinated forward thrusts. These Plans reached their height of intellectual rigour with the Second Plan, conceived by a man named Prasanta Chandra Mahalanobis, who had previously founded the Indian Statistical Institute and who combined just the attributes guaranteed to endear him to Nehru: a learned appreciation of big systems, a degree in physics from Cambridge, and a love of ancient Indian philosophy. On his appointment to the Planning Commission, Mahalanobis visited England, the USA, France and the USSR to discuss with the world's leading statisticians and economists the question of how state investment could best reach the sectors that needed it, at the appropriate time and in the appropriate quantity, in order to ensure holistic long-term growth.

In Mahalanobis' conception, the essential strategic industries – such as oil and gas, atomic energy, defence, aircraft, iron and steel, electricity generation and transmission, heavy electricals, telecommunications, coal and strategic minerals – were the exclusive preserve of the state, while both state and private enterprises could operate within a second category – which included chemicals, pharmaceuticals, fertilisers, pulp and paper, and road transport. The remaining industries – such as consumer goods – were open to private companies. Private enterprise was subject to intense controls, however: businesses could not introduce new products, set up a new plant, fire workers or make major investments without acquiring specific government licenses. It was a highly restrictive regime but it turned out to be a rewarding one for established interests, and Indian big business was not generally opposed to it. Those big business houses that escaped nationalisation were kept under the watchful eye of the Congress

Party; in return for their docility they were given cosy access to commercial licenses, which kept competition away and ensured high profits even when, as was often the case, their actual products were of terrible quality. (The defectiveness of Indian material life in those years, perversely, became over time a further justification for the system, since if markets were open then foreign companies would flood India with products of diabolical perfection and Indian companies would be annihilated in their own land.)

But Nehru was not greatly preoccupied by the quality of consumer products. He was drawn to the monumental. He loved to be photographed with large dams, which produced two other essential developmental forces – electricity and irrigation – and for which he entertained exalted feelings: at the dedication to the nation of the vast Bhakra dam, he called it – for he was not only a modern but a secularist – "the new temple of resurgent India". The three great steel plants built during those years were also close to his heart, for they demonstrated India's ability to harness its own mineral resources and produce a vital industrial asset without outside assistance. He was eager for India to boast great institutions of research and higher learning: he showered money on the Cambridge-educated theoretical physicist Homi Bhabha, who set up two high-level research institutes – the Tata Institute of Fundamental Research and the Atomic Energy Establishment, Trombay – and he established the lavish Indian Institute of Technology and Indian Institute of Management networks to cultivate home-grown leaders for a technocratic future.

These institutions, in fact, would continue to play a critical role into our own century, for they turned out many of the men and women responsible not only for India's technology boom but indeed, since a large number of them ended up in Silicon Valley, for America's. But in general Nehru's vision of how the economy might flourish was less enduring than his vision of political life. As it turned out, the complexity of actual economic processes proved too great for even such gifted planners as his: the second Five-year Plan was abandoned because its theories broke down in the face of unexpected real-world developments such as foreign currency shortages and inflation. By the time of Nehru's death in 1964, and the end of the third Five-year Plan, the promise of the early years was looking remote: many sectors of the economy had been choked by regulatory restrictions and lack of capital, and the country was suffering severe agricultural shortages. Nehru left behind a thwarted economy, whose resuscitation was the subject of furious debates for nearly three decades thereafter.

Part of the reason these debates were so drawn out, however, was that Nehru's conception of India continued to enjoy an almost theological prestige, even as the economic system withered on which it was, to a great extent, based. It was a lofty, brahminical conception, which disdained money-making and worldly vanity; private enterprise, and the buying and selling of consumer products – especially luxury goods – were seen as vulgar and granted little freedom or respect within the nation's life. The nation itself was the proper object of aspiration, and the closed economy was a sort of injunction, too, against too much dwelling on the outside world. As Nehru's own cosmopolitanism ebbed away in the years following his death, there entered into Indian life a particular, self-involved texture as the wider world gradually became, even for the educated and affluent, more remote and prohibited. During the 1970s and much of the 1980s, for instance, foreign travel by private citizens, while technically allowed, was difficult even for the few who could afford an air ticket, because of the severe restrictions placed on currency exchange. An international phone call had to be booked a day in advance. Very few foreign companies could invest in Indian firms or set up Indian operations of their own, and imports of foreign products were largely banned.

Over time, such repression gave rise to strange fantasies about the outside, which, like prisoners' dreams, were enervating and ambiguous. On the one hand, there was a great frisson about everything international: those who did travel abroad during that period, for instance, were a tribe apart, and whole towns turned up at airports to welcome them home with garlands, and to glimpse the radios and perfumes they brought back from other lands. But, at the same time, there were genuine fears of the evil that foreign countries could do, and the barriers that protected India's innocence could seem powerfully reassuring. Thinking back on long periods of insidious foreign rule, India maintained a paranoia about the possibilities of foreign infiltration and corruption – Pakistan and the CIA, for instance, were supernaturally present as agents of ill-luck in Indian life.

Perhaps it may be understood from all of this why India could not contemplate the dismantling of its state controls and the embrace of global capital until there was simply no other choice – even though the Indian economy was conspicuously dysfunctional for decades, and even given the spectacular growth, during the 1970s and '80s, of such neighbours as South Korea and Taiwan. The idea was simply too blasphemous. And yet, by July 1991 the prevailing system was in tatters and there was, indeed, no other choice. The Congress Party was discredited by scandal and rocked by the recent assassination of its leader, Rajiv Gandhi, who was Nehru's grandson and a former prime minister – and the economy had reached a fatal crisis. Perennially unable to export enough to pay for what it imported, despite the old rhetoric of self-sufficiency, India's foreign exchange reserves dropped in the middle of that year to just over half a billion dollars – enough to pay for about three weeks of essential imports. In order to get through the situation, the government negotiated an emergency loan of $2 billion from the International Monetary Fund. This loan came at a price. Pure gold, first of all: the government was forced to secure the loan by pledging sixty-seven tonnes of its gold reserves as collateral; forty-seven tonnes were airlifted immediately to the Bank of England and twenty to the

Union Bank of Switzerland. The other condition of the loan was immediate free-market reforms.

Manmohan Singh had been appointed finance minister precisely because he had been calling for such reforms for many years, even when they were an anti-Indian taboo, and he seemed to be the person best equipped to implement them. What he announced in 1991, indeed, went far beyond the demands of the current crisis: it comprised a fully conceived system which had been developing in his mind since the 1960s, when he wrote his PhD thesis about foreign trade. This system heralded a new economic era to come and, as he made clear in his epochal budget speech, it could not be introduced too quickly: "Neither the Government nor the economy can live beyond its means year after year. The room for manoeuvre, to live on borrowed money or time, does not exist anymore. Any further postpone-ment of macroeconomic adjustment, long overdue, would mean that the balance of payments situation, now exceedingly difficult, would become unmanageable and inflation, already high, would exceed limits of tolerance."

Since this speech, the Indian economy has grown by as much as 10 per cent per annum, overtaking those of Canada and Russia to join the ten largest economies in the world. So it is striking in retrospect how cautious and apologetic Singh was in putting forward his system – a system which, from our posi-tion of hindsight, has the feeling of inevitability. He gave the strangest of performances, bending over backwards to his point: for though he laid out a clear plan for the deliberate and far-reaching destruction of the old economic regime, it was cush-ioned all around with paeans to socialism and to Nehru – as if the only viable way to present this departure was as continuity, even consummation. He seemed terribly anxious to suggest that his was a profoundly Indian project, and that 'traditional' attitudes towards the outside world would be preserved: he reiterated, for instance, the familiar abhorrence of the "mindless and heartless consumerism we have borrowed from the affluent societies of the West". And at the end, having declared that India would now integrate with the global economy, he issued his battle cry – "we shall overcome" – a quotation from a familiar protest song from the old days which, while it might have reassured his audiences that values were intact, was totally incongruous in the context: against which oppressor was it now directed? But it was a speech that was all the more revealing for its muddlement: for if Singh's metaphors were confusing in their present context it was because they were time-travelled from Nehru's own. No orator himself, it was clear through his cadences that the finance minister was trying to assert fidelity to the nation's great speech-maker:

> . . . as Victor Hugo once said, "no power on earth can stop an idea whose time has come". I suggest to this august House that the emergence of India as a major economic power in the world happens to be one such idea. Let the whole world hear it loud and clear. India is now wide awake. We shall prevail. We shall overcome.

Singh's implausible attempt to arouse here invoked Nehru's announcement of Indian independence from the battlements of Delhi's Red Fort. "At the stroke of the midnight hour," he had declaimed as 15 August 1947 chimed in, "when the world sleeps, India will awake to life and freedom." Since India had awoken so spectacularly in 1947 it was of course somewhat anti-climactic to announce, in 1991, that it was still awake, but you could see what he was trying to do.

For Singh's anxiety about how to own up to this revolution was well-founded. Already there had been outrage that the nation's gold had been flown to the vaults of the old colonial masters. And now there was widespread disquiet about the new strategy, and about the role of foreigners – the IMF – in its formulation. As the *New York Times* put it, "India, which still views itself as a socialist nonaligned leader, views [economic reforms] with pain, even embarrassment . . . This will be seen as a kind of interference with India's autonomy."[4]

In our era, when we have lost our sense of the global power of the Soviet-sponsored system – and indeed of the 'non-aligned' movement advocated, among others, by Nehru – we recognise only one kind of 'globalisation'. It is difficult for us to imagine anymore, therefore, how a vast nation could have chosen to remove itself from this particular form of globalism, or to remember how dangerous and disloyal a prospect embracing it might have seemed only twenty years ago. India's entry into the global system, like that of so many other countries around the same time, was not the smooth reversion to a natural state it is so often imagined to be in our now-seamless capitalist world (which has lost so much of its comprehension and empathy for variety and alternative). It was in many respects a humiliating defeat for everything on which the country's greatness stood, and it generated a schizophrenic legacy. India 'came into' globalisation in the same sense as someone 'comes into' an inheritance: with a sense both of new economic possibility, and of crippling bereavement. Money would arrive; but everything exalted and nurturing was passing away, and nothing could replace it except a flood of baseness.

Three

I drive past a billboard advertising a television business channel. It shows the radiant face of a businesswoman and the caption, "1 hour of viewing can impact your bottomline".

Since the photo ends at the woman's neckline and we cannot see her "bottomline", I assume the text is supposed to read "bottom line". But she does look very smug about something.

"The first people we interviewed declined the jobs we offered them because they thought we were loony to imagine we could work for international corporations out of India. They all thought Indian standards were too low."

I am sitting in the office of Raman Roy,* CEO of Quatrro, a business process outsourcing company. Raman has little round glasses and wears an informal checked shirt. In his early fifties, he has an avuncular, and strikingly egalitarian, manner.

"There were so many disbelievers," he continues. "They didn't believe that we were capable of that quality. They had a fundamental problem imagining that an Indian could do a white man's job. We still look up to white skin in this country."

* Real name.

But as things turned out, it could be quite the reverse.

"Sometimes our employees had to apologise for doing a better job than the people who taught them. That has changed how they think. They realise they don't have to feel they're inferior to anyone."

The opening of Nehru's Independence speech, one of the most quoted passages of all twentieth-century rhetoric, contains a glaring error.

When it is midnight in India "the world" does *not* sleep. When it is midnight in India it is tea time in London and cappuccino time in San Francisco. And, as it turned out after 1991, there were billions of dollars to be made from this rudimentary geographical fact.

If there was one commercial development that became iconic for the new, globalised India, it was 'business process outsourcing' (BPO). The idea was that, given the state of contemporary telecommunications, a company's various functions did not all have to be grouped in one place. They could now be distributed throughout global space with no loss to functionality. Enormous cost savings could be achieved by moving non-core activities to lower-wage locations. Though this redistribution had already begun elsewhere in the world, it was the entrepreneurs of post-liberalisation India, above all, who turned the theory into a world-changing reality. And one of these entrepreneurs was Raman Roy.

At the moment of liberalisation, Raman was working for American Express, one of the foreign companies that had remained in India since British times. In the new climate of the 1990s, Raman helped convince his US bosses to consolidate the company's Asia-Pacific accountancy work in Delhi, where costs were low, and educated English speakers plentiful.

Perhaps it is difficult to remember now just how unlikely this must have appeared at the time. India seemed remote and primitive to most Americans, and the idea of moving a significant chunk of an American financial giant there was unorthodox to say the least. But as with many eccentric ideas, this one helped the people concerned to see the world in a different way. Over time, American Express transferred more and more of their 'back office' operations to Delhi – and Raman realised that there was a hitherto unimagined kind of value locked up here.

By the middle of the 1990s, a number of immense forces were converging on this little experiment. In India, the lifting of restrictions on business and capital continued apace, and investment funds flowed in to fuel the resulting entrepreneurial frenzy. One group of companies that rose very quickly to prominence was the new IT firms, founded mostly in the south of the country. The most dazzling of these was Bangalore-based Infosys, which in 1999 was listed on Nasdaq, where its valuation a year later hit $30 billion. This ascendancy derived not simply from the fact that these companies were delivering software systems to global corporations at half the cost of their American counterparts. No: their Indian location allowed them to compress not just money but also, and just as importantly, time. Indian consultants worked alongside their US clients during the American day and then sent a brief to India, Indian software teams worked through *their* day – the US night – and American clients could view the results first thing in the morning. Two working days had been extracted from one. By the time Raman Roy was thinking about cutting up American corporations and placing their various functions in different parts of the world, he could see several other people in India who were trying to bend the world in similar ways.

It is no coincidence that such thinking arose in a formerly closed and state-controlled economy. The entrepreneurs who emerged from that environment were full of revolutionary zeal, and took great pleasure in erasing the national boundaries that had hemmed in their childhoods – to an extent, in fact, that unnerved many of the Americans and Europeans who subsequently found much of their lives administered from the other side of the world. These entrepreneurs were intelligent iconoclasts who believed in technology and corporations, and hoped to use the power thereof to overturn nearly everything of the India that had existed before 1991. And yet they were Indian, and when they looked at the world of American business they did so with a foreign, unaccustomed eye. "How is it they have never thought of doing it like this?" they said to themselves, and went on to change things.

Perhaps it helped that they came from a land where trading families had for centuries spread their members out to different places on the planet in order to spot the commercial gradients between them. When one talks to members of these families, even those who are highly parochial in their personal habits – arranging only intra-caste marriages for their children, for instance – one often discovers an astonishing indifference to location and distance. It is precisely the regimented nature of their family structures, in fact, that frees them to such a flexible and unsentimental relationship to place. There are no facts except cost and revenue, and if the latter exceeds the former then the deal is good, no matter how bizarre the geographical effects.

Not entirely coincidentally, this Indian form of globalism was unleashed just at the moment when it could merge with another major transformation in the global economy. American corporations had spent the previous decade moving manual work overseas, both as a cost-reduction exercise and as a political assault on American workers, who enjoyed more bargaining power than the far-flung characters who increasingly laboured in their stead. This idea of the globally dispersed, low-friction corporation had a heroic appeal to American – and many European – boardrooms of the time and, as new communications technologies began to erode the information distance between one place and any other, it was natural for them to ask if there were other, non-manual, functions that could be moved overseas, with similar financial and political gains. Since many of these functions demanded large numbers of English speakers, India, with its much lower cost base, was an obvious place to look to. Using Indian, instead of American, software developers showed that the idea had great potential, and the stage was set for American corporations to start breaking off parts of their own internal operations and sending them in the same direction.

The other factor in the emergence of Indian business process outsourcing was the existence, just outside India's capital city, of an enormous zone of high-tech real estate where all these chunks could land. This was the new suburb of Gurgaon. DLF, the real-estate company behind the development, had been slowly buying up plots of farmland to the south-west of Delhi since the early 1980s. When the restrictions on foreign companies coming into India were lifted, this territory revealed a value beyond imagination. Gurgaon supplied the essential infrastructure to a major realignment of global corporate forces. Bordering Delhi in the neighbouring state of Haryana, it was conveniently close to the capital's international airport and was far preferable to corporations than anywhere in Uttar Pradesh, the other neighbouring state, which was known for its criminal activity. By the end of the 1990s, corporations were setting up there in droves, many of them moving out of the land-choked corporate capital, Mumbai, to do so.

The trigger for this incredible rush to the Haryana brushland had come with the announcement by General Electric, the world's seventh-largest corporation, that it would set up a new operation in Gurgaon. Named GE Capital International Services, the new entity would run global back-office operations for GE Capital, GE's finance company. In 1996, Raman Roy got a call asking if he would be interested in further developing his experiments at American Express at 'GECIS'. He went to Delhi's Oberoi Hotel to discuss the prospect with the president and CEO of GE Capital, Gary Wendt.

In an era of dazzling corporate energies, Wendt was a prime mover who understood the radical opportunities associated with global deregulation. At the beginning of his command, GE Capital had no operations outside the United States: by the time he came to Delhi it was spread over forty-five countries. Under Wendt, financial services had become the largest and most profitable part of the General Electric group, overtaking every other division of what was, in its origins, a manufacturing company. He had achieved this in part because he was an operational genius who understood how costs and revenues could be entirely restructured in the global era.

"That guy was a maverick," says Raman. "He was so quick to realise the potential of what we'd done at American Express. He asked me, 'What do you think we'll lose if this thing doesn't work?' I added 3 million to the number we'd already talked about and said '$10 million.' 'Fine,' he said. 'That's loose change. I'm going to put the money into an account for you and nobody will ask you how you spent it. Just set up something like you did at American Express.' Without him it never would have happened. I would never have got approvals for the enormous money I paid for satellite dishes and everything else."[5]

Raman had been working at the rock face of outsourcing for a decade when he arrived at GECIS and he had a more detailed conception than his American bosses of where this line of enquiry could go. In 1998, he set up a makeshift experiment in the Gurgaon office. It was India's first international call centre. Sitting in that office, workers handled credit card customer service calls from the United States. His fellow board members at GE in India had expressly forbidden him to pursue this experiment, so he concealed it from them and invited Gary Wendt to come and have a look.

"It was modelled on one of those old hairdressing shops. I rigged up curtains to separate the workers. If my colleagues had seen what I was doing I would have been fired. There was sensitive information on the screens and the whole thing was very ramshackle. I had no budgets – I started with just twenty people.

"When Gary Wendt came to visit he looked at this hairdressing shop and he was stunned. I can still see him coming down the stairs and shaking his head. He said, 'I don't think you understand what a revolution you've started'. He went away and became an evangelist for it in GE. Our cost per unit was less than 50 per cent of the existing and our quality was higher. In the US they were employing school drop-outs; we were employing people with college degrees. Before long we were providing services not just to GE Capital but to the whole General Electric group.

"It required massive lobbying to get to that point. International telecommunications were still a government monopoly, and the government was suspicious. When I went to ask for international bandwidth for that first hairdressing shop they thought I must be involved in espionage, because no one had ever requested that much capacity before. And though it was possible to rent a private international line, it was illegal to connect it to any public network, which would bypass the government monopoly – the fine was something like $150,000 per day. It took us eight months to get an exemption from that, and even then they only gave us permission for a pilot. They didn't comprehend what we were doing. We had to print out definitions of call centres from the internet and show them to government officials so they would understand what we were trying to do."

Raman is one of those people who have the satisfaction of seeing their own quiet realisation becoming a global revolution. "The original ambition," he says, "our ultimate horizon for this, stretched to about a thousand people. But it grew far beyond that. It became hundreds of thousands of people and it changed the whole society." Before long the rush for these jobs was such that the company was forced to alert the police whenever they were holding interviews, so great were the crowds outside the office. People came from far away with their whole families, and they would sit outside the office for days. The company had to hand out food and water.

GECIS delivered a wide range of services to General Electric companies. Customer service phone calls were only a small part of the corporate functions transferred to India, which became increasingly more complex and specialised as time went on. Systems and training were developed to a high level of effectiveness, and Indian workers did not have only mindless and repetitive tasks to fulfil: many of them went to the US for briefings and became valued employees of the global organisation.

After a while Raman began to feel that a much greater opportunity was being missed. "It was great to have the trappings of corporate life, big cars and clubs and everything, but I saw the possibility of doing something much bigger. I told GE that the real opportunity was to provide outsourced services to other corporations but they wanted to keep it for themselves. So in 2000 I set up Spectramind, which provided these services to all the big corporations – Microsoft, Dell, HP, Cisco, AOL, American Express, Citibank. Within a few years GE followed suit. They sold GECIS and it became an independent company called Genpact providing outsourced services to all."

Still headquartered in Gurgaon, Genpact is now, with annual revenues in excess of a billion dollars, as large as some of its Fortune 1000 clients. It has acquired other outsourcing companies in places as far-flung as Guatemala, China, Poland, South Africa and the Philippines, employs over fifty thousand people around the world and provides outsourced services in some thirty languages. It is so good at what it does that it has begun to make significant acquisitions in the United States. Because of its specialisation it can run non-core corporate functions more efficiently and to a higher level of quality than most corporations can do themselves. It has taken over substantial parts, for instance, of Walgreens' accountancy, which it now operates as outsourced functions in America.

After Spectramind was acquired by Indian computer giant Wipro, Raman, still restless in big corporate culture, left to set up Quatrro. As wages rise in India and some of the more basic outsourced work is moved to other countries, Quatrro has looked further and further up the value chain. The several thousand people it employs to supply their expertise to the world's companies include medical doctors, lawyers, engineers and journalists. And Quatrro targets a different market. "No one was servicing small and medium-sized American companies," Raman says. "They need all kinds of services they don't want to set up for themselves – from risk management to tax reporting. And there are a lot of them. The fees are much smaller: my average client only pays $5,000 a month. But I have 10,000 clients."

Raman has presumably amassed a significant personal fortune, but that seems to be the least of his satisfactions. What excites him is change. He invests from his own wealth in the projects of younger entrepreneurs, for entrepreneurialism, he feels, is the world's most powerful redeeming force.

"The BPO industry was catalytic. Nowadays, this industry earns about $15 billion in India. It employs 800,000 people, with an indirect employment of 4 million. And it's no coincidence that people started writing novels and making films about those people because they were in many ways the vanguard of the new India. They were hard-working, technology-savvy and they were exposed to the global environment. They were part of a massive change.

"Until the 1990s there were so few opportunities that many people stayed in education and did an MA just to save face. To conceal the fact that they were basically unemployed. So when we set up GECIS we found a big educated population in Delhi waiting for us to absorb them. But we soon ran out of local people and had to look further afield. In those days, more than half of Gurgaon apartments were occupied by people who had migrated from smaller towns to work in our industry.

"These people wanted to live different lives. We benefitted from the new aspirations that people absorbed from television in those years: suddenly young people wanted to work and have their own money. In the BPO industry, people found financial independence at a young age, and that completely transformed their lives. Especially in the case of women. This was one of the first places in the country to have a thriving evening scene for young, single people. And it was a very good scene as well, very different from Delhi, which is dominated by bureaucrats and family wealth. Go to a party in Gurgaon and you will find much more intelligence and much more humility. This is where the future comes from."

At the beginning of our century, a young man arrived in Delhi. There were many like him, and he could have come from pretty much anywhere, but he came from Kolkata. His name was Siddhartha.

Siddhartha was one of the great numbers of middle-class youths who rattled around, frustrated, in so many Indian cities of that time. His upbringing was sheltered and conservative, and he failed in his attempts to join the ranks of hustling entrepreneurs who were taking over the trading economy in those years. The era of well-paid, life-long government employment, for which Siddhartha's personality would have been well-suited, was long over, while his timidity and unexceptional academic record kept him far outside the circles of corporate executives – who provided the new image of middle-class achievement.

"We knew nothing about Delhi when we arrived. We just came with a bagful of clothes and we stayed in a tiny apartment that belonged to one of our friends. It was a Muslim area and we were Hindus, scared of anything unexpected. The streets were very dirty and full of cows. I had no job to come to but we had exhausted our options in Kolkata and we thought we might have better prospects here. People used to say in Kolkata that you can grow more in Delhi and Mumbai. And for middle-class people, Delhi is much more attractive than Mumbai. People who work prefer Delhi; people who act prefer Mumbai."

Bold gestures did not come easily to Siddhartha but he was encouraged in this one by the fact that his younger brother had come to Delhi before him and got a job within a week simply by wandering around and asking in stores.

"That's why I came here. But it's not easy to find a job that matches your expectations. That's something I didn't realise. At that time my mother was an assistant in a clothes shop in Kolkata, my brother had got a job in a bookshop in Delhi, and I thought if I start working in another shop we won't get anywhere. So I tried to get into a business. I went for an interview for a sales job that was advertised in the newspaper. I took a bus all the way across Delhi and got completely lost looking for the address. When I finally arrived I was drenched in sweat and they instantly rejected me. All the other candidates came on motorbikes and they had all the things you were supposed to have. I had nothing.

"After a while I didn't know what to do and I was running out of savings. So I went to the Oberoi Hotel, which was hiring bellboys. They offered me 200 rupees per night, working from eleven at night to seven in the morning.

"The first night, I arrived and they asked me to put on this uniform. So I put it on but I felt very awkward. And after three or four hours of that job I thought, 'This isn't me.' I hung up the uniform and left the hotel at three in the morning. I walked all the way home. Fifteen kilometres. And the whole way I was wondering what I would do. How was I going to survive if my ego was so important?"

At this point of desperation, Siddhartha had a chance meeting with a family acquaintance who gave him a job in his decorating firm. The work involved going from site to site checking on the progress of painters and carpenters, and the salary was Rs 2,500 [$52] per month.

Siddhartha hated this job. But it bought him time. Time enough for him to hear a phrase he had never heard before: 'business process outsourcing'.

"By the term 'BPO' I understood 'call centre' – I didn't know that companies outsourced many functions other than customer service. So I wanted to work in a call centre. I spoke English fluently, but when I interviewed with the international call centres they said, 'Your accent is too strong.' So then I looked for Indian call centres and I got a job with Tata Indicom. The shift lasted from eleven at night to eight in the morning. They would pick us up in a bus and take us to the call centre. Customers would call with problems – their text messages weren't working, their calls were cutting out – and we would solve them. I volunteered for the night shift because the volume of calls during the day was almost impossible, and also, if I worked at night, I would have the whole day to look for other jobs. For months I hardly saw my brother because I got home when he was leaving for work and he got home just as I left.

"Working at night was interesting. We were all men on the night shift and half the callers were women who wanted to chat. Relationships would form: we started to recognise callers and to put their calls through to the person they wanted to speak to. You would hear people shouting across the room like this: 'Hey Karthik, Mrs Santoshi wants you to call her back.' 'Oh yes. It's her birthday today: I promised to call her.' These calls couldn't last long because everything was monitored. But some of these flirtations led to real relationships.

"There are disadvantages to working at night. The main one is that the manager never sees you. You are just head count. Just a number. All the people who worked in the day were being promoted and I decided I had to go and see the manager face to face. In corporations, unless you ask for things, you don't get them.

"First they told me to come back after a few days. So I did. Then they said 'We're not offering you a promotion'. I said, 'Why not? Here are the requirements you set for me and I have met them all.' I don't know what got in to me that day but I was very insistent. So he said 'Either you work or you leave, but there will be no promotion.' So I said, 'I'll leave then'. And I walked out."

We are sitting in Siddhartha's apartment. He lives in one of the housing complexes dubbed 'DDA flats' after the Delhi Development Authority which built them. Conceived in the 1950s, and modelled on apartment complexes in the Soviet Bloc, new clusters of DDA flats were built all over Delhi until the 1980s without significant change to their design. The quality, however, dropped off greatly in the latter years, as the DDA's idealism evaporated: the early developments, such as the one we are in, still strike one as tranquil and well-made, while the ones built later are falling down.

For those middle-class families who migrated to the capital between the 1960s and 1980s – the teachers, academics and doctors, for instance, who staffed the capital's great new institutions – DDA flats provided the quintessential domestic landscape. Their acres of yellow stippled walls, their banks of mailboxes, their grassy courtyards with flowers and children's swings, their maze of staircases always labelled with the same mass-produced digits – many of them half painted over, now – are the backdrop to so many Delhi childhoods.

It is a weekend afternoon, and we are sitting in front of the living room window which overlooks the garden where a gardener is watering rows of potted plants. Siddhartha's mother is preparing lunch in the kitchen. His brother is watching cricket.

"Afterwards I realised what a huge blunder I'd made. I was right back where I'd started. I didn't know what to do. I couldn't go back to them and say, 'Sorry I didn't mean it.' So I started trying to get another job. It was really difficult. I was sitting at home all day and pretending to my mother in Kolkata that I was going to work, since I hadn't told her what had happened."

Finally, Siddhartha saw an ad in the paper for a job fair. He went along and was invited to Gurgaon for an interview with GECIS.

"I had no idea how to go to Gurgaon back then. I left at six in the morning to make sure I got there by nine. And I got the job. My shift coincided with the US day which meant I worked from eight in the evening to four in the morning, processing all the insurance claims.

"I was very happy. I mean, we were all very elated. I was getting a monthly salary from a foreign corporation. Before that I was outsourced – I was not on the payrolls of Tata Indicom but of the call centre which serviced them. So one of the questions I asked in my interview with GE was whether I would be on the company's payroll. And that was the start of everything.

"Soon after I started working with GECIS, GE sold its stake in the company and it was renamed Genpact. It was no longer part of GE and it could provide services to other companies as well. I began working on the business development team and we reached out to companies like Pfizer, Wachovia and Cadbury. Because we had been working for GE for so many years, it was easy to convince other global companies to send their back-end processes to Gurgaon."

Siddhartha had his break. He was managing Genpact's work for Pfizer, and he had a respectable income. His brother was also working for a call centre by now – and between them they were earning about $1,500 a month, of which they saved a half.

"My mother quit her job in Kolkata and came to stay with us. Before that, as two bachelors, we were compromising on a lot of things but when a female member of the family is around, you can't do that. We moved into a better apartment. I went on business trips to Europe and America. The following year, I got a job with Barclays Bank. We bought a plot of land in Kolkata to build a house on. We moved into this place."

Siddhartha is not without a sense of good fortune.

"Since globalisation, everything has changed for the middle classes. I saw the earlier generation in Kolkata – people who were in their thirties when I was a teenager – and they never used to get a job. They would graduate from college and then they all became private tutors. That was the only work they could get. Once in a while, someone used to get a corporate job and move away from Kolkata, and everyone used to talk about those people. They were the exceptions. But now, because of the BPO world, people get a job very easily. In that sense, young people's lives have become very good."

Siddhartha's mother summons us to lunch. We go through to the dining room, where three places are laid out for the men. Siddhartha's mother will serve us and eat later. We sit down in front of pots of steaming rice, chicken and daal.

"I tell him," his mother says as she serves mountains of rice onto each plate, "that it's time to get married. Now we are comfortable, it's time to think about finding a wife! For ten years neither of them has done anything except work. They haven't enjoyed themselves at all."

Siddhartha says nothing. He waits for his mother to leave the room.

"For a long time I didn't think about getting married because I didn't want anyone to interfere with my work and my savings. But now I want to get married and I cannot. Arranged marriages are impossible for me because I can't make a life-long decision about a woman based on an hour's conversation. At the same time, all the women of my own age are already married. And I'm not a flamboyant person who knows how to go out and talk to young women.

"The people who are in their twenties now don't know what the real India was. They live frivolously because they have never seen reality. They have never seen the hardship of life. People have stopped taking life seriously because they know they can easily get a job. I don't enjoy talking to this generation. I find it more satisfying talking to older people, who have seen hardship. They talk more sense."

Siddhartha harbours great ambivalence about the world that has provided him with his material basis. It seems full of moral threat to him, and the fact he is not married is just a part of the general, almost monastic, seclusion he maintains outside work. Though he has devoted all of the last decade's energies to accessing the rewards of the new business machine, he has at the

same time been anxious to keep its social and spiritual implica-
tions at bay. He never attends the many parties and outings
organised by his youthful colleagues. After ten years in the capital,
Siddhartha's mistrust of its culture remains intact. He hopes one
day to return to Kolkata and to live once more among people
with values like his.

"I don't see those values in Delhi. I would never marry a
woman who comes into the office with her shoulders bare. A
woman can be very attractive without baring herself. In Kolkata
you hardly ever see women wearing clothes that are so revealing.
What possible reason could there be for wearing such clothes?
India has a culture. We are not America. India has a culture of
its own but we are in danger of losing it because we don't value
anything anymore. Everything comes too easily now, and all
people think about is spending money and having fun."

Perhaps this is why, after ten years of living in Delhi, Siddhartha
and his brother have hardly a possession to their name. This is
a spectacularly empty apartment. A few folding chairs, a small
television and an air cooler are pretty much the only additions
they have made to the landlord's basic furniture. There are battery-
operated clocks on the walls of each room but nothing else. In
the mother's bedroom is a small shrine and a photograph of her
dead husband. Clothes and personal effects are locked away in
steel armoires. The few objects on the built-in bookshelf in the
corner of the living room serve only to emphasise how large
and empty it is. There is a small model of the Eiffel Tower and
a propped-up set of coasters, which have never been taken out
of their plastic box, showing the landmarks and boulevards of
Paris. There is a statue of Ganesh, a plastic plant and five Bengali
novels.

It feels as if they are living in permanent temporariness,
acquiring nothing that might stand as an obstacle between them
and their eventual retreat from this cultureless place.

"There has to be some culture which is inherited from our
ancestors. Just take the example of these pubs. Indian culture has

never been used to this. Now the young are going there and it's become part of their lifestyle. So if they were managing with 20,000 rupees a month, now they need 30,000. I'm not saying you shouldn't go to pubs but you must not lose yourself and your culture. Otherwise it will be a dog-eat-dog world."

When, recently, I attended the celebration of Siddhartha's arranged nuptials, it occurred to me that he has in one sense conspicuously preserved the culture of his ancestors. Siddhartha, in fact, is my cousin, and shares with me a long-dead Bengali grandfather with an almost neurotic admiration for the English language. The family's facility with English persisted through the generations, and helped enable Siddhartha, so many decades later, to secure his job in a Delhi call centre.

Four

At the first party I went to in Delhi, I saw a couple
smooching, and I asked myself, *How can anybody do that in
the open?* It was a shock to me. But it was nice. I understood what sort of opportunities there were for me here.
I could have an unconventional youth and an unconventional career.

– Ramesh

The advent of the corporation unleashed powerful new energies
into the lives, especially, of young people. After 1991, the entire
capitalist infrastructure needed to be built, and there was exciting
work to be found in every domain. As the capital of Indian
journalism, Delhi played host to an explosion of new newspapers,
magazines, TV stations and advertising agencies, and young people
with degrees in subjects hitherto considered useless, such as
English literature or history, now found themselves running
companies, commanding high salaries – and working extremely
hard. Their parents, who had often worked in government
jobs requiring not more than forty hours of their week, looked
on in bewilderment as their offspring returned from the office
at 11 p.m. only to receive further telephone instructions from

sleepless bosses. Nor could these parents comprehend the nonchalance with which their children leapt every year or so from one job to another, driving up their income each time. They had grown up in the belief that avoiding risk was the most important principle, and that if you found a good job you kept it for life. But these young people seemed to be drawn inexorably towards the desecration of the status quo, as if the receipt of capitalism's true blessings depended on it.

Many young people stayed late in the office not only because they had to but just because they liked it. It was an era when the corporation often seemed to be life-giving in a way that the family was not, and many of them turned to it for entirely non-professional needs, including, simply, a place to be away from the family home. The corporate mission was new and heroic, and could provide collegial relationships that seemed intrepid and profound, and young people spoke often about how their parents or spouses did not understand what they did which meant, now, who they were. In those early years of corporate euphoria, the corporation often became a kind of family of its own, and young executives began to develop a kind of affected corporate-speak that was intended to mark them out as separate from the ethos of their blood relatives. They no longer had a *reputation*, they had a *brand*. Things they did well were *core competencies*. They did not wonder, they *brainstormed*. Their DNA came from the corporation, whose traits they attempted to adopt more and more as their own.

This energy, with which such people sought their sense of purpose from the new institutions of global capitalism, had much to do with the withering of previous ideals. Such corporate enthusiasm could often be observed most powerfully, in fact, in the very families that had most whole-heartedly embraced the earlier ethos of frugality, service and nation. Many of those families had ended up feeling deceived, for when the system lost all its drapery in the 1970s it seemed there was nothing beneath save the struggle for power and money, and it no longer felt so easy to disdain those who cherished such things. In the wake of the high-minded Nehruvian vision were many disappointed middle-class people, and one legacy of this was the discrediting of ideals themselves. Many of those who came of age in the 1980s and '90s ridiculed their parents for believing in abstractions, and they embraced the principle of profit with relief. It was a new reality principle, and they remade themselves eagerly around it.

Ramesh's father worked in the government bureaucracy in a small town in Rajasthan. Ramesh was stifled by the conservative, parochial world of his childhood, and it was with a great sense of occasion that he departed for Delhi to study for an MBA. After that he stayed in the city, drifting through administrative jobs with newspapers without any particular sense of purpose. When he began his career in advertising, it was like a shot in the arm.

"I only figured out who I was when I landed up in advertising. Before that, it was a ten-to-five job and at five o'clock you packed your bag, went home and spent the whole evening sitting around with your family. In advertising, I go home at one o'clock in the morning. Sometimes I don't go home for two or three days. I keep a towel and a toothbrush in the car. Because my work is so exciting."

Ramesh seems ridiculously happy. I have rarely met anyone who finds the world so entirely positive. And he credits it to his work, which he speaks about almost as a kind of discipline of the soul.

"The only way you can be effective is if you start living those brands, if you become those brands. It is like Buddhism. It enters every part of you, it takes over your personal life as well. I explain my brands to my parents, my wife, my friends. It almost pours out of me because I carry my brands inside me."

When she became pregnant with their child, Ramesh's wife wanted them to leave Delhi and go back to where their families lived. But he could not do it.

"I felt very disturbed there, I couldn't find any peace of mind. So I convinced my wife to stay in Delhi. Otherwise I would have suffocated. It was difficult for her. She expected me to be around, and I was coming back every day at midnight. It took her a long time to reconcile herself to that. I took small steps to make her understand, just like an advertising campaign. I used analogies. When she was pregnant she used to complain about my working hours. I said, 'Look at your situation. You have a life inside you. I have that *every day*. I feel that pain every day with my campaigns. I know the kind of happiness that comes when you see that life emerge from you.' So then she understood, and now she is happy about what I am doing."

There is no doubt that Ramesh was working hard. But a lot of his time was also going into relationships with colleagues.

"We're a team of twelve people and we're very close. We stand up for each other. If any of us has a problem in his personal life, we all stand up for him. We all work hard and it's one for all, all for one. When something good happens at work, we all go out for drinks and celebrate as a team."

Young people like Ramesh were rapidly converted to the two universal drugs of corporate capitalism: caffeine and alcohol.

In the early 2000s the most visible new consumer development was probably the new café chains, which could hardly build outlets quickly enough to absorb the young people looking for a place to be out. Cafés allowed very different kinds of conversations from home or office, and at weekends they were packed with happy chatter. Compared to bars – which implied alcohol and late nights – cafés were a relatively innocuous reason for young people from conservative families to breach the boundary of the home, which represented, for many such families, the dividing line between the wholesome and life-affirming – inside – and the corrupt and poisonous – outside; the new conviviality of coffee bars gave many young people a different, even opposite, sense of things. And like every other Indian metropolis, Delhi, which, being in the north of India, had no particular historical relationship to coffee, was suddenly awash in the stuff, its smell filling every shopping mall and office block, brown liquid pouring into the veins of this new sleep-deprived generation – who, as often as not, did not *drink* from a cup but, like their American counterparts, *sucked* at a sealed and odourless container, as if they nestled at capitalism's plastic breast.

But after office hours, many of these people did need something more intoxicating. Private hesitations about alcohol evaporated widely during this decade, even though many young people chose not to tell their parents exactly what they were up to. In the early 2000s, groups of young people drinking openly together in bars still looked strangely forced: girls sat on one side of the table, giggling with each other, while boys tried to look unconcerned, and glasses of beer sat uncomfortably in everyone's hands. But this passed quickly as the new culture of work and socialising imposed its own narcotic rhythm. Women, too, ignored the page of 'mocktails' that were intended for them, and for many people of both sexes alcohol became essential to getting through the stressful tussle of work and family. Bars proliferated absolutely everywhere during the decade and they were full every evening with professionals – these re-engineered human beings of twenty-first century India – working off steam.

In bohemian circles, young people were going through an even more wholesale questioning of received values and structures. Most of the people I met when I arrived in Delhi had been living away from their parents since their late teens. This was not usual in north Indian middle-class families. In many cases it had required significant courage to make this move, and years later it had still not become accepted: those parents never visited the apartments in which their offspring carried on such illegitimate lives, often they did not even know where their children were living, or with whom, and in their own circles they felt obliged to invent excuses for their absence from the family home. Only marriage could redeem this situation; but rather few of these people seemed to marry. Many of them had been pushed out of their parents' house in the first place by this unwelcome pressure. Their desire to do creative work – the kind of work for which their parents often had little sympathy or comprehension – was only a sub-set of their more general ambition to re-create life itself. Creativity was all: not only as a professional asset that resulted in creative products, but also as the guiding principle of lives that were directed towards a wholesale re-imagination of ethics, sensibilities and relationships. Many of them had grown up watching their parents in unhappy marriages, some of them had seen child abuse and violence go on unpunished behind the closed doors of the family – and there was a widespread sense that the outer forms of north Indian respectability had become hypocritical and bankrupt. In choosing to do artistic work – thus flouting the risk-averse culture of their families and potentially foregoing the material rewards for which, in the expanding post-1991 economy, their talents should have readied them – in choosing unconventional lifestyles – living away from home and putting their emotional faith in new, elective families – they were conspicuously attempting to reproduce as little of their parents' ethos as possible. They lived out improvised kinds of romantic relationships, they began to build a gay scene – and they devoted extensive thought and discussion to the question of friendship. Having come from backgrounds, often, in which family was all and friendship only a provisional and opportunistic affair, many Delhi artists and intellectuals sought to re-imagine friendship as a more absolute and primordial kind of bond.

Some of these people had grown up in Delhi, some had not. But for all of them, Delhi in those years offered the equation of easy incomes and cheap living that is essential to artistic communities everywhere. People who could write arrived from all over the country, and indeed from many other countries, to earn money from the new magazines and newspapers so they could work, after hours, on other projects. Artists secured injections of cash by doing graphic design for the burgeoning advertising industry, filmmakers by working in TV news – at a time when new channels had twenty-four hours of programming to fill and a severe lack of people who knew anything about cameras. Some funded their lives of frugality and alternative sexuality by lending their creativity to the extravagant wedding parties of the city's rich. Delhi's world-class universities and research institutes were another powerful magnet for bright young people: they too offered forms of employment compatible with the dissident life, as did the capital's foreign embassies and cultural centres.

And life, in the 1990s, cost little. Houses in the most tranquil parts of the city had often been built with small apartments on the roofs intended for servants. This arrangement reflected an earlier, more paternalistic relationship between wealthier families and their domestic staff – but outlooks had changed and this relationship had turned balder with the years: now the city had such an abundance of poor migrants from the countryside, who were lodged in slums so conveniently close to affluent neighbourhoods, that the rich could cheaply buy any services they needed without having to go to the trouble of accommodating servants and taking on responsibilities for their families. (Often, they also campaigned for the slums near their streets to be demolished; sometimes it actually happened and they were astonished and outraged when their maids then stopped turning up for work.) Instead they could turn those servant quarters to rent. In those days, these rooftop apartments, too small and inconvenient for a family, but often endowed with dreamy terraces that were perfect for smoking dope on in the winter sun, went for about $50 a month – an amount that people with marketable skills could earn easily, and with time left over – and they filled up with young men and women wanting to be on their own and to live a creative life.

By definition, such people were a sub-culture, unrepresentative of the city as a whole. Part of the very reason why they thrived in Delhi, in fact, was that no one was interested in them. The very apathy of the middle-class city, its culture of indifference and looking after one's own, allowed people whose lives had always been excessively monitored and commented upon to discover in its self-absorbed enclaves a precious kind of freedom: anonymity.

But many of them were possessed with great energy and talent, and as they rose to visibility and influence, they took on disproportionate significance in the city's culture. They were, as one prominent artist from among their number puts it, Delhi's 'bastards': people without position or lineage who staked their lives on a different kind of future and, in many cases, came out on top. People half a generation younger looked up to them with respect and adoration, because they had added a whole new range of feelings and possibilities for life to an all-too formulaic city, and they had helped to make this barren place of bureaucracy and immigrants into twenty-first century India's cultural centre.

Manish Arora* is now a successful fashion designer, but when he came to Delhi in 1991 he had no idea what he wanted to do. All he knew was he had to get out of his parents' house in Bombay and live on his own.

"Living alone was not a very common thing in the family I come from. You lived with your parents until you got married. It was a big deal even to express that I might want to study in Delhi."

"Was it about sex?"

"I'd been having sex since I was thirteen or fourteen. That wasn't a problem. I suppose sex became easier when I came to Delhi. But that wasn't the reason. I was seventeen, I was studying

* Real name.

commerce in Bombay, and I wasn't very good at it, I wasn't happy. I happened to see an advertisement in the newspaper about this institute in Delhi – the National Institute of Fashion Technology – and I thought, 'Why not apply?' My cousins were in Delhi: they sent me the form and I went along for the entrance exam, not thinking at all about what I was doing. I turned up and there were hundreds of applicants and they all came with lots of equipment for drawing and painting – and I had just a pen in my pocket, that's all. I didn't even know the exam lasted for seven hours. I remember running to a public phone in the break to tell my mother I was still alive.

"Afterwards, they invited me to Delhi for an interview. Even then I didn't think much about it. My parents didn't either: 'It's an excuse to go and meet his cousins.' And even after the interview, I never stopped to think I'd be selected. But when I got back to Bombay, a letter was waiting for me, offering me a place. In those days there was only one campus and they took just thirty students a year from all over India. So I was very happy. But even when I began, I didn't take it very seriously. I failed the first semester. But at some point in the middle – I don't know what happened, but it struck me: *I've found the right place.* And then it all began."

One has the sense, looking at Manish's clothes, that they are the product of a mind that is preternaturally free. They are vivid and outré – they have something of the circus, Bombay kitsch and Pop art – and they bring you in touch with fantastic joy. But they are cut, embroidered and finished with the precision of a miniature painting: Manish is also a traditionalist, and the brilliant use he makes of longstanding Indian techniques shows how deeply he has absorbed their discipline. This balance of freedom and constraint generates in him, it would appear, a ferocious productivity: alongside his own brand, Manish Arora, he designs a sportswear line, Fish Fry, which is manufactured by Reebok, and innumerable one-off collections for other companies.

Recently, his undertakings were multiplied when he was invited to become creative director for Paco Rabanne in Paris. It was the first time any French fashion house had given creative control to a designer from Asia: the fact that this one looked to Manish to revive its long-flagging fortunes said much about not only his own originality but also the changing relationship of French fashion to the world. Manish now lives between Paris and Delhi.

"Even though they're now in Mumbai, my parents are actually from Punjab. Both their families came across at Partition. My father's been working in Mumbai for forty years but they haven't absorbed a single thing of the city: they're still like anybody's parents would be in a small town in Punjab. My mother has never left India. They are very naive.

"I am their only child, so it's very important to them that I've become successful. Now they don't mind that I'm not married! All is forgotten suddenly. That's one reason I have to keep doing well so they are charged about me. But they don't have a clue what I do. They're just happy to see my picture in the newspaper. They don't know I have a job with Paco Rabanne, for example. They just know their son has a job in Paris, which is good enough for them. You understand now – they're that kind of parents. They don't even know who Paco Rabanne is. And in a very nice way. I'm very happy it's like that.

"But I had horrifying moments when I was a child. My parents didn't get along and divorce didn't exist in my family – it still doesn't in the kind of background I come from. You fight but you live with each other your whole life. Of course now they're old so it's all become fine but my childhood was ruined. So that was one of the reasons why I left Bombay because I was disturbed mentally as a child. I loved Delhi because it gave me freedom from all that, and great friends, and a place to work myself out."

Manish cackles with ironic laughter to deflect such solemn talk. He is a small man – we look eye to eye – and there is something about his pointed face, which tapers into a grey goatee, something about his jaunty rising eyebrows and deep-set shining eyes, that gives him a faintly diabolical air. You feel that his confidence derives from the fact that he has at some point in his life marshalled great forces of self-sufficiency to get through.

"But I think today I could say that's why I've tried to do what I wanted to. If everything had been fine with my family when I was a child, maybe I would have been the most boring person today. I would just be doing some stupid business and I'd be married to a woman to hide the fact I was gay. But no: I wanted to leave, and I give that a lot of credit for what I am today. Because I told myself deep inside that I want to get out of this whole thing and be proud of myself. Maybe the fact I was lacking attention from my parents is what drove me to seek attention from everybody else. Which means: doing well in your own field so that you get appreciated. You can be greedy like that. Sometimes you can work hard only to be appreciated. And maybe that's why I've never been interested in money. What I need from life is people constantly telling me that I am great at my work. And that I've genuinely earned it − not because I acted in one movie and became an overnight hit. I guess that's what I live for. Because I didn't get much appreciation as a child.

"Another very drastic experience I had in Delhi was in my twenties. I was totally obsessed for years with one person. I would have done any damn thing to be with that man. To the extent of crazy things. It was not a little crush: it went on for five or six years. My friends told me I was blind, I was obsessed, but it just went on. It was horrible. And suddenly − I don't know what happened to me − I got out after five years and I looked at the rest of my life and I said, 'Wow. *Now* . . . ' You know that kind of moment? You need to save yourself. These things forced me to be successful, to want something far more than money.

"I don't need much money. I don't have kids to invest for. As long as I can meet my friends, I'm happy. I am not the kind who wants fancy cars. The typical Delhi male − straight or gay

– just wants to have the right car to drive into the hotel and park at the porch and get out of it with everyone looking at him. He buys his Porsche just for that moment. Maybe I've spent too much time in France, but I don't care about that. In Paris you can walk into a famous artist's party and there will be the richest and the poorest people, all at the same level. Nobody gives a damn. Or you can be very rich and still ride the oldest scooter because you love it. That doesn't exist here. Here, if you have money, even if you don't like a car you'll buy it because it is meant to be the best. I love that about France. They don't just value you for the money you have. Here they ask you straight away: 'What do you do?' It's the first question they always ask you."

As one might expect, Manish works like a man possessed.

"I live for my work. I believe in that and nothing else comes in between. I'm completely focussed. So that gives me opportunity to take care of the whole business of fashion, not just designing. I have the time to do all that. In Paris, being a designer is a job. It's a job, like being a lawyer. In Paris I wake up at 6.30; I work from 8.30. I carry my own clothes: I carry boxes of clothes in the Metro. Can you imagine a designer here who would carry his own clothes? Here the designers think they're superstars. They forget their job, which is to make better clothes every season. It's a job. It's fucking hard work. Just because you're in the Indian newspapers all the time, you don't forget, you don't act like a star. Have you seen how much the newspapers write about fashion designers? Don't they have anything better to do?

"India has not become fashion-conscious. No one knows about fashion. No one knows enough about themselves to be conscious of what they want. All that has happened is that people now have money and they are aware of brand names. When you meet people in Delhi who are supposed to be the fashionistas or divas: they have the right products in their hand but they know nothing. It is not like Japan. Even there, fashion is not so old but people understand fashion. Ask a woman in Delhi why she carries a Louis Vuitton bag, and she'll tell you that's the bag you're supposed to carry. Ask a woman in Japan, and she'll tell you the whole history of Louis Vuitton.

"But when I started out in Delhi, this ignorance was helpful. Now I'm in Paris so much I feel I started out in the right place at the right time. I was working in Delhi as an assistant to well-known Indian designers, and everyone was quite naive. I learned everything by doing it because I didn't know anything. For example, I didn't know – it's very stupid but it's true – I had never seen *Interview* magazine until my clothes were on the cover. I didn't get intimidated by magazines because I never saw them. My naivety has worked in my favour because I always have so much more to learn. A guy in London already knows everything when he starts and it's more difficult for him to do his own work and prove himself again and again. If I had been in London, maybe I'd be burned out by now."

He takes out his laptop and shows me a video of his latest show in Paris, which was organised as a magic show. He explains how the show is put together: how a collection is conceived to cater simultaneously to buyers from Europe, America, Asia and the Middle East. His sentences begin, "I know you're not interested, but . . . " – and he goes on to explain materials and textures, how this was sewn, how that was designed on a computer and laser-cut. He talks about the clothes he made for Lady Gaga.

"I wish my parents could understand what I do. But that's the problem with many people I have in my life: I'm growing so fast because of my experiences that no one else understands. The kind of knowledge I am gaining every day is making me so mentally rich, it's making me so sharp, it makes me able to deal with every situation and every kind of person. I designed 200 stores for Nespresso: imagine dealing with a coffee company for eight months. I've watched them making Mercedes cars. It's amazing how much you learn. I'm surprised every day at my life. Every day. Paco Rabanne can't believe my enthusiasm: *they're* surprised by *me* because growing up here you're used to everything, you know? Nothing is a problem. I can listen to the opinions of ten people and convince all of them and still do what I want. Two years ago I would not have been able to do that. It's come from working with brands like Nespresso where they have restrictions and policies and dos and don'ts – it's all made me so polished that I can handle anything now.

"I still tell myself: '*Fuck! I'm the designer at Paco Rabanne!*' I feel like that – why shouldn't I share it? It's a great feeling. It's amazing that I can feel like that. Of course I have to work like a bitch. But I'm ready."

His friends have been calling him for a while. He is awaited elsewhere.

"I don't love Delhi as I used to," he says. "Ten years ago I really loved it. Perhaps I wasn't so aware of what was going on. But nowadays you open the newspapers and it's terrible, the things that happen here. I'm flying back to Paris tomorrow night, and I can't wait. But I'll tell you one thing about Delhi: the gay scene is amazing now. There's a party every night of the week, and people are out there in hundreds and thousands sometimes. When I came here there was none of that. The only way gay men could have sex was to fuck horny taxi drivers who had left their wives back in the village. There was no way of finding other gay men. Only straight men who were sexually frustrated. They went to the park in Connaught Place where frustrated truck drivers waited to get their cocks sucked. But now it's easy to meet gay people. There's no other city in India with a scene like Delhi, and I would say it's better than many cities in the west. My boyfriend is from Bologna: there are more options in Delhi today than in Bologna to go out to gay parties or gay bars. And now that it's legal, people are more confident. There are young men in those bars who can't afford to be there but they save all their money to go because they think they have a right to it. It's amazing."

Manish is ready to leave. He tells me, by way of rounding up, that I dress terribly and advises me to get a makeover. I'm slightly rueful. I made a bit of an effort to meet this fashion designer.

As we pay the bill, I ask him if he has found the appreciation he was looking for.

"I have a fan in Tokyo. I love Tokyo: it's the place where people are the most different from the rest of the world. My biggest fan is from there. She is crazy. She literally breathes for me. The minute she learns I'm sick, she starts crying. Anywhere I do a show, anywhere in the world, she will fly from Tokyo just for one day to see it. For her last birthday I was the surprise. They flew me down just to be there at her party. She is what a real fan is. If there's somebody who loves me in the whole world, it's her."

It has been said that there are some who need to be loved by one person, some who need the love of many, and others who need to be loved by the entire world. But even when you fall into the last category, it seems, it is in the attentions of a single individual that the love of the multitude becomes manifest.[6]

Five

Two sisters who had locked themselves inside their Noida residence for the past seven months and were living in inhuman conditions were rescued by the local police on Tuesday. The sisters, both in their forties, were rushed to hospital, where the condition of one of them was described as critical owing to severe malnutrition and dehydration.

Both sisters have PhDs and were until recently successful professionals. They are said to have fallen into severe depression after their father, an army officer, passed away a few years ago. The sisters also have an estranged brother living separately in Delhi. He and his family reportedly had no contact with the sisters for the past four years. The death of the family's pet dog a few months ago is said to have aggravated their depression. The sisters had lost their mother much earlier.

A doctor in the hospital said, "The sisters arrived in an extremely emaciated condition. The elder sister was unconscious and suffering from internal and oral bleeding. The other sister is very disoriented in terms of time and space."

– News item, April 2011[7]

In the older centres of the global market, observers felt they knew exactly what all these developments in far-off India meant. The technology companies, the cafés, the mixed-gender groups of professionals drinking after work, the alternative lifestyles: Americans recognised it all immediately as – America. Knowing publications such as the *New York Times* 'explained' to their readers how the landscape of the rising Asian giant was, through the spread of cappuccino drinking, rapidly becoming just like their own. 'How India Became America'[8] went the title of one such article:

> Recently, both Starbucks and Amazon announced that they would be entering the Indian market [. . .] As one Indian newspaper put it, this could be "the final stamp of globalization". For me, though, the arrival of these two companies, so emblematic of American consumerism, and so emblematic, too, of the West Coast techie culture that has infiltrated India's own booming technology sector, is a sign of something more distinctive. It signals the latest episode in India's remarkable process of Americanization.

Cold-War suspicion between India and the United States was laid exuberantly to rest in March 2000, when Bill Clinton made the first state visit to India of any US president since 1978. His tour came at the peak of the Nasdaq's technology-fuelled boom, and Clinton was quick to acknowledge the contribution Indians had made to this extraordinary period of American capitalism. "Indian–Americans now run more than 750 companies in Silicon Valley alone," he said, singling out for tribute tech godfathers Vinod Khosla, who had graduated from the Indian Institute of Technology in Delhi before going to Stanford and co-founding Sun Microsystems, and Vinod Dham, who had studied at the Delhi College of Engineering, migrated to the US and master-minded the development of Intel's Pentium chip. But the president added, "We're moving from a brain drain to a brain gain in India because many are coming home." India, he said, citing the successes of companies such as Infosys, is "fast becoming one of the world's software superpowers, proving that in a globalised world, developing nations not only can succeed, developing nations can lead."[9]

Clinton's benedictions resembled those, not of a drily detached superpower, but of an emotional older sibling. America and India shared, after all, so much of their DNA: America, too, had won independence from Britain, albeit 170 years before India; and the fact that the two countries now enjoyed such close business ties stemmed in part from the language they both inherited from this history. Both were democracies; both were extremely diverse and found their unity in a liberal constitution. And both seemed to display the same inborn predisposition towards free enterprise. In a statement that could have been a declaration of the indispensability of brotherly love, Clinton concluded, "A lot of our future depends upon whether we have the right kind of partnership with India."

It was a theme that Indian ideologues would develop elaborately over the coming decade. As China rose, as wars against Islam brought America into engagement with India's neighbours Pakistan and Afghanistan, Indian elites made a fervent case for the 'natural' partnership of their country with the superpower. "In terms of the scale and ambition of our respective political experiments, we can only be compared to one another," said Indian historian Ramachandra Guha to *Time* magazine.[10] The argument could of course be profoundly self-serving, as was demonstrated with its most conspicuous outcome, the Indo-US nuclear deal of 2008, which, since India refused to sign the Nuclear Non-Proliferation Treaty, went against existing American law, but which Indians skilfully lobbied for nonetheless on the basis that India's interests, in these days of Asian instability, were an essential outpost of America's own. "The nuclear deal [is one] that the Indians regard as basic recognition of their status as a major power," approved Fareed Zakaria, columnist at *Newsweek* and conspicuous promoter of the Indo–US partnership, and even if it destabilised the global nuclear equilibrium, it could present no grounds for anxiety since "India's objectives are exactly aligned with America's."[11]

As America's global predominance fell subject to an increasing range of challenges, the US too found it soothing to imagine India as a 'second America'. If the centre of global power was to shift to Asia, if American hegemony was to decline, perhaps India could provide the guarantee that American values continue to reign. The future managers of the world might look somewhat different, but inside they were exactly the same. The future of the world, in other words, presented no unpleasant surprises. It would be exactly like the present.

But American newspapers' bucolic descriptions of couples in shopping malls and bourbon-drinking corporate executives listening to jazz seemed, in their emphasis, profoundly foreign to those who were actually living through India's transformation. 'Globalisation' was not homogenisation, nor even Americanisation. The presence of American brand names did nothing to alter the fact that India was a vastly poorer country than the US, whose relationship to Western capitalism was full of historical ambivalence – and what was emerging in India looked like nothing ever seen in America. Even those Indians who sipped coffees in shopping malls felt a very different content to that activity from the one felt on the other side of the world. The shopping mall was only one part of a carved-up landscape, inner and outer – for there was no continuity between the world inside the mall and the one on the other side of its walls, where street traders, shanty towns and traffic jams awaited the departing consumer. The mall itself, moreover, had arrived as part of a rapacious economic torrent that had turned everything upside-down, destroying things human and divine, scattering objects and energies, and setting down alien needs and rituals in the rubble. Global capitalism might have appeared serene and civilised in its ancient heartlands but this was not how it felt when it suddenly burst in somewhere new. This is why the system failed to produce, at its edges, those tranquil, docile citizens that Westerners so often assumed were an inherent part of the package.

Crudely materialist accounts of India's rising middle classes assumed that, since they now had incomes many times larger than twenty years ago, they must be that many times happier. But many of the things that drained life of its happiness had also swelled proportionately in that time, and many people did not actually feel any kind of spiritual profit. It was true that there was an exhilarating freedom to earn and to buy. But there were, correspondingly, very few guarantees: if something went wrong you were on your own. The middle classes who benefitted from that new market freedom often realised only too late that, though their salaries might be high, they lived more vulnerable lives, in many respects, than the poorest members of many another society.

I park in the car park of one of Delhi's new corporate hospitals and walk towards the building. As I arrive, I am shocked to see a dead woman lying face down on a stretcher right outside the main entrance. She blocks the door, and I have to skirt around her to go in. She is heavy-set and only middle-aged. I sit down in the waiting room, where I'm supposed to meet some people. They haven't arrived yet and through the glass I regard the stretcher with continued disquiet. I decide to go out and see what is going on.

Standing with the dead woman is a young man who turns out to be her son.

"She was in this hospital for three weeks. After they discharged her we took her home, but her condition got worse and she died early this morning. We didn't know what to do. So we brought her here."

He has been crying. He adjusts the scarf that has been thrown over her, the better to cover her face.

"We asked for a stretcher and we got her out of the car, but when we tried to take her inside they stopped us. They said she was none of their business anymore. So we don't know what to do."

We both consider her, lying under the hot morning sun.

A car pulls up in front of the entrance. It is the man's brother. He gets out, and between them they lift the woman off the stretcher and try to get her into the back of the car. She is a big woman and it is a tiny car. The two distressed men are unable to bend her legs, and they cannot force her through the opening onto the back seat. It is an unbearable scene.

At that moment, another family member drives up. He embraces the two men hurriedly and considers the scene. He is furious. He storms into the hospital and emerges with two members of the staff. A vociferous argument ensues, during which the hospital representative repeats, "She is not a patient in this hospital. We cannot take responsibility for her."

"Their mother has just died!" the relative shouts. "They need your help! How do you expect them to move her?"

A crowd has gathered, and the situation becomes impossible for the hospital staff, who concede defeat. A few minutes later an ambulance pulls up, the dead woman is loaded inside, and a small procession sets off for the cremation ground. The crowd disperses and I sit back down in the waiting room.

It is a well-appointed room, with the sort of good fittings and bad paintings that grace such rooms all over the world. Over the entrance is the sign displayed in every Indian hospital which informs patients that it is illegal to engage in 'pre-natal sex determination' – this being an important, though far from water-tight, measure against female foeticide. Since this is a corporate hospital, there are all kinds of helpful corporate flourishes: a suggestion box, for instance, and an information desk with a friendly 'May I help you?' sign over it. A TV screen shows computer animations of medical procedures that can be purchased here. Posters advertise laser surgery for vision defects, and various treatments for scars, stretch marks and wrinkles; the happy, healthy families in the pictures are, as they are in so many contemporary Indian advertisements, white.

Corporate hospitals like this one have been a conspicuous addition to the Indian landscape. Until the 1980s, all hospitals were run by the state. India had a distinguished medical fraternity and several of these government hospitals, such as Delhi's All-India Institute of Medical Sciences, set up by Nehru in the 1950s as the nation's flagship research institute, had international reputations for medical excellence. These older institutions still provide care to the majority, but precisely for this reason they are unable to offer the sophisticated medical apparatus that has become so familiar to the middle classes through American hospital TV dramas. For this 'world-class' care, the affluent turn to the new corporate hospitals, which are nearly all majority-owned by billionaire business families – members of the entrenched power elite with the political connections required to negotiate the acquisition of the necessary tracts of urban real estate. Three such healthcare moguls live in Delhi and belong to one Punjabi family – whose members arrived in the capital as refugees from Partition, as is the case with most of the city's leading business families – which collectively runs finance companies, insurance companies, clinical research companies, film production companies and airlines – as well as hundreds of hospitals, not only in India but all across the world. In India, these corporate hospitals have not only generated an entirely new healthcare experience for the Indian middle classes – stylish, well-equipped and, of course, expensive – but have also gone a long way to pioneer, through medical tourism and telemedicine, entirely new kinds of global healthcare marketplaces.

The room is full of people. Here and there I can spot frail sufferers of dengue fever in the company of solicitous family members: it is just after the monsoon, and therefore peak mosquito season. Opposite me is an old man in a wheelchair: his wife speaks on her mobile while his son strokes his hand and speaks reassuringly into his ear. Next to me three Australian women, wearing Indian clothes and jangling with anklets, debate what time they need to arrive at the airport.

An imposing woman enters through the front door and waves at me. She is dressed in a sari and wears large glasses. I have met her only once, at a party. Her name is Aarti. She comes over to me with two young companions whom she introduces loudly.

"This is Amit, whom I told you about," she says, "and his cousin Shibani."

We greet each other. Shibani smiles politely; Amit seems ill at ease. I propose that we repair to the hospital café, and we head off in that direction. Aarti chats fluidly to me as we walk past all the people waiting outside consulting rooms. I see an Arab family in pristine robes and think to myself that it is often in hospitals that one realises how many foreigners live in this city. We come to the café, which is a franchise of a well-known chain and which therefore exudes the same nauseating smell as every other café under this name. It comes from the muffins, which they microwave until they are burning hot and serve with a knife and fork.

The TV is on silent, and set to MTV. Everyone orders cappuccinos.

"You all met in this hospital, is that right?" I ask as we sit down.

"We met in the intensive care unit," says Aarti. "We were there every day, and we shared our stories."

I would put her in her late fifties. She comes from the city's propertied Punjabi elite and speaks loudly and with confidence. Amit's speech is mouse-like in comparison.

"I never thought I would come here again," he says.

I ask him what happened to his mother but he defers to his cousin.

"He went through such trauma after his mother's death," she says, "that he couldn't work for months. Now he works very hard because he doesn't like to be in the house anymore."

She recounts the details. A couple of years ago, Amit's forty-four-year-old mother began to have difficulty swallowing, and he took her to one of Delhi's big corporate hospitals. When, after two months of tests, the doctors could not work out what was wrong, they advised him to take her to see the experts at the All-India Institute of Medical Sciences. But there was no room there and the specialists had no time. Half of them were quitting to work for the corporate hospital in which we are now sitting. One of them told Amit to consult him here, which he did. The specialist conducted three days of tests and presented a diagnosis: Amit's mother was suffering from polymyositis, an inflammatory muscle disease.

Shibani and Amit are in their mid-twenties. Shibani is quiet and serious; she wears a slim-cut salwar kameez. Amit wears a shirt and jeans. While Shibani is talking, he wordlessly shows me a photograph of his mother on his mobile phone. A rotund, smiling woman in a sari.

"That was before all this began," says Shibani.

She continues her narrative.

"The doctor immediately told us he wanted to give her an injection that would cost 4 lakhs [$8,000]. Amit did not have that money, so he called his uncle to ask if he could borrow it. The doctor told us this would restore his mother's muscles and there was no alternative, so we had to do it."

The injection he was proposing was intravenous immuno-globulin, which has been shown to assist recovery from poly-myositis. This therapy is still poorly understood, however, and it is unusual to offer it before administering corticosteroids. After administering the injection, the doctor sent Amit's mother home, giving Amit and Shibani instructions for feeding her with protein powders through a tube in her nose. At home, however, her lungs were filling up with the constant flow of saliva which she could neither swallow nor spit out. Afraid that she might drown, they rushed her back to the same hospital in the middle of the night. There she was given an oxygen mask and diagnosed with pneumonia. The next day, more tests revealed that she also had a kidney infection. She was immediately transferred to the intensive care unit.

The doctor remained calm about all of this. He said,

"I knew this would happen. But if I had told you all the side effects of the immunoglobulin, you wouldn't have gone ahead with it."

He put Amit's mother on renal dialysis. A temporary tube in her arm was replaced by a permanent one in her chest. Then the doctor set about trying to rescue her respiratory system from the saliva flow. He administered another dose of immunoglobulin to strengthen her lungs. Then he performed a tracheostomy and inserted a tube to divert saliva away from the windpipe.

"They said it would only be needed for fifteen days," says Shibani. "But after fifteen days they said she needed a permanent tube and the one they had put in was only a temporary tube. The permanent tube cost another 75,000 rupees [$1,500].

"We were spending so much money. The day rate for staying in the intensive care unit was 16,000 rupees [$320]. Oxygen and dialysis came to as much as 45,000 rupees per day [$900]. Every night, Amit had to visit relatives all over the city to borrow money. People were giving us cash from their wedding funds.

"You don't know what to do. When you have the patient lying on the bed, the person who has brought you up, you are so emotional you cannot think. And this is how they get you.

"It was going on for weeks. Every day they would say, 'Your mother is recovering.' Our hopes would rise. Then they would say, 'She is not recovering.'"

We are a quiet group. Shibani's voice is soft, and we are all gathered around it. Amit looks into his half-drunk coffee as he listens; Aarti's gaze takes in the hot morning outside, and the manicured garden.

"Meanwhile her blood platelet levels had sunk to critical levels. And her saliva was still not controlled, so that she could no longer even talk, let alone eat. The doctor proposed another drug which would cost 1.7 lakhs [$3,400]. They administered this drug, which was supposed to restore her system and control her saliva flow. It had no effect. The doctors said to us, 'Of course it is not working. All the medicine is being flushed out of her body by the dialysis.'

"It was hell in there. People were dying at such a rate in the intensive care unit that there was panic all the time, and no one to take care of Amit's mother. The doctors never came to see her. They had no link at all to their patients. We were not allowed to go into the ward to see her. They never told us anything except, 'She needs more medicine.' There was nothing we could do except pay the bills. Every evening we received the bill for the day and we handed over the cash we had borrowed from our family. When you went to the accounts department, you saw massive trunks of 1,000 and 500 rupee notes being carried out to the bank."

Aarti laughs wryly. Shibani continues,

"We asked to take her out of intensive care, which was so expensive, so they put her in a normal ward where we could spend time with her. But she had reached a terrible state. She had bedsores and she was continually crying. All she would say was, 'Take me out of here!'

"We asked the doctors what we should do. They said, 'She is not eating. We need to put a hole in her stomach so we can feed her through it.' While we were discussing this with them, a nurse came in to tell us that Amit's mother had passed away."

Tears begin to pour down Amit's face as Shibani recalls this moment.

She says, "And you know what the doctor said to us? He said, 'Perhaps if we put her back into intensive care and put her on a ventilator, she'll revive. We can try that.' So I said, 'On one condition. I want to stay with her the whole time and watch what you do.' And the doctor said, 'Families are not allowed into the intensive care unit.' So we said, 'Then we won't do it.' And he said, 'Of course, if you don't want your mother to live, then

. . . I mean there is a 1 per cent chance that she will live – who are you to decide that she should not survive? But if you don't have money . . . '

"But we were done. It was over. We told the doctor, and he left us.

"We went in to see Amit's mother. Immediately someone came to collect the outstanding money. They talked to us across her dead body. 'You have 2 lakhs [$4,000] outstanding. Please pay.' They had no respect. They talked over her body. In India we respect the dead, you know? They were so rude."

Amit intervenes. "When we cremated my mother, the priest told me her bones had turned to powder."

Shibani is fiery with the rage all these memories have aroused.

"People are dying for no reason," she says. "At least we have a little money. We met people who were kicked out of the hospital when their insurance money was used up, and the doctors hardly bothered to sew them up. Of course, people who have no money at all don't have a chance."

"These hospitals are totally corrupt," says Aarti. "Patients are only profit. Nothing else. Anything they can't understand they call cancer because then they can pump you with the most expensive medicines. This religious, spiritual country – the humanity is going out of it. Very little good is being done but a lot of harm is being done."

"What happened to your husband?" I ask her.

"He died here too. Just before Amit's mother. He was a very good man. We had forty-three years of beautiful companionship. These days very few people can say that. I was married to a man who never stopped thinking about me and looking out for me."

I realise Aarti must be older than she looks.

"He came from a well-known family. There were famous journalists and academics in the family, and film stars. He had a successful career and we moved in good circles. Anybody who's anybody in Delhi, I know them."

Aarti has to take a minute to establish her class position. Her story has additional weight because she is *someone*.

"My side of the family is well-known too," she says. "Both my grandfathers were titled. My father's father was from Jalandhar. He became chief engineer of the railways: he was knighted and received an OBE. They were a famous Delhi family who used to be very close to Indira Gandhi. My mother's family came from Lahore – they lost everything in 1947 and came over to stay in Delhi. My grandfather did very well in business and acquired a grand mansion in the diplomatic enclave."

She is so Delhi. It drives me crazy.

"My husband was never sick. He was 6'1" and strapping. He never wore glasses. He never went to a dentist in his life and his teeth were all his own. When he was seventy years old he used to thrash thirty-five-year-olds on the badminton court. He never took a rest in the afternoon. During the forty-three years we were married, apart from a few colds and a back injury, I don't remember him ever being ill.

"In October 2009 everything went wrong. On 4 November he went into hospital and by 5 February of the following year, he was gone.

"The problem was never diagnosed, though I sent his tests to dozens of doctors. It started with a viral fever and then he became very weak. A low-grade fever continued for some time. A multitude of tests were done. We were sent to see endocrinologists who gave him expensive drugs. At first those drugs put him in a cold sweat and then they gave him a stroke.

"You see, he never took medication in his life. If he had to take an aspirin he used to cut it in half. He couldn't take so much medicine. They started pumping antibiotics into his system four times a day just because it cost 5,000 rupees [$100] a time. I said, 'What are you doing? You are only thinking about drugs and money, but I love him and I can see what it's doing to him.'

"They started chemotherapy without a diagnosis! They had no idea what was wrong with him. The doctors were so well-known, I felt I had to do what they said. But each time I listened to the doctor, my husband got worse. And it was only when I didn't listen that he got any better.

"I took him out of that hospital and went to another. I went with all his test results but they wanted to test everything again – there was incredible over-testing. They said they wanted to do a biopsy of his lymph nodes, which had become swollen with all the medication. It would be a simple procedure with a local anaesthetic.

"The night before it was supposed to happen I was sleeping in his hospital room when I suddenly woke up. It was dark, it must have been one in the morning, and I saw there was a beautiful nurse standing in the room. If you saw her you would say, 'What a beautiful woman!' So I opened my eyes and saw this extremely beautiful woman standing by my husband's bed. She had brought a form for him to sign, authorising the hospital to do a much more expensive procedure under general anaesthetic. Can you imagine? My husband was almost delirious with the drugs, and he would have woken up in the middle of the night to see this angel in his room asking him to sign a piece of paper? I told her to leave, that this wasn't what the doctor had told us, and I took my husband out of that hospital the next morning."

The combination of high costs and low information that characterises this system is an insidious one, and leads to a paranoid panic which only makes things worse. Patients consult twenty doctors because they trust none of them. They abort therapies and change hospitals, with the result that there is no sustained treatment.

"When we arrived in the next hospital, my husband began to recover. They gave less medication. His platelet levels had dipped to 45,000 per microlitre before we came there – they are supposed to be above 150,000 – but they began to rise again. After a few days, he was ready to leave hospital. But they decided they had to get more revenue out of him, and they faked his blood test result.

"He was ready to leave: he was putting on his scarf. He hated being in hospital and was very happy to be leaving. Usually, the blood tests came up automatically on the monitor in his room. On that morning they did not. He was getting his coat on but we couldn't leave before the test results arrived. There was no reason to worry – his platelet count had risen from 45,000 to 90,000 while he had been in that hospital.

"I went to ask why the results had not come. No one could tell me. The doctor said, 'Let me call the lab myself.' He looked at me and without listening to anything on the other end he told me that my husband's platelet count had fallen to 43,000 and that he needed an emergency transfusion.

"I went into a panic. If his levels had fallen so much in ten hours, how much further could they fall? There was no question of going home – he could go into a coma. 'I'm sorry my love,' I said, 'but you have to have a transfusion.' I was panicking and not thinking that anything might be wrong. I had to find a donor quickly. My nephew rushed from Gurgaon to donate platelets. He was so sweet. He came as soon as he could. When he learned he had to give five litres of blood he went white, but he still gave it. He is like my third son now. I will never forget what he did.

"By the evening, everything was ready for the transfusion. Before going ahead, they did another blood test as per procedure. I demanded to see the results of that test. My husband's platelet count was 90,000. Which meant it had never fallen in the first place! They had not given us the results in the morning just so they could sell a blood transfusion for 50,000 rupees [$1,000].

"During this whole time there had been a Sikh doctor in Texas who was monitoring our situation. He was a cancer specialist who had treated one of my friends. He was the only doctor who paid real attention to the reports I sent. Every evening he would call up at his own expense to find out what was happening. There was so much kindness in his voice. He knew what was going to happen and gave me advice about it. He said, 'He could start developing fluid in his lungs – you have to be careful.' So I told the doctors but they didn't care about anything we said, the bastards – and then he got fluid in his lungs. The doctor from Texas told me to make sure he wasn't given any steroids and then when he came to this hospital they started giving him massive doses and his system packed up.

"It was this hospital that killed him. They were so trigger-happy with medicines that they killed him. Before that, he had started picking up. When he went into the intensive care unit here – which is when I met Amit and Shibani – it finished him. I left him for a few minutes and when I came back he had tubes stuck in everywhere, and he was grunting and breathing terribly. He had burn marks on either side of his neck, which I never found an explanation for. I took him out of intensive care: I said he'll die in my arms, not with all these strange faces peering at him. They'd put a central line in him because they didn't have the patience to deal with the oedema from where the drip went in. I went back over the documents and saw that two minutes after they'd done that his heart had stopped beating.

"After he died I started my own investigation. In the early days I could only take a bit at a time because I would break down with the pain. But now I am starting to be much more serious. I am researching everything. Knowledge is never wasted. Money is wasted. Partying and merrymaking can be wasted. But knowledge, never.

"Twenty years ago, my husband's sister persuaded their father to sign the family house over to her so she could sell it to developers without my husband's permission. I went on a war footing. I had my own thriving business at the time but I put the whole thing on hold to throw myself into the legal battle. My husband couldn't do it: he was ready to collapse, seeing his sister and father turn against him. For two years I did nothing else. I read legal textbooks and taught myself the law. I learned how everything worked. I learned to manoeuvre through the lawyer-judges nexus. And I fought the case myself. I was up against a big racket of builders and real-estate people but I won the case in two years. I made everyone's life hell for all that time and in the end they had their hands together, pleading with me to leave them alone. No one could believe a case like this could be finished in two years – usually they take twenty. I had pulled out documents that no one could believe, ancient property files lost in Old Delhi.

"I learned the law then and I will learn medicine now. I helped at least twenty people after my court case and I will help many more when I find out what happened to my husband. I am hungry for knowledge. I worship knowledge. For me anyone is a superior person who can answer the questions that are troubling me.

"We didn't have health insurance. We paid everything ourselves. The hospitals wanted to put him on a ventilator for a month so they could charge us 30 lakhs [$60,000]. They tried to put him on dialysis because they had a new dialysis machine. But there was nothing wrong with his kidneys.

"Terrible things went on. I met a woman who had come in for a heart attack. Her arms were blue from the wrist to the shoulder from tests. How many tests do you need to do to a woman with a heart attack? But you can't ask any of those questions. Doctors have complete legal immunity: they ask you to sign forms at every stage indemnifying them. They are always offering you some wonder drug or other that will solve every-thing and will cost lakhs and lakhs. And after you have spent 40 or 50 lakhs and you are exhausted, they hand you a dead body and tell you to get out."

Our coffee cups are cold.

Shibani and Amit are nodding to themselves. There is some-thing remarkable about the complicity between these two cousins. Shibani is so meek in her appearance, and yet so powerful and impressive.

"You did everything you possibly could for your mother and for your aunt," I say to them. "That must have meant something to her."

Shibani glances at Amit.

"Actually we are not cousins," she says. "We are in a relation-ship. But since we are not married, no one thinks I can play a legitimate role in this story of Amit's mother, so we say we are cousins. The first doctors said to me, 'She's not your mother and you are not married to this man, so who are you to care for her?' But I had to take care of Amit's mother, because he was working."

Aarti is surprised at this twist in their story, but she says nothing. The coffee grinder roars for a few seconds in the back-ground. Everyone waits patiently through the silence in our conversation, not wanting to move.

Aarti says, "My husband was a tango dancer, a waltz dancer, a sportsman. He was a very hearty man. He was in love with life. When things started going wrong, he said to me, 'If my legs go, I don't want to live anymore.' I said to him, 'I'll take care of you. We've been blessed with forty-three healthy years together. What does it matter if one of us is sick now? We can go on for many years more. I will give up everything to take care of you.'

"That's what I did for those three months. He was never left alone. I never let them park him in a corridor which is what they always do. I said, 'He is not queuing in a corridor on his bed where everyone can stare at him. He will stay in his room and come down when the doctor is ready.'

"But at the end, when I went into the intensive care unit here and saw him full of pipes I broke down and I said, 'Go, go, my love, don't stay in this world anymore. This is no life for you.' And I took him out of there and back to his room. And I put on some beautiful devotional music from our Sikh tradi-tion and I massaged his head all night. He was at peace, he was not grunting or making noises. He just slipped away. I stayed with him all night – but he did not die then. He knew that if he died, I would be left all on my own. He waited until the next afternoon, when everyone was there around us and he knew he could leave me with people who loved me. Even in death he was so considerate.

"I gave him a beautiful death. In all of this, that's my only satisfaction."

Aarti speaks with great matter-of-factness about all this. There is no outward emotion – except, perhaps, a certain zeal, for she is a woman in whom adversity releases great retributive energy.

"For forty-three years," she says, "he gave me roses every Valentine's Day. Once when we were in Bombay and he couldn't afford twelve, he bought six. Other years he bought twelve or even twenty-four.

"This year I was talking to my sister in London and I said, 'I'll have to get used to not having roses on Valentine's Day.' But on the fourteenth, I arrived home in the evening and there was a massive bunch of roses from her. Her note said, 'Aarti, he never left you. He will always love you. These are from him.'"

For most people in the world, medical adversity represents the greatest source of financial crisis, and India has never been any different. Until liberalisation, however, the cost of healthcare was lower by several orders of magnitude, not only because doctors charged lower fees, but also because the whole business was significantly less technologically intense. Magnetic Resonance Imaging (MRI) scanning machines, for instance, were rare, and most doctors made their diagnoses without access to expensive tests of these sorts. Drugs and therapeutic equipment, similarly, were both more rudimentary and cheaper before liberalisation allowed the entry into India of the world's major pharmaceutical companies. So if serious health problems inevitably presented periods of financial stress, the cost levels were such that middle-class people could usually meet them by pooling the resources of family and friends.

The system worked also because doctors had high levels of

prestige and credibility. While many government hospital doctors supplemented their income by offering private consultations at home in the evenings, in the hospital itself they worked for a fixed salary and had no financial stake in the diagnoses and treatments they offered. Their medical judgement was, in their patient's eyes, uncompromised. There was every reason to feel secure, when consulting a doctor, that his or her interest was similar to one's own.

After liberalisation this equilibrium was significantly disrupted. Government hospitals had by this time become conspicuously under-resourced, and the middle classes flocked to the new corporate hospitals. But the costs here were such that, in the case of the most extreme and drawn-out of illnesses, even affluent families could stand to lose everything they possessed. And though the middle classes began in the same period to invest in the new health insurance packages offered by private financial institutions, these were often adequate only for relatively minor treatments. Even the most comprehensive of them excluded treatment for several chronic diseases – various kinds of cancer, all illnesses resulting from HIV, anything at all that struck past the age of sixty-five – and total re-imbursement in one year to any one patient was usually capped at a relatively low level, usually between $5,000 and $20,000. The most devastating financial territory was entirely unsecured.

This already-dangerous situation was exacerbated by the new suspicions introduced by the conspicuous profit motive of corporate hospitals. There was no doubt that these institutions were *corporations*: they looked like corporations, they expanded – and bought and sold each other – with corporate speed, and they were administered by some of the country's major financial interests. Patients in these hospitals were fully aware of the aggression with which big Indian businesses operated; they also knew that corporations were something of a fiefdom, whose practices went largely unscrutinised by any independent body – and they were therefore racked with uncertainty as to the nature of what was happening to them. Was this expense necessary to treat their condition or was the corporation simply trying to suck up their money?

As everyone knows who has moved from one country to another, the last thing one becomes accustomed to is a new healthcare system; and the shift to this new healthcare regime in India would have produced suspicion even if its integrity were beyond reproach – and in many cases, of course, it was. But there was considerable disquiet within the medical establishment too, and many doctors confirmed that the storm in patients' heads was not only in their heads. A surgeon from a leading government hospital felt that his entire profession was under threat from the new corporate hospitals.

"They are money machines," he said. "They are about revenue maximisation, pure and simple, and they have led to a dangerous collapse in medical judgement and ethics.

"Let me give you an example. A leading surgeon left his job at the government hospital where I work to join one of the big corporate hospitals. He was offered a salary of 2.4 crores a year [$480,000], which was ten times his previous salary, but it was dependent on him delivering 12 crores [$2.4 million] of revenue to the hospital. Now, if he did the maximum possible number of operations in a year, he still would not deliver 50 per cent of that figure. So the rest had to be delivered by diagnostic tests. Which is why there has been such a huge escalation in tests. Patients are sent to do repeated MRI scans so that doctors can meet targets. Some patients have very high radiation exposure as a result of all this.

"Certain surgical procedures are carried out almost without indication. Anyone who has upper abdominal pain has their gall bladder removed. Forty per cent of these procedures are unnecessary. But the patient doesn't know that. It's usually not possible for a patient to find any evidence of malpractice.

"Look at the rates of Caesarian section. Some of the most famous obstetricians deliver 70 to 80 per cent of their babies by

Caesarian. There is hardly a hospital in this city that offers a natural birth service. Why? Caesarians make more money than normal births, of course, but more importantly they allow doctors to determine the schedule and to fit more women in. It's much more efficient.

"The pharmaceutical and medical equipment industries have a huge role in deciding treatment options because many of these doctors are working directly for those companies, which the patient doesn't know. Drug companies pay many oncologists 10 per cent of the value of the chemotherapy they prescribe; a typical figure would be a crore [$200,000] of prescriptions a month. Cancer of the pancreas is a favourite, because if you get to the stage where you need chemotherapy you are anyway going to die within six months, so doctors can prescribe whatever they like.

"These hospitals are very dark institutions, even at the business level. Land is acquired for them by the government at an enormously subsidised level, and often the government donates money towards the cost of setting up the hospital, on the condition that it allocates a third of beds to the poor. But the hospitals never honour such commitments: there is no question of them writing off those kinds of profits. Later on, they sell a share of their company to the public for hundreds of millions of dollars and the newspapers laud them as self-made billionaires. But their fortunes were built largely from public money."

He talks calmly, but with brimming outrage.

"You should write your entire book about this," he says to me. "I can't do it because all these people are my colleagues. But someone needs to write about all this. Pose as a patient and see what happens. Start telling people you need to buy a kidney and see where you are led. In my hospital I worked with an anaesthetist who was involved in a big kidney transplantation racket in Delhi. Kidney transplantation is very easy: you can do it in a normal flat. And India is the diabetes capital of the world, so many people are proceeding inexorably towards end-stage renal disease, which is completely wretched. Add to that a lot of poor people willing to sell a kidney and the outcome is obvious.

"The whole industry has become very sinister. Where does it find its cadavers, for instance? With all these new pharmaceutical companies and research laboratories, demand is growing on every side. Tissue banks need cadavers. Every company that manufactures implants needs to test them on cadavers. Now, the Mysore Anatomy Act of 1958 says that only unclaimed cadavers can be used for medical experimentation. But large-scale entrepreneurial medicine needs far more than this. So now you have bodies being stolen everywhere. They disappear from funeral homes and end up in surgeons' colleges and corporations."

I tell him how I recently met a man who supplied cadavers to a dental college. I asked him where he got them from and he told me he fished them out of the Hindon river, a tributary of the Yamuna. He just sat by the river every day waiting for corpses to float down.

The doctor smiles.

"That river flows through Ghaziabad. A lot of those people whose bodies end up advancing dental careers would have been killed in property wars. Bumped off by rivals. It's an appropriate image for Indian medicine today. Taking the chaos of our society and turning it into profit."

Six

A man is telling me about the decline of his marriage. Part of the story is an affair his wife was having at work. From the way he tells it, I do not quite believe in this affair. I make the statement deliberately bald to see if he will stand by it.

"So she was having an affair," I say. "That must have been—"

"At least I *thought* she was having an affair—"

"You *thought* she was having an affair?"

"She thought I was having an affair. So I thought she was having an affair."

I realise that he knows perfectly well she was not having an affair. But he *thought* it all the same, as a form of revenge.

Discontent was a persistent irritant in Delhi during this period, like a bad spice lodged in the city's proverbial belly.

Often this discontent was of a very material and obvious sort. The group of people who felt that the serene, propertied lifestyle depicted in advertising campaigns was intended for them – a minority of the population, certainly, but a substantial one – came to realise that life in the new India did not automatically turn out like that. The carefree adults, the sprawling kitchens, the moneyed youth – none of this seemed to come as easily as one was led to believe. In fact, it grew to seem more and more remote, for property prices rose more quickly even than good middle-class salaries.

This particular kind of discontent was sharp. The middle classes had a strong sense in those years that wealth was their due: it had been promised to them. And it had been promised now: this was India's moment, and it might not come again. This explains those newspaper articles during that period which documented 'unconventional' middle-class money-making: the students who supplemented their income by theft or prostitution and, much more widespread, those entrepreneurial corporate employees who found ingenious ways to redirect company money to themselves.

But there were many other forms of discontent too, and if these were more inscrutable, they probably had a more profound and distressing effect on people's lives. It was clear for instance that the family – that symbolic mainstay of Indian society, in whose name so many people embarked on this fury of accumulation in the first place – was under enormous stress. It was as if the torque of the new system was exerted asymmetrically on parents and children and, in particular, on men and women: the various units of the family were wrenched in different directions, and bonds deformed and broke. Nowhere was this more visible than in middle-class marriages, which were exploding in those years like so many nuptial firecrackers.

"I think it would have been better if my husband and I had lived separately from his mother," says Sukhvinder. "At least there wouldn't have been so much constant bickering. And I think my husband would have been a little bit more open to new ideas. He was very stuck living under that roof. He did what he had always done and in the way he had always done it. The word 'change' did not exist."

We are sitting under Mediterranean-style parasols on the roof of one of Delhi's upscale shopping malls. There are other tables around us where people speak on mobile phones and sip brightly coloured drinks.

Down below, the mall encloses a cosy courtyard of cafés and restaurants. There is a billboard showing a larger-than-life photo of the new Mercedes S-Class on one side and, on the other, a video wall showing fashion ads. The architecture mimics those Italian Renaissance drawings of perfectly geometrical cities: there are classical columns and porticoes, and a square piazza where docile people are pleasingly arranged. In the middle are fountains, which periodically start up a synchronised display accompanied by loud Johann Strauss waltzes; people stop their conversations during these episodes – they don't have much choice – to watch the plumes of water prettily conversing, copying each other, chasing each other like chorus girls. The waltz ends with crashing chords and all the fountains ejaculate simultaneously. It feels like everyone should get married at this point, or kiss, or something. But conversations just resume, and the piazza reverts to how it was before.

Delhi's malls began small and late, but as the 2000s wore on, they sucked up more and more of the city's resources and attention. Great amounts of public land were released to private developers, who built frenziedly – quickly covering up, for instance, the ancient ruins they came upon as they went – and by the end of the century's first decade, several great air-conditioned consumer strongholds had been added to the thousand-year catalogue of palaces built on this plain.

The new mall we are in has been erected just next to the airport – which is why low planes roar so frequently over our heads – and in many ways it has absorbed the spirit of its location. The marshalls who wave cars around the underground lot seem to have been borrowed from the runways next door: their arm signals make you feel you are perched in a cockpit. Like an airport, the mall is entirely cut off from the space around: if we take the trouble to look through the screen of trees along the wall on the other side of this terrace, we can see that the landscape around the succulent mall, with all its lawns and fountains, is like a CNN cliché of ravaged earth. Right now, a truck has come to deliver water to the large slum below us: women and children are rushing out of their houses with as many plastic containers as they can carry.

Inside the mall, the number of men and women wearing aviator sunglasses continues the feeling – as if buying French fashion or American technology were an activity only a shade less intrepid than flying a fighter jet. There is something aeronautic about everything – as if membership of the small minority of people who can shop here brings with it a desire to lift off from the chaotic sprawl of the contemporary Indian city into a kind of well-enclosed Duty Free in the sky. Through its refracted memories of European metropolitan achievement – the Italian piazza, the Viennese ballroom – the mall seems to present itself as part of a long history of ideal cities, but this ideal city, of course, is not a city at all. It is not even really 'in' the city, since it can only be accessed by highway, and then only by a very small proportion of the population. It is a place where all transactions seem to serve the same purpose, a place with bag scans and body checks at the entrance. Just as the ideal home for so many of Delhi's rich seems to be a five-star hotel, the ideal city seems to be an airport.

"My parents started looking for a husband for me as soon as I finished my MA," says Sukhvinder, who is tall, quick-witted and hilarious. "I'm Sikh, so we generally don't wait too long."

One should not imagine that arranged marriages are the burden of 'tradition' imposed by regressive parents on 'modern' and unwilling children, for the situation is often more complex than that. In many cases, the parents of those having arranged marriages today did not themselves have arranged marriages, nor have they forced their children into them. Many arranged marriages emerge therefore, not from tradition, but from the rush of contemporary circumstance. In these days of uncertainty and change, choosing to go it alone is for many people too isolated, and too risky, a prospect. Children who have moved very far from the ambit of their parents feel that *something* should tie them down. And arranged marriages provide many reassurances in an era so short of them: in such alliances, responsibility for the couple's prosperity and happiness belongs, not to the couple alone, but to the combined ranks of their families.

But for Sukhvinder there was added pressure because she had a cleft palate, which her parents felt would make it more difficult to find a husband for her. So she joined those thousands of family groups who at any one time are sitting across from another family group in Delhi's restaurants and hotels, trying to strike up a conversation.

"Every weekend I'd meet guys. Each time I would sit totally disinterested because you know you have this thing in your mind about a guy that you want to marry and all the guys I met were jerks. I don't know why everyone pretends to be extremely modern and *out there* and inside they're complete idiots if I may say so. They're in the party circle and very well dressed up and all of that, very expensive shades. And when they open their mouths you're like, '*Oh my God*.'"

Parents use many methods to find prospective spouses for their offspring. Professional matchmakers cover a particular caste group or social class: they circulate albums containing single men and women's résumés accompanied by photographs which, especially in the case of women, are minor masterpieces all of their own, the make-up professionally done beforehand, the carefully styled hair borne aloft on studio fans. But such matchmakers can serve only a small and well-delineated universe of partners. For a long time now, the 'matrimonial' pages of the newspapers have been the primary way to reach out into the city at large – and for traditionalists they are still the sole trusted route. In the last few years, however, online marriage agencies have stormed the market – in part because they also offer additional features such as detective and astrology services. Detectives check up on a person's marital and sexual past, and verify the information they provide – that they really are HIV-negative, for instance, or vegetarian, or perfectly sighted. Astrologers ensure that there are not terrible clashes between the birth stars of the two prospective partners.

"I wanted to get married to someone I could have a conversation with. After 'Hi', most of these guys had nothing to say. 'Don't show the real you,' is what my parents kept telling me, 'don't open your mouth too wide,' so I'm trying to keep my mouth shut and I'm sitting listening to these guys and they're like, 'So do you know how to cook?' and I'm like 'Cook? No. I've always worked.' '*Oh*.'"

It is difficult to convey in text the lobotomised tone in which Sukhvinder imitates her male interlocutors. Her renditions have me weeping with mirth.

"Then they would say, 'Do you intend to quit your job?' 'No.' '*Oh*. Because we don't have any women working in our family.' So I would say, 'I think this isn't happening then.' '*Oh*. You have *very* strong views.' I'm like, 'Yeah.' '*Oh*.' So the conversation used to end right there."

Sukhvinder and her sister are directors of their father's business, which manufactures equipment for the printing industry. She is in charge of operations, which means that her working day often ends late. Quick-thinking and sure of her judgements, it is easy to see why she would be good at what she does.

"So I finally met Dhruv, the guy I married. I couldn't point out any real flaws when we met the first time, and his family was not open to us meeting many more times. Because I'm a blabbermouth, I didn't realise he didn't talk. He just answered whatever I asked and that was about it, but he really had nothing to say. Mom and Dad wanted me to get married quickly because my sister was going through a rough patch in her marriage, and if something were to happen, I would be less eligible. So things moved quickly. My parents went to see their house and said it was nice. My father visited their factories, which seemed fine, though as we found out later they were not doing well at all.

"Things went badly from the very beginning. We were very different people. I told my husband before we got married, 'I drink and I smoke and I don't plan to quit. I understand the family you come from. If you think you have a problem with this, tell me now and we won't do this. We haven't got engaged yet, I'm not in love with you and I dare say you're not in love with me. So we can say what we think.' 'No, I'm absolutely cool with that,' he said. I said, 'Fine.'

"When we went on our honeymoon, I carried five boxes of smokes. On the way we had a stopover in Singapore. I really wanted to smoke, but he was more into shopping, so I didn't. So we got to Bali, we checked into the hotel, and the first thing I did was to light a cigarette, go out on the balcony and sit there looking at the view and thinking about this beautiful holiday. And he looked at me and he was quite taken aback; he hadn't seen me smoking before. He was like, 'Can't you put that thing down? Don't you want to rest a little bit? Don't you want to lie down and watch TV?'

"I said, 'I understand that a honeymoon is about lots of sex, but it's not only about sex. We have to plan out what we're going to do here because we may never come here again.' And I'd brought all these pamphlets from the airport, and I wanted him to look through them with me so we could decide what we wanted to do.

"He was very boring. I had to drag him along to scuba diving. The guy didn't know how to swim and he was nervous about it. So when I realised he was going to take a long time, I jumped in the water and spent a nice twenty minutes, and I came up and he was still sitting on the boat. He said, 'I'm just about to go.' Then I went down again and when I came back, he wasn't there, so I realised he must be under the water. I was tired and I got on the boat, and there was this guy smoking a rolled cigarette and I asked him if he had another one.

"So by the time my husband pops up, I was sitting and smoking, and he saw me and said, 'Where did you get that cigarette from? You didn't bring yours with you.' So I said, 'No they're his.' He was really shocked. He said, 'But you don't know him!' I said, 'Okay, sorry.' So I put out my cigarette.

"Actually it was finished anyway. I don't waste my smokes. Not for anyone in the world.

"I said, 'Let's not make an issue of this.'

"Then we went shopping. You know, usually when you go away for the first time as a married couple, you bring back presents for everyone, so I made a list of everyone in his family and mine. He wanted to buy a carved wooden statue for himself. He looked at statues for forty-five minutes. I was going crazy. He said, 'Don't get impatient.' Impatient? I wanted to pull his hair! I said, 'You choose your statue, I'm going to buy the presents.' I went and bought gifts for twenty-five people, came back, and he was still looking for his statue.

"He said, 'I don't just spend like you do. I'm careful about money.' I said, 'Being careful with money is one thing. I'm careful with money. But wasting your God-given time is something else.'

"That day I realised that I would never go shopping with him. So after we got back to Delhi, I took all his measurements and I used to go and get him everything he needed. Because I can't stand wasting time shopping.

"But later I realised that actually he wasn't doing so well for money, which is why he was uncomfortable about spending. His business was not doing well. After I realised that, I used to deliberately leave his wallet at home when we went out, so that if he liked something we could just get it and he wouldn't have to think too hard. And then I stopped shopping in front of him. Which made me feel a little guilty because more often than not, I had to sneak things inside the house and lie about when I'd bought them. But he developed a real inferiority complex about money and it became an issue between us.

"There was this time when I walked in on his uncle saying to him, 'You can go and take over their business and it will all be yours. They have so much property and it will all come to you eventually and you can really make a life out of your wife.' I did not like that conversation at all because in our family we've always given more priority to relationships than to money. Even when Papa was starting up the business and we were hard-up, money was never an issue. We went through a patch when my parents only ate one meal a day to save money. But it never affected us.

"Cash was never really an *issue* for us. If we had it, we had it; if we didn't, we didn't. In his family, money was a really big thing. Much bigger than relationships. Which was really weird for me. Why would someone give priority to something that might not be there tomorrow rather than to people who might help you in your old age or whatever? But that's how he was. So his inferiority complex came up. And because of that a lot of fights started happening and abusive language."

The sun is going down and the feel of evening descends on the terrace. The heat of the day evaporates, leaving the roar of the highway somehow more exposed. Great numbers of crows caw overhead. Waiters put candles out on the tables. Groups of twenty-somethings turn up for after-work drinks; like everyone else in this mall – except the ones who clean and guard it – they are high-caste and pale-skinned.

A woman is taking photographs of her colleagues on her phone, which flashes each time with improbable brilliance. She has her back to us; through her beige business suit I can see the precise outline of her black thong.

"Soon after I moved into my husband's house," Sukhvinder continues, "I realised that the dependency between him and his mother was intense, and it made me extremely uncomfortable. Especially because his father had died many years before, and he acted as a husband as well as a son towards his mother. I have absolutely no issues about a son having a good relationship with his mother, but his mother intervened in every aspect of our relationship. There are certain things that should remain between a husband and a wife. After every conversation I had with Dhruv, his mother used to taunt me for it the next day. And I used to be quite taken aback. 'You know about that too! What else do you know about?' So I spoke to him about it, but he was absolutely closed to the idea of me saying anything whatsoever about his mother.

"I used to sit down with her – I am an open person and I believe a lot in talking about stuff – so I used to sit with her and talk to her, thinking that I could be a friend to her, since she didn't have a companion. But it totally blew up in my face. Each time I used to talk with her, she used to go to my husband and say, 'She was trying to say some shit against you.'

"She thought I was trying to take her son away from her. She thought, since my family had more money, I would one day buy her son off, move to a different house and make him totally forget about her. Which is really weird. I was the one who always said we should never move out because otherwise his mother would be lonely. Her other son never talked to her. He treated her like shit. So I said to my husband, 'She's our responsibility and we'll take care of her.'

"But she would tell Dhruv, 'You don't know what she is plotting, I heard her talking on the phone, she is evil.' Which was ridiculous. I never made phone calls when I was in the house because I knew what it would lead to afterwards.

"I used to tell Dhruv: 'She doesn't believe in herself or the values that she's given you. Or the man she's made you into. Otherwise why would she be so insecure? You take care of her. She knows you care about her. What is she scared about? One mere girl walking into your house? I'm not here to break up your family.'

"I was supposed to get up in the morning, cook, pack everyone's lunch, drive an hour to work, run the factory and get out of there in time to buy vegetables for the evening meal and be home by 7 p.m. to cook the dinner. Initially I didn't know how to cook and she taught me, which I still thank her for. But if I got back at 7.01 she'd have taken her place in the kitchen and she wouldn't let me enter, and then there would be a huge scene. I had to be in the kitchen by 7 p.m. so that Dhruv would not face some almighty scene when he came home. Nobody wants to walk into a house after work where there's already bickering happening, and I realised the only way I could help Dhruv was if I turned up on time. There were days when I left the office at 4.30 p.m. I mean, when it's your own business, you can take certain liberties. But it became a big problem: you can't go too far.

"Then there came a time when he told me that his mother had a problem with me working. I said to him, 'I told you before I'm not going to give up working.' But then it was ruining everything that I'd worked on so much that for a month I didn't go to work at all.

"I was not allowed to have any social life. The only time I socialised was when I sometimes spent two days at my parents' house or in the car on the way home from work, when I used to call my friends. At home they hated any calls on my number. Sometimes a machine was being dispatched somewhere and got held up, and since I was in charge I couldn't just say, 'I'm not allowed to take calls at home.' So I would take the call, deal with the issue, and my mother-in-law would say, 'She's just trying to show that she works more than my sons. Just because she has so many people under her supervision doesn't mean my sons are no good.' Things like that caused glitches in Dhruv's mind. I don't think he had really thought about it like that until she said it.

"I couldn't hug boys even if they were my brothers. I just couldn't hug anybody. In my family we're very physically expressive. If my father was going out of town, we'd hug and kiss you, know? There was this time when Dhruv was leaving for work, so I hugged him. And he was like, 'Don't do that, Mummy's standing right there!' I was like, 'Goddammit, I'm married to you, okay?' Then he was like, 'No she'll talk to me later and say you shouldn't do those things standing outside.'

"It was a totally different school of thought. Like there was this time when I came back from work, and I parked my car outside the house and there were kids playing badminton in the street. So I picked up a racquet and joined in. She opened the door and started shouting at me right there. 'Get inside the house!' I came in and there was a huge argument. 'The daughter-in-law of the house doesn't do such things! I don't know what your parents have taught you.'

"Sex was another issue. Actually he was pretty comfortable about sex. More than I was. Not that I was a virgin when I got married, though that was the picture I had to portray, knowing the kind of family I was getting into. But in the beginning his mother wouldn't ever let us close the door of our bedroom. From day one she wanted us to have a kid – that's what Punjabi families are all about – and I used to tell her, 'You won't even allow us to close the door: how am I gonna give you a kid?' If we did shut the door, she would start banging on it. 'Knock' is too polite for what she used to do.

"She would say, 'What has happened that you have to close the door? If nothing bad is happening you shouldn't have to close the door.' We would just be sleeping or chatting inside – on those rare occasions when we actually chatted – and she would come and shout 'Please put the light on in there. I don't like you being in there with the light off.'

"Dhruv was totally casual about it. 'What's the problem?' he would say. 'We'll just open the door.' Several times I used to tell him, 'You tell your mother everything; why don't you tell her the sexual positions you've tried with me?' I used to make fun of him about it."

During her speech a man has come to our table and, without a word, sat down next to her. She has taken no notice of this man, so I assume she was expecting him, but I am slightly taken aback at the lack of reaction on anyone's part. Sukhvinder has not touched her phone since we made the decision to come to this café, so she cannot have informed him where she was. And yet he has found her and sat down beside her without any remark. I enjoy the aloofness they both display to locational issues. I have no idea who the man might be. He must be someone she knows well, since she continues to talk about intimate things in front of him.

"Dhruv's family were not Sikhs. They were Hindu Brahmins from West Punjab, and they surrounded themselves with priests and astrologers. After about four months of our marriage my mother-in-law started to tell Dhruv that her priest thought I was an evil force and things were going to go wrong. I was the reason his business was failing and all of that.

"She began to tell him I was doing black magic. I just laughed because I don't even believe in all that. But they started all these rituals to protect their home. There would constantly be weird things in the doorway when I arrived to stop the evil coming in, and since I came from a Sikh family, I had no idea what they were, so I would pick them up and throw them away, which only made them believe it more. My mother-in-law was terrified about bad stuff coming in from outside. She never ever left the house except to buy vegetables from a street vendor, and when she went out she had three pairs of shoes and she would change from one into the next and then into the next, to make sure there was no contact between the inside and the outside.

"One day she went through my things and she found this amulet that I'd been given by a Muslim friend. It was some Islamic symbol and I liked it, I found it interesting, you know? She took it away and showed it to her priest and he said, 'This is where all your problems are coming from.' And they did rituals to purify the amulet. And she told everyone in the house and they all started avoiding me. The entire family would look down on me. They were a Partition family and this was like Partition.

And I was Pakistan. What hurt me was not that everyone else believed these crazy things but that Dhruv did. He couldn't question anything his mother said.

"I really did not want to fail at my marriage and I tried everything I could. I thought I could change everything and make everyone happy. My mother-in-law had been mourning ever since her husband died fifteen years before. You won't believe it: when I moved into that house I realised that in the entire house there was not one photograph of Dhruv's father. Which made me feel they had not yet accepted that he was no longer in their lives, and I thought that was why they were so insane. So one day we were out shopping and I bought a beautiful frame, and I got a photograph blown up and I put it in the drawing room. When she saw it, she was hysterical. 'Get rid of that!' she screamed. I said, 'Look it's a beautiful frame and it's a beautiful picture of him. I thought it would make you happy.' And she screamed at Dhruv, 'This girl just wants to make sure I am crying all the time.'

"She used to sleep with her property papers under her ass because she thought I wanted to steal them. I don't like to say such things but secretly I was like, 'Have you seen the property my family has? I already have houses of my own. This house will be divided between five grandchildren. Do you think I care about stealing one-fifth of your shitty house from you?' But I thought that since she cared so much about money, I could maybe make her happy with money. So I opened a savings account and every month I used to deposit 5–10,000 rupees [$100–200] depending on what I had. I gave her the ATM card and said, 'You don't need to go to Dhruv whenever you need money. This is yours. I'm a part of the family too.' But I guess I was never part of the family. The entire month she'd be sulking, being completely bitchy – and just when the day came that I had to transfer the money, she was suddenly extremely sweet to me. It was visible you know, that sweet thing, sickening sweet. But I had no issues with it. I thought, 'If this is what buys peace in the house, you can keep my entire salary.'

"As things got worse, I used to say to my mother-in-law and my husband quite frequently: 'What exactly do you want me to do, how do you want me to behave? Give me a list, A–Z, and I'll stick to it? Because whatever I do makes you unhappy, but when I stop doing it, you're still unhappy.' I told her after a year, 'Every week I sat down with you and asked you what you wanted me to do, and every week there was a definite thing. And I actually made a note of each and every thing you wanted me to do. But each week it completely clashed with what you'd said the week before. It was as if you just wanted me to fail.'

"Dhruv had a younger brother who was a loudmouth. He was very rude to his mother, and he would hit her when they had arguments. All that really shook me because after the first time I saw him do that I thought, if he doesn't respect his own mother, he'll kill me tomorrow. It totally shook me. He kept on kicking her and boxing her, and I wrapped myself around her so she didn't get hurt because she had acute arthritis. But in her head her sons were perfect, and the following morning she called up one of her relatives and said, 'Sukhvinder was trying to hit me.' So I was like, *You bitch!* She could never ever see that her sons were doing something wrong, and if they did bad things, she forgot about them straight away.

"I couldn't understand this, and I always made the mistake of being brutally honest. If my husband and his mother were having an argument about something, Dhruv would bring me in and ask me, 'Which one of us is right, which one of us is wrong?' Now, if you ask me that sort of a question, I expect you're prepared for the answer. So I would say, 'I think she was wrong here and you were wrong here and—', and it would make both of them furious. They would both forget about the fact that they were fighting, and they would eat me alive. He would be like, 'How can you say that about my mother?' And she would say, 'How can you say that about my son?'

"Anyway, there came a time when I got home really late from

work. There's one time in the year when we show our products at a trade exhibition, and I have to work all hours. So I came back from the exhibition really late and I really wanted to go to the toilet. So I came back and I completely forgot about the slipper changing thing, I just ran to the toilet. She made a huge fuss and said all sorts of weird things to me. I said, 'I'm sorry. I genuinely forgot. I only wanted to go to the toilet.' 'No,' she said, 'you are up to something.' So I said, 'Forget it. You're not making any sense.' And I went to take a shower.

"While I was in the shower I heard all this shouting between the mother and the son. When I came out Dhruv said, 'You should not argue with Mummy.' I explained the situation to him. 'No,' he said, 'you slapped her.' I was like, '*I* slapped your *mother*?' He said, 'Yeah.' Then he said, 'Well you didn't slap her. You were *about* to slap her.' And I was like, 'If you think after a year and a half of marriage that I am capable of that, then God bless you.' And I went into the kitchen to start cooking.

"So he followed me in, took my hand and pulled me into the dining room. He said, 'We have to sort this out right now.' I said, 'I know I'm younger than you, but I understand one thing: when you're angry, we should not talk. It's just going to blow out of proportion, and then you're going to say things you don't mean and you'll feel sorry about it later. And I'll reciprocate and it will be a *who-hurts-who-most* game.' 'No, we are going to sort this out now.' So I was like, '*Fine*'. And we were talking – we were just talking – and he whacks me right across my face.

"He was really tall, 6'2", decently built. He whacked me and I fainted. I collapsed.

"Afterwards I was totally numb. I called my two girlfriends and I went to see them. And I howled and I howled and I howled, and I was like, 'Is this normal, is this normal? Does this normally happen in joint families?' – because my friends were from joint families while I was brought up in a nuclear family. And they were like, 'It's okay, he was just really angry.' They were just trying to calm me down because I was really out of my senses, but they were furious, you know – I could see the look on their faces. I didn't tell anyone else, not even my parents, because I couldn't decipher at that time whether it was a big thing. I was just totally lost.

"I thought I would just try to forget all about it. Start a new chapter. But each time there was a fight, I used to be really scared because I thought he might do it again. Sometimes it happened, sometimes it didn't. But over time, the frequency of whacking just kept increasing and it was extremely disconcerting, and I was falling into a depression and all of that. Then one day, after about four years of our marriage, I left and I never went back.

"Obviously I hadn't told my parents about the whacking and all that – so it took me about three months to convince them. No one apart from Dhruv and I and Dhruv's aunt, in whom I used to confide, knew what had happened. I didn't feel it was appropriate to tell my parents what went on in their family. So I said, 'There are things you don't know about, and I can assure you I'm not making a rash decision.' But eventually, after months of trying in vain to convince them, I told them about the frequent whacking. They were furious. They went to discuss everything with Dhruv's family. But I wasn't ever going to go back.

"For some time I was very angry. I really wanted to put him and his mother behind bars. But eventually I calmed down. For a long time I wished I could slap both of them really hard, just once. But now I don't even feel like doing that. It's his life. I believe in God and justice. I know I didn't do anything so drastically horrible in my marriage that things had to turn out the way they did. It's okay. I'm fine with it.

"I did give it my best. More than I ever thought I had inside me. But I lost respect for him. I didn't trust him, and after that it was over. Before the love could develop it turned into bitterness. So there was absolutely nothing.

"You know the moment at which I really lost respect for him? When I knew it was over? It was not when he was hitting me, strangely enough. It was something else.

"I always liked to have all the windows open but his family would keep them completely shut. I used to suffocate in there. And I have asthma, so sometimes it got really bad. One night I woke up, and I couldn't breathe and I was panicking. I shook Dhruv awake and asked him to pass me my inhaler, which was on his side of the bed. But he refused to get it, and I passed out. After that there was no going back."

She has been talking for a long time, and it is dark. People have come and gone. At the table next to us, an enormously rotund man with a ponytail has sat down with a beautiful woman a head taller than he. She has a chihuahua in her lap.

We pay the bill and head back inside the mall. I say farewell to Sukhvinder. I shake the hand of her companion, whose identity I still do not know.

I am thinking about all her stories. I get into the elevator to go down to the parking lot. Another man gets in with me: he is holding a Gucci shopping bag, whose enormous size brings a slight strut to his demeanour. It is a strange spectacle, these men from Delhi business families who demonstrate their masculinity by buying handbags.

The elevator doors slide open and I emerge into the brown light of the basement. The air is fetid and hot. The air conditioning cools the mall's interior to a mild non-place; it is down here that the heat of the north Indian plains seems to be stored. Immediately, I begin to sweat.

I get into the car and drive to the exit, where there is a payment booth. I hand my ticket to the man inside and wonder how many hours he has to spend in this sub-terranean oven. "Fifty rupees," he says to me, and I start fumbling in my pocket for change.

As I am doing so, the man reaches out of the window and picks something off my windscreen. It is a huge red flower, fallen from the silk cotton tree that grows outside my house. Lodged in the windscreen wiper, it has travelled with me all the way from the leafy city to this wasteland out of town.

The man inspects it as if it has just descended from outer space.

"Can I keep it?" he asks.

"Of course."

And he sets it on his ledge inside the booth, and gazes at it, enchanted, as if trees were long extinct, and known only through children's books.

Seven

Dressed in a kurta and a turban, the politician stands smilingly on the stage. "Is there anyone here who can tell me the name of Jawaharlal Nehru's daughter?" Everyone in the auditorium puts up their hand. "Indira Gandhi!" they cry. "That's right!" beams the politician.

"And now who can name the sons of Mahatma Gandhi?" he says.

There is a shame-faced silence. No hands rise.

The politician feigns amazement. "How interesting this is!" he says. "Everyone can remember the name of a daughter. But no one can remember the name of a son!"

He walks across the stage, surveying the audience.

"So why do we kill our unborn girls, my friends? Why do our young men grow up with no women to marry?"

When advertisements wanted to show you something freshly contemporary, they showed you a woman in a suit.

Young, professional women were the icons of the new India. Towards the bottom of the economic scale women had always worked, as they often had, also, at the very top; but many of those middle-class women who took up jobs in India's post-liberalisation economy were doing something novel. Many of them had to fight battles within their families to achieve it; and yet, in aggregate, the revolution was swiftly won – partly because even those who disliked it could see that everything was changing against them.

The years after liberalisation greatly increased the extent to which middle-class self-esteem in general derived from work and income, and it diminished, correspondingly, the force of those unpaid roles of homemaker and mother that had appeared so lofty in twentieth-century mythology. Young women enthusiastically followed the flux of the times, for they had much to gain and little to lose from the move outside the home. They were there-fore in many ways the most unequivocal adherents of the new India, which was why their minds were so unencumbered – and why they were so successful in the workplace. The corporate world was more egalitarian than might be assumed – Indian gender inequality never had the same structure as in the West, and the dynamics of the corporate office were not those of the home – and women rose quickly to the highest ranks of corporate India. They were in many ways the model corporate employees, for they had no stake in old, entrenched systems, they analysed situations calmly and objectively, and they felt no fear of change.

It was not the same with men. Men did have a stake in the previous arrangement. Their inner calm derived – in deeper ways than they knew – from the idea of a woman presiding over, and being *in*, the home. Suddenly women were not only out of the home all the time but also earned their own money and, in this crucial sense, had no need of male support. For men, therefore, the transformation of Indian society was laced with threat. If men appear more frequently in this book than women, in fact, it is because the great ambivalence of India's changes was often more directly visible in men's souls than in those of women. Women had to suffer the outbursts of these haunted men – and at times the suffering was considerable – but their own minds were more their own. Sukhvinder was the 'modern', self-possessed heroine of her story, and this is why it requires no great effort to identify with her. But if we wish to learn anything at all about the painful churn of values and feelings in early twenty-first century Delhi, we must try to understand what was going on in the heads of the people around her.

Just because Sukhvinder is 'modern' does not mean that her husband and mother-in-law were 'traditional'. Friction between young women and their mothers-in-law was of course well-established in a family system where wives moved into their husband's family home. Many mothers-in-law, after all, had themselves been brought at some point into an unfamiliar home, to be met there by several kinds of punishment and humiliation – and the cycle often proved to be tragically repetitive. But in earlier times, when older women were more secure in their status, they could also play the role of mentor to daughters-in-law seeking to learn what they knew.[12]

But in the early twenty-first century, older middle-class women like Sukhvinder's mother-in-law could be very far from secure in their status. They felt often that the kind of knowledge they possessed had little value in this new world where *values*, precisely, seemed to be disappearing in favour of one single *value*: that of money. Young women who worked excessively, socialised frequently, dressed unorthodoxly, and showed no interest in all those rituals and practices of the home for which their mothers-in-law had always been venerated, seemed to represent an implicit denigration of everything on which their status rested – and mothers-in-law could feel themselves, rightly or wrongly, to be fighting against these younger women for their own survival: 'If my son learns to love a woman like that, he will never love me again.' The ultimate nightmare was that the valueless daughter-in-law, excessively swayed by images of the new, rootless, consumer lifestyle, in which free-wheeling dual-income couples neglected all other ties, might insist on moving with her husband into a separate house, even on cutting off financial support to his irritating, useless parents – who in many cases had little income, after their retirement, except what came from him. The fact that women such as Sukhvinder's mother-in-law had in their own lives been denied the freedoms enjoyed by the 'new', professionally active, women who now entered their homes only intensified such insecurities. Their professional daughters-in-law stood as a living reminder of everything they had not been free to do themselves, and the nonchalance with which they treated their freedoms seemed like pure insolence.

Young married men usually had more in common with their wives, naturally, than with their mothers. Their wives often had rhythms and lifestyles quite similar to their own, and could talk with them about many of those everyday things their mothers knew nothing about: going out, products, the workplace. But it was precisely this worldliness that could leave men so ambivalent. Even as they enjoyed the lifestyle that came with two professional incomes, they were often unnerved by the amount their wives were out in the world. These men had often absorbed a singularly domestic image of femininity from their mothers, who themselves had never had much truck with the outside, and sought to provide instead a soothing domestic refuge from the male world of competition and struggle. Around young, professional women, they could therefore feel an unsettling kind of misrecognition. Young women did not even look like women of previous generations, for consumerism, with its diets, gyms and skinny publicity models, had ushered in not only different clothes, but entirely different bodies. Young men found it an alluring look, but it could trigger associations of decadence in them, and they were often confused to discover that they could not feel for female partners the emotions they thought they should feel.

This supremacy of the maternal ethos might appear strange. But it was no mean supremacy. In Hinduism, the dynamic and productive energies of the universe were female, not male, and in the act of procreation, individual mothers channelled the totality of these cosmic forces. Their motherhood drew on the same raw energy of the goddess that gave India's political 'mothers' – Indira Gandhi and all the monumental female politicians who came after her – such awe-inspiring stature. Mothers might have stayed home, but in their sons' minds especially, they were anything but meek. It was they who supplied all the motive energy for their sons' achievements, while also protecting them from the evil forces with which the outside world teemed; and if north Indian men frequently reiterated the words of Rudyard Kipling – 'God could not be everywhere, therefore he made mothers' – it was by no means emptily.

Conflicts between wives and mothers therefore terrified men. Many men, in fact, listed as their most important criterion in a prospective bride that she respect his mother as he did, for they knew they would be ripped down the middle by these two female forces should they go to war. Men sympathised with both women, but it was like that popular visual trick of 'rabbit or duck?': they could see each perspective separately but not both at the same time – and they were often not capable of any kind of synthesis. They might agree with their wives that there were mice in the house which sometimes chewed holes in clothes, but when their mothers showed them the hole in their T-shirt right above the heart, they could not deny it was evidence of the foulest black magic. Being a man in their mother's eyes and in their wife's eyes were two mutually exclusive things, and they were under immense pressure to choose one or the other. The fault line between these two positions cut through the most primordial, inarticulate parts of their being, and when the split happened it could take men beyond words. They leapt, very often, to the maternal side, because betrayal of mothers was more impossible to conceive. And they often turned to blows, gentle and violent men both, for they had no words with which to counter their far more clear-headed and articulate wives.

This new outbreak of punishment of women in the home was only part of a more general intensification of misogyny during this period. Nowhere in India was this so acute as in the north, and particularly in Delhi. If there was one crime that supplied an image for the twenty-first-century capital, it was rape. The newspapers dubbed Delhi India's 'rape capital', and women from other cities feared going there because of the city's reputation for sexual aggression.

It was not that rape was new, of course: it had always been around, as in the rest of the world. In Delhi, however, the primary locale had historically been the household, and the facts and extent of rape had therefore been considerably veiled. What was novel in the early twenty-first century was the very public spectacle of rape, combined with a terrifying sadism. Each rape case seemed to dig deeper and deeper into the depths of brutal possibility, and sensational sexual violence occupied more and more of the city's media and conversation. Women were abducted and raped in quasi-ritualistic fashion; some of their victims were left in the street in such mutilated and abject states that one was put in mind less of sex than of retribution, extermination and war.

And this was just the point. What was going on in Delhi was precisely that: a low-level, but widespread, war against women, whose new mobility made them not only the icons of India's social and economic changes but also the scapegoats.

Rapes were the most dramatic manifestation of this offensive, but a similar retributive menace could be seen in quite ordinary transactions. Women walking alone in the street huddled up and looked at the ground so as to avoid the massed stares of men, which were calculated to cow them in just this way. Sexy pictures of film stars and models on media websites regularly received comments such as, "Tell me why we should not rape women who dress like you? Is this what your parents brought you up for?" – which were duly signed by their male authors, who apparently saw no indignity in visiting those sectors of the internet in order to comment on them in this fashion. Women walking alone in the city at night or sitting alone in a bar were regularly approached by men asking, "How much?" In these and so many other situations there was a redoubling of men's efforts to remind women that their place was in the home, even as such a battle had become absurd in the context of the society they now lived in.

But this idea of women in the home carried a very specific and potent significance in India, which derived from the country's colonial history. During the nineteenth century, a stark division of roles had grown up between the genders. Colonial control of commerce and politics meant that men were obliged to compromise their Indian way of life in order to conduct their affairs – bending, when outside the home, to British law, language, dress, technology and social customs. It became the nationalist duty of women, then, to preserve on everyone else's behalf a pure and undiluted Indian existence – and this meant staying out of the corrupted public realm. Women were to remain in the home and maintain it as a bastion of spiritual purity: a defence against the colonisation of the soul, and a refuge in which married men could regenerate themselves. In the colonial context this was not necessarily a passive idea of women's roles; as one historian writes:

> We are tempted to put this down as 'conservatism', a mere defence of 'traditional' norms. But this would be a mistake. The colonial situation, and the ideological response of nationalism, introduced an entirely new substance to these terms [. . .] The world was where the European power had challenged the non-European peoples and, by virtue of its superior material culture, had subjugated them. But it had failed to colonize the inner, essential, identity of the East which lay in its distinctive, and superior, spiritual culture. That is where the East was undominated, sovereign, master of its own fate. [. . .] In the entire phase of the national struggle, the crucial need was to protect, preserve and strengthen the inner core of the national culture, its

spiritual essence. No encroachments by the colonizer must be allowed in that inner sanctum. In the world, imitation of and adaptation to western norms was a necessity; at home they were tantamount to annihilation of one's very identity.[13]

A very extensive emotional and historical network was held in place, then, by the idea of the spiritually pure – and confined – Indian woman, which was why this image of womanhood was sacralised in Indian popular culture throughout the twentieth century. For some, it was the foundation of India itself, for if women were to abandon their role in the home, its culture would become indistinguishable from the irreligious rest of the world – which would amount to the "annihilation of one's very identity". And crucially, men could not maintain this distinction for themselves: they derived their sense of self, in a sense, not from what they themselves possessed, but from what was held in trust for them by their mothers and wives – who could at any moment, also, allow it to crumble away.

Perhaps in this light it becomes easier to see why the unsentimental abandonment of the domestic sphere by great numbers of middle-class women might have turbulent repercussions. The 2000s were a period, after all, when Indian middle-class life was assailed by more general questions of identity – for many of its rhythms had become indistinguishable from the ones in those foreign lands against which India had traditionally defined itself – and it was felt in some quarters that the cosmos would go up in smoke if domestic traditions were not strenuously asserted. It was a period, too, when many older male entitlements were done away with by the new ethos of risk and competition, and when many men therefore suffered a disorienting loss of status and certainty. Everything, then, was in flux, and even men who were doing well in other respects often felt that the society around them was headed towards some kind of catastrophe, and they understood this as a problem of values, against whose loss they railed endlessly. Women – particularly women out in public – received the backlash. Retaliations in the home were only part of a generalised male attempt to take out these anxieties on young women, whose new independence and mobility was seen as a destabilising cause.

Politicians and journalists often tried to claim that the upsurge of rapes in the capital was due to the presence there of large numbers of poor migrants – people who, in the impoverished imagination of the middle classes, were entirely lacking in culture or values. Indian culture venerated mothers, wives and sisters, went the thought, and no 'properly raised' Indian man would ever think of subjecting them to improper acts. But the problem was almost the opposite of this, and far more discouraging. The problem derived, precisely, from that 'Indian culture' whose veneration of those idealised, domestic women also somehow implied an abhorrence for 'public' women (and the two senses of that word, when applied to women, inevitably merged). The violence originated not with men without culture or values, but with just those men who were most concerned with these things. It was obvious in the comments of policemen, judges and politicians, for instance, that, even as they were called upon to express outrage for these crimes, they could barely suppress their feeling that women who walk in the streets at night deserve anything they get. A significant number of rape cases were filed, indeed, against politicians themselves. These were men who had pledged their lives, in a certain sense, to the protection of 'values', and in twenty-first century Delhi, unfortunately, such men were not necessarily outraged by the punishment of women.

Delhi was in the grip of one of those mad moments in human history, in other words, when terrible violence is imagined by its perpetrators as constructive and principled. Violence against women in the changing world of post-liberalisation India came not just from a minority of uncultured misfits. It came from the mainstream, and from every social class. It came not from an absence of values at all, but from a psychotic excess.

"I come from a very wealthy family," says Anil. "My uncle is the head of a big tea company. We have plantations in Assam, and some of my uncles discovered oil on their plantations. They're billionaires. They live in a huge house in London, they have twenty-four servants. My family name is rare so everyone knows I must be related to them."

Anil is a Marwari: he comes from a community with its roots in Rajasthan which is known particularly for its business acumen. India's richest woman, Savitri Jindal, who inherited her husband's steel empire, is a Marwari, as is Britain's richest man, Lakshmi Mittal, another steel magnate. Marwaris are known also for the strictness with which they keep traditions of diet and family life. Their commercial success derives partly, in fact, from the great fidelity with which each generation takes over, not only the family business but also the abstinent, hard-working lifestyle that built it.

About thirty-five years old, Anil is quite extraordinarily rotund, and carries himself with that altered gait of people who must support an enormous stomach. His speech sticks in his mouth in a way that resembles a lisp but seems to affect all his consonants.

"I was working in Atlanta at the time my mom decided it was time I got married. I was running my business so I couldn't come to Delhi, and I got married through the newspaper. My mom wanted to make sure there was someone to take care of me. As soon as they put the ad out there were loads of applicants because of my name. So we chose a girl, I came back to Delhi to get married, and then we went to Mauritius on our honeymoon.

"The honeymoon was perfect. I didn't have all this fat in those days. In fact, I was a taekwondo black belt. She and I were both excellent dancers and when we used to dance together, everyone else used to stop dancing and watch. My wife was a great singer, so she sang at all the karaoke sessions and everyone loved it. She wasn't beautiful, but I didn't mind. She was perfect for that time we were on honeymoon – she used to massage my head at the end of the day, wash my clothes and polish my shoes, massage my feet."

We are sitting in the bar of Delhi's golf club.

Driving along the dusty, congested roads of central Delhi gives no sense of the verdant landscape behind the high walls that line them: it is only when you ascend, for instance, to the top of the Taj Hotel, that you can look down and see that these roads are but arid strips through an enormous expanse of green. The several-acre lawns of the politicians' bungalows add up to a great garden tract of their own. The Mughal tombs at either end of Lodhi Road have expansive grounds of lawns and fountains; between them is the pleasant botanical sprawl of Lodhi Gardens, home to diplomatic joggers and unmarried lovers, who go – the lovers, that is – to hold hands and kiss under its bushes.

But most verdant and extensive of all is the golf club, set up by the British in 1931, and extending over 220 acres in the middle of the city. Unknown to all but Delhi's elite, the club is so pampered and insulated that it has an ecosystem all of its own. Walking in past the Mercedes promotional diorama of glinting limousines, the roar of the street fades behind the cushion of forest. Flirting pairs of yellow butterflies, a species I have never seen elsewhere, flutter on every side. Three hundred species of birds fill the air with song. Peacocks wander lazily across the lawns as, in quieter moments, do sambar deer. The hedges are perfect, the Mughal tombs – their red sandstone heart-rending against the golfing green – the most lovingly maintained in the city.

Here, in the bar, sit Delhi's landowners, lawyers and businessmen, laughing, chatting and exchanging fraternal handshakes.

"When we got back from our honeymoon, she thought she was going to have a lifestyle like my uncle. She thought she was going to have twenty-four servants and a mansion in London. But we don't live like that. We're not from that side of the family.

I bought her a Toyota SUV and she was very disappointed. She thought she would get a Mercedes.

"We were only together for another twelve days. During that time she managed to persuade my mom to take her to the bank deposit box where she kept her jewellery. She said, 'Mom, could I borrow that necklace you wore to the wedding? It was so beautiful!' So my mom took her to the lock-up and she borrowed three necklaces, each one worth a crore [$200,000]. My mom said to her, 'Look: you have to be careful with these because they're worth a lot of money.' 'Of course I will.'

"After that she said she was going to her home town to spend a few days with her mother. I said, *Fine* – I thought maybe after the first sex, a woman wants to chat to her mother about it. But then she didn't come back. She kept making excuses and then her mother said to me on the phone, 'You don't seem to love her.' I said, 'What are you talking about? We've only been together twenty-eight days!'

"She said to my parents, 'Your son doesn't love our daughter. He only wants to work. He was checking email when he was in Mauritius on honeymoon.' I mean, what am I supposed to do? Can't a guy check email? As it was, she wanted to have sex five or six times a day, which is not normal, and I was having trouble keeping up.

"Eventually we got a divorce settlement where we paid her 10 lakhs [$20,000] and she gave the necklaces back. She had to give them back because we had all the receipts and photos and everything.

"I was really shaken up by this because divorce is really bad for Marwaris. You can do anything you like behind closed doors – you can beat your wife and everything – but you should not get divorced.

"When she left, I lost it. I started drinking heavily. I started eating meat, which I had never done. I put on a lot of weight. That's when I started doing this thing with prostitutes. I wanted to humiliate girls. And because my wife liked sex, I took it out on girls who liked sex.

"I did not sleep with these girls, I just humiliated them. If any of my friends wanted a prostitute, I would arrange it for them. I would do the deal with the guy and I would tell him that we had to be able to do anything to the girl, with any number of people, or the deal was off. I would go and pick up the girl and I would tell her to suck me in the car for free. It was all about humiliation: I came in her mouth not for pleasure but to humiliate her. When I delivered her to my friends we would sit around drinking whisky and I would ask her to strip in front of everyone and to do all kinds of humiliating things. To put money in her cunt.

"Because I did everything for my wife. I gave her everything she wanted. I gave up my business in the US to be with her. I gave her a Toyota SUV just because I wanted her to have it. I gave her the respect of society, being the wife of such a rich family of India. I gave her all that and she screwed me. What was I supposed to do?"

I ask Anil if he had girlfriends before his wife.

"I wouldn't say I was a virgin when I got married. But I only had girlfriends outside India, never in India. I never touched an Indian girl before I got married."

"The prostitutes. Were they Indian?"

"Yes."

Anil is preoccupied by boundaries, and by the purity of what lies within. It was acceptable for him to have pre-marital sex outside India, but not to corrupt the Indian woman. It was possible to do business with both American corporations and ultra-conservative Islamists – for he had made some of his money from deals with the Taliban in Afghanistan – but he had to keep his body pure of meat and alcohol. In getting married, however, Anil had relaxed his boundaries. He had opened up his intimate world to an outsider, and in return he had been utterly undone. He had found that the pure Indian woman of his imagination not only had a sexual appetite in excess of his own, but that she was capable of perfidy. In the resulting emotional chaos he began both to defile his own body and to extend a ceremonial kind of sadism towards Indian women.

He tells all of this quite naturally, and without any kind of apology. He does not seem to feel that he is morally compromised. In fact he lectures lengthily, even tediously, about morals.

"You should not have desires," he says. "You should make yourself enjoy what life has given you. I do meditation every day to control my desires. For instance, I could spend my time complaining that I was in Delhi and wishing I was somewhere else, but that would just make me unhappy. I hate the fact that Delhi has no respect for women. But you have to be content where you are. People are too full of desires. Women, especially. Women don't know how to control their desires.

"True happiness is about sacrifice. Love is about sacrifice. When you're in love with a person, you just want to sacrifice for that person. Like Radha did for Lord Krishna. Like Sita did for Rama. If someone asks for your life, give your life. If blood, give blood. Like Mahatma Gandhi said, if someone slaps you on one cheek, offer them the other cheek. But the problem is today, people don't have that much patience.

"Now I'm trying to improve my karma. I've stopped the business with prostitutes. I've given up meat. When your karma is good, you'll automatically bump into people who are profitable to you. But when it is bad, you meet people who will fleece you. So I'm being a good person, trying to help people however I can. For instance, my favourite masseur came to the house. He wanted socks. So I gave him my socks. He's a poor man: he comes every day and he gives me a full-body massage. Tomorrow if he wants a shirt, I'll give him a shirt. You do whatever you can. Goodness is in circulation like money. The amount of good and bad in the world always remains the same. It neither increases nor decreases, it only changes hands. It is never yours: you are only the custodian. If you don't use it, someone else will take it. If I do something good, I take the credit from you. You get minus, I get plus. It's like a double credit. It is up to you to get as much as you can from other people. The only way to get it is to take it from other people because it is like money: it circulates with people. When I give socks to my masseur, I take his goodness from him."

It is still subdued in the bar at this early hour of the evening, so it is difficult to ignore the man who shouts out to someone in the opposite corner, asking if he is going tonight to a dinner hosted by a prominent industrialist. He drops the name twice, loudly, and an elderly Sikh man stands up to protest.

"Cool it!" he calls out authoritatively. "We're all invited to the same dinner. We don't need to hear about it from you. If you want to come in here, learn how to behave!"

Eight

1857

My heart does not dwell in this ravaged land
Who can be happy in an unstable world?
. . .
Tell these regrets to go dwell somewhere else
Where is the space in this scorched heart?

> – From a poem written in his final exile by
> Bahadur Shah Zafar, last Mughal emperor[14]

If Delhi was so particularly fearful of a loss of values, it was partly because the region in which it lay had had its values destroyed many, many times. For centuries it had lain in the path of invaders from the north and west who were drawn by the riches of the sub-continent, a fact which had lent fragility to all things, tangible and intangible. A saying is still preserved in some Punjabi families: "Khadda peeta lahe da, baki ahmed shahe da" ("What we eat and drink is ours, the rest belongs to [the Afghan invader] Ahmed Shah"). Assume the worst, went the thinking, the better to survive: wealth will always be stolen away; just consume whatever you can so at least that part is not lost too. For many people, even those who profited from it, global capitalism was another of these foreign invasions, and while it did have people consuming madly, this did not quell the anxiety of loss.

It is common to talk about Delhi as an ancient city, beginning with its supposed origins as the city of Indraprastha described in the *Mahabharata* – but it is not strictly that. There is little physical continuity between the many cities of Delhi: none was incorporated organically into the next. Cities were sacked by invaders and left uninhabitable, or they ran out of water immediately after their construction and had to be abandoned – and stones were then carted from each of these settlements to build the next. Each time a new power came to this place, it shifted ground and built afresh, draining the last life out of what existed before and leaving it to decay. This singular discontent with the already existing did not end in modern times: the British built 'new Delhi' in the wilderness, and global capital started from scratch with Gurgaon. The spirit of this place has always been staccato, and full of fractures.

The greatest period of stability came under the Mughals, a dynasty originally from central Asia, whose legendary wealth and magnificence reached their height in the seventeenth century. It was at this time that the emperor Shah Jahan removed his capital from Agra and brought it to Delhi, where he built a new metropolis on the banks of the Yamuna river. Laid out over the ruins of a city sacked in the fourteenth century, this glistening paradise of domes and gardens sprang up, stupefyingly, in less than one decade. Nowadays this city – Shahjahanabad – is called 'Old Delhi', to distinguish it from 'New Delhi', the city built by the British after they moved their capital here in 1911; but in the days of its magnificence, it seemed that obsolescence could never visit such dewy bowers, such inordinate splendour, such implausible avenues, with their rose-water fountains, exquisite merchandise and royal processions.

But Mughal decline, when it came, was as steep as the ascent.

During the eighteenth century, the emperor's power dissolved amid royal infighting, corruption and military obsolescence; great parts of the empire, such as Hyderabad and Bengal, broke off into independence, and most of the rest was snapped up by the new sub-continental empire of the Maratha kings. Delhi was repeatedly attacked, most devastatingly in 1739, by the Persian imperial army which, under Nadir Shah, looted the city and slaughtered 20,000 of its inhabitants. This debacle demonstrated just how complete was the end of Mughal might: Nadir Shah returned to Persia with the Peacock Throne, built for Shah Jahan with over a tonne of pure gold and inset with 230 kilogrammes of gems, including the most famous in the world, the Koh-i-Noor diamond.

A century after that assault, an English traveller named Emma Roberts, standing atop the Qutub Minar, could see the dimmed effulgence of Shahjahanabad in the distance. In contrast to the enormous extent of what *she* called 'old Delhi' – the collapsed cities of the medieval dynasties (which she refers to collectively as the Pathans) and of the early Mughals – it could still, nonetheless, inspire awe:

> The capital of the Mughal empire . . . the modern city, or Shahjahanabad, the designation by which it is distinguished by the natives, who have not yet fallen into the European habit of calling it New Delhi . . . stands in the centre of a sandy plain, surrounded on every side with the ruins of old Delhi, curiously contrasted with a new suburb, the villas belonging to Europeans attached to the residency, and with the cantonments lately erected for three regiments of sepoys . . . From the summit [of the Qutub Minar] the view is of the most sublime description; a desert, covered with ruins full of awful beauty, surrounds it on all sides, watered by the snake-like Yamuna, which winds its huge silvery folds along the crumbling remains of palaces and tombs. In the back-ground rise the dark lofty walls and frowning towers

of an ancient fortress, the stronghold of the Pathan chiefs; and the eye, wandering over the stupendous and still beautiful fragments of former grandeur, rests at last upon the white and glittering mosques and minarets of the modern city, closing in the distance, and finely contrasting, by its luxuriant groves and richly flowering gardens, with the loneliness and desolation of the scene beneath.

Before the Mohammadan invasion, [this collection of collapsed cities] had been a place of great renown, many of the remains of Hindu architecture dividing the interest with those of the Muslim conquerors: the sepulchres of one hundred and eighty thousand saints and martyrs, belonging to the faithful, were, it is said, to be found amidst the wrecks of temples and palaces, before all had crumbled into the undistinguishable mass which now renders the greater part of the scene so desolate . . .

From the outside the view [of Shahjahanabad] is splendid; domes and mosques, cupolas and minarets, with the imperial palace frowning like a mountain of red granite, appear in the midst of groves of clustering trees, so thickly planted that the buildings have been compared, in Oriental imagery, to rocks of pearls and rubies, rising from an emerald sea. In approaching the city from the east bank of the Yamuna, the prospect realizes all that the imagination has pictured of Oriental magnificence; mosques and minarets glittering in the sun, some garlanded with wild creepers, others arrayed in all the pomp of gold, the exterior of the cupolas being covered with brilliant metal, and from Mount Mejnoon, over which a fine road now passes, the shining waters of the Yamuna gleaming in the distance, insulating Salimgarh, and disappearing behind the halls of the peacock-throne, the palace of the emperors, add another beautiful feature to the scene . . . [But] the glory of the Mughals has faded away, and their greatness departed . . . The celebrated gardens of Shalimar, with their cypress avenues, sparkling fountains, roseate bowers, and the delicious shade of their dark cedars, on which Shah Jahan, the most tasteful monarch in the world, is said to have lavished a crore of rupees (a million sterling), have been almost wholly surrendered to waste and desolation.[15]

The wistfulness that touches this outsider's account was as nothing compared to the paroxysm of nostalgia that had taken over the city itself. In the years preceding Emma Roberts' visit, the aristocracy of autumnal Shahjahanbad found much of its remaining purpose in the writing and appreciation of a poetry which expresses more extravagantly perhaps than any other the sweet pain of passing. It was written both in Persian, the language of the Mughal court, and in Urdu, a language indigenous to India that had arisen over the previous thousand or so years from the encounter of the Sanskritic Delhi dialect with the Persian, Arabic and Turkish of western invaders. In this sense this poetry bore a family resemblance to poetry from those invading lands, in which the transitory nature of the worldly – of love, beauty and pleasure – had been an established theme for centuries. It was a theme that spoke, ultimately, of the wrench of devotion: for the devout poet must live among the passing wonders of the temporal world, all the time knowing that he must ultimately retreat from them into eternity. But the travails of eighteenth-century India added to this philosophical disposition a particularly experiential edge. There is nothing metaphorical about the "desolation" in this poem by Mir Taqi Mir, who was forced to flee the city after another Persian sacking, this time in 1756; arriving in splendid Lucknow, he was greeted by robed poets who looked with disdain at his rags:

To which place do I belong? You, men of the East, ask
And taunt and tease a poor man.
Delhi, which was once a city unique in the world:
The chosen and the gifted made it home.
Now it has been razed and ruined by the hammer of fate.
I come from that desolation.[16]

It says much about the spirit of Delhi that this mood, this sense of living in the aftermath, has dominated the city's literature until our own time. The capital of a fast-growing and dizzyingly populous nation it might be, but Delhi's writers have consistently seen it as a city of ruins and they have directed their creativity to expressing that particular spiritual emaciation that comes from being cut off from one's own past. This is both the reality and the fantasy of Delhi: the city is always already destroyed. The strange edge of desperation that the most distant outsiders seem to acquire when they come here derives from this – as if everyone becomes, by virtue of being in Delhi, a survivor, someone living on after the loss of everything they held dear. Maybe the present book, so apparently taken up with contemporary things, merely reproduces this ancient literary mood, for my ultimate experience of this city where nothing endures is also that of being bereft. Perhaps my father would say the same.

The high-flown regret of the eighteenth century was intensi-fied into apocalypse some twenty years after Emma Roberts' visit, when the magnificently senescent city about which she rhapsodised was definitively smashed by her compatriots.

By that time the major force in the sub-continent was the British East India Company, a massive monopoly engaged in the production and trade of commodities such as silk, cotton, indigo, saltpetre and opium. Such an enterprise required significant control over Indian land, labour and law, and, during the course of the eighteenth century, the corporation had engaged in ambi-tious military campaigns to achieve this, conquering much of the sub-continent and subduing the Marathas. The Mughal emperor had become a cipher: his own armies disbanded, he now lived in the Red Fort under the protection of the Company's forces.

In 1857, the Delhi 'sepoys' – Indian soldiers serving in the Company's armies, whose cantonments Roberts had seen from the Qutub Minar – joined in a sudden uprising against the Company administration. Sepoys in Delhi killed British soldiers and officials and took over the walled city. The British, shaken and terrified, regrouped, blew their way into the city with explosives and, after a devastating battle, suppressed the rebels. There followed an orgy of looting and revenge that terrified even the perpetrators. Tens of thousands of residents of the city were hung or shot, and many more fled. Though the uprising had involved Hindu and Muslim rebels equally, British reprisals were directed most severely against the latter, because they controlled the political establishment, and because there were fears of a holy war in the name of the Muslim emperor. The emperor was tried and exiled to Rangoon; several members of his family were executed. Most Muslim refugees were prevented from ever returning to Delhi; years later they were still squatting in ruined Mughal tombs to the south, exposed and dispossessed – some of them among the most cultivated and, until recently, the richest, people in the world. Shahjahanabad's Mughal culture of gardens, harems, merchants and poetry was finished overnight.

Mirza Ghalib, a Muslim aristocrat, the greatest of Shahjahanabad's many Urdu and Persian poets, described the aftermath of 1857 in his letters. Because of his affectionate relationship to the British, he had been allowed to stay in the city, but most of his friends had fled:

> . . . leaving behind them houses full of furnishings and treasures beyond price These . . . men of noble lineage had several houses and halls and palaces, all adjoining one another, and it is certain that if one measured the land on which they stood it would equal the area of a village, if not a town. These great palaces, left without a soul to attend them, were utterly looted and laid waste, though some of the less valuable, heavier things, such as the drapings of the large halls, and pavilions and canopies and . . . carpets, had been left as they were. Suddenly one night . . . these things caught fire. The flames rose high, and stone and timber,

doors and walls, were all consumed by fire. These buildings lie to the west of my house, and are so near that from my roof at midnight I could see everything in the light of the leaping flames, and feel the heat on my face and the smoke in my eyes, and the ash falling on my body, for a westerly wind was blowing at the time. Songs sung in a neighbour's house are, as it were, gifts which it sends; how then should not fire in a neighbour's house send gifts of ashes?

About the princes no more than this can be said, that some fell victim to the rifle bullet and were sent into the jaws of the dragon of death, and the souls of some froze in the noose of the hangman's rope, and some lie in prisons, and some are wanderers on the face of the earth.[17]

For Ghalib, the city was dead, and with it, its culture and even its languages. In clearing ground for their boulevards, barracks and military grounds, the British had destroyed not only houses and mosques but also priceless libraries, so that much of the physical record of Urdu literature had ceased to exist. The Muslim nobles who practised and patronised Urdu culture had disappeared too, and those who came to replace them were, as far as Ghalib was concerned, a barbaric rabble. Quoting a verse from a friend's letter in praise of Urdu – "My friend, this is the language Delhi people speak" – he wrote terminally:

My good sir, "Delhi people" now means Hindus, or artisans, or soldiers, or Punjabis or Englishmen. Which of these speak the language which you are praising? . . . The city has become a desert, and now that the wells are gone and water is something rare and precious, it will be a desert like that of Karbala. My God! Delhi people still pride themselves on Delhi language! What pathetic faith! My dear man, when Urdu Bazaar is no more, where is Urdu? By God, Delhi is no more a city, but a camp, a cantonment. No Fort, no city, no bazaars, no watercourses.[18]

"It's difficult to relate to the city of Delhi anymore," says Sadia Dehlvi,* "especially to the people of Delhi."

As a member of one of Delhi's old and august Muslim families, Sadia still looks back to the culture mourned by Ghalib in the years after 1857 as *her* culture.

She has written several books about Sufism, a breed of Islamic mysticism that entered the sub-continent from Persia around 1200 and produced a particularly vibrant intellectual, spiritual and aesthetic culture in north India, drawing on, and in turn influencing, the traditions of Hindus, Sikhs and Muslims alike. Such intermingling was facilitated by Sufism's universalist current, which rejected as false the appearance of division and difference, and proclaimed that the ultimate good was one, without label or preference. Sufi mystics also liked to eschew the authority of priests, and developed a moral language that rejected external rules and codes, asserting that right behaviour originated from inner wisdom and conscience. Fondly remembered by liberals, especially from the older elite, Sufism is remembered today as north India's now-departed aphrodisiac, which brought disparate groups together and spawned from their encounter a shared civilisation rich in music, philosophy and parables.

"One of the only places I really relate to, that I love from the core of my heart, is the shrine of Nizamuddin Auliya. It represents the continuity of the city, at least of the last 700 years: its culture, its soul, its language, its poetry. Go there today and you will see rich and poor, Hindu and Muslim, Indians and foreigners – because Hazrat Nizamuddin continues to foster a culture of equality just as he did in his lifetime."

The fourteenth-century saint, Nizamuddin Auliya, is a towering figure in the history of Delhi, and one of the few personalities to supply any true coherence to its scattered history. The anniversary of Nizamuddin's death still brings to his shrine pilgrims from all over north India, who sleep for a week on the streets

* Real name.

around, cooking their meals on the sidewalks and sleeping, for safety, under the few hundred buses in which they have made their journey.

Preaching renunciation, love and the unity of all forms of spiritual life, Nizamuddin kept away from those in power and advised his followers to do the same, but he was an outspoken political commentator – not only excoriating rulers for injustice but also praising them for wise government; he said, for instance, of the sultan Iltutmish that "more than his wars or his conquests, it is with the water supply he has built for the people of Delhi that he has won his place in heaven." Most conspicuously, perhaps, Nizamuddin Auliya was instrumental in fostering, through his disciple Amir Khusrau the ecstatic music form known as 'qawwali', which fused Indian, Arabic and Persian styles of music to bring novelty to the music assemblies at Nizamuddin's hospice. Qawwali became the characteristic form of Sufi devotional expression, one that dismayed orthodox Muslims because it was self-consciously pluralistic, drawing on older, Hindu, styles of music and poetry, and thus establishing a spiritual community that crossed religious divides. To this day, qawwalis are sung at Nizamuddin's shrine every Thursday evening by some of the same families whose ancestors were trained in the art by Amir Khusrau 700 years ago.

Sadia's house is in nearby Nizamuddin East, part of the neighbourhood named after the saint, an area of parks and blossoms, whose dreamy views of Mughal tombs and aristocratically unfashionable shops endear it to foreign newspaper correspondents.

"My family has been in Delhi since the days of the emperor Shah Jahan. We were successful merchants, and we owned almost the whole of Sadar Bazaar, where we controlled much of the wholesale trade. We had our own law courts: we didn't use the British courts. Even now my family avoids filing cases in the official legal system."

Sadia's remark about legal processes also says much about the currents from which she has emerged. In the wake of its arrival,

British law was regarded by the Mughal establishment as a foreign, godless and illegitimate imposition, and Sufi mystics instructed their followers that they had no moral responsibility to tell the truth in British courts. Sadia's family seems to have lived ever since on the leeward side of this historical breach.

The strength of feeling directed against the British legal system, and the fact that it never secured widespread assent in north India, had to do, indeed, with its failure to acknowledge such local sources of moral authority as the Sufis. Part of the social power of Sufism in the Mughal period derived from the fact that it acted as a democratising political force: Sufi saints enjoyed such popular prestige that they could act as a curb on the unfettered power of the Mughal throne. Emperors consulted them on ethical and political matters, and were reluctant to go against their word, which carried the force of the universal. In this way was established a recognisably consensual mechanism for just rule, in what was otherwise a dictatorship.

More recent legal systems, from the British onwards, have of course provided less space for such kinds of intermediaries. And still today, when the political and legal establishment is often seen as corrupt, self-serving and removed from the needs of ordinary people, there is a widespread hankering for fearless, saintly figures who might speak to rulers with cosmic authority, and change everything in a word.

"When I grew up, our house was always full of music and poetry. My family ran a publishing house: we published many magazines in Urdu and Hindi, including a famous Urdu cultural magazine called *Shama*; it had a huge circulation and we were very well-known. We had a beautiful bungalow where all the poets and film stars used to come. There was no cultural figure of any importance who did not spend time at our house. Writers and artists like Ismat Chughtai, Qurratulain Haider, Amrita Pritam, Faiz Ahmed Faiz, Gulzar, M.F. Hussain, Satish Gujral, and many others. Films stars such as Nargis Dutt, Raj Kapoor, Meena Kumari, Dilip Kumar, Dharmendra . . .

"With the collapse of Urdu, our magazines folded one by one. We sold our ancestral home some years ago. That was the house my family settled in when they came from the old city; it was the house where I was born. It was bought by Mayawati, the chief minister of Uttar Pradesh.

"I am not interested in trying to revive the family business. That era has gone. I am happy with my own. I am happy to focus on what is inside me and to write on spirituality. Ours is a wonderful city, a modern city: I don't want to be negative. But our soul is affected. Something has snapped. I can't identify it."

And indeed perhaps it is unidentifiable, this thing that has snapped. Perhaps it derives not from an event but from some condition of the city, this feeling that everything meaningful has already been destroyed – for Sadia's lament is almost comically similar in content to those of Ghalib a century and a half before.

"How do you expect Delhi to care about its own history when no one can read the languages it is written in? Its entire history is written in Urdu and Persian. The government deliberately killed Urdu after 1947 because they treated it as a Muslim language. But Urdu had nothing to do with religion: it was the language of Delhi, of everyone in Delhi. Pakistan took Urdu for its national language, but Urdu did not originate in any region of Pakistan. I mourn the loss of the language more than anything else. When you want to destroy a people, you take away their language.

"Delhi people used to be very particular about beautiful language. They were fond of poetry and they had real poets. Delhi used to be about beautiful cuisine. It used to be gentle. It was about beautiful living. When the rains began, the shopkeepers shut their shops and went out to enjoy the weather in the open spaces in Mehrauli. They made time for good food. They loved pigeon racing and listening to the storytellers on the steps of the Jama Masjid. They had few marketing skills, which is why they died out. They believed in exquisiteness: they made carpets and furniture, they worked as bookbinders. In Urdu, we call it 'saleeqa', a refined sensibility."

As Ghalib was, Sadia is greatly preoccupied by the uncultivated outsiders, those without any care for such a sensibility.

"The first blow to Delhi's culture came with the British, and then with the influx of Punjabis who came in after Partition. The original people of Delhi did not know what hit them after 1947: they were completely rattled by the loudness, aggression and entrepreneurship of the migrant Punjabis. My parents were shocked: 'Where have they come from, these people? Why are they so loud? What is this food they eat?' They tried to preserve the pre-1947 culture. They constantly corrected our language. 'We have a language,' they used to say. 'We have a refined language. We have to use it.' Punjabis took all the land of the city, they killed its language and etiquette. They ate tandoori chicken and butter chicken. Butter chicken! Those were things that I only saw outside our house, never inside.

"Of course, later on I became more receptive to other cultures. But I am glad that I was brought up in the old Delhi culture, because it was a good culture. It was a culture of hospitality. Giving water to anyone who came to your door. Giving up your own room for your guests, feeding them well, giving them shawls to wrap themselves in.

"Partition devastated the city, damaging its ethos forever. Look at our fabulous monuments: apart from the five or six that have been identified as tourist spots, the rest are just falling down. They're garbage dumps. Hardly anything of beauty has been made since Partition. Look at the five-star hotels. You need to be beautiful to create beauty, and I don't think people have that inner beauty anymore. Now our city is about aggression, rage, inequality, corruption and personal gain. It's about consumerism and shopping malls. There is little space to reflect and polish the heart. We have no beauty to leave to our children."

The walls of this room are covered with paintings of Urdu calligraphy. Sadia's teenage son practices music in the other room: medieval Sufi music that he updates on his guitar. Sadia speaks quickly, switching between Urdu and English, her sentences falling over each other because she has rehearsed them many times in her head.

"I used to enjoy going to parties, because people used to be more genuine. Today you have people looking over your shoulder, talking to you but wondering all the time who they need to give their card to. I don't associate with networking culture. And real prejudices have come to the surface since 9/11. At first I thought I was being too sensitive, but I wasn't. I saw it in people who were part of my own circle of friends. It's difficult to meet them now because inside they have a deep bias against Muslims. They say truly bizarre things these days. They want to know why we can't stop being so *Muslim*."

Two of Sadia's friends from Pakistan, a couple, are sitting in the room with us. The husband runs a company that makes facsimiles of Mughal jewellery, which are fashionable in Pakistani society. The craftsmen who can still make them are not in Pakistan, however, but in India, and he comes frequently to work with them.

"My friends went to a party last night," says Sadia. "And some Punjabi woman met them – she was Punjabi, wasn't she? – yes, and she said she was scared of Pakistanis and they said to her, 'Why don't you come to Pakistan?' And she said, 'No we're too scared. Someone might let a bomb off in your house.' And she started laughing. 'And our husbands would never let us stay among Pakistani men!' And I said how can anyone allow that type of conversation with a guest? I mean, it is most inelegant! If someone had said that in my house, I would have said, 'I'm sorry, you cannot talk like that to my guest!'"

The friend adds,

"And her husband had even been to Pakistan! And he came back with stories of all the good things you can experience there!"

"Anyone who comes here from Pakistan has to hear these things," says Sadia. "Before, at least, people kept such thoughts to themselves, but now they're open about them. That's why

I don't go out anymore. I can't listen to people talking like that.

"Look at how Muslims live in this city. Look at all the young Muslims who are turned away whenever they try to rent an apartment. Did you know pizza companies don't deliver to Muslim areas? I was at a friend's house and I called to order a pizza, and the man said, 'Madam, we don't deliver in those areas.' 'What do you mean by *those areas*?' I shouted at him."

She addresses her friend from Lahore.

"What did that woman tell you at the party last night? She asked you if you wanted a ride home and you told her you were staying in Nizamuddin. And this woman – she's a friend of theirs! – said, 'Are you crazy? I can't go to a Muslim area at eleven at night!' Can you believe it? These are people who studied at the best schools. And they think it is unsafe to come to Nizamuddin. These are the people who live in Jor Bagh, who wear high fashion, drink wine and send their children to American universities. They want to believe they are secular but they are not. They say it constantly because it is their fantasy about themselves."

Sadia is making a fuss over her Pakistani friends while they are here, showing them that in her house, at least, the old culture is still alive. They talk about the fabulous meals they have had with her. In a couple of days, an evening of Sufi music is to happen in her house. She invites me to come too: her son will play, and a young qawwali singer she has taken under her wing. There will be musicians from Iran.

"I have been so exhausted recently," she says. "I wanted to have an evening to replenish my soul, with people I love around me, and with music and poetry."

Nine

1911

I do not deny the glamour of the name of Delhi or the stories that cling about its dead and forgotten cities. But I venture to say this, that if we want to draw happy omens for the future the less we say about the history of Delhi the better. Modern Delhi is only 250 years old. It was only the capital of the Moguls in the expiring years of their régime, and it was only the capital of their collective rule for little more than 100 years. Of course, there were capitals there before it, but all have perished, one after another. We know that the whole environment of Delhi is a mass of deserted ruins and graves, and they present to the visitor, I think, the most solemn picture you can conceive of the mutability of human greatness . . . His Majesty's Government will be on much surer ground if instead of saying anything about the dead capitals of the past they try to create a living capital in the future.

– Lord Curzon, former viceroy of India, speaking in the House of Lords in February 1912 against the British government's recent decision to move the Indian capital from Calcutta to Delhi[19]

With the assaults of 1857, another metropolis, it seemed, had joined the perennial fate of cities built at Delhi. And in the years thereafter, Delhi became an image for European travellers of the impermanence and folly of human ambition. In 1912, an Italian poet landed there in search of heat to ease his tuberculosis. Journeying southwards from Shahjahanabad across the plain that led to the Qutub Minar, he witnessed a:

> . . . transition from the living city to the city of the dead. Finally there are no more houses inhabited by humans; those populated by monkeys have begun . . . The ruins extend into infinity; the entire steppe, as far as the eye can see and beyond, is the vast cemetery of a city destroyed and rebuilt ten times over in the space of four thousand years . . . Here, in this desert of rubbish, the reigning chaos of neglect and oblivion is such that the researcher must have the giddy sensation of being hurled five hundred, a thousand, thirty thousand years back into the abyss of time: from the final Islamic splendour of the Great Moghol to the dark Brahminism of the imposing early Jain and Pali structures, in the dim night of the Vedic origins . . .
>
> I find native and European scholars on the job: archaeologists, experts, architects making models and taking measurements. England is readying for a colossal undertaking: breaking into the bone cave these dead cities are immured within, restoring the ruins, and reordering them decorously in the light of day. A worthy undertaking, yet one I doubt will be favourable to the poetry of these memories. I do indeed thank heaven I am able to visit them today in their state of desolate neglect.[20]

But the poet viewed these goings-on through a tuberculose haze. The "colossal undertaking" for which England was readying was not one of restoration. Their project, like so many Delhi rulers before them, was to level and build again. From that year onwards, the great majority of these "unending ruins" was razed and the next 'New Delhi' spread out, like a fresh table cloth over the remains of yesterday's dinner, on top.

The declaration by King George V that the capital of British India would be moved from Calcutta to Delhi had come in 1911. Calcutta had become a problematic centre for the British. Educated Bengalis, increasingly dismayed by their political dispossession, had made the British capital also the principal laboratory of anti-imperial thought. Gauche attempts to control Bengali unrest through policies of 'divide and rule' had back-fired. The British decided to run elsewhere, and Delhi was the obvious choice. In a letter of 1911, the viceroy, Lord Hardinge, wrote:

> Delhi is still a name to conjure with. It is intimately associated in the minds of Hindus with sacred legends which go back even beyond the dawn of history . . . The Purana Kila still marks the site of the city which they founded and called Indraprastha, barely three miles from the south gate of the modern city of Delhi. To the Mahommedans it would be a source of unbounded grat-ification to see the ancient capital of the Moguls restored to its proud position as the seat of Empire. Throughout India, as far south as the Mahommedan conquest extended, every walled town has its 'Delhi gate' . . . The change would strike the imagination of the people of India as nothing else could do, and would send a wave of enthu-siasm throughout the country, and would be accepted by all as the assertion of an unfaltering determination to maintain British rule in India. It would be hailed with joy by the Ruling Chiefs and the races of Northern India, and would be warmly welcomed by the vast majority of Indians throughout the continent.[21]

But despite these appeals to Delhi's glorious past, the British were determined to build there a city that would negate everything it had previously been. The imperialists would design a city so geometrically European that it would defeat, with its very layout, the benighted orientalism of all its past and set the stage for a new, enlightened future.

In the British city there would be none of those narrow streets with which Shahjahanabad – and numberless other places with a similar climate, from Toledo to Venice to Baghdad – had prevented direct sun from reaching pedestrians. Such tiny lanes, with their unpredictable twists and windowless walls, filled Englishmen with unease. British urban theory was still governed by nineteenth-century 'miasmic' myths of pathology, which held that diseases arose out of bad or stale air, and, from the British perspective, Shahjahanabad was a breeding ground, not only for the insidious spells and complots of the oriental, whom white men would never be able to pursue through such winding alleys, but also for foul vapours, madness and disease. The British city would be conceived to attract light and air to disperse the miasma: the architect, Edwin Lutyens, was a lover of the English countryside and took his inspiration from the theories of Ebenezer Howard, whose book propounding the material and spiritual advantages of garden cities was just then generating an intellectual movement on both sides of the Atlantic. Lutyens determined that Delhi would be a combination of city and countryside, like Howard's utopia: buildings would be sparse, low, and separated by expansive gardens; wide roads and parks would keep the city fresh and well ventilated; a large lake, formed by damming the Yamuna, would give city dwellers access to water and open skies (though this part of the plan was never realised). All in all, a reversal: where Shahjahanabad's streets were narrow and labyrinthine, New Delhi would have vast, geometrical avenues; where commerce in the old city took place in a profusion of packed bazaars, it would be confined in the new to a pillared circle, eventually named Connaught Circus. Where

Shahjahanabad was a city, it could be said, New Delhi was a bureaucratic village – for though it would contain administrative buildings of stupendous size and grandeur, its dispersed, pastoral layout, whose open spaces were emptily monumental, left few places for any kind of urban bustle. There was almost no provision in the plan for venues of pleasure and congregation, nor for merchants and their trades, nor for housing for the poor – all of which had been conspicuous features of the old city.

Like previous building projects on this left bank of the Yamuna river, New Delhi was a heroic enterprise. Thirty thousand workers levelled the land with pickaxes and explosives, while trains brought continual shipments of stone and steel on purpose-built railway lines. Dust and noise erupted in choking clouds from the twenty-two-acre masonry yard where stone was sawn and chiselled into shape, while smoke poured out from the dozens of kilns where the bricks were fired. From the Italian poet's "vast cemetery" emerged the sketch of a city, at the centre of which sprawled an implausibly vast hexagonal plaza from whose points diverged six boulevards of astonishing breadth towards the ancient cities of Delhi. Observers must have had a sense of folly, for while the first levels of the buildings gave proof of stupefying scale and bewildering style, the city itself remained utterly conceptual, without inhabitants or culture. It was as radical as new beginnings could be: it was not at all certain how, or even if, it could work. When the First World War drained the enterprise of money and energy there were many calls, in fact, for its abandonment; but still the work pressed on, and the new capital of British India was finished within two decades.

It was a city of surprisingly graceful buildings – far more so than those built in London at the same time – and it recalled, quite self-consciously, the ethereal splendour of Athens and Washington, DC. As it came to life, the alien city, whose sapling-lined avenues petered out into the dusty brush, also introduced to this place an entirely unaccustomed ethos.

In order to turn their majestic emptiness into a real city, the

British needed people to live in it, which few wished to do. Most of those managing the building project, British and Indian, lodged their families in the old city, or just outside its walls in Civil Lines, where there was commerce, social life and entertainment. In order to get these people – the suppliers of labour, stone, furniture, alcohol, food, and all the rest – to move into the new city, the administrators offered them large plots of land at a greatly discounted rate. So the contractors came. They snapped up sites in the centre of the city for their own mansions, and also bought up large areas of city land as investments. Rich already from the money they had made, by fair means and foul, during Delhi's construction, the estates they now owned in the centre of what was to become a major capital city guaranteed their families wealth and prestige for a century to come. These contractors, in fact, became Delhi's new aristocracy.

They were a very different group of people from the effete aristocrats of Shahjahanabad's twilight. Mostly they were Sikh businessmen from Punjab, men of the world who had made their money in diverse ways – as feudal agriculturalists, as traders, as bandits – and if they muscled in on the British bonanza at all it was because they were masters of that activity which has defined Delhi's business elite ever since: securing contracts. They were brawny, monumental characters who loved political hustle, and their descendants still speak with awe of the entrepreneurial audacity through which their dynasties were made. The grandson of Ranjit Singh, who built such structures as the Council House, now called the Parliament Building, and who owned Delhi's lavish Imperial Hotel, recalls a figure wholly as enterprising as the British themselves.

"My grandfather's next-door neighbour on Curzon Road was Sir Lala Shri Ram, the owner of Delhi Cloth Mills. Both men had the habit of taking tea on their lawns at six-thirty in the morning. One morning in 1932, Sir Lala rushed round to Ranjit's house during the tea hour. His manner was unusually urgent. He was dressed in a three-piece suit and hat, carried a cane, and was followed by an assistant with a ledger book. 'Have you seen the news, Singh?' he cried.

"At that time, the British were trying to take the Asian sugar trade away from the Dutch, who supplied most of India's sugar from Java, which was part of the Dutch East Indies. In 1932, the British launched an assault on Dutch sugar by imposing huge tariffs on its import into the empire. This created an immediate opportunity for anyone who could produce sugar in India. And, since the Javanese sugar industry would be immediately ruined, there would be Javanese sugar refineries to buy for a song.

"As Sir Lala told him all this, my grandfather quietly took notes. After their meeting he worked the numbers out for himself and saw that Sir Lala had spotted a real opportunity. That very day he wrote a letter to his brother-in-law, who lived a life of leisure on a feudal estate in Chamba, enclosing a credit note for 400,000 rupees.

"The brother-in-law took a train to Calcutta, and from there a steamer to Java. He visited four sugar refineries and chose the best. He had it taken apart, shipped in pieces to India, and erected in Laksar in the United Provinces. He supervised the whole process, until the refinery was entirely reassembled. Then he went back to reading literature on his estate. He had no interest in making sugar. He was just in it for the lark.

"Ranjit put his brother in charge of the business. It still runs today. I am a shareholder in it.

"I wish I had recorded him telling this story on camera. Because for him it was so simple. There was nothing extraordinary about it at all. Just go to Java, buy the thing and bring it back. He was incredible.

"But he always maintained a simple lifestyle. He only kept one Jaguar. He never bought himself a plane or anything like that. He had the best suits from Savile Row but in his behaviour he was very down-to-earth. He had left behind a feudal environment, and he knew how easy it would be to fall back into it. One of his cousins in Punjab had 12,000 acres of land and a fleet of Rolls-Royces; he saw that entire fortune disappear in a couple of generations. Those feudal landlords lived in a bubble: the only things they cared about were money, cars, champagne and hunting. I can have a four-hour conversation with those men about weapons.

"That was Ranjit's nightmare. He always told everyone in his family that they had to study and work: 'If you don't have a profession you'll become feudal and lose everything.' And it happened. There were family members who sold priceless properties and blew everything on parties. One cousin had a continual party for thirty years."

From this final recollection we understand well how the fortunes of Delhi's original contractors have diverged so greatly over the years. Some of their descendants still reign over Delhi life from their estates in the city's centre. Others have faded away. Property has been divided up and sold. A quantity of energy goes into internecine legal battles over what remains. Land has simply disappeared, great tracts that were occupied and built on by others over the years, the title deeds lost to time, the energy for contestation lost. Many of these people now live straitened lives in wings of divided mansions, maintaining their status with occasional outings of the silver tea service and a haughty disdain for the new money that has replaced their old. Their faces are lined with the burden of family suicides, madness and alcoholism. They have eccentric paranoia about the past, hiding their whisky from the portrait on the wall of their magisterial great-grandfather, Sir something-or-other, who built the house in which now they skulk.

Houses under legal dispute cannot be sold, and they are too expensive to maintain. Mansions lie empty around Connaught Place, their electricity long cut off, attended only by retainers who clean and guard their somnolent grounds. Far from the hurtling pulse of the city – which nonetheless is only on the other side of the wall – these people live desultorily in 30-million-dollar properties, occasionally sweeping the lawn of leaves, and cooking on a wood fire. They prise apart the bars of the rusted gates to make a way out into the street, but they almost never leave. They sleep in the sun. Sometimes they raise their heads to throw futile stones at a trespassing dog, which is as sleepy as they. They watch their children play in the sprawling, ramshackle grounds. They sleep some more. They watch their children's children, in turn, playing in the grounds.

If the new aristocrats were a departure from the old, their arrival in British Delhi represented a significant departure, also, in their own lives. Their ability to continue getting contracts depended on their successful integration into the new world of British society, and integrate they did, leaving behind what they had previously been.

They had grown up, for instance, in houses built in the court-yard style that had come to north India from central Asia. The empty space of these courtyard houses was not at the edges but in the centre, where there was an open courtyard, often with trees and fountains, which provided a common area for the entire, extended family. Around the courtyard was the house, with private lodgings for different branches of the family, and sometimes separate day quarters for the family's women. It was an attractive style which still appears in the dreams of some of Delhi's elders, who were born in such houses but have lived nearly all their subsequent lives in dwellings turned inside-out. But in the 1920s, having to receive the British at their homes, Delhi's contractors put Asiatic accommodation unsentimentally behind them to build lawn-skirted mansions with large drawing rooms where men and women could consort, unsegregated 'à l'anglaise'.

The rewards of Anglicisation were great. The British, concerned to cultivate this new aristocracy, awarded them not only business contracts but also knighthoods and other state honours. They gave them membership of their clubs and helped them send their sons to Oxford and Cambridge. And so a new ruling class emerged which rapidly took on Englishness. They internalised the codes of English dress. They played tennis and golf, and went hunting at the weekend. They had picnics on blankets and high tea on polished silver.

But their success depended above all on their ability to re-invent their language. The novelist Khushwant Singh, who was the son of one of the building contractors, writes:

> My father, Sobha Singh . . . was way ahead of his times. He sensed that if he had to get on with the English, he must know their language. He advertised for a tutor . . . Within three or four years, he was able to speak the language fluently. He tried to get my mother to pick up English too. He hired an Anglo-Indian lady, Mrs Wright, to teach her. After months of slogging at it, my mother picked up a few words: good morning, good evening, good night and thank you. And she used to make fun of herself and converted the thank you to 'thankus very muchus'. Trying to train her how to mix with the English was a near disaster . . . He gave up the battle to Anglicise her.
>
> My father was a six-footer and slimly built. My mother barely five feet tall. He was very particular about his attire. He wore English suits: coat and striped trousers, bow tie or silk ties and dinner jackets. I never saw him in shervanis and chooridars. The only Indian thing he wore was a tehmat when he retired for the night. He loved to eat and drink well: a huge breakfast of cornflakes, eggs, toast and fruit; a couple of gins and tonic before lunch which was also substantial; tea included cakes or pastry; he liked a couple of Scotches before dinner which was again an elaborate multiple-dish affair followed by a cognac or two.[22]

The culture these people had grown up with was the joint Hindu and Muslim culture of north India, which, as we have seen, gave pride of place to fine language. Most of them had grown up speaking and writing several of the related languages of this region: Urdu, which was written in the Arabic script; Hindustani, which was pretty much identical but written in the Sanskrit-derived Devanagari script; Punjabi, which was written in the Gurmukhi script, a cousin of Devanagari – and possibly one or two of several other local tongues. Nor was language, even for businessmen such as they, merely a tool to get things done. They were lovers of poetry and song, and many of them wrote poetry themselves – usually in Urdu which, though it might not have been their first language, was generally considered the best language for poetry. Suddenly, however, they led their lives in their weakest language of all, or one they did not even know: English. They barked at each other in the clubby argot of the British bureaucrats and military men with whom they fraternised ("six-footer") and their previous culture dwindled within them. English took over, and though they passed on fabulous estates to their descendants they could not pass on their own tongues.

When you look at photographs of the newly completed British administrative complex, enormous and pristinely modern, and surrounded by miles and miles of nothing, you cannot help feeling there is something delusional about it – as there had been about many other cities built in this place. And indeed, in this sense, the British were entirely traditional Delhi rulers. They were forced to abandon their capital – in less time, in their case, than it had taken to build. In 1947, they hastily moved out, and the administrators of independent India moved in.

Unwittingly or not, these administrators finished what the British had begun: the destruction of north India's ancient shared Hindu and Muslim culture. In agony after the mutilations of Partition, the new state was determined to eradicate all reminders of its wounds. The shared culture would be forgotten, and its traces of Islam stamped out. Language was an essential sphere of operations.

The 1950 constitution set out as an explicit objective the propagation of a new language, 'Hindi'. Hindi was a re-invention of traditional Hindustani – the north Indian language of which Urdu, since it had been taken to the highest levels of literary and philosophical exploration, was the most sophisticated version – which would be fabricated by expunging, to the greatest extent possible, all influences of Persian, Arabic and Turkish and by replacing them with words retrieved or coined from Sanskrit. Indian tongues, henceforth, would not produce Muslim sounds. Nor would Indian hands shape Muslim letters: the writing of this language in the Arabic script was discontinued, and Hindi was only written in Devanagari, a script indigenous to India. The Central Hindi Directorate was set up to patrol the back lanes of this language and police its borders. Official communiqués – school textbooks, for instance, or news reports on All India Radio – were manufactured as showpieces of the new language: awkward, academic showpieces whose Sanskritic excess resembled no real person's speech.

Perhaps one imagines that an independent country is more vocal than one colonised. Perhaps one imagines independence as a moment when previously silent voices burst forth with conversation and song. But in north India the truth was more complex. People no longer read the works of Hindustani's greatest exponents, which contained too many unapproved elements and which were written in an alphabet which they could very soon no longer decipher. Punjabi households, previously so proudly literary, began to dislike books themselves. Most books, books that did not directly further one's career, represented an expense without return. They represented, in fact, a threat to the post-Partition household, in which rebuilding the family's material base was the only legitimate preoccupation: esoteric concerns and fictional worlds were now considered a dangerous influence from which parents should preserve their children. In the new, fearful, ethos of the family, moreover, parents felt uneasy about the self-sufficiency of a child with a book: they wanted their children to need them as they needed their children, and they shut off avenues to solitude and reverie.

Delhi upheld its reputation as a city where languages came to die: for not only did Partition refugees forget Urdu in one generation, they even had difficulty passing on their mother tongue of Punjabi, which few of their grandchildren knew except in snatches. Many members of its middle classes ended up speaking no language well – neither English, which was increasingly, nonetheless, the language of professional life, nor Hindi, which they spoke at home but in which they had little vocabulary outside the needs of the everyday. The care of language was seen as worthless and effeminate, and a certain vagueness of speech, a deliberate ignorance of grammar, became the style. Books and newspapers were full of errors of spelling and grammar, to say nothing of advertisements and street signs. It became difficult to find people to translate between Indian languages; for a high-level command of, say, literary English and literary Hindi, was hardly ever united in the same person. The old broadness of outlook died out. People knew less and less what people who were not like them thought about, and classes and castes became more isolated and suspicious.

It was often poor migrants from the small towns who preserved the idea of beautiful speech. The landed Partition refugees counted their houses and saved-up money, and they rejoiced in their superiority to these ragged, later arrivals; but sometimes they heard the speech of the working classes, who had come in from other places where the poetic, ecstatic elements of Hindustani had not become foreign – and they realised how inarticulate they themselves had become.

Perhaps the love for poetry and fine language, which now had no object, was transferred to Bombay cinema, which enjoyed cultish adoration in the decades following Partition. It was to the Bombay film studios that many of the migrant Urdu poets and playwrights then headed, and there they created a cinema of delicate feeling in which heroes spoke in exquisite, Persianate Hindi and sang love songs whose metaphors recalled the heights of Urdu poetry. The three male superstars of the era, Raj Kapoor, Dilip Kumar and Dev Anand, all arrived in Bombay from what is now Pakistan, and, if Hindi cinema from the 1950s and '60s still carries such emotional charge, even among people who were born long after it, it is because it remained a last refuge of romantic, poetic aspects of Hindustani culture that were largely driven underground by the severer ethos of the independent nation. Significantly, perhaps, Bombay cinema was one of the few domains of Indian public life where Muslim men were unabashedly adored – even though they donned Hindu stage names.

It is instructive that this cinema also had cult appeal across the entire Soviet Bloc, where audiences were governed by other mirthless regimes and where, moreover, they had in the 1930s and '40s lived through mass traumas of their own. For it was a cinema that existed slightly outside the everyday world, a cinema that operated as if the previous things, the finer things, endured (its stories were almost entirely silent about Partition, for instance, as if it had not been born from that throe). It was of extraordinary poignancy to people, wherever they might be, for whom those things had been lost.

Defence Colony is one of south Delhi's leafiest and most desirable neighbourhoods. Its spacious plots were given out in the years following Indian independence to officers in the armed services. The original inhabitants are now elderly and lead lives of archaic rhythms: brisk walks in Defence Colony's many parks at six in the morning – sometimes accompanied by sessions of energetic clapping or synchronised group laughter – followed by breakfast and the newspaper on the balcony at seven. Lunch and dog walks are coordinated by the 'boys' who work in the house, the sons and grandsons, often, of servants known and trusted from army days. Tea and biscuits arrive on the terrace with military regularity in the afternoon. Dinner and bed happen early for these five o'clock risers, but there may be time for an evening drink at the local club, where reminiscences are shared about the escapades of yore. They will talk about military college in the 1940s, before Partition split the army, too, into India and Pakistan. Half their college mates became the enemy at that point, and they fought them in three major wars, but this did not impede ancient affections (which sometimes even included surreptitious cooperation across the lines: "Hold off on such-and-such target, old boy: my sister's son is holed up there") and still now they preserve friendships with their former colleagues on the other side of the border. They talk of long-gone whisky-quaffing superiors with Wodehousian nicknames.

They are sturdy men and women with a powerful sense, both, of duty and pleasure. "When there wasn't a war on," one of the aged – but immaculate and beautiful – military wives said to me once, her accent Sandhurst, her glass full of gin-and-tonic, "it was the best life you could imagine. All of us together on a military base, drinks and billiards in the evening, and lots of tall men in uniform . . . "

Frugal people with comfortable homes and respectable pensions, there was nothing particularly wanting in these people's lives. They enjoyed social prestige and connections, their children were well educated, well married and well employed. Unexpectedly, however, in their old age, they surpassed adequacy, and became rich.

In the property boom of the early 2000s, the plots they were living on reached values of $2 million, then $3 million, then $4 million. These numbers were gossiped around the neighbourhood. Few of them really wanted a change in their lives, but there was pressure to release this value, often from their children, who were in the prime of their careers. The old-timers moved out and rented elsewhere as, one by one, the houses came down. They were idiosyncratic houses, often designed by the owners, but they had some grace and proportion: large, high-ceilinged rooms, roof terraces for the winter sun, and airy ground-floor rooms for the summer, well shaded by gardens of trees. Over a short period of time most of them were reduced to rubble, and Defence Colony rows became gap-toothed. Shacks came up in the holes, to house builders and their families: dark-skinned country children played in the streets by day, while at night melancholic songs could be heard as the women roasted rotis on wood fires. As the buildings rose, the labourers' accommodation rapidly improved: soon they lived in five-star apartments, their laundry strung merrily across marble halls, even their songs more joyful. And then the work was complete and these families went somewhere else to live in tents again.

The new buildings were very different from the old: great fortresses of international-style apartments. There were no more gardens, which would have been an impossible sacrifice of real estate; there were no more open-air verandas, sun-deflecting white-washed walls, shading trees, or any other signs of the architectural intelligence that had previously accumulated, over many centuries, in this harsh-seasoned place. These new colossi towered over the trees, their stone faces grimly to the sun, the greenhouse effect of their floor-to-ceiling windows off-set by great batteries of air conditioners. High walls, security keypads and CCTV cameras completed the promise of 'international living'.

The original owners retained a couple of apartments in these blocks for themselves and their children. The others they sold for $1 million each.

All this explains why, as I approach the house of Colonel Oberoi, the street is like a building site. The dust of demolition and construction powders the tongue. The air screams with the roar of masonry saws on Italian marble (the epithet, in fact, is unnecessary: all marble here is Italian, wherever it comes from). In front of one of the houses, a team operates a specialised drill for sinking still deeper the illegal private wells that all these houses use to bypass the rationing of the municipal water supply: as the water table runs dry, these wells, which until recently ran fifty feet below the surface, must now sink to 200 feet. The companies who possess the expertise and equipment to drill to those depths have more work than they can handle.

I am late for Colonel Oberoi, and my apologetic telephone call from the car did nothing to appease him. "I will give you five minutes to get here," he growled down the phone.

Colonel Oberoi's house has not been knocked down. It is one of the rare original houses still to be standing. Colonel Oberoi designed it himself, and it is highly eccentric: an attempt to fit an old-style courtyard design into a New Delhi row-house plot.

"My mother insisted on a courtyard," he says, "when we built this in the fifties."

For a house that has been occupied for more than fifty years, there is an astonishing lack of *stuff*. The walls are bare, as are the light bulbs. On the sideboard are several photos of grandchildren and military award ceremonies.

The Colonel is over ninety and has been retired for decades. He is slightly deaf, so his military bark is even more stentorian. He wears a rumpled safari suit – the uniform, in earlier times, of Indian public servants. He sits down at a writing desk on which there are notes written in Urdu in notebooks that he has made himself by recycling the blank sides of A4 printed pages: the pages are cut into four and stapled together at the spine. He gestures to me to sit across the desk from him.

"In the villages where I grew up," he says, "the houses all had courtyards. You entered from the street into the courtyard, where there would be cattle and hay, and beds for sleeping outside. The rooms were in a line along the far end of the courtyard: they were all on the ground floor, and built of mud and wooden beams. The roof jutted far out over the edge of the building so that the rooms were always in shade. All these rooms were bedrooms: the living area was the courtyard. If people came to visit, there would be tea in the courtyard around a table. We didn't host grand events at home – for weddings and religious events there was a community centre which we all helped to build and maintain."

Colonel Oberoi grew up in a tribal district of North-West Frontier Province, a place of extraordinary natural beauty where the peaks of the Himalayas are always within sight and the Indus river is at its proudest and most lush. In August 1947, this region became part of Pakistan, and Colonel Oberoi's family became Partition refugees.

"At that time I was posted in Bombay for military training. My family was stuck in Mardan, near the Khyber Pass, and they couldn't set out for India because my wife was pregnant. They were looked after by a Muslim colleague of mine, a Captain Jabbar who hosted them in his military accommodation and made sure they were safe: my sister and her husband, two cousins and their children, and my aunt and mother. The news coming out of those places was terrible and I was very concerned. Two weeks after Independence I went to the evacuee organisation in Amritsar. Friends of mine who had family in Lahore were given military escorts to cross the border and fetch them, but Mardan was too far away for that. I was very worried and didn't know what to do. Finally they made provision to airlift my family out. I still remember the moment when the announcement came over the loudspeakers: 'Lieutenant Oberoi's family will be airlifted out.'

"But my family was not ready to be airlifted. My wife couldn't move. So she had to wait until our eldest son was born, which didn't happen till October. By that time it was too late for the airlift. So Captain Jabbar personally escorted them to Peshawar, where he handed them over to the care of a Major from Haryana, who brought my family over the border in a regimental train. Delhi was chaos at that time – all the trains had been stopped. I could not get to Delhi and nor could they. It took another month before we were finally reunited."

As he talks, Colonel Oberoi draws extensively. Plans of houses, maps of family movements.

"I wasn't based in Delhi in those years: I was moving everywhere with the army. In 1949 I was sent to England on a long gunnery staff course. After that, I was posted all over India. But I had no accommodation of my own, which was a big problem. My extended family was still staying in a one-room house with a relative in Delhi. Delhi was full of refugees: a couple of hundred thousand people were still living under tents and thatched roofs in the various camps while the government tried to find housing for them. A colleague of mine told me to ask about evacuee property. They showed me a house that had been abandoned by a Muslim family and I went to the resettlement director to ask if it could be allotted to me. He said I was ineligible because I was posted outside Delhi. 'But we are building a defence colony,' he said, 'where you might qualify for a plot.'"

The authorities made it easy for army men to buy these plots by offering instalment plans over several years. In the post-Independence conception of Delhi, it was to be a city of high-minded people committed to the national cause, and the choicest of the new 'colonies' that sprouted quickly on all sides of the British bureaucratic city designed by Lutyens were given over to people from outside the government whose work was essential to the nation: in addition to Defence Colony there were neighbourhoods reserved for journalists, lawyers and the like. Businesspeople, by contrast, whose activities were considered more vulgar and self-serving, were housed in the comparatively remote neighbourhoods of west Delhi.

"I sat down and wrote a petition letter. The next day they called and told me that my application had been successful. I bought the plot. When I came back to Delhi, we built this house."

I have come to see Colonel Oberoi to look around his court-yard house built, anachronistically, in the new city, but he wishes to end our meeting at the time we agreed – in spite of the fact that I turned up late and missed half of it – so there is no time for the tour. It is time for his walk to the market. We stand up.

I ask him what he is writing in his notebooks.

"This is my poetry," he says.

"You write in Urdu?"

"I write in many languages. My mother tongue was Saraiki, a dialect of Punjabi spoken in the place I was born. I used to play with boys from the tribes who spoke Pashto. As a boy in the 1920s I spoke six languages every day: Saraiki, Punjabi, Hindi, Pashto, English and Urdu. I used to write letters in three languages using three different scripts: Hindi to my mother and sister, English to my friends, and Urdu to my uncles. I write English poetry too. But Urdu is the best language for poetry."

With the mention of poetry, Colonel Oberoi forgets his haste to leave. He wants to read to me. He goes to the bookshelf to get a stack of notebooks full of poetry.

"I have been writing poetry for seventy years," he says.

Much of it has been composed in old, unused diaries. He flicks through them, looking for the poems he wishes to read. There is something touching about these volumes, whose days and months are printed in grey English from left to right and from what readers of the Latin script consider front to back, and which are filled with hand-written poetry written the other way – the poetry cutting backwards through the days. He reads in a deep and musical voice, pausing after each poem. They are odd verses which give expression to unusual curiosities. "All the emotions we feel for other human beings, do they have any place in paradise? For if there is nothing to bind us together there, it is no paradise to me."

Jaise nadee ke bahaav main ek pathroon ka jaloos hai
Bahe jaa rahe hain ludak ludak

Wajood use na thahraav hai
Na lagaav hai na dosti hai
Na hai dushmanee
Chaahat nahin, nafrat nahin
Jannat hai uska naam agar jannat hamein nahin chahiye.

Like the march of stones
Tossing and tumbling in the current of a river
Without identity or roots
Without attachments of friendship
Or of enmity
No desire, no hatred —
If that's what you call heaven
I want none of it.[23]

Severe and regimented in his general dealings, something tender and mellifluous emerges from Colonel Oberoi in our conversation about poetry. It comes, in part, from the memory of stupendous nature in the mind of this man who has lived so long in what has become one of the world's largest conurbations. But his Urdu poetry asserts also his allegiance to a lost culture, one that Hindus like him once shared with Muslims, a cosmopolitan, multilingual culture in which poetry and the life of the spirit found more ample expression.

"How did you feel about Partition?" I ask, after the recitation.

"In the initial stages I felt very bitter. I mean, we were hoping for independence and what did we get? A country cut in half."

And he elaborates with a domestic metaphor that will return again and again.

"Two brothers ended up fighting and dividing the plot."

His bitterness finds its target in the politicians who oversaw the division of British India.

"We in the services had a code of behaviour. The welfare of the people and the country comes first, your own, last. This oath was emblazoned on the walls of our military academy. But politicians did not live like that. They thought of their own interests, and hang the country."

"Did you feel bitter towards Muslims?"

"Why would I? I had grown up with those people, and they were caught in the same situation that we were. The younger generation was taught to hate Muslims. That kinship we had is not there now: they grew up hearing horror stories. But we love those people."

He strokes his bushy white moustache and says, "Can I offer you some tea?"

Ten

1947

The car honks merrily as it approaches the main intersection, as if there were only ten other cars on the streets, as if such signals were not entirely drowned in the hubbub. Having broadcast its alert, it then drives serenely, and without looking, into the furious path of 16 million people and their traffic.

There is nothing urban about this place, I think. No metropolitan ethos emerges from all these multitudes who live together. So many of the people who created the modern city came as refugees from small towns and villages, and even after decades in Delhi, that is where they still live.

The Dominion of India came into being on 15 August 1947. Perforated by hundreds of principalities, which as yet retained their independence from it, the new territory looked like a moth-eaten remnant, torn away as it had been from a much larger swathe called the British Indian Empire, which, over the middle decades of the twentieth century, gave rise progressively to four new nations: Burma (1938), India and Pakistan (1947) and, with the rupture of this last, Bangladesh (1971).

The British Indian *Empire* was so called not because it was part of the British empire – though it was that – but because it was itself a super-territory, comprising an enormous array of nationalities and cultures. With a population roughly equivalent to Europe's, and a similar range of languages, it could easily, in other circumstances, have given rise to as many countries as that western flank of the landmass – or many more. In this sense, the old empire presented fewer conceptual challenges than the issuing nations. Empires do not need to conceal the fact that they are the artificial result of transnational might. A 'nation', by contrast, must rest on some natural logic, which is its perennial problem. Like most of the hundred or so other new nations of the twentieth century, the nascent states of south Asia had no historical basis except in imperial conquest, nor did they possess any single language, culture or ethnicity that could give them coherence. They were both too big and too small to match any category of experience – and their new administrators were greatly preoccupied by the search for symbols and slogans that would redefine their lumpy agglomerations as self-evident homelands.

The name 'Pakistan' was one such attempt to conjure coherence out of variance. It was an acronym of disparate territories, coined by a Cambridge student named Choudhary Rahmat Ali, who wrote in 1933 of the dream of providing a separate nation for the "thirty million Muslim brethren who live in PAKSTAN – by which we mean the five Northern units of India, viz: **P**unjab, North-West Frontier Province (**A**fghan Province), **K**ashmir, **S**ind, and Baluchis**tan**." Having settled on this neologism, Mohammad Ali Jinnah, who became Pakistan's first head of state, was furious when he discovered that the other new country across the border was going to call itself 'India'. He had imagined that his neighbours would throw out the British word and all its colonial associations, and, like Pakistan, bring in an untouched name for the era to come. By calling themselves 'India', they

passed off their infant state as an antique and pretended that all
the history associated with that name was theirs, that all the
millennia of competition for the lands beyond the Indus river
– Pakistan's river! – all the region's great civilisations, whether
they had existed within the territory of this new India or not,
were the inheritance, solely, of their shrunken land.

India not only took the name; India got Delhi. Delhi was the
city to which both of the last two empires had moved their
capital, and these empires, great builders both, had fashioned the
kind of monumental buildings and vistas that provided instant
national dignity. While the government of Pakistan camped for
over a decade in Karachi, waiting for a new capital to be
constructed, Indian officials could use the impressive parliamen-
tary infrastructure built to symbolise British authority in India,
to which the British empire had devoted several of its best
architects and millions of pounds. As British administrators packed
their bags and boarded ships, India's new ministers moved into
the bougainvillea-bedecked bungalows they left behind.

But the city would never again resemble the administrative
cantonment the British had known. For, as the flags of independent India were hoisted over their garden city, it was immediately overwhelmed by hundreds of thousands of people fleeing
the terrors of the empire's partition. And it is out of this, more
than anything else, that the contemporary city was born.

The partition of the British sub-continental territory into a
new 'India' and 'Pakistan' caused what has been called "one of
the great human convulsions of history".[24] Within the space of
a few months, 14 million people moved one way or the other
across the new borders in the north-west and the east. As many
as 12 million of those refugees crossed the north-western border,
which came within 400 kilometres of Delhi and divided into
two the state of Punjab: Hindus and Sikhs, mainly, moving to

the Indian side, Muslims to the Pakistani. Many of them moved for fear of the violent treatment they would receive as religious minorities in whichever of the two new states was walling up around them, and indeed the unscrambling of these conjoined religious populations was accompanied by staggering violence. Some 1 million people died in the partition of British India – some of hunger and disease, but most in the mass killings whose astringent memory still lurks in Punjabi households – not only in India and Pakistan, but all over the world. Muslims in what became India, and Hindus and Sikhs in what became Pakistan, were cut down in their houses and in the streets; they were pulled out of departing cars and buses and murdered. In what was to become a cliché of Partition storytelling, trains of refugees attempting to escape were stormed and everyone aboard slaughtered: the trains still ran, arriving at the other end like omens from hell. Seventy-five thousand women were raped or abducted in this monumental mêlée, a fact that still plays its part in structuring relationships between the sexes in this part of the sub-continent. The partition was, in brief, a massive catastrophe, one of the several instances in the twentieth century when suffering and death on an inconceivable scale were caused by bureaucratic pen strokes – pen strokes, in this case, of the British government and the governments-in-waiting of India and Pakistan, none of which has ever taken responsibility for its part in uprooting and killing so many.

What caused such an orgy of violence? These are events whose core is difficult to access in any entirely satisfying way. Even the perpetrators find them unintelligible in retrospect, for they were somehow, in that moment, the instruments rather than the authors of the fury; since then, it has released them from its grip and left them as bewildered as anyone else. Certainly, no utilitarian explanation – self-defence, for instance, or struggles over property – can do justice to the extraordinary fervour of Partition violence. For what took over such previously contented, peaceful cities as Amritsar and Lahore was a spontaneous mass fantasy of the sort that eludes such everyday causation. The object of this fantasy, it would seem, was the total annihilation of other religious communities – communities with whom social life had always been intimately shared, but who suddenly seemed, now everything was being shaken out by a border, hideous (the German word 'unheimlich', usually translated as 'uncanny' but literally 'un-home-like', would fit well here). This is what one must conclude from the sterilising bent of the violence – for, as in the similar rampages that have erupted over the political separation of other almost indistinguishable communities, such as in the former Yugoslavia, this was not simply a formless frenzy. It had a specific structure that was targeted not only against a community but also, terribly, against its reproductive potential: not only indiscriminate slaughter, but also the repeated exposure of unborn foetuses, the ceremonial display of castrated penises – and rape on a colossal scale, whose purpose was genetic subjugation: *their children will not be their own.*

Did these communities simply hate each other? Did the suspension of civility simply allow the emergence of murderous passions that had always existed? Of course, there had always been conflicts and tensions. People understood themselves through their membership of distinct communities of religion and caste, and the resulting divisions and suspicions were exploited by every ruling regime – not only the Mughals and the British but also, later, the various state and federal governments of independent India – with predictably corrosive results. It is perhaps not surprising that the word 'communal', which in every other part of the English-speaking world speaks of things harmonious and shared, is in India used to talk of social break-down: because the 'community' is thought of as necessarily partial and chauvinistic, its interests always at odds with those of society at large.

But many of these everyday conflicts were just as intense within religious groups as they were between them – Hindus of different castes, for instance, were often embattled. And curiously the overwhelming memory of pre-Partition culture in north India is not one of enmity. It is one rather of inter-religious respect and harmony: people like Colonel Oberoi – and my own father – lived with a sense of expansiveness and plenitude in the mixed religious environment of British India and think back on it with fondness and regret. The culture that existed there had been created by all the religions together, over many centuries, and, whatever the historical conflicts between them, their shared world was richer than the divided one which followed. And that is the point.

It is difficult to express to people who have not known it how shattering is the death of a culture – which is to say the annihilation of everything through which a society comes into being, and therefore of its members' very selves. The Partition of 1947 killed a culture – an old, shared culture – and the physical-life violence was part of a mad frenzy to survive this psychic death. The new regime of independent nations was narrower than the old culture, and in order for people to squeeze in, a great sacrifice was required: a process of purification and eradication that was essentially infinite because its true theatre was not external but in the self. It was not only Muslims who were afraid of having no place in the new India: Hindus, also, were too Muslim to live there. In their rampages, they killed not Muslims but *Islam*: the Islam of which they had always been part, the Islam they carried within themselves, the Islam they had to annihilate if they were ever to belong.

Even hatred is not such a powerful cause for violence as is commonly supposed. Love and survival are far more potent forces. The violence of Partition was the violence of people trying to survive – not only physically, but spiritually and politically. And their survival depended on the sacrifice of a love which had become, in the modern world, forbidden.

For the general mass of people, fear and violence broke out with little warning and there was no time to plan an escape: they locked their houses and set out in cars, buses and trains – but most of all on foot, in great columns hundreds of thousands strong, Muslims one way, Hindus and Sikhs the other, with no idea of what the future would bring, or if they would ever return. With some exceptions, the survivors of this terrible exodus lost everything they could not carry – houses, effects, land, businesses – and their lives after 1947 were begun again from zero.

On the Indian side of the border, refugees settled where they could. Some stayed with members of their extended family. Many were housed in refugee camps, some for as long as five years. A rapidly assembled camp at Kurukshetra in Punjab accommodated 200,000 people, who quickly turned it into a temporary city, bustling with schools, hospitals, markets and religious festivals – festivals, some of them, which commemorated events in the *Mahabharata*, the ancient epic that described a devastating war fought in that very place, Kurukshetra, between two branches of a single family; the contemporary resonances must have been clear to all.

Over time the greatest number of these refugees settled in Delhi. It was easier to force a way into Delhi than anywhere else: as the capital of the new nation, Delhi displayed the greatest resolve in providing shelter, welfare and business loans to Partition refugees; as a recent city built in the middle of great stretches of open land, it also had the most flexibility to offer permanent housing. During the first half of the twentieth century, which saw the building of the British capital, Delhi's population had crept up from about 150,000 to just under a million; after Partition, a million new residents were added overnight, and more Partition refugees continued to arrive for many years. The great work of the city after 1947 was the carving up of plots for these new arrivals on land acquired by the state from previous landowners – often the 1911 aristocracy – for the purpose.

As in all moments of great chaos and rupture, there were not only losers. Properties vacated by fleeing Muslims, especially in Old Delhi, were commandeered by Hindu neighbours who had prepared themselves for just such an operation; there are many landowning families in Delhi who cannot cogently explain the origin of their wealth. The state, too, seized a great amount of property from departing refugees, including assets of immense value belonging to the old Muslim aristocracy. In general, however, elites had a better time than everyone else, and not only because they had the money to get out. More than anything else, they had access to information. Most people had no idea what was going to happen and could only follow rumours, but those with access to the political establishment could ascertain much more concretely what the future held and how they might come out on top. People who owned major estates and businesses were particularly motivated to obtain up-to-date intelligence about the gathering Partition rhetoric, and many of them sold early on just to be safe. Such elites were also able to appropriate state resources for their private purposes: it was the army, often, that helped them to move their family members and assets southwards and eastwards into territories that would lie in 'India', were a partition to happen. Many of them bought property in Delhi and established a business position before the onslaught, and their descendants are still among the richest people in the city.

By its winners and losers, by the culture of those who arrived and by the absence of those who left, it is Partition, more than anything else, that marks the birth of what can be recognised as contemporary Delhi culture. The contemporary city was born out of trauma on a massive scale, and its culture is a traumatised culture. Even those who were born long after Partition, even those, such as myself, who arrived in Delhi from other places and histories, find themselves, before long, taking on many of the post-traumatic tics which are so prominent in the city's behaviour. This is why the city seems so emotionally broken – and so threatening – to those who arrive from other Indian cities.

Far more than the Jewish holocaust, whose stories were propagated by a myriad of political, legal and documentary processes, the events of the partition of British India remain, for the most part, locked in silence. The holocaust carried great rallying force for the new state of Israel, but for India and Pakistan, Partition violence was the shame that besmirched their independence, and they did not advertise it. In neither country are there official archives of Partition experiences, state memorials or remembrance ceremonies. In private life, the people who lived through those events typically told no one what they had done or seen. By now, prosthetic memories have taken the place of real recollection, for the chain of experience that leads back to those events is cut off. Every Indian Partition family tells the same stories: the armed Muslims descending in hordes on terrified households, the women jumping into wells rather than be dishonoured, the rivers of blood, the miraculous escapes of babies overlooked in the slaughter, the villages where "they did not leave any girl" – for euphemism speaks more powerfully of horror than direct speech. "They came brandishing naked talwars," they say, referring to an ornate curved sword associated with medieval Muslim rulers – and thus showing how the specific terror of 1947 collapses in the telling into an eternal, mythical vulnerability. For the Sikh and Hindu families who emerged from that catastrophe, what remains is a sense of transcendental horror, which is identified with Islam itself. The people who were adult at the time of Partition had real-life experience of Muslims, which set limits to their imaginings. Their children did not, and they peopled the void of adult silences with the most terrifying and obscene monsters. They reproduced those silences around their own children, so that even as all facts receded, the residual trauma, like DDT in the food chain, became more concentrated with time. Delhi was tormented by a catastrophe that would not go away, no matter how many years went by.

Fleeing to Delhi from Islam, these families were very conscious of making their new lives on Muslim land, and even as they sought to seal themselves off from the past, the evil continued to seep up from the ground. The new colonies in which they were settled in the 1950s were reclaimed from ancient Muslim graveyards (remember Emma Roberts looking down upon "the sepulchres of one hundred and eighty thousand saints and martyrs, belonging to the faithful"), and Islamic ghosts drifted into their nightmares. Though they brought priests to exorcise these ghosts, though they covered their lintels in charms and talismans, the onslaught of evil was simply too great for them to live at ease. They wore rings and amulets to protect themselves but still they looked upon the ground with horror. They did not dig in this earth: their gardens were full of flowers in pots and trees in concrete tubs, for they did not like the idea of what might emerge if they broke the surface to plant. Fathers told their children not to pick up any stone because it might have been used by a Muslim to perform 'istibra' – the ritual cleansing of the penis after urination. The earth was corrupted.

The 'Punjabi culture' which Partition refugees brought to Delhi is often satirised for its preoccupation with money, property and outward display. But this is as much a 'post-traumatic' culture as a Punjabi culture. It is the diametric opposite, in fact, of the Sufi outlook that so influenced the culture of this part of the world in previous times, for which only the inner life was authentic and everything else – power, money, possessions – was to be treated with detachment. Things had turned upside-down. The population somehow resembled one of those trauma patients who adopts a personality opposite to their own so as not to be susceptible to the same hurt again. *That older personality, all that tolerance and eloquence, was effeminate,* they seemed to say, *and it only got us screwed. Now we will care about nothing that we cannot touch, and we will let nothing stand in the way of us getting more of it.*

Delhi drivers spend much of their time gazing into the stationary back window of the car in front, whose angle is perfect for viewing the patient sky: in those back windows, lone clouds drift and fork-tailed kites circle. But it is also in back windows that people place their signature, as if to fight off the anonymity of the vehicular ocean. Sometimes the words are personable: "Sunita and Rakesh", for instance. Sometimes verbosely confrontational: "Are you racing past me so you can wait longer at the next red light?" Boys like to seem bad: "I am your worst nightmare", or "I drive like this to PISS YOU OFF!" Smarter cars project global gravitas: "Duke University" or, sometimes, "My child is at Northwestern". American universities actually make stickers like that. Often the import is spiritual: "Jesus Loves You" comes along sometimes, pictures of Sai Baba frequently. The sword advertises Sikh martial valour. Once I saw a crescent moon with a scimitar: in a place that has long been convinced – long before 9/11 – of Islam's inherent bellicosity, it struck me as an invitation to trouble, and I realised why I had never seen such a thing before.

The most common signature of all, however, is "Rama" – the single word accompanied, sometimes, by a bow strung with fierce-topped arrows.

Rama was an avatar of the god Vishnu, who took on human form to save the world from the demon Ravana, whose power had swelled to cosmic dimensions as a result of his many thousands of years of meditation, self-denial and physical discipline. Ultimately, Rama destroyed Ravana and was crowned emperor of the world, which he purified and ruled over for 11,000 years. Rama's triumphant return to his capital of Ayodhya after the defeat of Ravana is remembered every year in the festival of Diwali, possibly the most significant and popular of all mainstream Hindu festivals, and the millennia of his reign are remembered as the blissful time of the earth, when there was universal virtue, when the emperor was attentive to all complaints, and there was peace and justice for all.

This idea of Hindu power and virtue has obviously acquired an additional edge with centuries of rule by non-Hindu invaders. There exists a Hindu melancholy, which finds in Rama an image of what life could have been in this part of the world if the last millennium had been different: to put the name of Rama on the back of your car is, in part, to protest against everything that has gone wrong in those thousand years, which includes the corrupt and unresponsive governments of today. Traumatised places dream of transcendental heroes who can reverse the assaults of history.

But it is possible that Rama appeals to Delhi drivers not only because of his martial power, and the fantasy he holds out of Hindu recovery. Perhaps he also holds a more intimate appeal.

The cliché about Rama is that he is the perfect man, the incarnation of all virtues. So much so that pregnant women read aloud the epic of his life – the *Ramayana* – to teach his perfection to their unborn children – sons, they hope. What is striking about this wisdom is that it seems, on first sight, to fit so poorly with the stories we actually know about Rama, in which he seems like a deeply flawed and fragile man.

A great warrior and son of the king's first wife, Rama grows up as heir to the Ayodhya throne. The second wife, however, gets the king to grant her an unconditional request, which she redeems thus: Rama should be sent into exile so that her own son, Bharata, might take the throne. The promise may not be withdrawn but Rama raises no protest: he departs with his wife, Sita, and his brother, Lakshmana, to endure years of unhappiness and hardship in the forest. During this time, Rama meets a wandering widow, Surpanakha, who falls in love with his beauty. She approaches him amorously but he tells her he is married to Sita and rejects her; he and Lakshmana then begin to make fun of her for her ugliness. Surpanakha attacks Sita out of jealousy and Lakshmana cuts off her nose.

Surpanakha, however, is the sister of the great demon, Ravana, whose wrath is aroused by this disfiguring of his sister. He abducts Sita and takes her away to his spectacular palace in Lanka. Ravana, who has acquired his power through scholarship and devotion to Shiva, attempts to seduce Sita with promises of wealth and luxury, but she rejects all his advances. Eventually Rama and

Lakshmana invade Lanka with the help of the monkey god Hanuman, kill Ravana and rescue Sita.

But Rama is plagued by doubts as to what might have happened between Ravana and Sita while she has been away, and he refuses to take her back. Weeping, Sita decides to demonstrate her purity by plunging into fire. She emerges from the fire unharmed, Rama is overjoyed and returns with Sita to Ayodhya where he is given his rightful throne and the era of virtue begins.

The people of Ayodhya, however, are unnerved by the example Rama has set: they feel that the women of the kingdom will be corrupted if they see their king welcome back a wife who has lived with a demon. Having not the confidence of his own independent judgement, Rama exiles Sita to the forest, where she gives birth to his twin boys and is taken in by a sage. When Rama later encounters the sage and hears news of Sita and their children, he is moved by the memory of his wife, and he asks her to come to him and prove, once again, her virtue. The sage swears that she has been true to him, and all the gods descend from heaven to say the same, but Rama still requires more assurance. Sita says, "As truly as I have never, even with one thought, contemplated another man than Rama, may Goddess Earth open her arms to me!" – and with that the earth opens and she is swallowed up. Nothing short of Sita's death can convince Rama, apparently, that she is pure: now his love floods out of him unrestrainedly and he prays for her to be restored to him, but it is too late.

Rama is a character of extraordinary drives, no doubt: his willingness to abandon his political ambition to subsist in the forest demonstrates a startling commitment to the word of his father. But one cannot help feeling that there is something missing from Rama, even in this: is his obedience not rather obsessive, as if he lacks vision and is looking for some cause, even a negative one, so as not to be lost? Does he not seem like someone empty of values who therefore becomes brittle and loveless, and an extremist of rules? He is a severe character, Rama, who leaves one rather cold: he says little, and almost nothing that might inspire or warm. He is most content in self-denial: it is not amid the adversity of the forest but precisely when everything is restored to Rama – his wife, his city and his throne – that he begins to fall apart. Though he will fight fanatically for the recovery of his wife – because he understands the offence of a broken rule – when she comes home to him he hates her, not for what she has done but what has been done to her. It is dangerous to be loved by a man like this: he may raise armies for you when you are stolen away, but when you are by his side he is plagued by suspicions and spite. He is haunted by the idea that others may not have denied themselves as he has, by visions of the extravagant pleasures that they might enjoy.

It is interesting that one hardly ever sees the name of Krishna written up in the back window of a car, for the eighth avatar of Vishnu would seem, on the face of it, a far more attractive ego ideal than the seventh. Where Rama is perfect according to custom, Krishna is theoretically and theologically so: he is the 'perfect incarnation', incorporating all sixteen attributes of human perfection. Rama displays only thirteen; the three he lacks are: an unparalleled capacity for romantic love, an irresistible skill in music, and an extraordinary sweetness and sensuousness of person-ality.[25] Like Rama, Krishna is a warrior and a man of wisdom and moral seriousness, but he also has all the humour, eloquence and breadth of spirit that Rama lacks. He is unabashed about his sensuousness and his desires: his love for women is erotic and overpowering, and he knows the poetic ache of yearning for a lover far away. Like Rama, Krishna is beautiful, but women who desire him end up not with their noses cut off but loved and serenaded by the music of his flute.

But despite the immense numbers of his erotic conquests, there is something almost effeminate about Krishna's sentimental plenitude, his flute playing in the woods. Is this why he fails to be a satisfying mascot for our go-getting age? Or at least for its men? Go to celebrations of the major Krishna festivals and you will be surrounded by women and children looking at images of a playful infant and a flute-playing, sensitive man. It is at the festivals of Rama that you will find men in the lead, setting their flames, for instance, to the effigies of Ravana set up for the night of Dussehra. It occurs to me that, if 'Rama' is written up in the back of so many car windows in Delhi, it may not only be because he is a remote and unattainable hero. It may be also because he is someone very close, someone touchingly flawed, someone whose outbursts of spasmodic violence, precisely, make him a reassuringly familiar role model.

Colonised countries often imagine their liberation in terms of phallic recovery. Excluded from the government of their country under the British, campaigners for India's self-rule complained of the Indian male's political emasculation and infantilisation, and longed for a time when he could be made complete again. At just the moment when the dreamed-of recovery arrived, however, and Indians assumed political control of their own nation, they were, in this northern part of the country, unmanned forever, and in far more lurid and unforgettable ways. Some were literally castrated in the violence of Partition; many more had their male mastery outrageously mocked as their women were raped, murdered, disfigured and carried away. The gnawing emasculation of colonialism had proved to be temporary, but it had ended in a violent carnage whose genital mutilations, real and figurative, were impossible to reverse. It is the memory of these wounds that provides historical depth to everything we have seen about the fragility of north Indian men, who leave their women pining for the emotional completeness of men from Bombay − or other, more far-flung locales.

For many north Indian families, the abduction of women, especially, is not merely a mythological tale. Tens of thousands of women were seized during the partition, and they remained with their captors while the rest of their families travelled to the other side of the new border.

If the new state of India was so concerned to recover abducted Sikh and Hindu women from Pakistan it was because Indian manhood depended on it: as mythology made clear, there was no male duty more essential than the rescue of a stolen woman. Just as each individual abduction was an insult to a father or a husband, the totality of abductions was seen as an insult to the authority of the state; and it was essential for the new nation's sense of its own virility that the lost women be brought home. The Congress declared in November 1947:

> . . . during these disorders large numbers of women have been abducted on either side and there have been forcible conversions on a large scale. No civilized people can recognize such conversions and there is nothing more heinous than abduction of women. Every effort, therefore, must be made to restore women to their original homes, with the co-operation of the Governments concerned.[26]

Thousands of women were located and transported to their parental families in the ensuing process, which involved large-scale investigations on both sides. What it did not take account of, however, was the wishes of the women themselves, many of whom did not want to be removed. In many cases, after all, years had gone by, and life had moved on. When the agents of the state came to uproot them, they often said they were content with their new religion, they were happy with their new husbands, they now had children, they did not want to lose everything again – but they were carted over the border anyway. This despite the real terror that returning 'home' inspired in many of these women. As social workers reported to the government from their interactions with abducted women:

Sir, we the social workers who are closely associated with the work are confronted with many questions when we approach a woman. The women say, 'You have come to save us; you say you have come to take us back to our relatives. You tell us that our relatives are eagerly waiting to receive us. You do not know our society. It is hell. They will kill us. Therefore, do not send us back.'[27]

These women were entirely justified in their fears. Among Hindu families, in the stories that people told of Partition horrors, 'pure' women had jumped into wells rather than allow Muslims to dishonour them – they had, like Sita, allowed the earth to swallow them up, and demonstrated their virtue with their death. That was the way the epic was supposed to end. These women who sought a place back in their own families after years in the demon's palace caused immense consternation. Many of these women had experienced the love of Muslim men – whose sexual potency appeared, in Hindu nightmares, demonic – and there was no way to recognise them anymore as legitimate Hindu women. They were worse than dead: they were alive, and they presented to their fathers, brothers and husbands an unbearable reminder of their own masculine failure. While some remained as outcasts, many more were turned away and some were indeed murdered. Nearly all were cut out of memory. Countless numbers of women from that time disappeared from family stories: children grew up with fleeting impressions of aunts and older sisters who were never seen or spoken of again.

The sense of historical castration did not disappear from north Indian society. Quite the opposite. One of the first rules that people who moved to Delhi learned was that you did not insult a man in public, or remind him of his shortcomings, for the consequences could be improbably severe. Almost every week someone died in the city because they confronted a man about his bad driving, or his loud behaviour, or his lewd remarks to a woman. As the *Hindustan Times* commented at the beginning of 2010, looking back at the murders of the previous year:

> A man murdered his neighbour for kicking his dog at Ranhola village in Outer Delhi. Another was killed for breaking the queue at a public toilet in Civil Lines, north Delhi. New Friends Colony in south Delhi witnessed murder when a man refused to let another make a call from his cell phone.
>
> The Delhi Police registered 523 cases of murder last year against 528 in 2008. Of these, 15 per cent were due to 'sudden provocation', legalese for Delhi's infamous bad temper, while 17 per cent were passion-related. Only 16 per cent were committed with criminal intent.
>
> "Last year saw some of the most bizarre murders as far as motive was concerned," Y.S. Dadwal, commissioner of police, said at the Annual Police Conference on January 2.
>
> Psychiatrists believe lack of a proper outlet for anger, as well as the absence of basic information on anger management is to blame. "Many things – from machismo to impulsiveness, part of every metro's culture – are behind such cases," said Dr Rajesh Sagar, senior psychiatrist, AIIMS.
>
> "People in the city are changing with it. They are finding it difficult to control emotion," said Dr Rajat Mitra of the NGO Swanchetan, which works with the Delhi Police. [28]

The capital was defined, increasingly, by a hyper-aggressive masculinity, which seemed to lose all constraint in the years after 1991. *Who are you to tell me what to do?* was what a man shouted as he hit another in the face: because with this age of global markets came an end to all limits on behaviour, and now no one, least of all a stranger, could tell you what to do. People used the word 'slave' a lot to describe the history that was no more: "We have been slaves for too long; now no one can order us around."

Delhi, where a rising breed of politician–businessman embodied most perfectly this new Indian brawn, became the stage for a new, psychotic model of manhood which jettisoned all social and even legal constraint in its concern for phallic prestige. The stories which dominated the city pages of the newspapers either side of the year 2000 concerned scions of powerful families who seemed to feel that the principal benefit that came with their social position was the free expression of furious masculine power. In 1999, for instance, Manu Sharma, son of a Congress member of parliament whose political position had helped him assemble a multibillion dollar empire of hotels, entertainment, sugar mills and agriculture, shot dead a well-known model, Jessica Lal, because she refused him a drink at the bar where she was serving in a celebrity party. Sharma had turned up with a group of friends which included Vikas Yadav, the son of another rich politician whose perennial success in evading prosecution for his gangsterism must have contributed to the young men's sense of invulnerability. Lal told the young men that they had come too late and the bar was closed. Sharma offered her 1,000 rupees [$20] and she replied that he still could not have even a sip of alcohol. "I could have a sip of you for a thousand rupees," replied Sharma, and took out a gun to threaten her. He fired a shot into the air and then a second shot into her head. He and his friends then left the bar.

The restaurant was crowded with witnesses, and Sharma himself told the TV cameras that he had shot her – "It was embarrassing to hear that even if I paid a thousand bucks I would not get a sip of drink." But in the trial that followed, he was acquitted of the murder, mainly because thirty-two witnesses withdrew their initial testimony. The trial was later opened, partly as a result of a sting operation by a critical newspaper, *Tehelka*, which produced evidence of coercion and bribery of witnesses by Manu Sharma's family, including his politician father, and Sharma was sentenced to life imprisonment.

Manu's friend Vikas Yadav later had his own turn in the

headlines. In 2002, Vikas and his brother, Vishal, apparently marched their sister's twenty-four-year-old boyfriend out of a wedding party, loaded him into their Tata SUV and murdered him. They did not like the relationship between their sister and this man and, as we know, losing control of the family's women was one of those things most likely to inflame north Indian masculine rage.

> When I saw Nitish at the party, Vishal and I decided this was a great opportunity to fix things, a chance we would not get again . . . I told Vishal to take Nitish outside. It was midnight. Vishal and I made Nitish sit in the front seat of our Tata Safari. Vishal and Sukhdev Pehalwan were sitting at the back. I was driving. We reached Balwant Rai Mehta Lane at around 1.30 a.m., and stopped. We made Nitish move to the back seat, now Vishal and Pehlwan held him tight. I drove again and stopped somewhere between Bulandsher and Khurja. Using all my strength, I hit Nitish's head with a hammer. He fainted and after a while he died. We drove one kilometre and then we threw his body onto the road. Vishal removed Nitish's cell phone from his kurta pocket. He also took Nitish's wristwatch and hid both these in the bushes that were nearby. I took the hammer that I used to murder Nitish and we hid that in the bushes too. Then we took the diesel from our car's tank, poured it on Nitish's body and we set it on fire. Then we drove to Delhi.[29]

Vikas Yadav had evaded conviction for murder in the past, but this time even his family's prowess in this domain was not enough to get him off, and both brothers were eventually sentenced to life imprisonment. But many other violent deaths in the prox-imity of Delhi's power youths, however, somehow disappeared abruptly from the newspapers or were tied up in some far-fetched resolution.

At the core of the city's soul was something dark and fatal. Like all dark things, however, Delhi held a powerful attraction. It promised terrible, forbidden pleasures. It was not only the families of 1947 refugees who manifested its cracked and volatile personality: newcomers too sensed the violence under the ground and quickly adopted the city's ways. Delhi's grip was nauseating and yet secretly delicious: you gave yourself to it, and you did not realise until you spoke to outsiders just how corrupt you had become. If people flocked to the city it was not because it held some promise of New York-style grandeur – "If I can make it there, I'll make it anywhere" – even though "making it", in the financial sense, was of course critical. It was more than that. Delhi whispered promises, even to the purest souls, of violent and demonic pleasures. *Come to me, all ye who have been fucked*, it told them, *and I will show you how you can fuck others.*

One evening, I go to a qawwali concert in the gardens of the India International Centre, a well-known cultural institution in central Delhi. A group of musicians has come from Pakistan. They take their places as the day ends. Far above, bands of shrieking parakeets, which rediscover their sense of direction when the sun touches the horizon, fly home in straight lines across the sky. The first bats are flickering among the trees.

It is a weekday and the audience members have come from offices. Tight-lipped Hindu bureaucrats in blazers and ties shuffle around in the rows of plastic seats, hassled, and not yet present to the music.

The musicians take no account of the unrest around. Their music lifts off straight away to an extraordinary pitch of ecstasy and yearning, the voices soaring one after another to the yawning sky, drums filling the static garden with dance, hands clasping at heaven. The head qawwal is a man of extra-terrestrial magnetism:

portly and jowled, his fingers dart weightlessly, drawing sound in the air, and his voice is abundant with every kind of desire, spiritual and carnal. He wears a brilliant white kurta, embroidered around the neck, and a scarf which he tosses like a mane of golden hair.

Over the course of the first forty minutes or so, something amazing happens in the audience. The men begin to make twitches of enjoyment – but they are embarrassed at first, and they look around them quickly after each full-arm gesticulation, fearful of censure. But the spirit spreads and soon everyone is touched by it: their restraint leaves them and they leap from their chairs in elation, they are full-heartedly clapping, swaying and crying out. Something has entered them from the outside: their bodies are making unaccustomed movements and they are moaning with words from elsewhere. They are going to the stage to give money! – and the Hindu women cover their heads and bow before the foreigners, *Salaam!* Islam is pouring out of these people who lie awake at night terrified that their daughter might marry a Muslim. These people who were not even born in the days when these gestures were de rigueur, know them nonetheless.

Look at the men in the audience, these unimaginative men who love rules, who fast on Tuesdays and believe they are virtuous because they deny themselves pleasures; these suspicious men whose Brahminical anxieties keep them from eating out, mixing with strangers, or walking in the street, these dutiful men who work hard but speak poorly; look at these men who are so conditioned to murder the feminine within them that they cannot keep themselves from stamping on girls and women without – look at how they desire this Sufi on stage, the weeping tuneful beautiful Muslim whose passions overflow, the man of poetry and eloquence, the man of universal desire, the man who has not sacrificed his feeling, who has never learned that ecstasy and song are effeminate – look at how they take him into themselves and try to fill themselves with him. How his gestures infect their own, how his passion lights up their faces. Look how this Muslim can set a fire in the hearts of these Hindus and set them free – look how he can restore them to everything they have been.

Eleven

A rich jeweller bought himself a Lamborghini for 35 million rupees [$700,000]. Finding it was impossible to take it out on Delhi's crowded streets, he offered it for sale. It was bought for 22 million rupees [$440,000] by the twenty-seven-year-old son of a real-estate dealer. Newly married, the young man did not tell his family about the purchase; he hid the car and only drove it at night. At 5.30 one morning, driving at 200 kilometres an hour, he lost control of the car and crashed into barriers at the side of the road, killing himself and severely injuring a man on a bicycle.

The injured man was the fifty-five-year-old caretaker of a school who cycled an hour to work every morning because he found it healthier than travelling by bus. He had worked in the school for twenty years; each morning he had to arrive before everyone else because it was he who unlocked the doors.

On the morning of the accident, he was rushed to hospital with severe head injuries. The school offered financial assistance for his emergency surgery but further operations were required to save the man from paralysis. His son said he had no idea how the family might pay for this treatment, which, it was feared, might cost as much as 150,000 rupees [$3,000].

Looking for a new apartment, some years ago, I was taken with a beautiful place nestled close to one of Delhi's ancient cities. The rent was far more than I had budgeted, but it was so perfect that I spontaneously handed over deposit cheques to the owner, who was a Punjabi businessman. Eighty years old, he still ran the business he had set up, which manufactured large-scale electrical equipment for sale all over the world. He was successful, and owned many properties in Delhi. His wife served tea and sweets in celebration of our deal. He told the story of how he had fled Pakistan in 1947 as a young naval officer, established a business in Delhi, and set up livelihoods for his brothers, whom he brought, one by one, to the city.

"Now we don't talk to each other," he said. "Punjabi families support each other fanatically when things are bad. But when they become rich it all falls apart. That's why the Marwaris build the biggest business houses. They put the business first."

Lying awake in bed that night, I was filled with disbelief at what I had done. I could not afford this place. The next morning I called the landlord and said I was sorry but we couldn't go ahead with the deal. He said he was sorry too, not least because he had turned away other prospective tenants, and he asked if I could compensate him with half a month's rent. I agreed to stop off at his place with a cheque for that amount; he said he would at that point return the cheque I had given him on the previous day. After our conversation, nonetheless, I put a stop on that cheque.

An hour later he called me. "The price of severance has just gone up. You stopped your cheque at 10.04 this morning."

I asked him how he knew.

"Do you think I won't find such things out?"

And he proceeded to list, just so I understood what I was dealing with, the numbers and current balances of all my bank accounts.

"You have insulted me," he said. "Now I am expecting you to give me a cheque for two months' rent."

That was a lot of money. I argued that it was disproportionate to the loss he might have incurred.

"This is not about loss. It is about insult."

I said I was sorry that he took it that way, and asked if we could work out some kind of compromise.

"Mr Dasgupta, you will find that it is against Indian law to stop a cheque without informing the other party first. Of course it is up to you what you pay me. I will only say that I play golf at the Delhi Golf Club every morning with the country's most powerful lawyers and judges, and I can make it impossible for you to live and work in this city. You are a foreigner, after all."

And he added,

"I am not threatening you. I am just letting you know."

I sought legal advice. The lawyer I spoke to advised me to give him what he asked for. Stopping a cheque in such circumstances was indeed prohibited. "And a man like that can ruin your life."

The landlord called me about ten times that day. He was frantic at the slight he had received, and could not leave the issue alone. He threatened me, he cajoled me. He appealed to my sense of honour.

When I arrived at his place with my cheque book, he suddenly relaxed. He was jubilant, even. I gave him a cheque. He took a long time writing me a receipt so he could educate me about life.

"There are two important things to remember. Patriotism, which I learned from the navy. And honesty, which I learned from business. If you are not honest, you will never get anywhere."

He handed me back my original cheque.

"I will keep an eye on your bank account. There is nothing you will do in this city that I will not know about."

His was one of those large Delhi fortunes that are built up

discreetly on the basis of reputation and personal affinities. One of the ways that such things are maintained is that the smallest slight on your reputation is immediately stamped out and punished. You do not let it stand.

There is admiration, in contemporary fashion, for the smooth mind: the mind without 'issues' that is 'comfortable with itself'. True strength, it is thought, originates in minds like this; the work of becoming strong consists, therefore, in that kind of mental ironing we call therapy.

According to this, Delhi, with its jagged history and unresolved pain, should have been a place of weakness. Those who visited the city in the early twenty-first century, however, were struck in the opposite way: they were astonished at the confidence and ambition of its people. This is because 'resolving' trauma is not the only way to prevent it from incapacitating you. You can also use its energy to fuel an entirely different, and far more vigorous, response. You can become – since all of history, since all the world, is a battlefield – a warrior.

This was the way that many people, especially businesspeople, chose to see themselves after the partition; and the free-for-all of liberalisation only served to deepen the need for martial resolve. While most businesspeople in the West considered themselves to be civilians, their counterparts entering the global system in this place – and others like it – thought of themselves as soldiers. To others, they sometimes seemed to be unprincipled – to care little for the rules of society at large, for instance, or for those more vulnerable than themselves – but that was not their own conception of things. Of course they did not concern themselves with civilian considerations, for the warrior's vocation required them to soar above them. But like all warriors they operated, in fact, according to a strong code of ethics. Their operating unit was the family, and sustaining this as an effective martial force required wisdom, rectitude and sacrifice.

The people of this part of the world, as we have seen, were always tough, self-reliant and prepared for adversity. Partition did not crush this spirit; it only confirmed its premise. *Everything can be taken away.* Property and money had disappeared, which was the perennial fate of wealth, so Punjabis took up arms against ill-fortune and started to make everything back again. And in Delhi, which acquired a million new citizens immediately after the partition, there were commercial opportunities galore.

Entrepreneurs had enjoyed little visibility in the newly independent India. The 'good citizens' were its farmers, soldiers and workers and those professionals who served the nation as teachers, doctors, engineers and bureaucrats. But for the global economy of the future, perhaps, it was those who operated in a permanent state of exception – its entrepreneurial warriors – whose activities were the most significant.

When I show up to meet Rahul Kapoor,[30] I find that he is out at the gym. His grandfather, however, is at home, and he is delighted to have someone to whom he can show off the work that has just been completed in his bathroom. The room has been extended into the garden, so that it is now sunlit from three sides and very long. He raps his knuckles against the walls of the original part. "You see this? Italian marble." Then he walks into the extension and knocks again. The sound is hollow. "And this new section is just plasterboard which has been painted to *look* like Italian marble. Can you tell the difference?"

He laughs delightedly.

"Why don't you come into my study?" he says.

Somewhere above eighty years old, he is spectacularly sturdy and walks without impediment. He leads me into a small room flooded with daylight, where he bids me sit down. He does so himself, in a leather armchair, dons glasses, and presses the buttons of a mobile phone. I look around me at the silver-framed photographs of his grown-up grandchildren, who are all, men and women, strikingly attractive. In the middle of the room is a novelty table with a vast stone book for one of its legs. There is a large oil painting of village women on one wall and a sculpture of Ganesh on the other; above us is a chandelier decorated with glass roses.

"Hello, my dear," he says into the phone. "I am chatting with a very nice man who has come to see Rahul. Do you know when he will be back? He doesn't have his phone with him. Is that right? Wonderful. Thank you, my darling. I will see you soon. Very soon."

He turns to me.

"He'll be back any minute. Why don't you have some tea or coffee in the meantime?"

He presses a button and a servant appears, to whom my order is precisely transmitted.

"You must meet my wife. She was one of the most beautiful women in the city. I had to chase her for years. Because I wasn't a handsome man. Even now she is very beautiful."

I find myself thinking, as I have thought before, that men from this generation, the men who were adult before the partition, seem able to love women more fully than their sons and grandsons.

"And she is the greatest hostess. While you are discussing something, she will bring out fifty different plates of snacks. And the best thing is, she will take plates for all the drivers also. With all this construction work in the house, she always makes sure the workers have a meal and a cold drink."

Mr Kapoor is full of his wife. He is full of everything, in fact: he is happy to be alive.

He tells me about the young people in the photographs. Some

are in London, some in California. Some are working in the family business in Delhi.

"My grandchildren still want to go on holiday with me," he chuckles. "That makes me proud. Love is the most important thing. No matter how hard I was working, I always spent time with my children in the evenings."

I ask him what he tries to pass on to his grandchildren.

"I teach them what goodness is. How to treat people. I know the richest men in town. But I've looked after everybody. And one thing I'm very proud of is that no one who has walked into my room looking for help has ever gone away disappointed. These blessings come back to you."

Tea arrives on a tray with biscuits and a sugar bowl. I ask Mr Kapoor where his family came from.

"We were in Sialkot before the partition," he says. "We had a good situation there. In 1947 we ran away with just one change of clothes: we jumped in the car and came to Delhi."

Mr Kapoor was in his early twenties in 1947. He tells me how he revived his family's lost medical instruments business in their new home. It happened astonishingly quickly. It is clear that, even if many of his class lost their tangible assets in 1947, their social networks travelled with them almost intact, and they could still call upon the same kind of favours and introductions as before. The new housing extensions to Delhi were conceived, in fact, to preserve previous distinctions of rank, caste, ethnicity and profession, and networks could be recultivated with ease. And in a new capital city with a new population in need of every kind of product and commodity, those who had good contacts and entrepreneurial drive found themselves thriving almost before they had found a house to live in. By the early 1950s Mr Kapoor had established a monopoly across north India, and was well on his way to becoming rich.

"It wasn't very difficult, honestly, to do what I did," he says. "I just worked very hard and learned along the way. You have to enjoy what you do. Otherwise you should do something else."

By the 1960s, Mr Kapoor was rich enough to build a large hotel; several more real-estate investments were to follow. Partition refugees, who had been denuded of their assets, were magnetically drawn to the consolations of property, and they acquired as much of it as they could. In the long-term, this served them better than they could ever have imagined: with the recent boom in property prices, they have seen their fortunes turn fabulous. Mr Kapoor owns houses in Delhi's best neighbourhoods, and a farmhouse outside – a property portfolio whose worth must now lie between $50 and $100 million. It is this property boom that has generated, over the last few years, the extreme self-confidence of the city's propertied classes, who now find themselves rich on a global scale, and without doing very much. They differentiate themselves from everyone else in the city by their 'unearned income' – and if Delhi's exclusive restaurants are strangely full, on weekday afternoons, of carefree men and women of working age, it is because there is a lot of it.

I hear Rahul's voice in the hallway. He bursts into the room.

"I'm sorry," he says. "I was running late."

"Don't worry," says his grandfather calmly. "We are having a lovely time."

Rahul is sweaty from the gym and, since it is a mild day, he wants to sit outside. I pick up my cup of tea to follow him.

"Leave that," he says. "I'll have it brought out for you."

We go to sit on the terrace, which overlooks a walled garden surrounded by majestic trees. A cavernous reception room, all beige leather and marble, opens out here.

"What did you think of my grandfather?" Rahul says.

I offer some warm impressions.

"That guy has balls the size of this table," he says earnestly. "He built everything we have. That generation built things their whole lives and it adds up to a big story. Young people just fritter it away and it doesn't mean very much."

Rahul is slight, intense and twenty-five. He looks calculatedly stylish in his gym clothes. Drinks are brought for us on a tray: he sips a fresh lime soda.

"That generation was strong. My grandfather is nearly ninety and when I drink whisky with him, it's me who has to give up first."

Some construction work is going on at a nearby house; Rahul is extremely, even excessively, disturbed by the noise of a drill. He waits for the drill to stop before he begins his story. There is something fastidious about him.

"My family came from Sialkot, which is now in Pakistan. In British India, Sialkot was the centre of surgical instruments manufacturing. My family controlled that industry. When they left Sialkot in 1947, they spread out over India and started it up afresh.

"My other grandfather, my mother's father, was also a legendary character. He went to south India because he knew there would be little competition. He started off cycling round hospitals, selling products out of a trunk. His company is now by far the biggest medical instruments supplier in south India. It was a shrewd move for a Punjabi to go to the south: south Indians aren't good businessmen. They're academic types down there, not very tough. So if a hospital put out a tender, my grandfather and his brothers would guard the room where the documents had to be delivered and beat up anyone who tried to submit a competing proposal. They couldn't do anything. But once they all got together and ambushed him and beat him up for revenge.

"He was an amazing man. He was a big philanthropist who set up the best schools in Madras. The one bad thing about him was that he had a thing about Muslims. When he came across during the partition, his son was killed by Muslims. After that he tried to have a son many times but only succeeded in producing five daughters. So he hated Muslims till the end of his life. Just the mention of them would drive him into a rage. For a Punjabi man the one thing you have to do is produce an heir to take over your business. His business was shut down after his death. His daughters were spoiled rich girls who didn't want to do anything, and it's not good for men to go into their wives' family business — it's as if they're a failure."

Rahul's family, like the majority of Delhi's business elite, comes from the Punjabi khatri sub-caste, one that is equally divided between Hindus and Sikhs. It is probable that khatris were always members of the lowly trader caste, but they like to claim more aristocratic origins, saying that the word 'khatri' derives from 'kshatriya', the name of the superior warrior caste. They say that they were heroically oppressed during the thousand years of Muslim rule but that their spirit never flagged and, with the wealth and education they had acquired, they rose to important positions in the Mughal military administration. It was the chauvinistic emperor Aurangzeb, they say, who threw them out of his bureaucracy and forced them to become shopkeepers. Even in this commercial role, however, they retained their martial identity.

The way that Rahul remembers his grandfathers is typical of the way this identity functions today. Many young Punjabi businessmen are frustrated at the way their families have become lax with wealth and comfort, and they tell and re-tell the stories of their grandparents' impoverishment and subsequent recovery. They cling to this historical suffering, and the warlike vigour with which their grandparents faced it, in order to retain their own sense of martial purpose.

As Rahul's story indicates, however, not everyone can have been happy about the tactics with which Punjabi businessmen built up their empires. The victims of these tactics also saw them as warlike, and not in a positive sense. Many parts of the country resented the ferocity with which Punjabis sought to monopolise business.

"Until recently I didn't realise we were rich. My family had very middle-class values. My grandfather would always tell us to switch off the light. My mother got angry if we wasted food. They were very financially conservative. They put all their money in fixed deposits and just left it there. They never took loans. They didn't spend much money.

"When I went to our factory as a kid, thousands of people lined up to see us. So I felt like a prince. But I still didn't realise we were wealthy until I was in college. Then I became a shareholder in the family business: I went through the balance sheet, I saw what my father was paid and what we owned. That's when I found out.

"But now, with the rise of China, we have stopped producing anything. My father closed down our production and now we only sell other people's products. German, American and Chinese. My grandfather still runs a stethoscope factory, even though it makes losses, because he likes it. Even though he's old and he doesn't need to, he goes there every day because he is passionate about making stuff. I've never really seen anyone from my father's generation get passionate. They're happy but they have no ambition. They have their parties, they marry their kids into fancy families – they're all happy. Too happy. Each of them owns a big company, they sell products that cannot be matched and do not need marketing. One of my aunts owns the India monopoly for Nikon cameras. Money just keeps piling up without anyone doing anything."

Rahul studied at an Ivy League school in the US. In many ways he felt more at home there than here, and wondered for a while whether he should return. But his father wanted him to take over a chunk of the company, and at length he decided to take the plunge.

"Of course I thought about whether I should do something else. Sometimes, running this company, I just feel like I'll die. But there are compromises in every kind of life. And I thought: how many people get an opportunity like this? I could have got a job in the US, and now I might be some analyst trying to help a supermarket save 1 per cent of its costs. Then I would be only a part of the machine. But I want to *be* the machine. Or: I want to control the machine.

"My friends at college were mostly artistically inclined. What I will do by the time I'm thirty will be much, much more than what they will do. Business, money – it's all just a means to an end. I want to have a legacy. That's what I'm trying to say. I don't want to die without a legacy."

We talk about business strategy. He is undertaking a total overhaul of the company, extending its scope up- and downstream. Right now he is launching a chain of speciality hospitals, using tracts of land acquired by the family decades ago. Ultimately, it will be an international chain. After that he wants to invest in medical research and development, and perhaps acquire a foreign medical instruments manufacturer, so that the company can produce original products of its own and not just sell other people's. He speculates about new investments even as he's talking.

"That may not be the right thing to do. But that's how I'm thinking. I often get ahead of myself. There's no point in doing this unless you are playing at the level of the people at the top. So you have to think all the time."

His knee pumps up and down as he talks: there is enormous nervous energy about him. It comes partly from the fact that he is taking big risks within the family.

"In Punjabi business families it's very difficult to change direction because the family is risk-averse. You carry on doing what you know. You do the thing that is in your blood. For the old business there are thirty people I can ask for advice, but with these new ventures I have to start from scratch. But that's how I'm different from most of them. Most of them will never do anything significant because personal gain means too much to them. They're not willing to think far enough. Of course Indian businessmen have to continue their business tradition, and there's no question that out of ten businesspeople, three or four will definitely go far compared to their US or European counterparts because of the way that our families and society are structured. But if they're going to do something really great, they have to break out of their conservatism."

In order to do all this, Rahul has departed significantly from the traditional family ethic, again, by raising external financing. In this he is typical of his liberalisation generation, which holds a profoundly changed conception of money. Before that, money – 'dhan', or wealth – was static. It was symbolised in gold, and it was kept locked up. It was not gambled, spent, or invested in uncertain schemes. It could not grow but it could easily shrink, and so every expenditure, no matter how small, was a loss of potential. Punjabis fought over one rupee and 1 million rupees with the same fervour, for other people's profit was their loss. But with the era of markets, money has ceased to be tangible and static. It has become abstract and dynamic. *Putting money out* no longer leads, automatically, to loss: not doing so, in fact, is to lose out on the benefits of money's expanding universe. Suddenly, money breeds money, which is one of the reasons that the younger generations of north Indian families have suddenly lost their anxiety about buying stuff. There is always more money where that came from.

"What I will eventually do is demerge these companies and run them like a venture capitalist, investing capital as they need. Eventually I'll take some of them public. It's great to have a tightly held group but I'd rather have 40 per cent of 10,000 crores [$2 billion] than 100 per cent of 500 crores [$100 million].

"Let me tell you, this is not easy. I've just come back from financing meetings in London. It's very challenging to get investment from fifty-year-old guys when I'm so inexperienced. This project is turning all my hair grey. It's making me old."

"You look like a kid."

"How old do I look?"

"About twenty-one."

"Oh *thank* you. I feel like I look fifty years old. I feel like I am fifty. I was looking in the mirror this morning, and I thought I was going bald."

It's as if Rahul feels he has made a Faustian bargain with his family firm. It will suck out all his youth and energy, and he will be condemned to a lifetime of looking with horror in the mirror. But, as he immediately says, in words that could have come directly from Goethe's play, it will give him enormous productive power:

"When I go there and see the huge piles of mud and the huge excavations where they're building the new hospital, it's so thrilling. If I can make this thing work, the satisfaction will be *unmatched*."

Those huge piles of mud, those excavations: these are the images that circulate in magazines as the horror of ruthless, relentless capital, constantly tearing down what exists in order to accumulate anew: more, bigger, further, quicker. But Rahul looks out on the gouged earth and sees himself completed, expanded, raised up.

"Sometimes I feel like I am just drowning. I am sinking and drowning. But sometimes I'm like, *Wow*."

I ask him why he needs to live life so dangerously. He becomes melancholic about the history of the family firm. It was split up among the men of his father's generation in ways he finds unjust.

"I should have been running a much larger group. When I think about that it pinches a little bit. So some of my motivation comes from wanting to compensate for the losses of the past. Crucial chunks were lost to us, and that burns."

"Being gay must affect your outlook too?"

"Well, that's another thing that motivates me to be better than everyone else. I *am* better than everyone else. I know it sounds conceited. And part of the reason is that I have to perform in order to defy all stereotypes – so they can never say, 'He's not really a man.' I'm not one of those burly Punjabis, so I have to prove myself."

In fact Rahul has all the qualities of the quintessential Punjabi businessman: a sense of historical slight, a struggle against the world, infinite ground to make up. It makes for his nervous energy, his impatience, his great ambition.

"You talked about a legacy. What is a legacy?"

"I mean, you can set up a school where they educate a hundred kids. You can give money to a charitable organisation. Those may be good things to do. But that is not a legacy. In the broad scheme of things it's so small that it's completely irrelevant. Have you seen what the Rockefellers did? That's a legacy. Every college and university in the US has something that the Rockefellers gave. Every person in that country is somehow touched by what they did. That's a fucking legacy.

"Look at the businessmen around you. Here. They build obscene houses. They have all these obese children who will eat themselves into an empty grave. Then there will be endless property disputes. And then what? *And then what?* What is their vision of life? You make money, then you die. You just accumulate a big fortune, and you go on and on and on, and you never do anything else. And then what? I mean how much money do I need? Once I have my apartment in New York and I fly everywhere first class, how much more do I really need? I'm going to change the world with my money. Which is why I need to make so much."

"So you're working for the benefit of those less fortunate than yourself?"

"I wouldn't say that. I mean, I did go to a liberal American college, and that's what I am in my heart. But when I'm running the company, I'm the stereotypically evil capitalist. I'm like a character from *Hard Times*. I order people about and tell them to polish my shoes. I make sure servants don't get above themselves."

It happens that I have come to see Rahul directly from one of the camps set up for the labourers who came to Delhi to work on the infrastructure for the Commonwealth Games, and I am still disturbed by the experience. I cannot help responding to Rahul's comment with an account of what I have seen in that pathetically overcrowded place. Workers and their families sleep in windowless corrugated iron shacks, and there are ten toilets for about 3,000 people. With the monsoon rains, the whole place is under water: wandering children have fallen into unseen holes in the ground and drowned; mosquitoes have reproduced exuberantly and spread malaria throughout the camp. I have spent the afternoon talking to those too sick to be out at work. They are not paid for the days they do not work, and cannot visit a doctor. They wonder if they will ever make it back to their far-off homes.

"It's not necessary that it be so bad," I say. "It's bad by design. It's obstinately bad. It's impossible not to feel it is sadistic."

"I'm sure if I were to see that I would feel the same," says Rahul. He pauses, thinking about his feelings, and adds, "But if I saw those people, I am sure I would also feel contempt."

Rahul's grandfather comes out into the driveway. He gives us a merry wave and climbs into the back of a Mercedes, which pulls away. Guards open the gates, and the car drives away. Rahul and I contemplate his departure.

"He's extraordinary," I say.

"He is," Rahul replies. "There's no one I respect more. But you shouldn't think he was always like this. In his own day, he was a bastard. Ran this family like a tyrant."

Family businesses had several clear advantages over more impersonal structures, and these derived not least from their martial culture. They bred not employees but cult members, whose motivation was not just money but glory. These members accepted authoritarian conditions that employees would not. Sons could be dispatched overnight to spend years on the other side of the world. Wives managed the substantial social and familial duties of a wealthy businessman so that he did not need to. It was a dynamic structure that exploited its human resources in a far more primordial way than the average corporation. Fully owned, usually, by the family itself, no one else interfered with business strategy, and major decisions could be taken over dinner.

So the family did indeed require 'running'. Parenting was a critical business skill. Paternal authority was essential, but when the entire business depended on sons taking over from their fathers, this authority could not be naively applied. Fathers knew that if their sons knew nothing except authority, they would either run away or become idiots. They choreographed an elegant dance with their teenage offspring, therefore, which allowed substantial liberties along the way, and even gave youngsters the idea, when they finally came home to join the business, that they had chosen it of their own free will. Mothers were often exceptional personalities, deploying an astonishing range of resources to manage these complex human dynamics, and ensuring that the inflexible family structure was nonetheless abundant with spiritual and chivalric meaning.

One of the advantages of all this is that there was great continuity of purpose in business families, even through the white-hot economic environment of the post-liberalisation period. They did not have to deal with the metaphysical shock that struck more liberal, 'middle-class' families over the same period, for whom everything suddenly changed. In business families, sons did work just like their fathers, and marriages were reassuringly patriarchal – so it was possible to watch calmly as the rest of Indian society tottered in disorientation, and to profit from the chaos. As we have seen, north Indian business families have always considered themselves to be at war, and the sight of calamity and destruction revives their spirits. The early twenty-first-century shake-up allowed the more forward-thinking of these families to greatly increase their economic reach. They understood, as many of the middle classes did not, that endless accumulation required the constant production of the new, which could only happen through perennial destruction. This is what

Dostoevsky was referring to when he observed, in London in 1862, "that apparent disorder that is in actuality the highest degree of bourgeois order".[31] The business family was a structure that was designed to ride undismayed through the storm of disorder, and to profit from it.

But the risks were high. One of the reasons that legend speaks so exuberantly of the perfect warrior is that he – or she – is an extremely rare occurrence. Knights are flawed and fragile, and often allow inscrutable urges to divert them from their calling.

Those young men whose fathers briefly sponsored their interests in photography or music – buying them the most expensive cameras or drum kits, allowing them the freedom of girlfriends and months of travel – gave themselves intensely to these pleasures because they knew they would expire; and when the time came to get married and join the family firm, they did so obediently, because their life had never been about 'personal fulfilment' or any such civilian nonsense: the warrior ethos was built on sacrifice, and they had always known they would eventually have to give themselves to their calling. It was painful to leave behind girlfriends and lifestyles they loved, but it was precisely this pain that sharpened their martial resolve. They threw themselves into work with the torrid sense that otherwise they would die.

And yet. It did not always work. So many things could go wrong. If fathers were painfully preoccupied with their sons' characters and life choices, it was because reproducing the warrior ethos from one generation to the next was extremely difficult. Sometimes alcohol and other addictions came to take the place of all those things young men had allowed themselves to dream of. They beat the wives who had been thrust on them, who, in their turn, turned to addictions to cope with a life in which bearing children was their main significance.

In some cases, the situation became fatal. I heard of a businessman who had no heir and therefore adopted a son from one of his brothers, who had several. The boy was already in his teens: he was good at sports and had no interest in commerce. His real parents felt it was better if they did not see him so he would settle in better with his new environment, and his new parents began to groom him to take over an enormous business. They married him to a wealthy girl from another business family. He told his family he was not happy, but they did not realise how serious he was. Eventually, the burden of what he knew he could not do became too great for him, and he killed himself.

The great expansion of powers that business families experienced in the early twenty-first century also made the transfer of authority to the younger generation more fraught. The forces were greater and more volatile, and Delhi was full of a significant number of failed and dissolute knights.

Simran says, "I did realise my husband drank a lot. Everybody drinks a lot from time to time and it's okay, but this was a little more. It began to have effects on our life. His was a Punjabi business family and they had given him a division of the business to look after. He couldn't handle it. He was drinking a lot. He was never violent, just switched off. Hung-over, never going to work. His family members would hound me on the phone – 'Where is he, why isn't he picking up his phone?' – and I was lying all the time: 'He's not feeling well, he's got an upset stomach, he's lying down.' I couldn't deal with it.

"I took time to have my children. I wasn't sure I wanted to bring children into my marriage. Because my husband was an alcoholic. But I loved him.

"The family was trying to figure out ways to make Prashant feel good about himself so he would stop drinking and take on his responsibilities. They started pressurising my father-in-law, saying he's married now, he's nicely settled, he's in charge of part of the business, give him some shares in the family firm so he becomes more responsible. So my father-in-law gave him his first shares as a gift. And the first thing he did? Buy a Lamborghini

Murciélago. Which was great, and he was feeling so important and happy. But I just kept getting this feeling that something wasn't right.

"Things didn't change and eventually Prashant got kicked out of the family firm for his alcoholic behaviour. He had done something silly. So he left and he didn't know what he was going to do. My in-laws kicked us out of their home as well, and we moved into a rented apartment. He was redundant and was just drinking and sleeping. Our life was starting to fall apart.

"Then something terrible happened: I went into a coma and had to have brain surgery, and I wasn't allowed to have children for two years. He was very shaken by what had happened and he decided he was going to clean up his act. He went to rehab in England.

"By the time he came back, my medication was over, we were allowed to have children, he was completely clean. And that was great, and that's when we decided to start a family. My son came along, Prashant was a great father, his business started doing well, he came up with the most fantastic product anyone can imagine. I was very proud of him.

"But I was beginning to have issues with him again. He lost interest in his business and would go to work very late every day. It would piss me off because he would sleep till midday, none of the rooms would be cleaned. By the time he got up, his breakfast had been cleared away because it was already lunch-time and— . . . but I tried to deal with it. Once in a while I'd tell him: 'Prashant, you want your shares in the company, you want your father to respect you, so you've got to act responsibly. You can't just sit with your mouth open under the mango tree: nothing is gonna fall in. Go to work every day, it's not a big deal, you know? You're on the internet talking on Skype to random ladies or watching movies till four in the morning. Obviously you're gonna sleep all day. So start acting responsibly. Your children need to see that. Discipline, routine.'

"We also had loads of conflicts over money. Prashant was

raised frugally. I mean, he had the best of everything: travel, education, and all of that. But he always felt deprived for some reason. So that's why he had this whole ridiculous thing with his Lamborghini. I would always say to him things like, 'Money doesn't grow on trees' or 'Money doesn't buy you love' and he would go ballistic. He felt I was limiting him. Everywhere we went he would be like, 'Oh nice watch, let's buy it!' and I would say, 'Oh my God, it costs as much as a house! What is wrong with you?' And he would get angry, so I would say, 'Can I think about it for a couple of days?' Before spending $60,000 on a watch! And he would hate me for it. He hated the fact I was natural and didn't wear crazy fancy stuff and that people still liked me. All his friends really liked me and so did his parents. He was horrified by that because all his life he had never felt accepted and that's why he put on these airs. When he saw me wearing ordinary clothes and looking like myself, it irritated him like a wound. He said I looked like a beggar, and I couldn't sit in his Lambo looking like that. I have a Breguet and a Rolex but I wear a big Swatch. I like its big dial. I'm a Swatch girl. Like this scarf I'm wearing cost me 400 rupees [$8].

"So I was already irritated with him. It was showing in my behaviour. And I was fat – something he couldn't handle – because I'd just had my babies. Then we had all these problems with a priest. My brother's factory had just burned down: he makes metal handicrafts for export. So this friend of ours introduced this priest to my brother, saying there must be something wrong with the lay-out of your house. You know about 'vastu', which is how your house is oriented for good or bad luck. So I thought, why don't we get this priest to look at the vastu of our house, since our life was going wrong too. So we brought him into our life. He was very happy to be associated with this big family and over time he started realising he had this good-looking-don't-know-their-heads-from-their-backsides couple who have a lot of money, so let's use them. He started really irritating me."

There is a fly in Simran's tea and she is distracted. She asks a waiter to bring her another cup.

"Where was I?" she asks. "I'm sorry, I have problems with my memory. I've been through ten-and-a-half hours of brain surgery, and I keep forgetting where I was."

"You were talking about the priest."

"Right. Later on I found out that this vastu man, this priest who everyone talks about with so much respect, actually does a lot of black magic. Things had fallen apart with Prashant and he decided to leave me. I don't know what happened. I confronted him and that made things worse, and he left. And the priest asked me what was going on and I said, 'You *know* what's going on: Prashant is with this Czech woman and he's gone to live with her. You should know, you speak to him every day.' So he asked me to do something ridiculous, which didn't sound right to me. Black magic. He said, 'If you do this, this woman will be out of your life.' He said he would make me something of metal with her name on it and I had to pour boiling water on it every day. Sounds scary, doesn't it! I said, 'I can't do that sort of thing. I'm a simple person. Let her live! Let her live with my husband and eat up all his money. I don't care. I don't want to kill anybody. My husband's gone haywire and I'm not going to stop him. If he sees the light at some point and comes back, I'll see if I want to go there. As of now I've got my own responsibilities: keep a clear conscience, spend time with my children, raise them into great adults, into responsible secure, good citizens – that's my focus and it doesn't matter what he does.' So I never did it.

"Prashant had been acting strangely for a while. He had stopped giving us an itinerary for his overseas trips, which was what the whole family did: they put up an itinerary for their trips with back-up phone numbers and everything. Prashant had stopped doing that. So my father-in-law would ask me where he was and I would say 'Last time I heard he was in Frankfurt.' And my father-in-law said, 'Don't you speak to him every day?'

I said, 'He never answers his phone.' And he started figuring it out. I told him what I knew and he said, 'Something isn't right because Prashant just took a ridiculous amount of money out of the bank, which he was planning to take with him. I had to confiscate a suitcase of money from our assistant who was taking it to Prashant. It's just not on – there are all kinds of people who will come after him, including the tax people.'

"So my father-in-law confiscated all his money. And they had this huge fight about it. And my father-in-law said, 'I'm not giving it back.' Because he could see that Prashant was doing something wrong. So Prashant got on the plane and hasn't come back. He's lost, for sure. I don't know if he wants a higher life than the high life that he has. Or, he's looking to renounce everything eventually. No: I think he just wants his money back, that's all he wants.

"His father knows what's going on and he's very upset. He's taken care of me and my children, he gives me a monthly allowance, and he's helped me take legal action against his son to secure properties.

"He is spending $100,000 a month in London. So he has immense money needs and his company is losing money because he's not there. So he needs to liquidate property, which is difficult because everything is in my name too. Once he came to me and threatened me holding an ink pen to my cheek like a dagger, saying, 'Sign now!' I said, 'Can I smoke a cigarette and think about it?' and he said, 'Sign now!' and I did because my kids were next door and I was afraid of what he would do. And my father-in-law said, 'Why did you sign?' and I told him the situation and he understood. So then we put an injunction on the other properties and Prashant was mad. There's one very valuable property and he thought he would sell it, buy a beautiful farmhouse in England, have thirty cars and live happily ever after. What can I do? He wants to sell everything and do what? Put all his money down the toilet. I need to educate my children. I need to run a home. I need money to invest in a business for my own self-respect because I feel embarrassed about taking money from my father-in-law.

"For a long time after that pen incident I went around with bodyguards because I was terrified of what Prashant might do to get property out of me. I've hidden my kids' passports because I'm scared he might send his mother to take them away. His mother is a very beautiful woman: five foot ten, blond hair, beautiful hands, perfect features – she's a stunner, you know? She's very fair-skinned because her family hails from the north-west of Pakistan. She's from a very humble home but she was married to my father-in-law for her good looks. They never fell in love. So she lives in London and she says – she used to sing opera – she says she sings opera at the Royal Albert Hall but that's just fantasy; she drinks herself crazy, that's what she does.

"But Prashant is very close to his mother and I can just see her coming to get my kids. She would say, 'Come with me to London and you can ride around in my pink Jaguar and I'll take you shopping to Harrods and I'll take you to Disneyland,' and of course they would go with her.

"I don't know what's going to happen. I don't know if he'll come back. I'm just trying to take care of things as best I can. I have wonderful kids, and just being a mom makes me feel fantastic. I'm just scared all the time. I'm scared he'll say I'm crazy because of my brain surgery, and he'll take my kids away.

"Did I tell you about my brain surgery? He was responsible for that too. It happened after he bought his Lamborghini.

"I have a condition called AVM," says Simran. "Arteriovenous malformation. It's pretty common and it's no big deal: just thin arteries in part of your brain. You can live with it forever without any problems. It doesn't handicap you or anything.

"I remember it was my father-in-law's birthday and we had drinks at home. Afterwards, we said goodbye to all the guests and I went to sleep. The next morning Prashant was in a golf tournament. So he woke up early and he'd been drinking all night – I'd gone to sleep and he'd stayed up drinking, watching

TV and whatever. On his own. And then the next day he left early for the golf tournament and apparently packed a bottle of vodka in his golf bag. And he left his mobile at home so I couldn't get in touch with him. So I called his friends to ask if he'd arrived safely and they said, 'No but we can see him cruising in his Lamborghini with a bottle of vodka – he's so cool – he's such a stud, he's such a rockstar. He's drinking a bottle of vodka and cruising.' I was like, 'You think that's funny?' They're like, 'He's a wacko, your husband, but we love him!' – you know, for them it was a joke. So that stressed me out. He'd been drinking all night. And he was drinking while he was driving. He was driving one hour away from Delhi. I was so stressed. And my blood pressure went up and burst the artery in my brain. And I went to sleep and I didn't wake up for twenty-two hours. My mother-in-law kept telling my maid, 'She just can't handle her drink: keep giving her water and she'll be fine.' And then my mom called and she was worried. She called the doctor and the doctor said, 'Take her to hospital immediately.' And my mother-in-law said, 'No, I know Simran' – as if she does – 'Simran can't handle her drink so let her sleep.' Then the doctor called back and she said, 'Oh, she's still sleeping,' and the doctor said, 'I'm telling you there's something grossly wrong with her, she needs to go to hospital.' Then my mom called up and said, 'I don't care about you, I'm taking my daughter.' She came and wrapped me up in a blanket. I wasn't waking up. By now I was just out. The doctors couldn't talk to me. They put me in the MRI machine and said, 'If you had brought her five minutes later we would have lost her.' It was zero hour.

"I was in a coma for nine days. My chances of coming out of it were very low. Because the burst artery was in the area of speech and memory, they said, 'If she ever wakes up, either she won't remember anything or she won't be able to speak again. She might just be cuckoo and you'll have to deal with that. And there's a 10 per cent chance that she'll be okay. So you know what? – we've done what we've can; all you have left are prayers.

And our best wishes.' So what really saved me was the prayer. There were 101 priests chanting for me. Prashant's grandmother and my grandmother put all of them together. And everybody's kindness, and people who wanted me to live, and all the positive energy – I survived and I was absolutely fine, and I was in that 10 per cent of completely normal people."

Twelve

A young woman is preparing to deliver the opening speech at a film festival when she realises she has left the text at home. She asks her boyfriend to rush home and get it. He speeds off on a bicycle: the house is nearby, and he is able to make it back within ten minutes.

Guards stop him at the entrance to the cultural centre, telling him that bikes are not allowed inside. He protests that he has to deliver something very urgently. When he makes to hurry past them, they set upon him with sticks, beating him around his head and body.

By the time he has recovered himself, he is too late to deliver the piece of paper. He enters the auditorium and sits down next to me as his girlfriend improvises onstage. He is hyperventilating; when I turn to look at him, I realise his head is running with blood. We go outside and make our way to the office of the director of the centre.

"I am sorry about your injuries," he says, after hearing the story. "But I would say to you that if you had spoken in English none of this would have happened. They saw that you were on a bike and you spoke to them in Hindi. How were they supposed to know you were middle class?"

The mountain of garbage at Bhalswa Colony is awe-inspiring. Only nature, one would imagine, might produce something so vast. It towers over the landscape, a long, gruff cliff along whose flank zigzags a shallow road where overflowing trucks rumble slowly to the summit. From below you can see them driving along the cliff's flat top, unloading their cargo of trash, feeding the mountain with more. All around them, mere specks from down below, are the people whose work it is to pick out from this megapolis-scale pile of refuse what can still be used.

Around me is an open plain where trash is sorted. The sacks full of plastic bottles are each the size of a car. In one area are piles of cushions, mattresses and sofas which boys are cutting open for the cotton stuffing inside. There is another area where resounding, syncopated hammers flatten out steel dustbins and casings from old air conditioners. There are phenomenal piles of twisted tyres.

It has rained recently and the ground is waterlogged. Pigs and dogs bathe in the water, which stinks of chemicals.

We are in the far north of the city. Walking here is uncanny after the city jam because there is just so much space. The sky is vast above and there is an almost pastoral openness to the landscape. The land slopes down to a reservoir where buffalos soak and storks keep watch on the banks. Buffalo manure has been collected for fuel, village style: here and there are conical piles the size of a large man, which are sheathed in tarpaulin against the rain.

Bhalswa Colony itself is squeezed into a tiny area of this generous tract of ground, a thick mass of brick cubes piled unevenly on top of each other, and reaching out, like saplings in a forest, into any unoccupied patch of air. The houses are flecked with lime green: the bricks have been taken from previous buildings whose painted walls survive here in fragments. From outside, the entire township seems blind: there are no windows in the walls, so the houses cannot see the giant sacks of trash that surround them on every side.

As we walk towards the colony, everyone emerging from it seems to be in uniform. A crowd of laughing school girls in blue dresses, for a start, their hair in wagging bunches tied with ribbon. And a music band, all military hats and epaulettes, departing with trumpets and drums for some distant nuptial.

I am walking with Meenakshi, who is not from this colony, though she is its self-appointed guardian. In her early thirties, she talks hurriedly and with gravity.

"When they had the idea of creating a city, they had to invite people to run it from elsewhere because they had no labourers. You can't run a city if you live in a mansion. A city is run by people who live in huts and slums. Rickshaw drivers, vegetable vendors, cobblers, construction workers, other working people: these are the people who run any city.

"So people from Bihar, Rajasthan and Uttar Pradesh who didn't have work moved from their villages to Delhi. In Delhi they found they had work but they did not have anywhere to live. So they began to make little houses for themselves on areas of vacant land on the edges of the city. Since they represented a vote bank for the government, the government decided to register them as voters in Delhi and to provide them with water, electricity and ration cards. Their families began to join them and they lived a normal life for thirty years.

"People kept coming to Delhi. There was lots of work. The Delhi Metro required thousands of workers. They built huts for themselves under the government's eyes and the government said nothing. But then the government thought: 'They are dirty people, they don't look nice in our city.' The city had grown, the areas where they were living were no longer on the periphery, and the government wanted to profit from that land. So they came to those people and told them they were illegal and they had to go.

"One of these settlements was on the banks of the Yamuna river and it housed some 30,000 families. In the year 2000, they decided to evict them from that place so that they could make the city beautiful. On that site they built the new headquarters for the Delhi government, which is one of the ugliest buildings in the world.

"Of those 30,000 families, 20,000 were declared illegal and were simply kicked out with nowhere to go. No one knows where they went. The others were resettled in various places around the periphery of the city. If they had come to Delhi before 1990 they were given six-by-three metre plots, if between 1990 and 1998 they were given four-by-three metre plots. Families had to pay 7,000 rupees (then $160) for these plots.

"Some of the families that were resettled came here to Bhalswa. But the relocation plan was very cunning. Of the 30,000 families in the Yamuna settlement, only 529 were sent to Bhalswa. The others were sent to other places. They made sure the townships were split up into different places so that they would not be able to unite.

"At the same time, they were destroying other settlements and many of those people came to Bhalswa too. The ones from Nizamuddin were Muslims. The ones from the Yamuna bank were Hindu. There were people from dalit communities. All of them had different cultures and religious practices, and the government knew that if they were all made to live in one place they would definitely fight each other. It was very intelligent.

"What does 'resettlement' mean to you? I'll tell you what it means to me. Resettlement means that people are settled in a complete manner. It means that all the facilities they had in the first place are provided to them in the new place.

"But it was nothing like that. People were evicted from townships they had built over forty years and thrown into places where there were not even the most basic requirements for life. There were no shops. No ration stores. No schools. No buses. Forget about electricity or water. The land was totally bare. There was nothing. The first people to come had to begin from scratch. The government provided nothing.

"Children had to drop out of school, as there were no schools there. Most men lost their jobs. Rickshaw drivers were thrown thirty-five kilometres from their homes into a wilderness where no one ever went. Of course they had no passengers. The same with the shopkeepers. They couldn't source vegetables anymore, and they had no customers. Everything was finished.

"The women of that slum used to work as housemaids in middle-class houses in south Delhi. They could not let this work go because their husbands had no income. So they used to leave home at 5 a.m. and travel all the way down to their places of work and come back at six in the evening. They could not take care of their children, who were at home since they had no schools to go to."

We enter the streets of the settlement, which are strikingly well-made compared to the streets of rich south Delhi neighbourhoods. The surface is brick, with a gentle camber. Bright yellow and blue washing is hung across the street; bicycles are parked in front of the houses. Inside, people are making household brooms: in one house they are cutting bristles, in another they are making the handles. There is a smell of frying garlic.

Meenakshi stops at a front door and calls in, "Hello! Have you received your ration card yet?"

"Yes. It came a while ago!"

"Why didn't you tell me?" She is quite irritated. "You have to tell me these things!"

The task Meenakshi has set for herself – for no one has invited her to do it – is to be the political representative of this community. She is the one who organises their official documents – many of them cannot read or write – lobbies on their behalf with the city authorities and, when necessary, organises political action. It is a role, I can see, that possesses her utterly.

"As I told you before, all these communities were from different cultures. The government planned to build for them apartment blocks with common spaces in between. We said this layout would create problems because everyone would fight over those common spaces. The Muslims would want to slaughter animals there, which would offend the Brahmins, who would want to use the same space for prayers and devotions. There would definitely be clashes.

"The residents said they wanted individual houses, and refused to accept the government plan. The government said it had been designed by a Scandinavian architect and so it could not be changed. They said, 'If you don't accept this plan we will just leave you there in the wilderness.' So the residents said, 'We have been living in the wilderness for six months, there is no reason why we cannot continue.' So for one whole year they lived in small tents under the open sky. They protested. They went to court, to the media, they went on marches. Finally they forced the government to abandon its plan. The government drew up a plan of row houses, allocated plots to individuals and left them on their own."

We stop at a house, and enter. It belongs to a woman named Jahanara, who is sitting on a mat on the floor with a friend, Saraswati. Both have been closely involved with Meenakshi's political campaigns on behalf of this settlement.

It is late morning, and the room is bright with the sunshine streaming through the open door. It seems large because there is almost nothing in it beyond a fridge and a stove. The walls are painted cream, and glow with the sunlight reflecting off the floor. At the back, stairs go up to the floor above.

Jahanara offers tea and gets up to make it. Meenakshi continues.

"You can see how terrible this area is. The land is marshy and prone to flooding. The first people to settle here had to dig drainage ditches before they could build anything. And even so this area is always flooded in the rainy season. This year a child died in the flood: the water came up above the houses. And even so there is no water to drink. The water in the reservoir is salty. And the groundwater here tastes of acid because the chemicals from the trash pile seep deep into the ground. It is so toxic that even mosquitoes can't survive in it. It's pure acid, and it burns. The kids all have rashes from bathing in it, and the women have terrible vaginal inflammations.

"These people built this town with their own hands. They could not wait years for the government to build streets and sewers so they did it themselves. They had to lobby for every brick and every bag of cement. They had to lobby for electricity. After ten years they are still lobbying. They still do not have a secondary school here. The nearest school will not accept these children because they are '*slum kids*'. So they have to travel far away to a school where there are 100 children in every class and there is nowhere to sit, no water and no toilet. It's very hard for those children who are trying to go to school. Have you seen the road into this colony? After the rains, it becomes completely impassable."

"Why did we come to this city?" interjects Jahanara. "First for work, because there was nothing in our villages in Uttar Pradesh. We knew people who were taken by labour contractors to Delhi, and they started getting good money, so eventually many of us followed. And the second reason we came was for schools. We cannot read or write, and we wanted our children to be better educated. In the village, the schools were far away. You couldn't check that your child was actually going to school. And it was dangerous for girls to travel that far. That's why we thought it was better to live with our husbands in the city. That's why we came. To give a better future to our children. Especially our daughters.

"When we arrived we managed to get our two children into a school in Delhi. But it was far away and the teachers didn't understand their situation. They failed our children because they didn't want slum children in their school. The children got disheartened and left their studies halfway through. Now they are working as labourers. That is the worst thing about all of this. Our children lost their education."

In the house opposite, a young woman has just emerged from the bathroom wearing a flaming pink sari. Her hair is wet: she stands in front of a mirror combing it. She puts cream on her face. She takes a long time over these rituals. Then she takes a broom and begins to sweep the floor of her house. With these narrow lanes and these windowless houses lit by open doors, everything is visible.

We drink tea in the room. Saraswati plays meditatively with Jahanara's toes. Both women are dressed in cotton salwar kameez. Saraswati has a row of metal and plastic bangles up to her elbow. She says,

"My husband's sister and her husband left our village for Delhi, and we did not hear from them again. My mother-in-law was very worried. She wept every day for her daughter because she didn't hear from her for two years. She kept asking my husband to go to Delhi to find her. So he went. He looked all over this huge city, asking in every settlement if anyone had heard of his sister and her husband. After many weeks he arrived in a place on the other side of the Yamuna river. He asked if anyone knew them and someone said, 'They live here.' They told him to wait by the well. When he got there he saw some women were fetching water. He called out to them and asked, 'Sisters, does a person by this name live here?' Now his sister was one of their number, and she heard him say her name. She ran over to him, and when she saw him she began to weep. 'Brother, what are you doing here?' she said. My husband said, 'Why didn't you make any contact with us for two years? Mother has been so worried that she has become ill.' And she said, 'My husband gets no holidays so we cannot come back. But I wrote you so many letters and I never received a response.' He cried, 'But we didn't get any of your letters!'

"After that, my brother-in-law helped him get a job in Delhi. My husband began to work on the construction of the new bridge across the Yamuna. But after five months he lost that job and he had nothing to do. One day, he found a chair. He decided he would set up as a barber on the riverbank. There was no township at that time. There was nothing except a huge pit of trash. My husband was a barber in a place where there were no people. He waited all day with his chair in the middle of a huge wasteland. The area was completely desolate and at night it was in total darkness.

"He hardly earned any money during the day, so he had to work all night as well. He was given a night job removing the trash that built up every day around the Yamuna bridge construction site. In that darkness he had to get into the river and swim to the site. He could not see anything, he just had to swim in the endless black. He worked through the night pulling corpses out of the river from where they had got stuck, and carrying away every kind of garbage. They paid him 500 rupees [$10] a month for that.

"Eventually, the government filled in the trash pit on the Yamuna bank with soil and flattened the area, and my husband and his brother-in-law built a hut on the site. More people came to live there. But my husband was feeling lonely, and he could no longer eat. He could not stop thinking about his children. Only his children made him feel that he was not totally alone in the world. So he asked me to come to Delhi to join him.

"We lived there for almost twenty-five years. Little by little we made that place worth living in. We built everything, brick by brick. We made a two-storey home there. Eventually, the place had everything – electricity, piped water, a government school and, right nearby, a government hospital. And then they knocked down everything we had built so they could make an office for the chief minister.

"They promised us that we would own a real house with toilets and bathrooms, and we would no longer be slum people. Everyone hates slum people and we were happy: they said the word 'slum' will be erased from your lives. They said they would take us to a new place which would have good schools, parks, water and electricity. Our children were very happy too. None of us knew at that time that this was all fake.

"They charged us 7,000 rupees [$140] for our new house:

many of us had to borrow that money or sell jewellery. But they refused to show us the place beforehand. They loaded us all into a truck; on the way, we asked the truck driver, 'Where are we going, is the place good? Are people nice there?' He said nothing to us. How could he? He was just doing his duty after all. And when we arrived here, it was just empty marshland. The house they had promised us did not exist. The truck driver himself said, 'This place is not good for you. How can you live here?' Some of us had arrived with bricks from our previous houses, but most of us didn't have even that. The whole place was flooded and there were snakes and rats everywhere. It took six trucks of mud and more than five thousand bricks to bring the land out of the water."

There is a great precision of detail in their stories of construction. They know how to make a sewer or a doorway, and they know how much cement and how many bricks such things take. If these women are so imposing, in fact, it has something to do with the fact that no part of their lives is delegated. They are not specialised. They are their own builders, town planners and politicians. They have an intimate and comprehensive understanding of all those aspects of life that remain vague and remote to other people. They seem to own themselves in a way that most people I know do not.

Jahanara tells a similar story. When she came to Delhi, she settled in the Muslim slum around Nizamuddin.

"There is a big well there and we lived near it. There was a vacant area at that time and the local boss built a slum with the help of the local police. First we had a tea stall. Soon the place became lively and we made a makeshift hotel there. We had water and electricity, and because Nizamuddin railway station was very near, a lot of people came to eat in our hotel.

"Then they came to us to say that whatever good you do and whatever money you make here, you will always be called slum people. They told us they were going to take us to a new place which would have good schools, parks, water and electricity.

We were told that we would have our own house in this place with toilets and bathrooms. Our children were very happy. We didn't know at that time that it was all a lie.

"They asked to break down the houses we had built with our own hands. There were some among us who said they didn't trust the promises this boss was making. But one night around 3 a.m. he broke down his own three-storey house with his own hands. People started to panic. They said, 'If the government officials come to demolish our houses we will lose all our belongings in the mess. It's better if we demolish them ourselves.' So we did. Then they loaded our belongings into a truck and threw us here."

The pitch of our conversation is curiously tranquil. It is a beautiful morning and the women speak calmly, affirming each other's accounts here and there as if each one spoke for the other. One senses that they are *together* in a way that few middle-class people are. Precariousness is so much the defining quality of their lives that mutuality is the only form of survival, and even in their grammar the 'I' rarely breaks ranks with the 'we'.

Meenakshi shows me files full of the letters and photographs they have sent off to various government departments in their attempt to make Bhalswa liveable.

"It's still going on after ten years. We still do not have some of the most basic things. We are still lobbying for ration cards. These are the most important thing in anybody's life. If they have rations, they can at least eat bread, even if it is just with salt. Without this they cannot survive. You know what the inflation rate is at present? They cannot afford to buy anything from the open market.

"These things actually irritate you. Each time we walk into the office of the Municipal Corporation, the bureaucrat there wrinkles his face in disgust and says, 'Why does this garbage keep coming back to me?' How long can you go on fighting with that? The people here can either spend their days fighting for water or they can do their daily work and earn some money for their families.

"I have found out that the government spends 56,000 rupees [$1,200] per month providing water tankers to us. That's nearly 7 lakhs [$14,000] a year. It would take just half of that amount to make a proper pipeline into this settlement. But they don't want to do that. They know that without water this will never be a proper settlement, and they will be able to move everyone out again."

For most middle-class families, government has retreated drastically from social and economic life over the last two decades, to the point that they hardly see it anymore. They like it like this: they idealise government withdrawal and 'deregulation'. Many of them do not realise how much work the city government does to protect their class from the enormous mass of poverty that surrounds them, which is firmly prevented from having any claim on city space or resources. It is the poor who understand how the city is truly managed. They have a far greater intimacy with government and, indeed, a far greater bureaucratic burden. As I understand, looking through these files: the work Meenakshi has taken on is monumental.

In the house opposite, a man emerges into the room, the husband of the woman in the pink sari. He is wrapped in a towel, his chest bare. He is muscular, with thick, wild hair and a silver necklace shining against his dark skin. He is heavy with sleep and moves slowly. He comes to sit on the steps outside. The rings on his fingers glint in the sun.

"It has been difficult for the men," says Meenakshi. "They all lost their jobs when they came here. No one wants to employ men for domestic work. Nowadays there is some daily work that the men can do. They shell peas, for instance. That gives them 30 rupees [$0.60] for a day's work, and that is usually with the help of the whole family. Some men make brooms and sell them the residential areas nearby. Some have started working on construction sites. But that's not the majority.

"So most of them sit at home, and they get depressed. Their minds get completely blocked. They resent their wives who are always away working. They beat them. They don't like them getting involved in political work: they turn up at our meetings drunk and abusive. They shout at us: 'You women can't do anything. You can't change a thing.'

"And this community is badly affected by drugs. I am not talking about one or two families, I am talking about the whole community. Even children are affected. They don't have school so they don't have anything to do and slowly they get affected. They sniff the glue which is used to make shoes. There is a tablet that costs one rupee and it makes children forget everything that is happening. The cheapest drugs give them the utmost happiness.

"The men drink and they smoke brown sugar. As soon as they see their wives with any money, they take it to buy drink. They come home with their bottles hidden in their clothes. I ask them, 'Do you really want to buy that bottle when you don't have any food to eat in your home?'"

Saraswati says sarcastically, "The government is doing a wonderful job here. They haven't started any hospitals or schools but they instantly opened a liquor store. They even posted a policeman to guard it. Schools cost the government money but liquor stores give them revenues.

"People say we are always blaming the government. Why would we not blame them? The things on which our life depends, the government is taking away from us. And the things that can kill us, the things which make our homes bankrupt, the government is opening new shops to provide those things. It is providing those things very generously."

In the house opposite, the girl in the pink sari has taken delivery of many hundred newly made plastic brooms, which she is now wrapping individually in plastic sleeves. Her husband is sitting on the steps outside smoking.

Meenakshi says, "So here is the thing. You can see the streets and houses that people have made here. After ten years they now have something of value. But now the government has declared *this* place illegal and says they have to leave. The land which was provided *by the government* is now illegal. Because they only gave them permission for ten years. They will not give poor people a permanent place in the city."

"When you came here, you must have walked across the empty land," says Saraswati. "Now the government wants to build flats on that land, and they want to get us out. Why do they want to build flats there? Because *we* have spent ten years making this place habitable. We are the ones who drained the land, who built the streets, who organised the electricity supply, who got the buses to run here. It is we who have made this land valuable enough for the government to sell. We will not leave it. We have built two cities already in our lives and we will not build another."

"We will not go," echoes Jahanara. "They tricked us once. They will not do so again."

Meenakshi says, "When they told us they wanted everyone to leave, people from Bhalswa knew if they didn't fight they would be left with nothing. For this they were prepared to be beaten by the police. So we decided to hold a protest during the Commonwealth Games to try and embarrass the government into finding another solution. While millions of rupees were being spent on a huge sports event that benefitted no one, the people who needed money were not getting it; in fact the government was taking money away from them and knocking down their houses. So we decided to go out, the whole community, and block the main highway that runs near here. Students and teachers from Delhi University organised the protest with us: many of them are interested in our situation, which no one else is.

"Bhalswa was badly affected by the flood at that time but everyone decided it was essential to participate in the protest. Around 5,000 women came out of their houses and blocked the road. For forty minutes, the traffic was jammed on the highway. First the police came from one station and then they called up other stations. The assistant commissioner ordered the police to attack us with batons. Women were badly beaten up and one had to go to hospital with broken bones. We called an ambulance but they refused to help us. Students from Delhi University were arrested.

"I should say that our women also fought the police. They snatched police batons and hit back. To our great shock, the police identified one of these women and began to intimidate her. They got hold of her son and found out where she worked. Later, the police went to the place where she worked and told her never to do anything like that again. They like to target individuals, because individuals are not strong on their own. But we are never going to give up."

"When they come to ask us for our vote, they don't come in cars," says Jahanara. "They come on foot and they say to us, 'Sister, please take care of us.' It is we who win them elections and make emperors of them. The money they grab is our money. So it is our right to fight the government. We are also citizens of this country.

"We have all had many threats. Men came to our house with big sticks and threatened my husband. They said, 'Control your wife or you will face serious consequences.' After that my husband started fighting with me. I told him not to get involved in all this: I was the one who was taking care of the family.

"They are the government. They can lodge false cases against us and send us to jail any day. They control everything. If they sanction 10 crore rupees for us, only 2 crores will reach us. The only thing I am afraid of is the government. They will try to seize everything we have."

Saraswati is enraged.

"If I ever meet the chief minister of Delhi, I will hit her so hard she can't even imagine! They brought us here on the basis of lies. If they had shown us this land before, we would never have come here. This is the place where all of Delhi's trash is dumped and she thinks we can be dumped here too. Someone make her live here, then she will realise what it is. And now they want us to leave again! If they try to force us to leave this place, we will break their heads. We had to sell our house in the village to get this plot. Many of us are still paying back loans to moneylenders ten years later for those 7,000 rupees that bought us nothing. We are not leaving."

The postman comes to drop a letter. His arm has been severed at the elbow.

Meenakshi says, "The majority of the people, the people who actually run this city, are being eliminated from it. They are not welcome here anymore. The city is being remade for rich people. Only people who have cars can live here. Look at the structure: the flyovers, malls, hotels, and other luxuries. It is all meant for people with money. Look how much money is spent on flyovers, and who is using them? Only those with money. What use are they to people who walk? You cannot walk on them. People who walk cannot move in this city: there is no place for them.

"The Metro only links those places where there are offices or posh neighbourhoods. It doesn't link any places where working-class or poor people live. So the Metro just supports people who have money. A poor man can't afford a Metro ticket. And poor people travel with a lot of stuff: they cannot take it on the Metro. They have to travel by bus.

"But now they have introduced new buses which cannot serve the poor. They are pretty green buses and they brought them in to make the city look good for the Commonwealth Games. They have special low floors to make it easy for people to get on – even people in a wheelchair can get on. But these buses can only travel on flat roads. So they have cancelled all the buses that used to come to this colony. The transport people simply say that there is no road and we can't come there.

"Everything is getting worse. Everything. Ultimately it is not only the poor who will suffer. I come from a middle-class family and I can tell you from my personal experience that in the near future even a middle-class family won't be able to raise their children in Delhi. The people of Bhalswa are afraid for their future, but I too have a deep fear inside me. Because I don't know what will happen to any of us in the future. It's not only the poor."

Saraswati says, "Sometimes we wonder if we should ever have left the village. Many of those who stayed behind have ended up better off. Many of the men went to do construction work in Saudi Arabia or Dubai where they make more money. We don't have anything. Whatever we had earlier we sold for a better place in Delhi. We thought one day we would have our own flat in Delhi."

Jahanara says, "The villages have also changed since we left. The schools have become better. Our relatives who stayed behind raised their children better than we did. The villages have seen a big change in the last few years.

"But we can never go back. We sold our property in the village, and whatever we still have has been taken by our relatives. It's better to fight with the government than with your family. In a fight with your family, you will die. So we will stay here. No matter what they do."

Meenakshi walks with me as I depart.

"How did you get here?" she asks.

"I took an auto-rickshaw from the Metro station."

"You're lucky," she says. "Most of them won't come here."

As we walk through the township I realise that the streets we entered by were the very best. Others are in far worse condition. Some of the road surfaces have been washed away in the rains, and residents are laying fresh concrete to mend them. The streets where the ragpickers live are full of piles of trash that is being sorted in homes. At the end of the township is a den where men smoke crack behind a tarpaulin. Their kids sit around outside. One girl makes a pattern out of the pieces of a broken plant pot. Other kids are at work sorting garbage or arranging in boxes the jamun fruit they have picked from trees. Chickens forage. The puddles are covered with strange swarms of tiny flies such as I have never seen before: at the slightest movement the entire swarm takes off, but it stays together, a cloud-organism, and then lands all in one go on the puddle again.

The only way out of this place is a community bus. We get on. The thing travels at a fantastically slow pace around the potholes, stopping every few minutes to let people on or off. It takes us an hour to get out of Bhalswa. This is partly because of a big argument over unpaid fares, which leads the driver to stop the bus in protest until the three men in question either get off or pay. They refuse to do either. It is Meenakshi who intervenes. She offers to pay their fares for them. But they prefer to get off the bus than pay, and do so.

It is impossible to communicate how remote and inaccessible this place is, though it is in the middle of one of the world's largest cities. It is easy to understand how national borders might separate populations with very different access to the global economy but more difficult to conceive of how such divisions might run through a single city. But in this metropolis where many people are totally restructuring the global economy with their capital, ideas and labour, and where you can sometimes feel, therefore, that you are sitting where all the forces of the globe converge, there are populations that are entirely irrelevant to that system. Bhalswa is not a place of capitalist oppression – in fact, many of its residents would love a bit more of that. It is a place of unwanted lives, of people who can find almost no connection to the economic boom that surrounds them. They are a 'surplus' population that has nowhere to go, and all they can do is try to survive the shunting around from one trash pile to the next.

Meenakshi and I take the Metro to Connaught Place and sit in the Indian Coffee House, an institution set up in Nehru's time and run by a national cooperative of coffee workers, where you can still find a hot drink for 5 rupees.[32] Meenakshi will not order anything, however. She carries a flask of water in her backpack.

"My father came from a village in Uttarakhand. Our situation was like the people you met today. Farming was very precarious in our village. It was terrace farming, which doesn't yield much food. It was very dependent on the rains. My grandfather died when my father was two, so my father and uncles did different kinds of work to earn a living: they grazed other people's cattle and worked in other people's fields. It was miserable and they were starving. When my father was seven, he ran away to Delhi with my uncle.

"At that time, people in the city were more genuine. A man who saw the plight of my father and my uncle took them to a Jain ashram, where they lived. They studied there. My father left his studies when he was fifteen and started working as a labourer. He cleared the bushes around the Old Fort and every day his hands bled terribly. Then he went to work in the house of a Muslim family in Aligarh. And then he was selected to work for the Intelligence Bureau.

"He never really told us what kind of work he did for them. He said he started out as a dishwasher. In the village they used to say, 'He has a lot of attitude for a dishwasher!' But he managed to get a training while he was doing such menial work, and eventually he was given proper responsibilities. When he retired from the Intelligence Bureau, he was an inspector.

"There were more opportunities in those days. Nowadays people would not get the kind of options my father got.

"While I was growing up, he was sent away from Delhi. He was posted to a village in the border regions, where his job was to arrest illegal immigrants. He pursued them ferociously. He had spies and informants who would give him information about people who had crossed the border illegally.

"I did not feel good in the village. I had to go to a school with a broken building and write on a small board. It was the only school for eight villages and even so there were only forty children in the school. I was the only girl in my class. We were taught under a tree. It was very awkward, the transition from the city school to the village school. I lagged behind and when I came back to Delhi, I failed in English. Even today, I am not confident enough to look into someone's eyes and speak English.

"After high school, my father said I could not study further so I went to work in a factory. I was sixteen years old. It was a textiles factory and I was involved with some of the designs. I thought I wanted to do fashion design but it didn't appeal to me at all. All I could think about was the women who worked there, who were in hell. They worked more than twelve hours a day and in return they got nothing. I organised for the workers to be given proper clothing to wear and campaigned for them to receive the minimum wage. For three years I fought with the company owner and finally we won, and the company granted them a fixed salary with a few holidays every year. Of course, they fired me and kept my salary. But it made me more confident and I did a lot of different things after that.

"Later on I went to do a degree at Delhi University and then a Master's. But when I look back, I don't find myself at par with the world. I feel far behind it. Had I studied in a good school and not wasted the crucial years of my life, I would have been a better person today. When I visualise myself in the world, I feel I have nowhere to stand.

"There are things we are born with. I have something in me, you have something in you. My thing is that I have always been alone. I have not met other people who think like me. I was always eating alone, sitting alone, thinking alone. When I was fifteen or sixteen, I started writing poems. When you are alone and you think that nobody understands you, you feel heavy. But when you put your thoughts on paper, you feel light."

Meenakshi takes out a notebook and reads out some poems that she has written. They speak of terrible, destructive forces. A man at the table next to us is listening intently. He is enormously impressed by Meenakshi, whose masculine demeanour cannot conceal the fact that she is beautiful. He gets up to congratulate her and to ask her all about herself. He wants to sit at our table and talk to her. But her silence is formidable, and he retreats to where he came from.

She speaks about her childhood.

"In the village there used to be powerful people who would beat less powerful people. There were also many caste restrictions. I was a Brahmin and there were many things I could not do. If a Brahmin did manual work, another Brahmin could not eat his food. These things used to hurt my mind somehow. I saw the things that happened to girls and never to their brothers. When I came to the city, I was friends with a Muslim girl in my class. I used to eat her lunch and she used to eat mine. When I told my father, he said I had become no one, neither Hindu nor Muslim. Then I decided that I wouldn't tell them anything. Slowly the thought of revolt sparked in me. I used to think about these things the whole night. I used to ask, 'Who invented these boundaries? Why do they exist?' But there was nobody to answer these questions. So this was what gave me new thinking."

I suspect it would be difficult to get to know Meenakshi well. She is extraordinarily self-contained. Through the furious energy of her labour one can sense an intense but inchoate inner search. It refreshes me to hear her talk. She too is part of this city. She reminds me of what I love in the friends I have here: a fierce intelligence searching for a better arrangement of the world. This too is Delhi culture, but it is what you could call the city's minor culture. It rarely rises to the surface of things.

"After my Master's I started working for an NGO which sent me to work in Bhalswa. That changed my life."

Meenakshi, whose father worked hard to provide for his family a middle-class life, finds her ultimate fulfilment in proximity to the poor. As she talks about the work she does for this community, I wonder in which direction the dependency goes: do they need her or does she need them?

Meenakshi found herself at ideological odds with the NGO

she was working for. "They are not actually interested in people," she says, "only in their own projects. Because it is projects that give them money, not people." In the end her disagreements grew too much for the NGO, and she was fired. Remarkably, she carried on doing the same work for the Bhalswa community, now without position or salary.

"I have dedicated my life to this work. I am a single person, so I can give everything to what I do. I work eighty-hour weeks and I still bring work home because there is no end. When I have money I give it to this work. I live with my parents and I have no needs. I left my earlier life in a textile export business because I didn't like it. I don't want to be in a capitalist world, simply earning money and looking at my life like a bank balance. I love to work for people. I like work that can help someone or actually shape someone's life.

"If I stood today for the council elections at Bhalswa, I would certainly win. Even my brother says that I should do this so that I can earn a lot of money and change my lifestyle. But I don't want to do this. My brother says that trying to understand me is like beating your head on a stone.

"I don't know what will happen to me in the future. But I know that my life will never be 'normal'. I know it will continue to be as it is now. A prolonged fight. So I try to prepare myself for the future by living without things. Now I have many things because I live with my parents, but I try to live without milk, without fruit, because I know that in the future I may not be able to have those things. I try to see whether I will be able to survive if I have to live alone, or without food.

"My father is very unhappy that I spend all my time in a slum. He is suspicious of migrants and the poor. At the place where he worked, if he saw four people talking, he would start to wonder what they were talking about. Are they talking against the country? He thinks like the intelligence services. If he hears people speaking Bengali, he will assume they are illegal immigrants from Bangladesh because he is trained like that.

"His thinking is middle class, so I don't discuss things with him. There's no use fighting with him about issues he cannot understand. He says I have turned into a slum girl. I feel bad about this but I can't help it. I know what I am doing. I know I have no money, but I still feel I am better than that other world.

"When I was a child, my mother used to tell me, 'When you die, no one will even ask about you.' I used to reply to her, 'Mother, when I die there will be a thousand people weeping behind my body.'"

Thirteen

[The bourgeoisie] has pitilessly torn asunder the motley
feudal ties that bound man to his 'natural superiors', and
has left remaining no other nexus between man and man
than naked self-interest, than callous 'cash payment' . . . It
has resolved personal worth into exchange value, and in
place of the numberless indefeasible chartered freedoms,
has set up that single, unconscionable freedom — Free
Trade.

> – Karl Marx and Friedrich Engels,
> *The Communist Manifesto*, 1848

It will come as no surprise that the warrior ethos did not allow
much room for concern about the weak. Life was war. Too bad
for the ones who could not fight.

The members of the flourishing bourgeoisie that is the subject
of this book constituted, of course, a small minority of the Delhi
population. They owed much of their prosperity, indeed, to the
fact that they were situated in the middle of an ocean of poverty.
Sweeping away from Delhi's south-eastern edge was the vast
swathe of Uttar Pradesh and Bihar, where 300 million people
earned an average of $500 per year. Not only were they very

poor, they were also politically weak and their lives were getting worse. They constituted therefore a cheap and near-infinite resource for the labour-intensive industries – such as construction, mining and manufacturing – that made Delhi wealthy.

The fact that their lives were getting worse was not despite the boom in the Indian economy but because of it. The boom was fuelled, in part, by a corporate occupation of the countryside which pitted big money against poor agricultural and tribal communities, turning rural India into a turbulent and volatile battleground. Expanding business needed land, and most of India's land was in the hands of small farmers, whose legal ownership of it had been well secured during the Nehru years. Since most farmers owned only a hectare or two each, and since most of them did not wish to sell, acquiring hundreds or thousands of hectares of contiguous land was almost impossible to pull off legally and within business-like timeframes. So the post-liberalisation period was witness to various forms of seizure involving millions of hectares of rural land.

Sometimes this was achieved by so-called land mafias. Many large fortunes were acquired in those years by 'land-aggregators' who got farmers off their land with gang violence, or who used connections in the political establishment not only to arbitrarily re-allocate land but also to enforce the order with state resources – such as the police. But often the land grab was enacted by the state according to the terms of the Land Acquisition Act of 1894, an instrument introduced by the British empire to legalise the expropriation of lands from their historical owners to the colonial power – and indeed the rampage of Indian elites in their own country bore a significant resemblance to that of nineteenth-century European imperialists in other countries. Land was repossessed under an authoritarian law, little or no compensation was given to the people who previously made their living from it, and it was sold on, often at ten times the price, to corporations, which then used it in ways that actively destroyed the living of that place – employing the former landowners, now conveniently destitute, as construction workers, miners and factory labour.

Farmers who protested against the forcible acquisition of their land for the purposes of Special Economic Zones or automobile factories sometimes found themselves jailed or, in extreme cases, shot. But such a large-scale and devastating revolution could not proceed without widespread resistance. At any one point there were hundreds of protests across the country over land appropriation. Most distressingly for the political establishment, an armed Maoist rebellion swept the country's most devastated rural regions, and in many places usurped all state control. By 2006, armed groups were organised throughout the eastern states of Bihar, Jharkhand, West Bengal and Andhra Pradesh, and were said to occupy a fifth of India's forests. Prime minister Manmohan Singh declared in that year that they represented the 'single biggest security challenge ever faced by our country'[33] – which was something of a shock to urban elites, most of whom found it difficult to imagine, by that time, that they shared their country with hundreds of millions of beleaguered farmers, hunter–gatherers and other such mythological creatures.

But the wars of which they remained, for the most part, so blissfully ignorant were violent and consequential. In the mineral-rich state of Chhattisgarh, the government sold mining leases for land on which large populations subsisted by hunting and gathering; in order to clear these people away, the state government used the services of a people's militia, the Salwa Judum or 'Purification Hunt'. The Salwa Judum was an armed movement fostered by the mainstream political parties in the hope that it could drain and defeat the Maoist insurgency that was threatening the state in those desperate years; under the impetus of this new political mission it went beserk, looting and burning villages, raping and killing and herding tribal populations into prison camps. Hundreds of thousands fled the onslaught, thus transporting conflict and competition over resources to other places.

But even those rural communities who managed to escape such land battles found that it was increasingly difficult to survive doing what they had previously done. Given their dependence on the rains – the right amount at the right time – many farmers had been for a long time balanced precariously between success and failure. The processes unleashed by liberalisation helped to tip them irreversibly to the side of the latter.

This was partly because of altered ecological conditions, particularly as regarded water. The expanding cities found themselves in a greater and greater water deficit, and had to pull it in from further and further afield, drying out villages and agriculture to a radius of hundreds of kilometres. New factories in the countryside needed large and predictable water supplies – some of them made fizzy drinks, after all, or even bottled water – and the corporations looking to make these investments did so only if the state would guarantee these supplies through wet times and dry. Where the availability of water was already precarious, it could now become unviable.

But liberalisation also changed the economics of agriculture, introducing new earning options to farmers which also carried with them much higher levels of risk. Many farmers were anyway pushed towards such new options because the high-intensity farming introduced in the 1960s – the 'Green Revolution' – had by that time exhausted their land and they were obliged to explore the possibility of new crops and chemical supplements. At the same time, the arrival of global corporations looking to India's farmers to supply raw materials for processed foods presented them with new revenue and indeed lifestyle opportunities. Many farmers therefore opted to stop growing food and to pursue higher returns by growing cash crops such as sugar cane, coffee, cotton, spices or flowers. But this left a financially vulnerable group highly exposed to market fluctuations – the price of food, for instance, which they now had to buy, soared during those years – and sometimes the gamble ended in ruin.

Also, in the years after 1991, successive Indian governments signed up to international trade agreements that committed them to accepting and enforcing foreign corporations' demands regarding the use of their products; these included protection for the new generations of patented seeds issued by global biotech corporations. Farmers subscribed to these products in large numbers precisely because agricultural conditions were so bad and the seeds were offered as a solution. But according to the licenses, these seeds had to be bought each season from the manufacturers, and many of them were engineered to produce sterile offspring, so that farmers could not, as they traditionally had, save seeds from one season to plant the next. The seeds were also designed, often, to be used in conjunction with certain fertiliser and pesticide products which required not only significant cash outlay but also extensive training, which was usually lacking. In an environmental context that was already becoming more stern, many farmers exhausted their land with the new chemicals and entered an impossible spiral of debt, usually incurred to local money-lenders who charged extremely high rates of interest (in this, as in so many things, the poor paid more than the rich for the same resource).

Together, all these things were fatal. In the first decade of the twenty-first century, some 15,000 Indian farmers committed suicide every year. The only way out.

Given the great numbers of people affected by the crisis of the Indian countryside, slight exacerbations were enough to unleash very large tides of refugees who departed, naturally enough, for the cities. Most of the 7 million who were added to Delhi's population between the censuses of 1991 and 2011 were poor rural migrants such as these. They were the stock characters of modernity's now-venerable story: the shattered tribes whose land had been cut open for minerals, the desperate farmers who could no longer feed themselves from the land, and the embroiderers, potters and wood carvers – sometimes the last of ancient lines – whose work had been made obsolete by new factories.

Some of these people ended up protecting and enhancing the very wealth that had derailed their lives in the first place – for

Delhi's affluent households were hungry for servants. The fact that it was so easy to purchase cheap labour, in fact, was essential to urban middle-class identity. Even modestly off families often employed a chauffeur, while a maid to come early in the morning and clean the floors of the previous day's dust was de rigueur. Wealthier households had security guards sitting permanently in plastic chairs outside their gates, their main qualification for this non-job being that they were alive rather than, say, not.

This entourage of labour gave the rich dignity in their own eyes, and defined for them, indeed, what was seemly. It was not normal or appropriate for wealthy people to do certain things for themselves, and this had an impact on the very shape of the city. The fact that there was nowhere to park, for instance, did not bother them because they did not drive themselves: their chauffeurs dropped them off in front of a restaurant and circled until they came out. The fact that every ordinary task, from posting a letter to buying a train ticket, involved so much interminable jostling in crowds received no middle-class censure, because these were things they almost never did. In general, a kind of affected incompetence characterised the behaviour of the city's rich, who would ring for a servant to look for their car keys, or summon a waiter to pick up the wine bottle that stood in front of them and pour its contents into their glass.

The power to employ labour was real power. Much of the daily effort of middle-class Europeans and Americans was foreign to their Indian counterparts – washing the dishes, doing the laundry, making the kids' dinner – who could often be more productive in other domains as a result. And yet their relationships with their domestic servants were frequently, and bizarrely, resentful. If you listened to middle-class people complaining about their maids, you could be forgiven for feeling that the role of these women was not to perform essential labour in the house but rather to lose keys, steal jewellery, break dishes, waste electricity, ruin clothes, put things in the wrong place, teach bad habits to the children, allow fruit to go rotten and, above all, to destroy everyone else's life by missing a day's work because – so they said – they were sick, or their children had been mauled by wild dogs or electrocuted by live lines submerged in the flood, or their slum was being demolished or their husband had died or their sister was getting married in some godforsaken village – or some other equally improbable tale. Such maid-inflicted woes were a staple of middle-class conversation, to the extent that one wondered why so many privileged people seemed to be so invested in the perfidy of the poor. There seemed to be some historical intensity to the way in which the middle classes placed the blame for everything that was wrong in their lives on the heads of their maids. A few generations ago, after all, many of Delhi's propertied classes were themselves refugees, and it was as if, looking into the eyes of these new migrants who now cooked their meals and looked after their children, they were put in mind of violent and unpleasant things they would rather not remember.

The corollary of all this was that, in middle-class minds, servants did not deserve their salaries. Servants' salaries were not a reflection of their contribution to the household but rather a kind of charitable donation given in spite of their incompetence. The middle classes were fond of seeing themselves as under-appreciated benefactors and their image of the poor was not as a productive engine but as a pack of parasites living off their own intelligence and hard work. It was they, the middle classes, who contributed real value to the economy, and they were determined to ensure that the fruits of that economy's growth remain confined to their own kind. Even as their own incomes multiplied manifold, they fought furiously against pay rises for the people who served them. When you moved into a new middle-class neighbourhood, the old residents, some of them owners of million-dollar properties, would come to tell you that the garbage collector would charge Rs 100 [$2] per month but you were only to give him Rs 50 [$1], "otherwise the price will go up for all of us". The scandal of a maid who was asking for her Rs 2,000 [$40] monthly salary to be raised to Rs 3,000 was frequently discussed over Rs 3,000 dinners.

The people who were complaining about these things presumably knew that working-class rents were rising as quickly as everyone else's; they certainly knew that the price of food was going up by as much as 12 per cent a year. But these demands from working-class people were still seen as pure opportunism. Being 'fleeced' by the poor was a near-obsession with the city's middle classes, who described the vegetable sellers who came to their doors as 'thieves', while rickshaw drivers were all out, so the truism went, to 'take you for a ride'. India's boom belonged to the middle classes: it was their moment, and they would fight furiously for it. In a country where the mean income was $1,400 per year, the slightest move to average out incomes would be catastrophic for the few who earned, say, $60,000 per year. So the 90 per cent were excommunicated from the middle-class project of India's rise, and their claims on better incomes and better lives pronounced illegitimate. As if in reaction to the perennial dictum of the post-Independence period – "Remember the poor!" – it was now, so it seemed, time to forget.

And yet it goes without saying that the poor were instrumental to the new accumulation of middle-class wealth. The disaster of the Indian countryside unleashed not only a handy supply of domestic servants; it also generated a vast supply of labour for construction firms and factory owners. The labour of these millions produced fortunes for factory owners, of course, but it also funded the management consultancy firms and advertising agencies where professionals worked, it produced the gratifying stock market returns from the mining and construction companies in which they had their investments, and it built the roads on which the car-owning classes drove and the houses in which they lived. But once again, the balance was firmly in the hands of elites, because of the sheer quantity of willing labouring hands. Employers never had to worry about where the next workers would come from. They could pay almost nothing, and demand pretty much any level of toil. It was common for factory workers to work sixteen hours a day, seven days a week, thirty days a month. Most were not paid the minimum wage of $4 per day, and almost none were granted pensions or insurance. The fact that Indian factories were now producing for consumers all over the world added to the intensity of workers' lives but made almost no difference to their salaries: if liberalisation brought extra revenues into the system, they were generally taken by contractors, not by the workers themselves.

The decade following liberalisation, in fact, saw an aggressive assault by industrialists on workers' bargaining power. At the beginning of that decade, some 90 per cent of workers in the factories around Delhi were employed on a permanent basis, which meant not only that they enjoyed higher salaries but also pensions, health insurance and various legal protections. Many workers worked an entire career in one factory. But with the new pressures of globalisation, this situation became increasingly unattractive to factory owners, who sought pretexts to fire permanent workers, often en masse. By 2000, 70 or 80 per cent of workers were temporary, and their legal and economic situation correspondingly more precarious. Workers could not make individual complaints about their situation, since there was a long line of people waiting to take their place, but mass protests were dealt with harshly and often with the assistance of police batons and tear gas – the police seemed always to stand unquestioningly by the side of factory owners even when protests were provoked by worker deaths or by reports of bizarre and sadistic violence on the part of the management.

Unlike in China, where so many workers were housed and fed in dormitories and bussed to the factory, Indian employers made little investment in workers' lives outside the workplace. Workers had only makeshift shelter to return to, often without running water, and it was therefore difficult to achieve even the bare minimum of self-preservation – staying healthy and getting enough rest to return to work a few hours later. Needless to say, factories produced a great accumulation of human detritus: those who had fallen sick and could no longer work, those who had, aged thirty-five, grown too old, those who had lost fingers and hands in machines and who could do little, henceforth, except beg in the streets.

But this uncontrolled situation was inconvenient for employers too, because their workers had no stake in their enterprise, and came and went without warning. They suddenly went back to Bihar when employment prospects there were rumoured to have improved, they took a week off for a religious festival – or they simply moved to the factory next door when the owner temporarily offered higher wages in order to complete an urgent order. Textile manufacturers supplying major Western chain stores had sixty to ninety days to produce and deliver their clothes on pain of harsh penalties; ensuring, in such labour conditions, that everything happened on time presented enormous problems. But employers seemed to think of their workers as alien, and incurably insubordinate beings, and did not believe in the possibility of coming to any kind of accommodation with them. The only interface they had with the inscrutable worker psyche was money, so this was where they applied their pressure. In some factories, workers who were paid the minimum wage of around Rs 6,000 [$120] per month had one-third of that amount categorised as an 'attendance bonus', which was withheld if they missed a single day of work, even for sickness. But even such measures could never entirely preserve the mechanised and predictable space of the factory from the immense turbulence whence it derived its human resource. These workers were living on every kind of edge, and were stalked by emergencies of all sorts – as were their parents, siblings, wives and children in far-off parts of the country (unlike in China, most factory workers were men). Even when the financial consequences were as serious as they were, it was frequently impossible for them to work all their waking hours for thirty days in one month.

The situation of the poor in twenty-first century India certainly owed much to local dynamics: traditional caste hierarchies, for instance, and the failure of human sympathy to pass between the city and the countryside. But in many respects the poor who laboured here were not just 'India's' poor. They belonged to the world. By the early twenty-first century, in fact, it could be said that much of the global economy was running off the desperation of the Asian countryside. If the 1990s had seen so much manufacturing moved to places like India and China it was because of, and not in spite of, the authoritarian system that operated in both those places, albeit in different ways. 'Normal' bourgeois life, whether in Delhi or New York, required one to consume immense amounts of embedded labour, which was only possible if that labour was kept very cheap. The force that was pressing down on Indian and Chinese labour, ultimately, was not the class contempt of wealthy Indians so much as the global consumerist logic of *new, fast and cheap*. This logic was merciless, and insatiable in its thirst for human labour. The death of rural life in Asia, which affected many hundreds of millions of people, provided the hopeless reservoir on which this logic could draw.

As one unusually self-critical textile factory owner observed to me, reflecting on the system in which she played a nodal role, "There used to be a time when you could be a capitalist with personality. You could make your own decisions about what kind of ethos you wanted to create. Now it does not matter if you are a 'nice' person. It is completely irrelevant. We live in an age when we all know what we do is disgusting but we still carry on doing it. The system we are part of feeds on desperation. And any system that demands such levels of desperation will produce more and more disorder, and the only way to keep everything in check will be the increasing militarisation of the world."

When asked about how he would solve the problems of the countryside, a Congress finance minister said, essentially, that he would liquidate it: 85 per cent of Indians, he said, now needed to live in cities. He said these words at a time when 70 per cent, or more than 700 million people, lived in the countryside: his breezy percentages conjured up upheavals of mythic proportions. They reflected the fact that urban elites had lost the ability to imagine the countryside, and therefore the vast majority of their own compatriots, and they wished it would simply disappear. Pastoral billboards advertising real estate developments called 'Provence' and the like presented India's countryside as just so much empty 'Lebensraum' waiting for the middle classes to move in. But what city people had ceased to understand was that agriculture could support far more people than industry and that, with its destruction, India would be faced with a violent crisis. The cheapness of labour in early twenty-first-century India derived from the fact that there was a huge *excess*, which meant not only that it was easily available but also, by definition, that it could not all be used. A great number of India's poor were not sucked up by the capitalist machine. They were just left over. Like the residents of Bhalswa, they maintained only the most tenuous connection to the frenzy of the mainstream economy, and were squirrelled away in an improbable parallel universe of lassitude and decline.

"We are storing up immense problems for ourselves," observes the owner of a large private equity fund. "People talk about India's 'population dividend', referring to the advantages that recent high birth rates might deliver in terms of a youthful, energetic population. But I am unable to see it like that. We have 15 to 20 million people entering the labour market every year and there is nothing for them to do. The only thing that can absorb such numbers is electronics and textile manufacturing on a scale out of all proportion to what we have.

"We make a lot of our IT industries, but India's IT and BPO sectors together only employ 2 million people. Retail and restaurants have created new jobs, but those account only for another 4 to 5 million people. Compare that to China's electronics and textiles manufacturing, which employs 100 million people. India has failed entirely to get hold of this kind of business, and there is no indication that we can offer jobs to our young people. It is a colossal failure."

This failure raised profound questions about the future of societies such as India's. More historically minded observers thought back to the destruction of rural life during the industrial revolution in Europe, which also produced enormous waves of newly destitute people to the cities – far more, again, than could be employed in new factories and mines, far more even than could be accommodated in prisons, workhouses or workforces on infrastructure projects. The carving up of traditional agrarian lifestyles was for the majority a catastrophe that would only be healed many generations after their own, and during their lifetime they could expect no better fate than membership of the thronging, surplus 'underclass'. But nineteenth-century Europe allowed itself an astonishing possibility which twenty-first-century Asia could not, and that was the 'New World'. North America in particular, but also Brazil, Argentina and Australia, were essential to European industrialisation, acting as a safety valve for the great number of people that it rendered homeless and unemployed. Some 70 million people left Europe for the 'New World' between the Napoleonic Wars and the Second World War, which is to say one-third of the European population at the start of that period – and this is in addition to the fact that some 130 million Europeans also died in the two world wars. (In the same period, of course, many tens of millions of the 'New World's' native inhabitants were wiped out by a combination of war and disease.)

The situation was different in the twenty-first century. A third of India's population was close to 400 million people, and there was quite obviously no place on the planet where such a surplus could be stowed. How they would be integrated into a fast-changing society in a way that did not involve genocide or more world wars was still an open question.

It should not be imagined that immense intelligence and resources were not devoted to the resolution of this question, nor that there were no debates, conflicts or breakthroughs. On the contrary. Early twenty-first century India was, in addition to everything else, a giant laboratory of social and economic experiments, in which every sector of society participated. Farmers displayed great ingenuity in developing – sometimes with the help of the government or of the countless NGOs at work in the Indian countryside – new economic and agricultural strategies to reduce the precariousness of their situation so they might not join the mass exodus from the land. Factory workers became conspicuously more creative and organised in the way they contested the progressive erosion of their rights: by the end of the first decade of the twenty-first century, Gurgaon car manufacturers could no longer depend on workers fighting, ineffectually, all against all, and found themselves having to sit down to serious negotiations. The government too, despite its reputation for incompetence and corruption, was capable of visionary innovation. These years saw the introduction of the first-ever financial safety net for rural communities, which offered adults 100 days of guaranteed employment every year at a salary of Rs 100 per day – a vital measure for communities so assailed by financial unpredictability. This was the time also of the groundbreaking Right to Information Act, a transparency law which dramatically empowered poor communities, whose fate was so heavily decided, as we have seen, by the machinations of government: armed with this act they could now find out when they were being lied to, or by how much the money that reached them was less than what had been paid out.

And even the wealthy were furiously divided over what should be the style and human cost of India's economic transformation. Television scenes of farmers protesting against the seizure of fertile agricultural land and its conversion into factories, and of bloody showdowns between them and armed representatives of the state, caused people of all kinds to meditate on their relationship to this 'new India' – and some of those members of the urban, affluent classes who were most dismayed by these meditations worked to mitigate the harsh fall-out of change. NGOs, some of them with brilliantly creative visions of what modern life could be and how its benefits could be better distributed, sent educated people into the remotest corners of the country. Some of these were funded by foreign governments and foundations, which also pumped in billions of dollars of developmental aid over this period. The press remained, for the most part, free, and the media could be powerfully illuminating and acerbic with respect to contemporary society's inequities.

The first decade of the century also saw gathering waves of urban protest against its corruption and cruelty. It was increasingly common to see the city taken over by gatherings of a hundred thousand or more united in outrage towards society's ills or the machinations of its rulers. Though some of this discontent could be accommodated within the prevailing rubric of self-interest – middle-class resentment towards the fortunes made by corrupt politicians could be seen in this way, for instance – it was clear from the grief and euphoria on display at such gatherings that there was more than this at stake. There were other, humbler ambitions at play: the desire to live in a more tender society; the desire for a loftier idea of human relations, for something other, indeed, than self-interest; the desire for a respite from the world's conspicuous cruelty. Cruel societies are often the most dynamic and productive – nineteenth-century Europe was one of the most creative societies ever to exist – but even if you are one of those borne up on this dynamism, cruelty is less easy to live with than one imagines. Only the most hardened warriors are able to assume total ownership of their cruelty, and indeed of the mercilessness of capitalism. Middle-class Indians did not actually *want* to be responsible for cruelty any more than middle-class Canadians or Swedes did. It is part of the ideology of our 'neoliberal' moment that only self-aggrandising drives are 'natural' to human beings, but in fact sympathy for others is more difficult to defeat than we imagine.

It was remarkable, in Delhi, for example, how many women

from the richest families, women who treated their inferiors with deliberate fear and contempt, devoted their spare time to caring for stray dogs: taking out food and blankets for them, taking them to the vet when they were injured, taking them into their homes when they were sick. You couldn't help feeling, watching such women, that human beings were endowed with a specific quantum of sympathy, and if its expression were entirely blocked in one direction, it had to emerge from another.

But the question of what would happen to the great mass of India's economic refugees was impossibly taxing, and good feelings were not enough to solve it. It was a question, in fact, which undid the entire logic of India's new economy – and indeed of global capitalism itself. And yet it seemed impossible to imagine that there could be another way of organising things, for everything was now aligned in that way. So the only 'solution' to the question, ultimately, was to ignore it. And that, pretty much, was what middle-class India did. The hundreds of millions of their country's poor were dazzlingly absent from their world, not only as a matter of individual obliviousness but as a matter of policy. Delhi's official urban strategy was to not *see* those millions of people, to treat them as ghosts who periodically contributed their labour to the feast, but who did not themselves require food or shelter or anything else.

Worker housing – that simple acknowledgement that workers had a bodily existence – did not exist. Faridabad, the industrial city set up in 1947, had no worker housing, for instance: workers were expected to find or build a place wherever they could. This became the norm for all of the Delhi region's 'planned' cities – Okhla, Noida, Gurgaon – which had immense labour requirements but conspicuously – obstinately – no place for workers to live. It was as if labour were an immaterial force, one that magically operated machines and built houses, but one that had no physical existence, or needs, outside of these activities. Large numbers of workers bounced between Delhi and their villages: men, especially, left their families behind in the countryside and came for a few months to earn what cash they could working on a construction site or driving an auto-rickshaw, and they sought to spend as little as possible on accommodation or anything else. They rented basement rooms fifteen at a time, they lived in tents on construction sites, they slept in rickshaws or on the pavement. But this still left great numbers whose work kept them all year in the city and who had to find some way of subsisting in it. This is why the other great boom in Delhi, apart from its property prices, was that of informal living. In the late 1970s, it was estimated that Delhi's total slum population was 20,000. By the early twenty-first century, many millions – perhaps one half of the city's population – lived in some kind of unauthorised housing – slums, squatter settlements, lean-tos and the like – while many tens of thousands lived without any shelter at all.[34]

The places where the poor collected were constantly under attack by the authorities, who wanted to ensure at all costs that they never began to imagine some real claim on city space. After a devastating series of slum demolitions spearheaded in the 1970s by Nehru's grandson, Sanjay Gandhi, many of Delhi's working poor bought plots in new slum areas in order to secure their situation in a city that suddenly seemed much more inhospitable. Slums had a thriving real-estate market of purchases and rentals, much like the rest of the city in fact, with the exception that the entire enterprise was unauthorised: the land belonged, theoretically, to the government, which could dismantle the whole system at will and so deprive people of a lifetime of investment. And as we have seen, the turn of the twenty-first century was the time when the government called in all these dues. There was a new spate of slum demolitions, so that even those of Delhi's working classes who had come to the city in the 1970s and '80s often found themselves suddenly homeless. At a time when a hundred thousand or more poor migrants were washing up every year in Delhi from a rural situation that had become so desperate that they could no longer survive there, the total space where poor people could make a semi-permanent home in Delhi was systematically decreased. The 'surplus' piled up in the millions: people who could not go back and could not stay.

Some of those slum demolitions were by official order, in accordance with the Land Acquisition Act and under the banner of the 2010 Commonwealth Games; some of them were carried out after a series of suspiciously convenient fires destroyed the slums and scattered their residents. A number of these slums had been established soon after the demolitions of the 1970s, and by now they each housed 100,000 people who had, during that time, built themselves brick houses, water and sewage systems, schools, temples and mosques. They were vibrant townships that were an essential resource for the city as a whole, since they housed so many of its factory workers, domestic servants, security guards and the like. When bulldozers were sent in to these places, it brought to mind nothing so much as a devastating military assault. Grown men and women sat on the mountains of bricks, weeping at the destruction of what they had often built with their own hands; some of them argued with the police and bureaucrats who had come to superintend the process. Children roved what had once been streets, wide-eyed at the miracle of the razed houses and schools. Many of them had already been set to work gathering undamaged bricks for new builders to use: they piled them in great walls at the edge of the site and were paid 2 rupees for every hundred bricks. On the main road, Biblical lines of refugees set off with pots and pans and bundles of clothes, looking for a place to settle.

Those who could prove that they had lived in these places for many years were given land in compensation, though the process was tortuous. Since there was only a limited number of these plots the government was forced to inflate the requirements whenever they found out that too many people qualified. "We said you have to be able to prove that you have been living here since 2000. Well, now you have to prove you have been here since 1998 . . . " And when one visited the new areas – like Bhalswa – one was incredulous at the condition of the land and the distance from jobs. But most did not get any place to live at all. Some went back to villages to see what remained for them there. Some joined the human detritus living in underpasses around Connaught Place, blasted out of their minds, shivering under tattered blankets. Some joined the armies living under blue and yellow tarpaulin around factories and building sites.

In these latter places the punishment would go further. It was not enough to deny workers physical space. They should be given nothing, in fact, to suggest they were anything other than entirely dispensable units broken off from the infinity of India's masses. Often not even shoes or gloves, which might have given the mistaken impression that their bodily well-being was significant, were provided to the construction workers who built Delhi's much-vaunted real estate. Construction workers were regularly injured and even killed because they had no helmets or harnesses and only the most rudimentary information about what they were doing. During the 'beautification' of the city prior to the Commonwealth Games, one could see men, women and children painting kerbs and fences with their bare hands, their arms stained with paint up to their elbows. It was as if the whole thing were a cold joke played on the underclass, reminding them constantly that their existence, outside the pure fact of their labour, was nothing and would never be acknowledged. Building contractors, many of whom made enormous fortunes during the boom, did absolutely everything to shave bits off their workers' salaries. Not only did they not pay minimum wages – let alone the mandated social security payments – but they charged workers rent to erect tents on the building site and they deducted money for the boots and gloves they handed out. It was so emphatically petty that it felt that money was not even remotely the issue. It seemed to be not so much a financial strategy as a class lesson: people like you have no claims to comfort and safety, you are not people like us, you are on the outside of this story and you may never come in.

This strategy – of choosing not to think about the enormous

reservoir of human suffering off which the Indian boom fed – was mostly successful. Wealthy Indians did not spend too much time thinking about the plight of poor Indian workers, anymore than wealthy Americans or Australians did, for the level of remoteness was the same. But there were moments when the feeding frenzy came back to them in unexpected ways.

The suburb of Noida was conceived during the slum demolitions of the 1970s as a modern extension to the capital that would be able to absorb its population growth and industrial expansion. It lay just across the Yamuna river in the state of Uttar Pradesh, whose chief ministers gradually acquired land for the project and laid out the kind of grid-like structure suited to a rationally planned new town. By the late 1990s, Noida was a fully realised city, bustling with the new middle classes and their flats, offices and shopping malls.

In 2005, migrant labourers living in a slum area of Noida called Nithari began reporting to the police that their children were going missing. The police did not file these reports: these were poor people with no influence, tens or hundreds of thousands of such children were missing across the country and no one was going to spend time trying to track down these ones. Among the Nithari community, however, there were suspicions that some methodical predator was at large, and these suspicions began to close in on a house inhabited by a businessman and his domestic servant. Behind this house was a large drainage ditch, and some were convinced that the remains of the missing children had been dumped there.

In December 2006, two men who had failed to interest the police in the story of their missing daughters approached the head of the local residents' association, who agreed to accompany them on an inspection of the ditch. As they began clearing out accumulated trash, they found a severed hand and called the police. Over the following days, the police retrieved from the drain evidence of a series of terrible murders: the complete and partial remains of four women, eleven girls and four boys, packed up, mostly, in some forty plastic bags. In the house were found surgical knives and gloves, blood-stained clothes and the school bags of several children. The businessman and his servant were both immediately arrested.

As it happened, a different lead had already led the police to start asking questions of the fifty-two-year-old businessman who lived in the house, Moninder Singh Pandher. Pandher was from a well-connected family in Punjab: he had attended Delhi's prestigious St Stephen's College and counted many members of the north Indian elite among his friends. Most people who knew him had only good things to say: he was life-loving and 'normal', they said – though his family relations were strained. He was separated from his wife and was entangled in a bitter land dispute with his brother which involved half-a-dozen separate legal cases; the brother's family, fearful of Pandher's political influence, had filed complaints to the police about possible abuses of justice that they suspected Pandher might commit.

Pandher lived as a bachelor in Noida, where his house was the venue for various politicians, bureaucrats and policemen to retire for late-night drinking sessions. In addition to this, he frequently invited call girls to his house for what journalists later called 'orgies'. A woman named Payal had not been seen since one of these assignations. Her concerned father, who received a fee for her services directly from a local madam, and knew about her movements, had alerted the police to Pandher's possible role in her disappearance. The police had seen that Pandher had spoken to Payal several times a day right up to her disappearance and had questioned him about her on three occasions over the previous six months, even, most recently, searching his house. Later, there was suspicion as to how Pandher had made this investigation go away: was it because the police were themselves involved in – beneficiaries of, even – his patronage of local prostitutes?

As DNA tests linked the recovered human remains to missing Nithari children, residents from the area gathered in large numbers outside Pandher's house. Parents carried photographs of their dead children. The crowds shouted abuse at the police and bombarded Pandher's residence with flower pots and bricks, breaking doors and windows. The police realised this was a situation of the greatest sensitivity and they quickly attempted to make up for their past omissions: various policemen were suspended for their failures to respond to complaints, and the drainage ditch was dug up in accordance with the demands of the Nithari residents.

The investigation was handed over by Uttar Pradesh officials to the Central Bureau of Investigation, which followed leads across state lines. They searched Pandher's properties in Ludhiana and Chandigarh, and re-opened the investigation of a series of child kidnappings in the latter place, which was Pandher's home-town. Pandher's well-documented patronage of prostitutes made it seem to some that he might be capable of any kind of perversion, and there was speculation that the mutilated bodies might be the leftovers of a pornography operation of a particularly horrifying kind. Police announcements that they had recovered photographs showing Pandher surrounded by naked children fuelled this speculation. But the children in the – perfectly innocent – photographs were revealed to be Pandher's grand-children, and this line of enquiry led nowhere.

But the sheer number of corpses led to the widespread suspicion that this affair centred not on the spasms of perverted desire but on some altogether more systematic, even industrial, enter-prise. For many it was evident from the beginning that the remains in the drain were the detritus of a large-scale organ-stealing enterprise. It was discovered that one of Pandher's neigh-bours was a doctor who had been accused – though never convicted – of such a trade some years before, and Nithari villagers, for whom organ stealing was a convincing explanation for what had happened, surrounded this second house and pelted it with stones.

Organ stealing was in the air at that time: a year after the Nithari discoveries, and while the trials were still going on, a multimillion-dollar kidney-stealing scheme was uncovered in Gurgaon. Poor migrants from Uttar Pradesh were lured to a private house on the pretext that they would be offered work; when they arrived they were offered money, reportedly Rs 30,000 [$600], for their kidneys. Those who refused were drugged and their kidneys were forcibly removed. These kidneys were then transplanted into wealthy patients from all over the world for a fee of some $50,000. It was later estimated that the racket had been going on for six years, during which time some six hundred transplants had been conducted. The doctor in charge, Amit Kumar, owned a large house on the outskirts of Toronto, where his family pursued the global bourgeois dream: SUV, swimming pool, children at private school. In 2008 he was arrested in Nepal, where he had gone into hiding.

When this latter case hit the Indian newspapers, the residents of Nithari became convinced that there was a connection with their own tragedies. They declared that they had seen Amit Kumar visiting Moninder Singh Pandher on several occasions; they also said that they had seen ambulances parked outside the latter's house and nurses emerging from inside. It was observed that many body parts were missing from the remains found in the ditch. As one father said, commenting on the remains of his eight-year-old daughter, "They found only the hands, legs and skull of my daughter. What happened to the torso?"[35]

The police quickly abandoned the idea that this was an organ-stealing operation. They found enough intact organs to make it unlikely, and they did not feel that the risk and inefficiency of such an operation fitted with Pandher's highly successful business in heavy machinery. But suspicions of organ-stealing persisted for a long time. It was a story that fitted many people's picture of the society in which they lived: a rich man with brutal indifference to the personhood of the poor steals their organs to give to people of his own class and to enrich himself. Indian journalists and their readers alike were used to seeking out the financial motive, which they felt was the prime mover in most mysteries. They were often unconvinced by mystical explanations such as psychopathologies, which seemed to them excessively American. It was in this direction, however, that things began to move.

Both Pandher and his housekeeper and cook, Surender Koli, were interrogated under the influence of a 'truth serum'. Since these statements were not admissible as evidence, they were not made public. But it seems that both men implicated themselves in the murders, and both were charged. The media engaged in endless speculation as to the nature of the relationship between the two men. How extraordinary, that two serial killers should find each other in this manner! A psychiatrist from Chennai commented, "In this case, it is probably coincidence, where an ordinary employer–employee relationship developed into a mutually beneficial one. The affluent one with the power and confidence to blatantly express himself, and the other, also with poor scruples and a dark side to match his master's, and who got the chance to find a dangerous outlet."[36] Stories went like this: Koli was given the responsibility of fulfilling Pandher's insatiable need for sex with poor and powerless women and girls. He went out to look for anyone he could find and brought them home. After Pandher had finished with them, Koli raped them and then killed them. Sometimes Koli brought boys by mistake, and they simply killed them.

A psychological profile compiled by the Directorate of Forensic Sciences described them as "emotionally deprived and sexually deviated men, separated from their wives and family, living in a single house and trying to cope on their own in their different ways, without feeling concerned for, or bothered about each other".[37]

In February 2009, Pandher and Koli were found guilty of the

murder of a fourteen-year-old girl named Rimpa Haldar and both were sentenced to death. Koli was subsequently found guilty of other murders, and awarded further death penalties.

But doubt was growing as to the contribution of the employer, who had at first been assumed to be the evil ring-leader of this bleak circus. Though as the Supreme Court judgement later put it, house number D-5, Sector 31 " . . . became a virtual slaughter house, where innocent children were regularly butchered,"[38] and though it was therefore impossible to believe that Pandher was ignorant of what was going on, despite the fact that he had been able to provide evidence that he was out of the country at the time of some of the killings, Koli's confessions had been so lurid as to remove all need for a second man's involvement.

In his statement, which he made voluntarily in court because he needed, he said, to "lighten himself", Koli described how he used to lure children, usually girls, into the house by promising them work or sweets. (Two girls from the community testified that he had attempted to lure them into the house, but they had refused to go with him.) Once they were inside the house he would strangle them. He would often attempt to copulate with the dead bodies, but by his own admission he failed to do so. He would then cut up the bodies, sometimes taking organs from them, cooking them and eating them. The first time he tried the liver of one of his victims, a young girl, he said, he vomited; but he continued to make meals of his victims. The remains he put in plastic bags and dumped in the drain outside.

In this statement he offered to take the police to places where they could recover more knives, personal effects and body parts; he later did so, and his leads turned out to be authentic.

Koli came from a small town in the Himalayan state of Uttarakhand where his wife – eight months pregnant at the time of the revelations – and young daughter remained while Koli worked as Pandher's housekeeper and servant. During Pandher's absences he had the house to himself; while Pandher was there he was frequently witness to debauched gatherings and, of course, the comings and goings of prostitutes. He cooked meals for Pandher's guests and knew exactly what was happening in the house. Sometimes, he said, Pandher spent the night with two or three girls in his bed. He claimed that all this used to build up in him an intense pressure of arousal and desire. As he said in his confession, "once Pandher's wife moved away to Chandigarh, Pandher started bringing call girls to the house daily. I would cook for the girls, and serve them. I would see them and crave sex. Later, bad thoughts entered my mind: to kill them and eat them." Mostly it was not these girls but others whom Koli killed: with Payal, however, Koli satisfied his urge to kill and "consume" one of Pandher's own sexual partners.

During one period of six months when the presence of a house guest made it impossible for Pandher to entertain prostitutes at home, Koli said that peace returned to him and he felt no impulse to kill.

Koli also told the police that he would often dream of a girl in a flowing white dress who laughed at him and taunted him. Each time he dreamt about her, he would tremble, lose his appetite and be unable to sleep until he found a victim, and relief.

Despite all this, when Pandher was acquitted of murder by the High Court in Allahabad at the end of 2009, there was widespread scepticism. One magazine pronounced, "despite the manner in which the Noida police bungled the case, there is little doubt that Pandher is as guilty as the man who actually carried out the serial killings, his accomplice Koli."[39] Journalists had their own class prejudices, according to which the poor had no vision of their own and could only obey the orders of their superiors, and Pandher's leadership was necessary to this conception. That the servant would end up taking the punishment for both of them was consistent with a widely accepted idea of Indian society, according to which the elite always managed to export the blame to a scapegoat when things went wrong.

Pandher's much-documented connections to the political and commercial elite of Punjab and Delhi, as well as the frequent presence at his parties of senior policemen, made it easy for many to imagine how he would have engineered his own acquittal.

Surender Koli's guilt is established beyond reasonable doubt. If Moninder Singh Pandher had an active role in these deaths, it has yet to be proved. But perhaps he had nothing to do with them. Perhaps the truth is just what it appeared to be. Perhaps Pandher was so inattentive to the lives of his subordinates that he really did not notice anything amiss, even as the domestic servant with whom he lived enticed at least seventeen young people from the surrounding streets into his home, murdered them, cut them up and disposed of the body parts behind the house.

But perhaps there is still hidden meaning in the story. Perhaps it is an allegory, and perhaps it is more terrible than anyone even thought.

Moninder Singh Pandher ran a JCB dealership in Noida. He supplied the kind of earth-moving equipment so much in demand in the Delhi region at that time – the equipment with which Delhi's slums were destroyed and the ground was prepared for the new landscape of elite housing and shopping. From this dealership he allegedly made some 30 lakhs [$60,000] a month. With this money he enjoyed raucous evenings with his club of influential men, the sexual services of as many poor women as he liked and, of course, the labour of Koli himself.

What erupted in Koli in reaction to all this was not some democratic sentiment whereby the privileges of the rich would be abolished. Quite the reverse: Koli wanted exactly what Pandher had, which was the power to consume the poor. And if he could not consume them with Pandher's abstract appetites, he would – literally – eat them.

Pandher's son, visiting his father during the months of Koli's crimes, observed a change in his father's servant. "When we hired

Surendra, he was docile and obedient. But there was something amiss about his behaviour lately. When I went to Noida in November, I found him cocky and rude, which was not what I had known him to be. Most of the times I found him talking on his mobile on the roof. I had told my mother about his cocky behaviour."[40] Perhaps Koli had ingested something of the spirit of the speaker's own class. Perhaps he wanted to be as cocky as the tiny percentage of crowing, wealthy, endlessly consuming elites with whom he had some acquaintance. Perhaps he wanted to emulate the appetites which defined those elites, and placed them so securely above everyone else.

I meet with a psychologist who was involved in counselling the parents of the Nithari victims.

"How could a place like that exist?" he says. "A lot of police officers were going there for parties. It channelled the worst aspects of the collusion between police and corrupt business. There were orgies and call girls, but no one was questioned when people started going missing. Such people have complete impunity. Businessmen like that pay off the police and arrange girls for them as part of their normal business operations.

"What kind of culture have such people created for us? They have treated everyone as abject, and people have therefore become abject.

"I was conducting a grief session for the parents of Nithari victims. Someone came into the room and announced that a politician had arrived outside. Everyone ran out of the room except one parent because rumours of compensation money were circulating. These rumours were untrue and after a while people began to file back in again. A discussion began in the room about the 5-lakh [$10,000] sums that had been rumoured. And parents said, 'If we had known there would be 5 lakhs for a dead child, we would have sent two children.'

"And I sat there and I thought, why have I bothered to come? Why am I here?

"You think that there are certain primordial events that eclipse all others. You think, for instance, that no suffering can be so great as that of a parent who has lost a child. But there are things that are even worse, forms of suffering so great that they harden people even to the death of their children. And you can see them everywhere in this country."

Miniature

Mangoes are surely the most literary fruit. Countless tales have been told, in this part of the world, about their magical power; many more concern the wily stratagems by which loveable thieves – or children, or monkeys – successfully purloin mangoes from the trees of miserly owners. The mango has a prominent place, too, in literature that touches on sexual desire, for though its pubescent lobe does not properly resemble any part of the human anatomy, male or female, it still manages to incite mysteriously erotic thoughts.

When, in the blinding heat of Delhi's May, mangoes begin to pile up on vendors carts, it is easy to feel they have fallen out of a fairytale. Imagine: it is forty-five Celsius in the afternoon, and even the sky is seared white. The wind blows in from the bitter plains like the blast from a clay oven, and no moisture can survive. Laundry hung outside has the water sucked out of it in five minutes by the parched air, which sucks at bodies too, drying out eyes and tongues, dehydrating the very innards.

Amid such universal desiccation, the unabashed, chin-dripping wetness of the many species of mango that suddenly pour into the city is a miracle. That merciless nature should supply such consolation for its own ravages, that it should display simultaneously such brute impact and such subtle deliquescence, is literary already. Like rags that turn to riches, or fools who outwit kings, mangoes attract stories because they overturn the general logic of the world.

Cut up into small cubes whose sunshine orange is their concession to the season, it is mangoes that appear on the table now. My friend Gautam and I take a bowl each and eat with relief. The fruits have come out of the fridge, and they restore our systems to some kind of balance after the climatic emergency from which we have just come in.

We sit in semi-darkness, for all the blinds are closed against the angry glare outside. A quiet glow emanates from the corner of the room, where a glass box containing a plastic model of the Taj Mahal fluoresces in alternating colours. The fan churns like the rotors of a helicopter.

Gautam and I have stopped here to pick up one of his friends, Ranjit. But he is not back from work; we sit in the front room and chat to his father, Baljeet, while his mother brings more snacks from the kitchen. We sit on sofas covered with white sheets. Ranjit's mother flicks on a fluorescent light in honour of our arrival, which bathes the room in green.

Baljeet is rotund, and gives his weight entirely to the support of a worn armchair. He wants to tell us about his latest scheme, in which there have been some encouraging recent developments. He takes out a scruffy bit of paper from the pocket of his white kurta and hands it to me, chuckling conspiratorially. It is a receipt for 2,000 rupees, and it is dated April 1980.

"This is a receipt from a DDA lottery."

The Delhi Development Authority was set up by Nehru's government as a consolidation of the capital's various planning and development agencies. It had sole responsibility for the city's development and, in order to fulfil this, it had the right to acquire land forcibly and at greatly reduced prices. It was a development monopoly, whose exclusivity was guaranteed by laws making it impossible for private individuals or companies to own more than a few acres of land within the Delhi borders. At various points, however, it released plots of land to individuals through lotteries. Entrants paid a non-refundable fee to enter the lottery and waited, sometimes years, to hear if they had been selected for a plot. If so, they could then buy it at a guaranteed rate.

"This lady entered a lottery in 1980 and she still hasn't heard anything. But this year she is likely to get a plot. I mean, she *will* get a plot. She doesn't know she'll get it of course. But I know because I have contacts in the DDA. So I am trying to buy her receipt from her. After thirty years she won't care about it anymore: she'll be happy to give it up. In fact she has already said she wants to sell. So the plot will be allotted to me. It should be worth about 15 lakhs [$30,000]."

He clasps the arms of his armchair as if it were a throne, and sits up, inspecting my face for signs of approbation.

"You have to know people in the DDA for this kind of business. DDA officials are transferred every two to three years to prevent corruption, so you have to keep building those relationships: take them out, take them gifts.

"When the plot is finally allotted to me, I'll pay all my contacts. Twenty thousand [$400] here, twenty thousand there."

In Baljeet's universe, this is what business is. Business is a lottery run by cheats, and anyone who gets involved had better be prepared for the consequences. This time you might be lucky enough to outwit others. Next time round, it will probably be different.

"I've made crores and I've lost crores. I've probably lost 60 lakhs [$120,000] in scams. One person sold me a property that didn't exist. I paid 40 lakhs [$80,000] for it. Most of that was cash: the paper value of the property was only 6 lakhs [$12,000]. So 34 lakhs [$68,000] just disappeared, but I filed a legal case for the other 6 lakhs. The DDA came back and told me I had no case. Some guy in the DDA was playing with two people over one property, and accepting money from both."

Baljeet retired some time ago from a long career with the

Bank of Maharashtra. Since this was one of the banks nation-alised during the prime ministership of Nehru's daughter, Indira Gandhi, Baljeet was effectively an employee of the Indian govern-ment. Much of his career was devoted to delivering on Mrs Gandhi's populist promises for the state-run banks: he worked in some of the remotest parts of the country to set up branches which were, in many cases, the first contact those regions had with formal banking services. In 1976, while still working for the bank, Baljeet began to speculate in property. This is what occupies his time, and especially his thoughts, now.

"Another time I bought a shop in the market near here. I started running the shop and it was going well. But what I didn't know – which the person who sold it to me did – was that it was soon going to be demolished. A powerful real estate developer wanted to build there. He had political support. And since my shop was an illegal construction – it wasn't within the approved limits of the market – it didn't officially exist and I could get no compensation for it. So I lost 23 lakhs [$46,000] there."

There is a gloomy silence.

Gautam says philosophically, "But you have done okay. You still have two houses. You've provided houses for both your sons."

Baljeet grunts lugubriously in response. He begins to describe another deal he lost out on.

"In 1976, when Sanjay Gandhi was trying to clean up Delhi, he shut down all the dairies within the city. The DDA appropri-ated land from villages on the outskirts and gave it to dairy farmers in compensation. But some of those areas are no longer on the outskirts at all: they've become very fancy since. So now the owners of those dairies are trying to get approvals to build on their land.

"The standard way to acquire a large amount of land," he says, "is to buy it at a highly subsidised rate for some public purpose – a school, a temple, some sports facilities – and then pay an official to get the land-use changed. But it's a gamble, because changing the land-use may not happen, and then you're stuck with a temple.

"Three or four years ago some people were trying to sell off their dairy at a greatly inflated cost because, they said, at some point the land-use could be altered and it could be developed as real estate. They had already divided the dairy into plots, which they were selling for 12 lakhs [$24,000] each."

Gautam says, "All of us were saying to him, '*Don't do it! Don't do it! That's not a good investment to be in.*' But then they did manage to change the land use!"

"Now they're selling houses on those plots for 7 crores [$1.4 million]," says Baljeet.

He laughs wryly.

"If you made money on every deal, everybody would be doing this business. It's high-risk. Every time you invest, you have to assume your money is gone. You have to say to yourself, 'It's gone.' And then it might come back four-fold."

He erupts into a coughing fit. He is not a healthy man.

"He always used to have a drink in his hand," says Gautam. "He was drinking every evening and smoking two or three packets of cigarettes a day. Then last year he developed severe lung problems and had to go to hospital. He almost died. Now he's given up."

Baljeet grins sheepishly and makes a gesture of resignation. He shifts the conversation back to business. He offers us the benefit of his experience: how to distinguish good deals from bad. How to carry around large amounts of cash.

"I never travel the same route twice. I vary my route every time. And I don't bring cash into the house. I keep it in a brief-case in the car. People never imagine that anyone would be so mad as to leave 30 lakhs [$60,000] in their car."

While we are talking, Baljeet's other son, Jimmy, drops in. He's been out walking his dog: he lives just around the corner, in the other family house. He wears stone-washed jeans and sunglasses, and he is sweating. His mother brings him a glass of water which he downs in one go and sets back on the tray she holds patiently in front of him. There is a great weight of gold on him: gold necklaces, gold bangles, gold watch. He is in the property business too. He starts telling Gautam about a new apartment complex that's just being built and that he thinks will do very well.

Baljeet cuffs the air in order to dismiss the opinions his son has hung there. He says to me, "He is not an expert like his father. He is way behind me."

As if in response, Jimmy begins to vaunt his foreign travel. His father has never left India and this is an area where Jimmy can one-up him. Jimmy travels to Dubai and Bangkok as often as he can. He talks about the stuff you can buy in Dubai. The gold markets.

"Do you take your wife with you when you go?" I ask.

"I've taken my wife to Dubai. For shopping. Not to Bangkok. Who takes their wife to Bangkok?"

There are dirty laughs.

"Anyway I don't let her drink," adds Jimmy. "So there wouldn't be any point."

He starts talking about online poker, which is his latest obsession. He looks at the floor as he speaks. He is a braggart, but a peculiarly edgy one. He is divided within himself, and one part of him clamps down on the other.

"Jimmy refuses to go to Europe," says Gautam, "because he's not confident of his English. I tell him there are lots of places in Europe where they don't speak English, but it doesn't change anything. As far as he's concerned, white people speak English."

Baljeet's wife brings out tea and pakoras. There is quiet in the room, for father and son have managed to silence each other. They are happy to listen to Gautam, who is a supremely relaxed conversationalist. He has recently bought a new car, and everyone enjoys stories of new cars.

"This guy who got it for me, he got my first car too. At that point I had a motorbike but it was giving me terrible back problems. I just happened to mention this to him and he said, 'Get a car!' He said if I had 75,000 rupees [$1,500], he could organise financing for the rest. I said, 'Let me think about it.'

"The next day he called me. 'Do you want to go ahead?' I said, 'Okay.' So he said, 'So what car do you want? What colour?' And so on. Then he called the garage. Five minutes later he called me back and said, 'The car will be outside your house in 45 minutes.' We hadn't exchanged a single piece of paperwork and a few minutes later a brand new car turned up in front of my house.

"So when I wanted to buy this car, I called him again. It cost 6 lakhs [$12,000]. I gave him a cheque for a lakh [$2,000], and he gave me the car. 'I'll take care of the rest,' he said. Once again, we didn't sign any paper. As soon as I got the car I drove it up into the mountains. While I was there this friend called me to say my cheque had bounced. I felt bad: it looked as if I had just given him a bad cheque, taken the car and run away. But he wasn't bothered in the least. 'Don't worry,' he kept saying on the phone. Like *he* was reassuring *me*."

Ranjit has shown up during this story. He apologises for being late. He quickly downs a cup of his mother's tea.

"Let's go," he says.

We say goodbye to the parents. Jimmy follows us out of the apartment so he can check up on his dog, which is tied up downstairs. It's a young mastiff, large and full of energy; it goes nearly hysterical when it seems us coming down the stairwell. We venture out under the gong of the sky. Jimmy lets the dog off the leash and even in this enervating heat it bounds majestically into the distance. We are in Shalimar Bagh, in the northern outskirts of Delhi, on the site of the long-forgotten gardens built by the emperor Shah Jahan; space is generous here – as it was in Bhalswa, which, though it is a separate universe, is only a twenty-minute walk away. In front of the apartment block, a great area of empty land slopes away to a surprisingly sparkling canal, which is itself a relic of the Mughal water system. The buildings are run down, but there is a sense of ease about things: the cars are parked indolently, and trees grow where they want.

As we walk, Jimmy asks me if I know anyone who might be interested in buying apartments. He gives lists of features: Italian marble floors, modular kitchens. He asks for my email address so he can send me the floor plans. We reach Gautam's car, which is so new that the seats are still covered in plastic. We get in, and I spell out my email address through the open door. As soon as I shut it, the air conditioning starts up with a *whoosh*, cool on our perspiration. We drive away, the sun descending over the canal, the mastiff racing optimistically after us.

"Jimmy's amazing," says Gautam. "He doesn't miss an opportunity. That guy does business with everyone. You want to borrow 5 lakhs [$10,000]? He'll get it for you that day. You want 20,000 tampons, he'll deliver them straight to your shop. He can forge any document you want. Anything you want to do in Shalimar Bagh he can hook you up. Who to talk to, how much to pay."

Ranjit is on the phone as we drive. He runs a small travel agency, and he is trying to sort out the crisis of a client who has been denied a visa to Canada. "This guy," says Ranjit between calls, "pays 70 lakhs [$140,000] income tax a year. He's a businessman with a wife and two children. But his travel history is weak. That's the problem."

The evening is only just beginning: we still have to pick up another of Gautam's friends from his shop in Sadar Bazaar, a large wholesale market near the railway station. The roads around there are packed with activity, and before long we have ground to a halt in the commercial mêlée. The driver in front of us takes advantage of the stasis to open his door and spit a red stream of paan onto the street. Cycle rickshaws manoeuvre around us, piled with chemicals in drums and stacks of printed packing boxes. I watch a group of women sitting on the sidewalk making brooms. Further down, mechanics are putting the finishing touches to a stretched "Hummer" limo. They have welded this thing together entirely from the parts of a Jeep. But it looks a lot like a Hummer and they have put a Hummer sign on the front. Now they are spray-painting it gold.

We inch forward. A cycle rickshaw is hemmed in next to us, the driver a bright-faced adolescent, dripping with sweat, who shrieks out loudly in a perfect imitation of a car horn. He wears a T-shirt which bears the words, "I can cure your virginity." We draw level with a textiles workshop whose owner sits on a bench outside gluing together paper bags which have been cut out of newspaper. I can see why he is not inside: he has divided the normal-height room into two levels so that he can fit in double the number of tailors at their machines. But it's impossible to stand upright in there.

Makeshift accommodation has been built on the roofs of these workshops, to which people climb up by ladder. Workers' underwear flutters overhead like so many grey flags. In every room you can see a great number of water vessels: gathering and storing water is the great enterprise hereabouts. The water pump by the side of the road is in constant operation. People flock to it with buckets, bottles, plastic drums. Next to it is a vast and luxurious peepul tree around whose trunk statues of Shiva and Durga have been propped up: a large woman sits there, her breasts exposed, babbling to herself.

We arrive at Pratap's metal shop. He is not there. We wait in the heat. The shop, whose front is open to the street, is not large enough to drive a small car into. Pratap's son, Amitabh, is perched on a huge stack of one-kilogramme nickel plates, talking on the phone. More plates are being unloaded in front of the shop: they clang loudly as they are put down, but this is incidental to the background din of car horns and auto-rickshaw engines. Amitabh must shout for his deals to go through.

Pratap buys metal in bulk and sells it to big consumers: manu-facturers of car components, bicycles, bathroom fittings, and the like. The whole business rests on the vagaries of metal prices, which are in constant flux. Amitabh's mobile phone is hung on the wall so he can watch the flickering prices on the London Metal Exchange throughout the day.

"It's very intense," says Amitabh, joining us. "You invest money in a quantity of metal and you have to make it back. But prices can fall at any time. Of course we read reports, we keep on top of everything that's going on in the metal markets. But it's basically unpredictable. And now we've started importing our own metal, in addition to what we buy from dealers. It takes a whole month for your metal to arrive, once you sign the deal. In that time anything can have happened to the price. And price is everything. If you are one rupee more expensive than the next guy, no one will buy from you.

"The mental pressure can be huge. Sometimes you make a crore [$200,000] in a few minutes, sometimes you lose it. Sometimes you have to sell property to cover losses. There are men in this business who drink a bottle of whisky every night to deal with the tension, and they take it out on their wives and kids. My dad was never like that. He never spoke about it at the end of the day, even when he'd lost a lot of money. He knows how to relax. He takes us for weekends in Hong Kong or Bangkok just so we can all chill out."

"How much does your business make?"

"We turn over about 100 crores [$20 million] a year."

"And it's just you and your dad?"

"And my cousin. My father brought his sister's son into the business too."

Pratap came to Delhi in 1980 from a small town in Uttar Pradesh. A friend of his from the same village had migrated some years before to Sadar Bazaar, where he found work as a broker with a successful metal trader dubbed the Metal King. The friend arranged for Pratap to apprentice with the same trader and, since brokers are entrusted with a lot of cash, he gave guarantees to his boss that he would pay for the losses should Pratap disappear. Pratap's monthly salary was 600 rupees (then $75).

"He worked hard and he learned. He had a dream. He saved his money: he used to walk three kilometres to work to save fifty paise (then $0.06). He wanted to eliminate the label 'broker'.

A broker is nothing. A broker gets ignored. Some of them earn a lot of money. But they are just middlemen, and if they come into the room, no one takes any notice. A businessman is something else. You give value to that person."

After fifteen years of learning and saving, Pratap struck out on his own. He bought his own stock and got himself this shop. He worked methodically, never risking too much, always knowing his limits.

"My father is happy with normal risk and normal profits. He doesn't like to lose too much sleep and take big risks. He says, 'Remember the Metal King!'"

A few years ago, the Metal King was ruined. He was over-exposed to nickel when the price of the metal crashed. He had debts of millions of dollars. He sold real estate to pay off his debts and then retired from the metal market. His sons had started a carpet manufacturing business, and he went to work with them.

"Just imagine. Twenty years you ruled that market, and then you lose everything. It's years now since he started working in carpets, but people still call him the Metal King."

We stand just outside the shop smoking cigarettes. Nearby, a man is frying samosas, which smell superb. A goat is chewing at a tuft of grass growing from the crack between the shop wall and the sidewalk: where its tail should be is a massive sagging tumour, which we discuss for a while. It holds a macabre fascination.

A big Toyota pulls up. Pratap's workers rush to move their bikes, which have been stacked in his parking space so that no one else occupy it. Pratap gets out of the car, a blazer slung over his shoulders like a cape. He has been exchanging news with other metal traders as he does every evening; any one of them who misses this session is at a disadvantage the next trading day. He stands for a moment, waving to us like a patriarch, and then ducks back inside the car to escape the heat. Gautam goes to get his car and pulls up outside the shop so Ranjit and I can get in.

"Are you coming?" I ask Amitabh.

"I'll stay and shut the shop," he says evasively. The suggestion that he should go drinking with his father is obviously out of place.

I get in the car and we set off behind Pratap.

"That Toyota he's driving?" says Gautam. "He had great difficulty buying it. He takes home 10 or 15 lakhs a day [$20,000–$30,000] but none of the money goes into the bank. He pays almost no taxes. There is no record of his money. So no one would give him a loan to buy his car. You can't buy a car with cash. Eventually he had to take a loan against his property just to buy a car."

It is dark now. Gautam plays old Hindi movie songs on his stereo.

"Don't think he's dishonest. It's quite the opposite. He has a very strict code of ethics and for him it is the state that is corrupt. He won't let himself be compromised by cheating policemen or tax officials. This unofficial economy – which is basically the entire economy round here – runs on a different moral system.

"But each year he pays more taxes," he continues. "Because it's getting difficult to function if you can't show taxable income. The government knows there are lots of people like Pratap who earn 100 crores [$20 million] and declare only 15 lakhs [$30,000] to the tax authorities. But they are moving gradually: for now all they want is to get them into the system so they know who they are. Ten years ago they were totally invisible. Now they all have tax identification numbers and they file returns. It's a big change."

Ranjit is on another call. He is trying to change the timing of a flight to Nairobi. A battered bus overtakes us, its flanks festooned with the vomit tracks of passengers rattling inside.

The traffic bunches around a wedding procession and for a moment we are jammed up against the wedding band. Thirty trumpets resound in unison to the beat of big drums hammered with simultaneous passion and boredom, and the street is full of leaping men in suits, their shoulders shuttering, horned fingers aloft. Aloft on his white horse, the bridegroom looks curiously lonely. On the dark street the procession is a glaring island: uniformed men carry bright lamps on their shoulders, the wires trailing from one to the next. At the rear, a man wheels a cart on which a juddering diesel generator grinds out the power for all this illumination.

On the other side of the glass from my nose is the bare midriff of a dancing man whose shirt is hoisted high by his thrusting arms. Around the waistband of his bouncing boxer shorts is printed a brand name with no vowels: MYYTPPPS.

Forcing our way through the streets we arrive, finally, at a proud restaurant crowned with red neon signs. Pratap's car pulls in ahead of us, and attendants, recognising him, jump to his assistance and ours. Both cars are whisked away by valets as we evacuate. We are in a red night glow. Above the entrance to the restaurant is an imposing statue of the god Hanuman. Behind his monkey head rises the moon, a quarter tonight. I think again, as I have so often, that no matter how many years I live in this place, I will never get used to that moon. I grew up with a moon propped up at a jaunty forty-five degrees. Here it lies on its back. The earth is round: we jut out from it at different angles to the sky.

We walk inside. Another statue of Hanuman greets us, garlanded with marigolds, but with this exception the restaurant has something of the feel of a strip club, with its parsimonious spot lighting and sweeping mirrored ceiling. The dining room itself is like a giant cavern, with tables stretching away – since the walls are black reflective glass – to apparent infinity. There are only men here: it is a businessman's haunt.

We sit around a large round table: more people are expected. I sit between Ranjit and Pratap. Waiters bend their ears to Pratap, who orders whiskies for everyone. I have already been told that this is his show. It's a tradition. He orders, he pays.

Ranjit is telling me about the first job he ever held.

"It was a lottery racket. Very sketchy. I worked for two brothers who had contacts inside the Nagaland state lottery. This was back in the 1990s. Every day they would pay 15 lakhs [then $50,000] to the lottery people to give them the last digit of the winning ticket before it was announced. Then they would buy up every single ticket ending with that number. We used to fan out all over India to get them. I used to cover Punjab and Haryana; I would take the 06.25 train to Jalandhar. When I arrived, I'd call my boss: 'Which number should I buy?' – '7' – and I'd go to the market and buy every ticket ending in seven. Then I'd get on another train, go to Amritsar and do the same. And the same for all the cities. The tickets cost 10 rupees, and every ticket with the correct last number won 70 rupees, so they made 60 rupees on every ticket I bought. Tickets that had two or three numbers correct won 50,000 or a lakh. The winning ticket won 10 lakhs. So after all their bribes, salaries and expenses, my bosses earned profits of around 20 lakhs per day [then about $70,000]. It was crazy. We worked in a vast office where there was constant free booze and people were on the phone the whole time. Eventually one of the brothers was killed in Nagaland when he went to hand over a suitcase of cash. A terrorist organisation demanded his money, he refused to hand it over, and they shot him. The whole operation shut down straight away. But imagine how much money they made over three years. The surviving brother runs restaurants all over Delhi."

"You should have seen Ranjit in those days," says Gautam. "He used to earn lots of money, he wore expensive clothes, he had a nice car. He always had a full tank of petrol: you could say to him, 'Let's drive to the Himalayas,' and we would just go. But he was very disturbed when that guy was shot."

A tray of whisky arrives. Ranjit is irritated that this dinner has been arranged on a Tuesday, which is one of his non-drinking days. Drinks are distributed to everyone else: now we are seven or eight at the table. Their first gulp after the working day is greedy. They praise Ranjit's abstention, however: "It is good to know you can do without it." They tell astonishing stories of alcoholic addiction, whose spectre looms large for all of them. This leads naturally to chat of heart disease, diabetes and renal failure.

Pratap contributes nothing to these conversations. "I lost 60 lakhs [$120,000] today," he says. "Can't you all stop chattering?"

But no one takes any notice. The music is too loud in here for people to hear each other across the table, so they talk to those around them. Ranjit continues his account.

"I decided to look for a real job. I had been earning good money but I knew there was no future in it. When you're doing something like that, you can't say to anyone, 'This is what I do.' So I began to think about learning a real trade."

"But you worked for that cable guy first." Gautam laughs. "Ranjit was a hired thug."

Ranjit is laughing too.

"That was when cable TV was just coming into Delhi. Every neighbourhood saw intense competition. I was employed by a cable operator to make sure no competitor came into his area. If they did, I would beat them up. I got into so many fights with that job. Once I was at a paan shop: a man came up and said, 'Why are you standing here?' and I said, 'Who are you to ask me why I'm standing here?' and three of us started beating him up. We only realised afterwards he was a policeman, and suddenly the police were all over the neighbourhood, beating people up to find out who had done it. We had to flee town."

Ranjit is a quiet man. It is difficult to imagine that his modest physique might be capable of such exploits.

"I had a friend who worked for a travel agency and he told me there were good prospects in travel. So I got a job with a travel agency. My salary was 1,300 rupees [then $42] a month. Before that, at the lottery, I used to earn 30,000 rupees [then $1,000] a month. But I wanted to learn something respectable. For the first six months I worked as an office assistant, serving water, making coffee, washing plates. Then I spent six months as the office runner, delivering tickets to customers. Then I worked in their courier business: I would accompany large loads to Bahrain, Abu Dhabi or Moscow. When I went to Bahrain I would leave on Saturday night with a thousand-rupee allowance and $50 for a Bahrain visa. But I didn't want to spend the $50 on the visa, so I would stay in the airport for two days until the return flight on Monday night. I would just sleep for two days.

"After that I began to manage travel for big corporate clients. Before that I didn't know how to talk to important people. I didn't even have a picture in my mind of what they looked like. These clients would spend 12 lakhs [then $30,000] on a trip, and I would have to monitor the entire schedule as they travelled. If a flight was delayed I would call them in the US, tell them the problem, and they would say, 'Get me on another flight.' It was very exciting."

Ranjit now runs his own travel company. He started two years ago with an investment of 1 lakh [$2,000]; now the company has capital of 40 lakhs [$80,000].

"I give excellent service. I work very hard and my money means something."

Pratap has ordered enormous quantities of food which now arrives, suddenly, in gleaming brass bowls: daal, butter chicken, kebabs, roti. Everyone digs in: this is the kind of food that has you slavering primordially when it is put under your nose.

Whisky keeps coming too, unaccustomed for me, but which I drink by way of conviviality.

Ranjit says, "When I watched my father and brother in the real estate business, I knew I didn't want to live like that. No standards. No permanent income. You have to drink every night with the police – my father would drink two or three bottles a day and come home dead. If you want to be in the property business you have to work like that. And every night you say, 'God, I did this today. Please forgive me.'

"I don't like that world. I don't like how those people have no respect for money: money comes easily and just disappears on clothes and drink and trips. If you work hard for your money, you will save that money.

"Not only that, but real estate people have no respect in society. You only need a table, three chairs and a phone to do that business. People say, 'If you can't do anything else, you do that.' My brother cannot sit still on a chair all day long and concentrate on a screen. He has to jump around all day and be on the phone.

"Now I'm happy with my life. I'll work as long as I live because I love this work. I want to make it on my own. I want to look after my children and give them a better education. The only thing I still need to sort out is my wife. I don't like her working so far away from me. I'm planning to train her in the travel agency business so she can work with me."

"Every day," says Gautam, "he drives two extra hours so he can drop her to her office before he goes to work, and pick her up again afterwards. He won't let her travel the streets on her own."

"But my closest relations are with my friends," says Ranjit. "Not with my family. Not even my wife. If I need help, I call my friends first. One thing I don't like is that I work so hard now, I don't see my friends as much as I used to. I keep asking Gautam if he wants to go on a trip. But he doesn't have time for me."

He says it with some edge. Actually it approaches a conflict in their relationship. Gautam has recently married a white American woman, of whom Ranjit does not totally approve, and sometimes it is awkward for them to be together.

"Ranjit never says it to me because he is a very nice man," says Gautam. "But inside him those issues are deep. Hindus and Muslims. He can't stand it if I have Muslim friends."

I am slightly confused. "But your wife is not Muslim," I say.

"Muslim, Christian – it's all the same. It's not Hindu. It's not Hindu culture. Ranjit is bothered by everything that disrupts

Hindu culture. For instance, I don't live with my parents and Ranjit always tells me this is not our culture, and I say, 'But my sister lives with them!' and he says, 'Don't try to escape your duty. It is the son who should take care of his parents. It's your responsibility.'"

I finish eating and run away from the table to wash my hands. With this food, the passage from pure animal craving to incapacitation and remorse is remarkably rapid. Afterwards you are desperate for hydration, because it is constituted, overwhelmingly, of oil. You drink glass after glass of water but it doesn't make any difference, because it will never penetrate the pure lipid you have become.

The conversation turns to cricket. Or, more particularly, the private lives of cricketers. Pratap, who is sitting on the other side of me, is unable to engage with this sporting gossip, and stares off into the distance. I try to rouse him from his silence. He tells me about his working life.

"It's getting very tough out there," he says. "It's becoming a winner-take-all market. Smaller guys are going under, and the fight at the top is more vicious."

"What can you do about it?"

"You can't plan beyond a point. No one knows the future. The main thing we have done is to diversify our income. From a metal trading business we began a metal import business. From those two businesses we began buying land outside Delhi for development. We also bought a property in Delhi which we run as a gym. We will always have several businesses, whatever happens. If one doesn't work, others will."

I ask Pratap if he considers himself a rich man.

"I have a lot of respect in my family," he says. "I have given money to many of my relatives, and I have given my sister's son a job. But I am not rich. In Sadar Bazaar terms I am one of the smallest traders. Many of them have been there for a century and they control far bigger markets."

"The *Forbes* list of billionaires only includes white money billionaires of course," I say. "Corporate billionaires, whose money is publicly accounted. But there must be many other billionaires who will never come to the attention of *Forbes*. Cash billionaires."

"How much is a billion dollars?" asks Pratap.

"Five thousand crores."

"Oh, there are several in Sadar Bazaar who have that. If you lower the bar to 1,000 crores, there are very many. But you would never know from looking at them."

This is a conversation that interests everyone. They all pitch in with their stories of fabulous wealth. Someone has read about a gold bathtub.

I ask, "Who is the richest person in Delhi?"

Several men shout, "Madhu Koda!" – which is a joke. Madhu Koda is the story of the moment: a poor-farmer's-son-turned-billionaire politician. The newspapers have been breathless with his life story. He began working as a miner and welder, entered politics in Bihar in the early 1990s and became a minister in Jharkhand when that state was carved out of the former. Minister with authority over mines and minerals, in fact, in a state whose enormous natural resources were just then, in the wake of liberalisation, attracting a stampede of mining corporations from all over the world. Later on, during his tenure as chief minister, Madhu Koda was arrested for possessing assets and investments valued at close to a billion dollars. He allegedly owned mines in Liberia, a $200 million real-estate development in Dubai, business investments in Sweden, Thailand and Indonesia – as well as resorts and houses all over India, including in two of Delhi's most exclusive neighbourhoods. This money was amassed, in part, by selling mining licenses to corporations for cash. It was part of a grand business plan, the newspapers reported, that was intended to culminate in respectability and a listing on Nasdaq, but it was impossible to keep a lid on it all that way.

It is in some ways a grimy tale, and yet it has also the thrilling glint that all rags-to-riches stories possess. And it is stunning evidence for the truth that politics, for India's poor, is the quickest and most accessible route to wealth. Stories of poor people making fortunes through business are much loved, but in practice they almost never happen. Politics, however, which offers so many quotas and breaks to those from the most marginalised sections of the population, has made many of India's poorest rich. If you have no money, status or connections and you want to get rich in your own lifetime, politics is the absolutely rational career choice. Corrupt politics, in this sense, is a corrective to the brutal inertia of the rest of society, which is why, for many, it is not so much a reason for despair as the main source of hope.

The reason it is funny to invoke Koda as the richest man in Delhi is that he has only just arrived here. He has been moved from a jail in Jharkhand to Delhi's Tihar Jail, in fact, so that he can continue to attend parliament. Which puts him in good company. The bus between Tihar Jail and the Parliament Building is not a lonely line to travel.

At some point in the conversation I am forced to make an exit so I can catch the last Metro. I bid farewell to the company, drunken by now. Gautam leaves with me, and drops me to the Metro station. It's deserted. I get into an empty carriage. The air conditioning is powerful, the ride smooth. I feel drowsy. At the other end, I pick up my car and head for home.

I am nearly at the house when I see a peculiar sight. A woman in a glittery nightclub negligée is walking down the dark street, so unsteadily that it seems she might fall at any moment, and behind her, two men are following at walking pace on a motorbike. I am not sure what to do. It is well after midnight, and the woman seems oblivious to everything around her: not drunk, but flying on the wings of some other potion. I draw level and put down the passenger window.

"Are you okay?" I ask. She looks in the window. She cannot focus too well on my face.

"What did you say?"

"I just asked if you were okay."

"Me? I'm fine!"

I watch her walk away. I put the window up. I look ahead, ready to drive on, and see that one of the men on the motorbike has run in front of my car, which he now proceeds to beat violently with both his palms. While he is doing so, the other man jerks open my car door and grabs my arm.

"Get out!"

"Why?"

"She is a prostitute. You are under arrest."

"For what?"

"What did you say to her?"

"I asked her if she was okay."

"How do you know her?"

"I don't."

"Get out of the car."

"Who are you?"

"We are police."

I get out of the car. I look around for the woman, who seems to have completely disappeared.

"Driver's license?"

I can't believe this situation. I get my driver's license out, and I watch while he inspects it.

"Which country is this from?"

"The UK," I say.

"You are British?"

"Yes," I say. He looks at me strangely. He begins writing down the number of my driving licence. While he is doing so, I hear my car engine rev, and turn round to watch it being driven away by the other man.

"Where's he going?" I cry.

"Police station." He is unperturbed. I am dumbfounded. He continues making his quiet notes. Then he hands me back my driver's license.

"Get on the bike."

I climb on the back of the motorbike, and he drives away at

speed in the direction already taken by my car. We whizz round dark corners and out into the neon sea of the main road. A U-turn, a side road, more dark corners, and finally the police station. My car is meekly parked out front, under a sign offering helpful advice to all who visit the Delhi police: "*A Person Who Has No Opinion Will Seldom Be Wrong*".

There seem to be two opposite conclusions to draw from this, and I honestly don't know which is the intended one.

I am led into a ramshackle office smelling of dust, sweat and stamp pads. A policeman is sitting behind a desk. He seems happy to see me in his net. My captor briefs him.

"What were you doing this evening?" the boss asks me.

"I was having dinner with friends."

"Girlfriends?" he says, smiling.

"Friends." I can see that he hopes I will turn out to be morally vulnerable. I resolve to act blasé. I don't have much money on me.

"So you leave one girlfriend and think you can pick up another girlfriend?"

I do not answer.

"Why would you stop to talk to a woman in the street? In the middle of the night."

We go over the details of the event again. He asks where I live, trying to place me in the Delhi galaxy. You never know with foreigners.

"Have you been drinking?" he asks.

"No," I lie.

"Shall we go to the hospital and check?"

"Okay," I say. This irritates him.

"What do you mean, 'Okay'?" he barks. "Show me your driving license."

I hand it to him and he makes a big show of inspecting every detail. I am not going to give him the satisfaction of hanging on his opinions. I look around. I'm actually a bit fascinated by this place, which is the most dilapidated seat of state power imaginable. Wires spill out of empty light sockets. There is a cardboard ceiling, in which holes have been rudely cut for the spinning fans to protrude. The walls are covered in phone numbers written at screwy angles and, behind every chair, dirty brown clouds where heads have leant. Someone has put up a sticker above a desk saying, "Sexi Hot Boy". In the corner of the room is a shrine with statues of various gods.

The office is just a cleared-out corner, in fact, of a giant storeroom. All around is the most enormous accumulation of police paraphernalia. Road signs, traffic cones. Rows of mega-phones on shelves. Piles of shoes and boots. Beds. Massive piles of old files.

Birdsong starts up in the room, which I realise is the ring tone of the policeman's mobile phone. He answers it. "Yes sir," he says solemnly. And again, "Yes sir." I can hear a raised voice on the other end and realise he is being reprimanded. I know the consequences for me will be bad if I stand and watch his indignity, so I wander out of the open back door into the court-yard outside. Another policeman is draping wet laundry over the handlebars of the old scooters which are parked here in great numbers. In fact, as my eyes adjust to the light and I can see out across the courtyard, I realise there is here the most enormous expanse of rotting vehicles. Abandoned scooters, cars and auto-rickshaws, all broken and twisted, and jammed in together. I wander into the darkness, round the corner of the building. The trees here are old and tall, and bats flit overhead. The wreckage goes on and on. There must be fifty or sixty rotting police vans. Rusting traffic lights and police barricades. Unbelievably, there are two small aeroplanes jammed in at the end, half overgrown with grass.

I head back to the building. The policeman ignores me when I come back into the room. He is typing with one finger on a computer keyboard. I sit down. Another man comes in and sits next to me. His walkie-talkie keeps erupting with voices of the night. Listlessly, he picks up a shred of newspaper from the floor and tries to make out what the ripped-off article is all about.

The man behind the desk acknowledges me at last. He says, "What would have happened if my men had not saved that woman from you?"

I feel he is running out of ammunition. He says, "Would you like everyone to know what you do at night?"

I try deference. I call him "Sir". I tell him again how it was.

He holds my driving license in the air and summons the cop sitting next to me.

"Photocopy."

The man takes my driving license to the photocopy machine in the corner, whose sparkling newness contrasts with the general decrepitude. He presses the copy button but nothing happens. He turns back to the man behind the desk.

"No paper."

The man behind the desk has a full packet of photocopy paper in front of him. He carefully takes from it one single sheet and hands it to his colleague, who opens the drawer of the machine and places it in the tray, closes the drawer, presses the button, and prints on it a copy of my driving license.

The boss hands me a pen.

"Sign," he says.

I sign the copy of my driving license. For some reason. He throws the original down on the desk.

"Never come back to this place," he says.

I retrieve my license and leave the room. I get in the car and drive home. This time I arrive successfully.

The house has been empty all day, and the air is stifling. By this stage in the year, the bricks of houses have accumulated so much heat that they continue to bake the rooms even at night. I turn on all the fans.

Then I go to the fridge and take out two ripe mangoes.

Fourteen

1984

In a new shopping mall you cannot escape the voice of a woman jabbering into a mike: " . . . seventy-eight Gandhis, seventy-nine Gandhis, eighty Gandhis, eighty-one Gandhis . . . "

You drift into a shop. You come out. The noise is still going on. Now her speech is more excited and rapid. She shouts, "one-forddy Gandhis one-forddy-one Gandhis, one-forddy-two Gandhis . . . "

You wonder what all this is about. You look for the voice. By the time you reach the central atrium, where she stands on a publicity podium with her arm around a beaming couple, her counting has reached near-hysterical excitement.

"Two twenny-seven Gandhis – two twenny-eight Gandhis – two TWENTY-NINE GANDHIS – we have a WINNER!"

The couple's two tubby kids are sprinting around in mad orbits, ecstatic with victory. The presenter holds up a wad of notes to the audience. "Look at all these Gandhis, people!"

The contest is this: they are giving away a free Reebok watch worth Rs 2,500 [$50] to whomever is carrying the most thousand-rupee notes – on which there is a picture of Mahatma Gandhi – at the mall this evening. The winning couple has pulled out from a handbag 229 of them [$4,600] thus demonstrating more fidelity than anyone else to the nation and its hermit-father.[41]

It should not be any surprise that this was a highly corrupt place.

Corruption does not stem primarily from wicked or greedy individuals; it comes from destroyed social relations, and, as we have seen, history had placed a great strain on Delhi's social relations.

Delhi had become a society that had, in its bleakest moments, ceased to believe in the idea of society – which was why the state, and religious identities, and other surrogates for 'society', were so fetishised. And when there is no society, you might as well despoil away, because you cannot harm a society that does not exist. If you don't do it, everyone else will, and for just the same reason.

It is often thought that it is effective law enforcement that keeps corruption in check, and of course this is partly the case. But it is also prevented by inner restraints and in Delhi these inner restraints had been significantly dismantled. You met them often, the old bureaucrats whose first words on meeting you were, "I never took anything from anyone, I could have made millions but I never took one rupee," and you could see what obsessive zeal it had required to keep hold of that principle. You wondered if they were still trying to convince themselves it had been a good idea.

Delhi's cynicism arose from its history, and from its age-old feeling that the human world existed to steal away, destroy and desecrate what you possess. It would have been corrupt in any circumstance. But the reason that, by the beginning of the twenty-first century, its corruption had reached the dizzying levels it had, was that it was the capital, and the seat of federal politics.

Jawaharlal Nehru died in 1964. He was succeeded by Lal Bahadur Shastri, another high-minded Congress man, who had been a close colleague of Nehru's ever since the freedom struggle. But Shastri survived Nehru by only two years, and in 1966 the party faced a succession question.

India had been in the hands of the one party since its inception, but cracks were appearing everywhere. The lofty momentum of the freedom struggle had run out, and, by the mid-1960s, the Indian reality was mired in dysfunction. Despite twenty years of managed development, the country was in the grip of an agricultural crisis, and depended heavily on food imports from its ideological foe, the United States – a measure which did not prevent a famine in the eastern state of Bihar in that same year, 1966. A mushrooming population was partially responsible for these deficits: while in 1947 the growth rate was just over 1 per cent per annum (doubling the population in seventy years), by 1966 it was nearly 2.5 per cent per annum (doubling the population in thirty years) – and India had become the preferred case study for the renewed Malthusian fears of the international managerial class. Meanwhile, wars with China (1962) and Pakistan (1965) had necessitated exceptional purchases of arms from abroad and further diminished India's already precarious foreign currency reserves; inflation now ran as high as 15 per cent. Partly as a result of these problems, many regions and communities had become disenchanted with the very idea of India: the state faced secessionist struggles in Andhra Pradesh and in the north-east, an increasingly militarised and desperate relationship with the region of Kashmir, and, in south India, widespread demonstrations, even self-immolations, in protest against the imposition of a foreign language, Hindi, as the lingua franca of politics (the policy from above was to phase out the other lingua franca, English, which would have greatly disadvantaged the non-Hindi-speaking south). In a *Hindustan Times* article entitled 'The Grimmest Situation in 19 Years', one senior journalist remarked, "The future of the country is dark for many reasons, all of them directly attributable to 19 years of Congress rule."[42]

It was a dangerous and volatile time, then, for the Congress Party, and one that required flexibility and pragmatism. The best way forward, in the view of the powerful collection of party bosses and chief ministers known by their opponents as 'the Syndicate', was to have a weak leader who could be controlled easily from behind the scenes. This was why, in 1966, they lent their support to the candidacy of Nehru's daughter, Indira. She was a woman and she was young – forty-eight – and they supposed she would put up little fight. They could not have been more wrong. Indira Gandhi – she was the widow of a Parsi politician and administrator named Feroze Gandhi – turned out to be one of the most ruthless political fighters of the twentieth century.

She had worked closely with her father during his premiership, but there is no sign that Nehru ever intended her to inherit his position: the idea of a ruling dynasty would have sat awkwardly with his democratic, anti-feudal sentiments. And he may not have considered Indira a plausible candidate: certainly she possessed very different attributes from her conspicuously – perhaps even squeamishly – cerebral father. She failed to complete, for instance, her degree at Oxford. The political speeches she gave were pragmatic and slogan-filled, and displayed none of her father's preoccupation with big ideas. And indeed her long period of influence – which lasted until her assassination in 1984 – turned Indian politics into so naked and brutal a struggle for power that post-Independence utopianism was entirely driven out. For most observers it has been difficult to believe, since her time, in any reason for political action that does not arise from the simple lust for power and money. Of any set of possible explanations for an event, in fact, the most craven will attract the widest belief.

The newly appointed Indira Gandhi responded to India's currency crisis by falling in line with World Bank and International Monetary Fund demands for the devaluation of the rupee. Hitherto pegged at 4.76 to the dollar, the rupee was, in March 1966, devalued by nearly 60 per cent to 7.5 to the dollar.

Such deference to capitalist imperialism was an offence to many, particularly those on the far left. It seemed to align the prime minister with the voice of free markets and free enterprise. This voice was increasingly articulate at that time: an emerging party, the Swatantra Party, had been set up to promote a free-market reaction to Nehruvian controls in 1959, while the Congress Party itself was moving further in this direction under the influence of the Syndicate, which was close – notoriously so – to big business.

It became clear in the 1967 elections that the free-market impulse carried little appeal with voters. The young and poor, who were particularly disenchanted with the ruling party, turned to the left (the communist and socialist parties) and towards parties of regional preferment (such as the Akali Dal in Punjab). Congress suffered terrible defeats.

After these elections, her prime ministership intact but fragile, Indira Gandhi suddenly took a startling and radical turn leftwards. She determined to crush the right-wing, business-oriented wing of the party – which included not only the Syndicate but also her rival for party leadership, Morarji Desai – and to make a new populist appeal to the electorate. Having built up her own power base, she fired Desai from his post as finance minister, nationalised the banks, banned contributions to political parties – a direct assault on the Syndicate, which drew income from corporate donations – and introduced even greater restrictions on big business and foreign capital.

In speech after speech, Indira Gandhi vowed to root out the insidious few who exploited the hapless many. Her rhetoric was populist, and though it was, in the light of her actions, only that – rhetoric – it was dazzlingly effective. She developed an extraordinary gift for communicating with crowds, and she channelled that peculiar power that is disdained only by those who have never seen a demagogue in action. She revolutionised the structure of Indian political relations by cutting out the business owners, trade union leaders and feudal landowners who had previously interfaced between politicians and the masses: in her campaign for the 1971 elections, under the banner of "*Garibi Hatao!*" ("Put an end to poverty!") she spoke to those masses directly. Her image acquired the aura of something primordial and awe-inspiring, and her victory in the 1971 elections was overwhelming.

She followed this up with a well-judged, and wildly popular, military intervention in the war between the two wings of Pakistan, East and West. This had begun as a secessionist campaign by the eastern wing, or 'Bangladesh', which had resulted in terrible retribution by forces from West Pakistan – an episode of terrifying genocide and hundreds of thousands of rapes that displayed again what wild energies circulated between these cut-off siblings of South Asia. After months of military escalation on both sides of the India–Pakistan borders, Pakistan bombed north India and a war began on both northern and eastern fronts.

Great international interests were at stake. The USSR provided support to India while the US, afraid that an Indian victory might spread Soviet influence further across the region, supported Pakistan. But the war was over in a few days. It was a decisive and powerfully symbolic victory for India, which took from Pakistan some 90,000 prisoners of war.

Indira Gandhi rode high, and her style became cultish. Her image was everywhere, and, like the goddess she appeared to be, she brought forth twin eruptions of creation and destruction which gave great symbolic charge to the imagination of India in those years. One was the Green Revolution, which had begun under her predecessor but which began to have a real impact on food production levels only in the early 1970s. Based on new fertilisers and high-yield crops, the Green Revolution transformed the wheat production, and indeed the entire economy, of the Delhi hinterland of Punjab and Haryana. The other achievement was a successful nuclear test explosion in 1974, which brought to its culmination the line of research initiated by Nehru back in the 1940s, and established India as the only nation to possess this technology outside of the original five nuclear nations – though it would not be until the 1990s that a nuclear missile became a military reality.

They were uncanny days, when giant symbols floated gaily above a sclerotic reality. When people speak dismissively today of the state controls and strangled energies of 'Nehruvian' India, it is often not the Nehru period but that of his daughter that they remember. Under Indira Gandhi, business was in a stranglehold, and corruption, already rife after twenty years of one-party rule, became an epidemic. With 'official' corruption now banned – that is to say, corporate donations to political parties, which was the normal mode for business to buy influence under Nehru – businesses resorted to buying off individuals, thus giving rise to the era of 'briefcase politics'. Politics became a business; bureaucracy provided the structure for a particularly intense and original kind of entrepreneurialism.

Ironically but predictably, it was at this moment when Delhi was most ideologically opposed to big business that big business began to gravitate towards Delhi, thus preparing the way for the capital's emergence as a commercial hub in the early twenty-first century. Under Nehru, Delhi had been an administrative town, as it had been under the British: business was afforded little place, entrepreneurs remained small in scale and big companies stayed away. Under Mrs Gandhi, however, it became impossible for big business to avoid Delhi. Approvals were required for absolutely everything and – since Indira co-opted great slabs of authority from the states in order to weaken her rivals and concentrate all power in herself – those who were far from Delhi started to feel cut off. Several British-era business houses from Calcutta moved to Delhi at that time, fleeing the strikes and commercial lockdown of West Bengal, which the Congress had lost in 1967 to a coalition of socialists and communists. Many companies from other north Indian states moved to Delhi in order to make political connections and so reach the next stage of their growth. Several companies which have today acquired global proportions started up in Delhi during Indira Gandhi's time. Even businessmen who remained in other centres began to keep houses and apartments in the capital (which contributed, later, to the incredible overvaluation of Delhi property). Delhi public life was infiltrated by a new fervour of networking and soliciting.

Delhi did not in general attract businesspeople with startling ideas; as we have seen, it was in Bangalore that the best software companies were set up, also during the Indira Gandhi era. No: the people who were pulled in to Delhi in those years were the ones who needed to hack into the political establishment in order for their business to work. This included those who sought control over basic resources – real estate, minerals, petrochemicals; those who operated in highly regulated areas – such as telecoms or media; or those for whom the state was a major client – such as construction or heavy industries. All of these needed powerful patrons in the political and bureaucratic machinery if they were to get land, resources and approvals, and if they were to avoid critical operational delays, harassment of every imaginable kind, and even total shutdown for some trumped-up reason or other.

The enclaves built for Delhi's high-ranking bureaucrats are invisible to most people. Set back from the road, and cut off by guard posts, they are pretty hamlets of quiet streets embraced by lush trees. Inside, chauffeurs dust off bureaucratic cars while gardeners water and prune the plants. The houses are well designed and maintained. There are different grades of accommodation for inhabitants of different ranks: the most splendid residences are large and cut off by hedges and private drives even from the rest of these cut-off places.

The house I come to is not one of these; it is on a street in a row of similar houses. But it is a comfortable dwelling, faintly reminiscent of the American suburbs: there is a basketball hoop at the end of the driveway. Meenu answers the door, apologetic for the fact that I have got so lost on my way. There is nothing for her to apologise for: these enclaves are designed to be found only by those who already know where they are.

The large sitting room we sit down in is strikingly empty of possessions. One has the feeling of a family that has moved many times and is ready to do so again, at a moment's notice.

Meenu's son runs out to see who the visitor is. He is delighted to have a stranger in the house, especially one as ignorant of contemporary ten-year-old-boy culture as I. He brings a succession of things he feels I need to know about: books, toys, games. He lies on the sofa with his feet up on the wall, telling me stories about his school. Meenu shoes him out of the room, saying, "Can I talk now?" He disappears for a while but will continue to launch illicit educational operations on me for the rest of the evening.

"I went to Jawaharlal Nehru University in Delhi," says Meenu, "and I just sort of fell into the civil service exams. My father was in the bureaucracy so it wasn't at all alien to me. I passed the exams on my first attempt, and I've been a bureaucrat since I was twenty-three."

Now in her late thirties, Meenu has an elegant, thoughtful face. She is dressed casually, in jeans and a white shirt, and her hair is cut short.

"It's the only kind of work I could be satisfied with," she says.

"Bureaucrats have a huge impact on ordinary lives, including people very far away."

Her husband, Amit, comes into the room. He is tall and slim, and as soon as he enters I have the sense that he and his wife share an intimate bond. He works in the railway administration just as she does, which is how they met. Unlike her, he is from Bihar, where his father worked for the government.

The migrants who swelled the population of Delhi in the years after 1947, were not all poor and uneducated. Not by any means. As the capital, Delhi drew educated people from every corner of the country. It had two large and excellent universities, several research hospitals, and national centres for dance, theatre and music. It hosted the headquarters for countless research centres and NGOs. It was the centre of Indian journalism. And it was the hub for politics and the bureaucracy. These systems, though they were essential to the city's make-up, were entirely cosmopolitan, and the local Punjabi majority had no hold over them.

"It is true that the bureaucracy is very corrupt," says Meenu. "I would say that 80 per cent of bureaucrats are corrupt. Fifteen years after entering the bureaucracy, many of my peers own ten houses and fleets of cars."

Needless to say, these assets were not bought with bureaucratic salaries, which rarely exceed $15,000 per year.

Amit joins in.

"People who aren't there to make money are terrorised. Especially in highly corrupt areas like customs, which is where I worked before. If you have a high-value position which you're not exploiting, if you're not handing out money to the people around you, you get serious threats. It's not so bad in the railways, where they just harass you by transferring you."

'Success' in the Indian bureaucracy generally means getting to a position where you can offer something that powerful people need, or, even better, where you can hold harsh threats over their heads. The customs and tax services are therefore the most energetically entrepreneurial of all. Senior figures in these services can amass fortunes of tens of millions of dollars. It is a cut-throat game, however, and it requires great acumen. The Indian bureaucracy is consistently listed as the most corrupt in Asia, and this is usually intended as a slight. But with big money at stake and a fantastically complex set of competing interests to negotiate, corrupt Indian bureaucrats are no dud. They have skills and drives which equip them very well, in fact, for twenty-first-century life.

"There are levels of moneymaking, of course," says Meenu. "At the bottom is 'speed money', which basically means collecting bribes for what you are supposed to do anyway. You don't actually do anything wrong, you just charge for it twice. For instance, if you're deciding the order that freight trains will depart in – and there is money riding on those trains because people are waiting for shipments – you can put the train first that was anyway going to go first and you'll still get 5,000 rupees [$100] speed money. Because people are so used to paying. It has sunk into the psyche that unless you pay it won't happen. When you enter the services your seniors tell you, 'Just do your job and money will come anyway'. Of course, if you put another train first you'll make 200,000 rupees [$4,000]."

One can appreciate the conviction with which market forces are applied. *Why not let the market decide in which order trains run?* The first slot is a commodity that can be auctioned, and whoever wants it the most, gets it. It is market capitalism in its purest form. The ability to create markets out of nothing, the ability to see that everything has a financial value: these things mark out India's bureaucrats, not just as the rod in capitalism's churning wheels, which is how they are usually portrayed, but also as a talented entrepreneurial class with a profound capitalist instinct.

"We were transferred to Ferozepur," Amit says, "the most corrupt centre of the northern railways. We told our boss, 'We don't want to go. It's very corrupt there.' Our boss was amazed. 'In Ferozepur,' he said, 'you only have to open your drawers and bundles of cash will fall in.' It was true. Even boxes of sweets you were given at festival time would be stuffed with cash. Those were some of the most desirable positions in the country and people would pay big money to get them, knowing they would earn ten or twenty times their salary in bribes."

"Another time, we were transferred to Bikaner," says Meenu, "and I had discretionary authority over people's jobs, which meant I was very powerful."

"Meenu was the first woman bureaucrat to be there," Amit adds. "Men didn't know how to address her. They used to call her *Sir*."

"When we arrived, all the small business owners came queuing up to offer favours. The dry cleaner said, 'Please use my shop,' and I asked him for a price list. He was very offended. 'It's free, Madam.' Because these people want access to senior bureaucrats and they will pay for it. The payback comes when they bring people to your house in your private time and ask for favours. 'Please don't send my brother-in-law to a less attractive posting.'

"For instance, the man who worked the platform going towards Delhi made a lot of money from tips and bribes from passengers wanting to get on the train, whereas the platform going in the other direction made much less. What most bureaucrats do is to rotate people among these jobs. So those who have the lucrative positions have to lobby to hold onto them.

"At another time, I was in charge of New Delhi railway station. Every day 1 lakh [$2,000] used to come up from the ticket windows and was distributed to officers."

"Have you ever bought a ticket at those windows?" says Amit. "Have you ever wondered why it's such a nightmare? It is deliberately kept like that. Half of Indian chaos is the deliberate strategy of the bureaucracy. Because if things were efficient, there would be no reason to pay bribes. Ticket counters in stations are big sources of unofficial money."

"At the centre of this business is the man behind the reservation window," explains Meenu. "When I arrived in Delhi I got a call from a cabinet minister who wanted to propose a particular candidate for this job. I was astonished that one of the most powerful people in the country would personally make a call about the ticket seller in New Delhi station whose salary is maybe 6,000 rupees [$120] a month.

"I wanted to improve work conditions in the station. I felt that my workers were not getting decent breaks. I went right back to the railway regulations written by the British, to see what the rules were about employee breaks, and I found that they were supposed to have two fifteen-minute breaks a day. I got rid of the tea boy who came round serving tea to people while they worked, and I set up a special tea room where people could relax in their breaks.

"But unknown to me, this caused a big problem. Because the real significance of the tea boy was not that he delivered tea but that he took away all the accumulated cash from the reservation windows. There could be a raid at any time and if you're caught with all that cash you have no way of explaining it. So the tea boy was the person who took it away and kept it until the end of the day. He was essential to their livelihood. They were furious when I took him away. I'm sure he's back again now.

"Such things made me very unpopular. I was disrupting the entire economy of the station, and everyone felt I was their enemy. Once the vigilance inspectors came round to check what was going on. They are the people who investigate corruption, and they're obviously highly corrupt. They collect bribes and they're foul-mouthed. They insult everyone. The unions wanted me to shut them out, which I refused to do: in fact, I was quite happy about them coming.

"The unions are very big in stations. They have links to the top and they're very powerful. They got 500 people to surround me, shouting in chorus, '*Meenu Sharma murdabad!*' ('Death to Meenu Sharma!'). Just because I let the vigilance inspectors in.

"Nowadays, the first thing I do when I go to a new posting is get rid of all the chairs in my office so that large numbers of people cannot sit down. They like to intimidate you like that. It's difficult to get people out when they are sitting.

"People also play the caste card a lot. There was a man who used to come to me every day when I was working in the station to say, 'My name is Sharma.' I used to think he was an idiot, telling me his name every day. I'm naive about these things. It took me so long to realise that he was telling me he was from the same caste community as me and therefore expected special favours.

"But I ended up gaining respect there. Because I made no exceptions. If you make exceptions, you make money, but you also arouse resentment. I would transfer everyone, according to the rules. No one could pay to avoid it.

"In my early years in the railway service, I had an amazing boss. He was a very intelligent man who really taught me how to do my job. His lesson to me was that all documentation had to be well argued. You couldn't just write, *Request rejected*. Enormous money was at stake and people could always come back afterwards and accuse you of things. *Why did you reject that request?* He was a wonderful mentor to me. He worked very hard, and he used to keep the most amazing documentation.

"Later on, I discovered he was exceedingly corrupt. He could make precise arguments for anything but they were always the arguments that earned him the most money. While I was working with him, he was looking to purchase cleaning equipment for Indian railway stations. He asked me to draw up a detailed comparison of all the products on the market. But what I only knew later was that one multinational company had paid him a large fee to give them the contract. He did very extensive research and then he wrote the tender such that only his client's equipment could fulfil it. It looked like an open tender, of course, but the guidelines only matched one company.

"He was very smart. He could never be caught on file. He worked very long hours – he used to call me at 6 a.m. from the office."

"People make a lot of money," says Amit. "They have the same problem as criminals: where do they hide their cash? A couple of weeks ago one of our senior colleagues was found with 10 lakhs [$20,000] concealed in his toilet cistern."

The bureaucracy is a vast cash generator, which is why there is so much cash in the Delhi economy. In central Delhi markets you see hundreds of banknotes in customers' wallets. The big jewellery stores feel like banks, which is, in a way, what they are: people use them to convert cash into gold, many thousands of dollars at a time. The cashiers' desks are noisy with the constant whirr of counting machines flicking banknotes.

The ultimate destination, however, for all this cash, is property. It is still common in Delhi for people to pay for 60 per cent of, say, a $4 million property in cash, a practice which has been clamped down upon much more quickly in, say, Mumbai. In Delhi the booming, multibillion-dollar property market owes its very existence to the constant need to offload large amounts of cash, so things do not change so fast. In any property deal the two key pieces of information are the price of the property and the proportions of 'white money' – declared money, paid by cheque or bank transfer, and 'black money' – cash.

Amit says, "Friends of my parents in Patna say to them, 'You have not one but two bureaucrats in the family! Soon you will have more cars and houses than you can count!' Unfortunately, they don't know us."

He grins.

"They gave me a job in vigilance," says Meenu, "investigating corruption. I registered charges against several senior bureaucrats, which was a huge insult. They removed me very quickly. They never expected me to do that.

"Getting a reputation as a difficult junior is a serious thing. If you don't laugh at a senior's jokes, if you're not corrupt enough, if you make your boss look bad in front of his boss – you get a reputation for being difficult, and you don't get promoted.

"At the same time, you need a lot of skill to play that game and honestly I don't have that skill. If someone does you a favour – a senior bureaucrat gives you a desirable posting for instance – how will you repay it? My boss called me and said, 'I'm taking my family on a trip to a resort in your district. I need a place to stay, transport, etc.' I didn't even realise what he was asking. I just said, 'Thank you for telling me.' But he expected me to organise free tickets and hotels for him. Later on, he punished me by transferring me five times in rapid succession and making my life hell. But the thing is that even if I had realised what he wanted, I wouldn't have known how to do it. He expected me to have a whole network of relationships with small business-people in the state – travel agents, hotel people – from whom I could ask favours. But it's a very complicated thing to maintain. Once you accept favours from those people, you're vulnerable to anything they ask."

"There was a businessman who was constantly offering to send me on luxurious trips," says Amit. "He would call me and say, 'Let me sponsor a trip to Goa for your family. Or would you prefer to go to Italy?' If I had accepted, he would have held it over my head for ever. He wanted me to push through a scheme for a new railway to Assam."

"This is a constant problem for bureaucrats. The ideal bureaucrat is able to avoid getting to close to any particular businessman, because if he does, it means he is unable to offer favours to others and he appears to be exclusive."

I ask them why they think things work like this. Amit says, "Politicians have become more invulnerable in these years of fragile coalition governments. The government needs its coalition partners so much, it will protect them from anything. They may be pathetic ministers but they are too important to the ruling coalition to be allowed to fail."

Meenu continues, "I blame it on the business class, which is always willing to pay for advancement. Everybody wants to be in the fast lane. If you go to the parties that the income tax people hold, it is as if the entire business class of Delhi is out to please them. They take these guys out and give them whatever they want."

"Party culture is very important," says Amit. "Networking is crucial to business and politics in Delhi, and these parties give you a heady feeling. Golf: who you play golf with is very important. Do you play with this secretary from this ministry or just someone lowly? That establishes your position. These days a bureaucrat can't just sit around, do his work and pull rank like in the old days. You have to go to the parties and network. Then you get to do favours for powerful people, which is where it all leads. It's such a buzz that many people don't even do it for money. They just want to be at the centre of the network."

At times one can feel, it is true, that this city's motto is: *I network, therefore I am.* People carry their networks with them everywhere, cite them, name-drop them, as if without them they would cease to exist. Facebook has slotted in perfectly into the life of the city, being only a technological representation of what already existed. Sometimes when you go to Delhi society parties you feel you are in a kind of Facebook reality game. People come up to you that you hardly know, they seem strangely, even excessively happy to see you again and greet you sentimentally. You didn't even realise you were friends, but after such a display you feel the need to show some curiosity. "How have you been?" you ask. But by then they have moved on, and they look at you in surprise, as if to say, "You? You're still here?" They are already scanning for the next encounter, and you realise that what has just happened is not something that belongs to the real world of bodies mingling and conversing in a space, but something that belongs to online. You have been 'poked'.

"Delhi is being taken over," says Meenu, "by contractors who know how to manipulate these systems. Bureaucrats are willing to sell themselves, partly because they come, increasingly, from deprived backgrounds. They have genuine problems, they feel they've suffered in the past, and they think it's their right to get something back from everyone else. If you talk to them, they're never doing it for themselves; they want to improve the lot of their whole community. And such people place a lot of significance on markers of status – chauffeurs, networks, contacts, invitations."

"Does no one fear getting caught?" I ask.

"Of course. They're *very* concerned about getting caught. It's very embarrassing to be caught. But what I've noticed recently is that this has stopped being a deterrent. Getting caught is increasingly unrelated to anything you have actually done. There's a kind of fatalism about it. Recently a senior bureaucrat came to give a training session and he asked attendees what might lead to them getting caught. 'Accepting bribes,' suggested the students. 'No.' 'Breaking procedure.' 'No.' 'Accepting favours.' 'No,' said the instructor. 'You will get caught when your destiny turns bad.' You hear that more and more often. Somebody else said recently, 'Being caught doing something wrong is like being hit by a car. It could have happened to anyone, but it happened to you. It's entirely random. There's no way you can predict it.'

"There is no longer any constraint except bad fate. Which you can't do anything about anyway. So you might as well carry on."

Indira Gandhi's cult of the self inevitably provoked resentment and consternation, and in 1975 she went to the Allahabad High Court to answer allegations of malpractice in the 1971 elections. The court decided against her on two counts, which thus rendered the election result void. An appeal was registered with the Supreme Court. Before any verdict could be reached, however, Mrs Gandhi declared a national state of emergency. Explaining this extreme measure on national radio, she said, "This is nothing to panic about. I am sure you are all conscious of the deep and widespread conspiracy, which has been brewing ever since I began to introduce certain progressive measures of benefit to the common man and woman of India."

A dictator by personality, Indira Gandhi flourished under the autocratic conditions of the Emergency. She jailed her opponents, including two future prime ministers and one future deputy prime minister – Morarji Desai, Atul Bihari Vajpayee and Lal Kishanchand Advani respectively – and the remarkable Jayaprakash Narayan, who had long been campaigning for a wholesale renewal of Indian political and social life through what he called a non-violent total revolution. Narayan's imprisonment provoked especial outrage, including in the international press, since he was a powerfully principled leader who had at one point been very close to the Nehru family – it was as if Mrs Gandhi were imprisoning an uncle – but the prime minister's rampage had hardly begun. She had always disliked the dispersal of powers inherent to India's federal structure: when state government terms ended in Tamil Nadu and Gujarat she cancelled elections and administered the states directly from Delhi. Freedom of the press was cancelled, and sweeping changes were made to the constitution to remove curbs on prime ministerial power. Amnesty International estimated that 140,000 people were imprisoned without trial and, in many cases, tortured, during the twenty months of the Emergency. The Emergency traumatised universities, many of which were vocal in their opposition; it also gave great moral standing to the Sikh parties and radical Hindu groups, many of which maintained principled criticism in the face of Indira Gandhi's onslaught.

For some, the Emergency did not seem so bad. There was a new-found, nervous order to social life, which stood in marked contrast to the political disruptions of the previous years. Business enjoyed the comparative regularity of labour and supplies, and the unusual efficiency of the bureaucracy in issuing licenses. It seemed to many that the experiment of Indian democracy was over, and some – such as that punning courtier who supplied the refrain, "Indira is India, and India is Indira" – began to sing the praises of the new dictatorship.

But in Delhi, the Emergency left a particularly violent imprint through the astonishing rise to power, during this period, of Indira's adored younger son, Sanjay. The first of Delhi's political bad boys, he was one of those dangerous patriots who love the idea of their country but hate its reality. He was plagued by nightmares of filthy, exponentially reproducing masses, and he longed to destroy, to root out, and to impose hygiene and order. Twenty-nine years old in 1975, balding, and with a curled mouth that seemed to display some dark and disturbing sensuality, Sanjay suddenly became his mother's closest adviser, and indeed began to enact, of his own personal will, major social policies. It is a sign of what dizzying extraordinary powers Indira Gandhi had managed to win for herself that her son, who held no political position of his own, was able to depend on such obedience from his coterie of powerful sycophants

In Delhi, he launched a major programme of slum demolition, which delighted the ambitious vice chairman of the Delhi Development Authority, Jagmohan Malhotra. Malhotra sent bull-dozers to demolish the slums of Old Delhi, producing a stream of 700,000 refugees who settled in the south and east of the city (where they would encounter a fresh wave of merciless demolition in the mid-2000s). But this upheaval was rendered all the more traumatic because these people were also especially targeted by Sanjay's other big scheme of male vasectomy. Administered through public servants, such as policemen and school teachers, who were required not only to go through the operation themselves, but also to deliver prescribed numbers of men for vasectomy every day if they wanted to keep their jobs and receive their salaries, this immediately turned into a brutal and arbitrary process whose burden fell disproportionately on the poorest and most powerless.

Among the poor Muslims of Old Delhi, these two schemes together brought back perennial fears that the purges of 1947 would one day be taken to their completion, and the tension escalated into the most terrifying battles between communities, police, demolition vehicles and vasectomy squads. The Indian state, which had arisen, in part, out of outrage against the excesses of the British against ordinary citizens, seemed to have parted its cloak to reveal some genocidal organ of its own – and there was thenceforth no level of sickness and cruelty where the imagination could not reach, especially where the poor were concerned.

But it was by no means only the poor who were targeted by Sanjay Gandhi's sterilisation scheme. It was supposedly a universal programme that was compulsory for all men who had already had three children or more, and some of the first people to whom it was applied were those to whom the government had easiest access: its own employees. Bureaucrats, policemen, school teachers – these people too were obliged to fall in line, often in so crude a way that the state was totally discredited, along with all its opinions about such private matters as childbearing.

For many of these middle-class families who had given them-selves to the Nehruvian ideal and who sought out work as servants of the state, the imposition of male vasectomy represented another kind of disappointment with the entire national project. In north India, especially, where men were still trying to escape the emasculations, real and figurative, of the partition thirty years before, this symbolic castration by the very state in which they had taken refuge, to which they had pledged their life energies, rankled deep.

On 31 October 1984, prime minister Indira Gandhi was assass-inated by her Sikh bodyguards, who shot her thirty times as she was taking a walk in her garden in the heart of bureaucratic Delhi. The bodyguards surrendered to arrest: one was immediately shot dead; two more were imprisoned in Tihar Jail where they were later hanged.

In the 1977 election, Mrs Gandhi had been voted out of

government to be replaced as prime minister by Morarji Desai, who now stood for the Janata Party, which had been newly constituted as an anti-Emergency coalition. But India's first ever non-Congress government quickly collapsed amid infighting, and in the elections of 1980, Indira Gandhi took the country back under the banner, no longer of helping the poor, nor really of any big idea save that of her own power. This power, however, required some positive manifestation. Indira needed to produce economic growth to retain her legitimacy, and her economic policies took a marked shift to the right. She surrounded herself with new business-friendly advisers, deregulated key commodities such as cement and sugar and took a big loan from the World Bank to boost productivity.

But her enterprise was beset by adversity. Indira's major source of personal strength, her son Sanjay, who was now a member of parliament himself, was killed shortly after the election while flying loops over Delhi in his private plane. She found herself embattled in the states, where parties catering to caste identities, religious ideals and hopes of regional autonomy were everywhere on the rise. A generation after Independence, Indian politics had grown beyond one-party federalism towards what some would call a more genuinely democratic variety, and Indira Gandhi found herself adopting strong-arm tactics to maintain the power of the centre.

Nowhere was this battle more serious than in Punjab, where demands for territory and autonomy had been growing under the leadership of the vehement and well-organised Akali Dal party. In order to divide the Akali Dal's support, Indira Gandhi supported the agitations of the ultra-Orthodox break-away leader Jarnail Singh Bhindranwale. But it soon became impossible to check the rise of Bhindranwale, who made increasingly overt calls for the armed liberation of Punjab from Hindus and from Delhi, and before long the Congress had a major problem on its hands. In 1981, a senior journalist who had been critical of Bhindranwale was assassinated. Bhindranwale was arrested, but

at the cost of the death of several of the civilians who gathered
to prevent it; widespread rejoicing broke out in Punjab when
he was released three weeks later for lack of evidence. The central
government had become hated and discredited, and in the wildness of 1980s politics no tactic, including political assassination,
was disallowed to the leader who would take it on.

Terrorist acts became more and more persistent, and in 1984
Mrs Gandhi decided to take military action. Bhindranwale and
his fighters took refuge in the Sikh holy of holies, the Golden
Temple in Amritsar, where they built up a great arsenal of arms
and defences. On the night of 5 June 1984, several regiments of
the Indian army stormed the temple. A huge battle ensued which
resulted in the death of Bhindranwale and hundreds of his men.

Ramachandra Guha writes:

> The Golden Temple is ten minutes' walk from Jallianwala
> Bagh where, in April 1919, a British brigadier ordered his
> troops to fire on a crowd of unarmed Indians . . . The
> incident occupies a hallowed place in nationalist myth and
> memory; the collective outrage it provoked was skilfully
> used by Mahatma Gandhi to launch a countrywide
> campaign against colonial rule. Operation Blue Star differed
> in intent − it was directed at armed rebels, rather than a
> peaceable gathering − but its consequences were not dissim-
> ilar. It left a collective wound in the psyche of the Sikhs,
> crystallizing a deep suspicion of the government of India.
> The Delhi regime was compared to previous oppressors
> and desecrators, such as the Mughals, and the eighteenth-
> century Afghan marauder Ahmad Shah Abdali. A reporter
> touring the Punjab countryside found a "sullen and alien-
> ated community". As one elderly Sikh put it, "Our inner
> self has been bruised. The base of our faith has been attacked,
> a whole tradition has been demolished." Now, even those
> Sikhs who had previously opposed Bhindranwale began to
> see him in a new light. For, whatever his past errors and

crimes, it was he and his men who had died defending the holy shrine from the vandals.[43]

And so: the murder in Delhi, a few weeks later, of the prime minister.

The city-wide anti-Sikh rampage of murder and destruction that followed this assassination blew open the troubled heart of the city. Sikhism was, far more than Islam, the sibling of Hinduism: its founder, Guru Nanak, was part of a sixteenth-century movement of reform and renewal within the Hindu religion. Until recently many Hindu Punjabi families gave their first-born son to the Sikh religion, often in fulfilment of a vow made when a childless couple prayed for children. Like the events of 1947, then, the violent eruption of 1984 had all the fervour of a struggle over the nature of the family. Sikh militancy had been fuelled by the sense that Hindus treated Sikhs as India's illegitimate offspring; Sikhs had in turn rejected an Indian state they described as "effeminate" and unleashed instead their own principle of virile, martial valour:

> In one of his speeches Bhindranwale propounded the idea that it was an insult for the Sikhs to be included in a nation that considered Mahatma Gandhi to be its father, for his techniques of fighting were quintessentially feminine. He (Gandhi) was symbolized by a charkha, the spinning wheel, which was a symbol of women. "Can those," asked the militant leader, "who are the sons of the valiant guru, whose symbol is the sword, ever accept a woman like Mahatma as their father? Those are the techniques of the weak, not of a race that has never bowed its head before any injustice—a race whose history is written in the blood of martyrs." . . . To be able to claim true descent from the proud Gurus (the ten acknowledged founders of the Sikh religion), it was argued, all corruption that had seeped into the Sikh character because of the closeness to

the Hindus was to be exorcised . . . The dangers of a "Hindu" history, it turned out, were not just that Sikhs were denied their rightful place in history but that the martial Sikhs became converted into a weak race: "The Sikhs have been softened and conditioned during the last fifty years to bear and put up with insults to their religion and all forms of other oppression, patiently and without demur, under the sinister preaching and spell of the narcotic cult of non-violence, much against the clear directive of their Gurus, their Prophets, not to turn the other cheek before a tyrant, not to take lying down any insult to their religion, their self-respect, and their human dignity."[44]

The Sikh male identity – which included the wearing of a beard, and the carrying of the sword (or, in a different context, the Kalashnikov) – thus brought him naturally into conflict with the Indian state and, ultimately, to the assassination of its female leader. But for many Hindus, the idea of the supreme mother was paramount, and Indira Gandhi's death was immediately seen as an obscene assault on *their* idea of the Indian 'family'. Leaping as outraged sons to avenge her death was a clear duty: "Indira Gandhi is our mother and these people have killed her," yelled the Hindu crowds.

It should be evident that, for both sides, this crisis of 1984 had everything to do with the unfinished business of Partition, which had done so much to call into question the masculine credentials of both siblings, Hinduism and Sikhism. It was thirty-seven years since Partition, and many of those involved in the present atrocities, on both sides, were seeing these scenes for the second times in their lives. Sikhs who had spent that time rebuilding their lives found themselves subjected to rape and murder all over again; once again they lost their homes and livelihoods. Hindus who had mulled for decades on the ignominy of their flight from West Punjab found themselves taking frenzied revenge on their one-time fellow refugees. The violence which began on 1 November 1984 was fuelled by paranoid rumours, some of which drew explicitly on the unresolved nightmares of 1947: trainloads of dead Hindus, it was said, were arriving from Punjab, where Sikhs had unleashed a campaign of annihilation. It was also rumoured that Sikh militants had poisoned the Delhi water supply, and there was a crisis of drinking water in the city; people travelled far to regions they thought unaffected to collect water for their families.

For four days the violence raged. Mobs patrolled the city with knives, guns and tanks of kerosene, which they used to incinerate people, houses and shops. It is not known how many people were killed; estimates range between 3,000 and 10,000. What was clear to all, however, was that the organs of the state were conspicuously lax in trying to quell the reprisals. It is all but certain, in fact, that members of the Congress Party sponsored the entire episode, handing out weapons and liquor to Hindu avengers and promising them rewards for murders. Congress MPs who owned gas stations provided kerosene for their operations, and in some cases sent vehicles stocked with kerosene to accompany them on their forays. Congress Party officials handed out lists of addresses of Sikh families so that they could be targeted systematically. Rather than acting to control Hindu mobs, the police further incited them with rumours that Sikhs were plotting to bring down the state. Hospitals refused to treat Sikh victims and police stations refused to file reports of crimes against Sikhs.

Indira's surviving son, Rajiv, who was sworn in as prime minister on the night of her death, gave his own infamous – and indifferent – explanation of this violence: "When a great tree falls, the earth shakes."

For the city of Delhi, the 'Sikh riots' turned 'the law' into an obscene nonsense. One commentator relates an incident in the west-Delhi neighbourhood of Sultanpuri, one of the areas where violence was at its most intense, where a Sikh community leader and his two sons were set on fire. The three men were shrieking for someone to bring water. Observing all this, the police inspector shouted that no one should think of coming to their assistance, but he said it in these terms: "if anyone dare[s] to come out and interfere with the law (*kanoon ke khilaf kisi ne hath uthaya* — literally, raise their hand against the law) he [will] be shot dead." The Hindu mob had become the law, the kerosene fire had become the law. Another policeman went around announcing by megaphone that any Hindus who were caught hiding Sikhs from the mob would have their houses burned down because it was *illegal* to do so.[45]

The discrediting of the law was complete. For people in Delhi, whatever other reason there might be to comply with the law, it could no longer be a moral one, for the law had no moral content whatsoever. This impression was only strengthened as successive investigations of the massacre failed to find significant evidence of wrongdoing in the Congress establishment: to this day, no one has been held accountable for what happened. The official response has been a thirty-year-long shrug. The law has no comment.

Delhi was corrupt anyway. But the riots now sent a definitive message that the law was a degenerate part of Indian social life and one's only moral duty was to oneself. One had to look after oneself, since no one else would do it, and now there were no legal constraints on how one should go about it. It is from this date that the 'compound' feel of Delhi's residential neighbourhoods dates. No more those gentle practices of the past – those middle-class boys who took beds down to the street to sleep incautiously in the open air on hot nights. Such trust of the outsider and the street was put away, and middle-class families replaced their thigh-high walls with ten-foot spiked steel gates. The subsequent boom in private electricity generators has to do not only with the erratic nature of Delhi's power supply but also with the mentality of self-reliance: no one else should be able to interfere with one's electricity. The same goes for private wells. The rumour of poison in the municipal water was only that, but its effects persist.

The riots were a breaking point for many. Many Sikh families left Delhi for ever after 1984. But for those that remained, and indeed for Hindus, Delhi would never feel the same again. For many of my generation, who were children or teenagers in 1984, the Sikh riots were the foundational coming-of-age experience, revealing, as they seemed to do, the deep truth of Delhi's social relations. Bloodshed, it seemed, had not ended with Indian independence. This time it could not be blamed on the British, or on Pakistan, or on the insider within. It was eternally inherent to the city.

Jaswant is a member of Delhi's Sikh aristocracy, the descendant of one of the contractors who built the 1911 city. In his early seventies, he has a rakish flair about him: he wears a floppy hat and carries sunglasses in his shirt pocket.

"In the 1970s, this lurking sense that the elite could do what the hell they wanted turned into a syndrome. People became giddy with power. They sucked up to Indira Gandhi, and Congress made sure they did well. So many of Delhi's big businessmen got their start during the Emergency, when those who supported Indira got big breaks and favours."

Jaswant is horrified by the Delhi elite of which he is a part, and his comportment is deliberately calculated, in part, to irritate and offend this class. Other members of his circle dislike him intensely. "He is mad," they say. "He does crazy things. In a party he just unzips his thing and starts pissing in the bushes in front of everyone. He dresses in a crazy way, talks in a crazier way. He has crazy parties."

Jaswant is indeed eccentric. His life has been full of turbulent, ambiguous relationships and immense private tragedies, and he has emerged from all of this more headstrong and contrary than ever. But among all the people I speak to about Delhi, he is unique in his readiness to speak about the violence and exclusion to which so many of them are immune because of their class. And in this respect his eccentricity seems well directed.

"Look at this Delhi culture. The refugees from West Punjab came to Delhi and they became cart pushers. They showed astonishing enterprise and they have amazing stories. But now they're filthy rich and they have no social conscience at all. They're racists, they've totally forgotten their own origins. They were refugees themselves but they have no care for the millions of refugees who are in Delhi today. Our north-eastern people who come to Delhi to work are molested and raped every day. It's horrible. I mean, my blood boils. I don't know how I stop myself from going out and throwing stones.

"If you want to know the personality of this city of Delhi, go to Kashmir or the north-east and see what happens under Delhi's orders. India only holds onto those territories by military brutality, intimidation and rape. If there were any rule of law, whole jails would be full of the Indian soldiers who have raped and mutilated. Including members of my own family, who have given the orders. But they are protected by the Armed Forces (Special Powers) Act. Of course this is antithetical to the constitution, which guarantees the right to life. But it doesn't matter anymore because there is no rule of law. This is a completely lawless society. Nobody is accountable to anybody. The people who run this country are all lawbreakers."

Jaswant's horror at what surrounds him was crystallised during the Sikh attacks of 1984, which did not pass by people like him. Delhi people had always sought out positions and connections to insulate themselves from the wildness of things, but the mobs of 1984 were willing to take on any Sikh target, no matter how powerful.

"After Indira Gandhi's assassination, with the encouragement of the press and politicians, not less than 15,000 Sikhs were killed in Delhi. The official figure was 3,000, but it was far more than that, and it happened in the most brutal way possible.

"The petrol station my family owned next to the Imperial

Hotel was surrounded and they were threatening to burn it. The manager called to tell me what was going on and I said, 'Why don't you call the police?' and the manager said, 'The police are the ones who are doing it!' Eventually the crowd was dispersed by shots fired from the Imperial Hotel.

"I was alone in the house with my kids. Hindu friends came to stay with me to help us. They knew what kind of state I was in, and they wanted to make sure I didn't do anything stupid. I gave way to self-harming behaviour. I decided to cut my own hair off rather than have state-sponsored goons do it. I smashed my parents' crystal and cut my hair off. I still have the hair.

"I lost faith in everyone. Including my friends who were trying to help but whose behaviour I found patronising. I was from Delhi and they were from outside. Who were they to protect me? My family built this damn city. I should have been protecting them.

"Two years later I was at a traffic light and my car stalled because it was cold. There was a motorcycle behind me and the rider was annoyed. He leaned in my open window and said, 'Did you Sikhs never learn your lesson?' There was not a hint of remorse in Hindus: they were delighted to have 'taught us a lesson', and they continued to display the most menacing, ghoulish behaviour.

"Another time I was walking in Connaught Place and a girl saw me in the street and asked if she could say something to me. I was afraid of the insult she was about to give me. But instead she said, 'Can I just say how handsome you look in your turban?' I was incredibly moved by her compliment, you can't imagine what it meant to me.

"But in general I was outraged by the fact that no one really came out against the genocide. All around me people were trying to suck up to the Congress and they refused to say anything against what had happened. Even the Sikhs. My brother was a socialite and a businessman, and he refused to be affected by any of this. He just went along with the dirty flow of the city.

"One time, at a party at the house of an ex-army officer – a man who later killed a guy he suspected of having an affair with his wife – I got into an argument about how the press should not have said that the bodyguards who murdered Indira were Sikh. And that man said to me, very coldly, 'You should watch what you say. You know what can happen to people like you.'

"I know those people well: the ex-army, the ex-navy, the ministers, the landowners. They're all violent, indecent people who make a mockery of the excellent education they have had. Arms dealers, contractors, suppliers of women to powerful men, all paying each other off, getting their pound of flesh. Arms dealing has a lot of prestige in this circle because it makes you rich and you can say you're being nationalistic, keeping the military supplied. That's what they say. They are proud of what they do. And their wives are proud of it too: if they have to sleep with a general or somebody, they'll do it.

"But they're also very nervous. They escape all the time: they escape into golf and bridge. They escape to London for the weekend. Their money escapes to the Channel Islands and Switzerland and Panama. They are an effete elite. They have all had bypass operations. They all have pacemakers. They are riddled with diabetes and arthritis. They are corrupt not just in their money-making but in their bodies and souls. They're very super-stitious: their fingers are covered with stones which are supposed to protect them from evil forces, and they have little gods and goddesses in every corner of their house. Because they don't know who they are, and their confusion expresses itself in preju-dice and violence."

Jaswant's romance with India's marginalised populations irri-tates a lot of his peers, who find it pretentious and perverse. But after what he experienced in 1984, Jaswant feels at home among such people in a way he does not among his own kind, who fill him, in fact, with the most profound despair. It is only among the poor and oppressed that he finds some reason for human optimism.

"What happened in Delhi in 1984 was an organised massacre of people and I don't think the city has a capacity to absorb what happened. The scars don't heal. In me, personally, the scars have not healed. The only release I have had is through my discovery of other people who have been subjected to that kind of violence – though in a much more sustained way – at the hands of the Indian state. Almost every village in Nagaland has been raped by the Indian army. Consistently. Their villages have been burnt and they have been relocated in other areas so that they are forced to encroach on other people's territory. That produces violence. Then the state comes in with violence to stop that violence. So the north-east is a cauldron.

"When I encountered those people, I realised that my suffering was nothing compared to theirs. They have suffered immeasurably, but that is their strength, their resilience. Their hands have been cut off and their villages destroyed but they still put their high-caste oppressors to shame because they have dignity. They are capable of looking after themselves. They are brilliant. They are survivors. When everything explodes, they will survive. The elite will not, because when all this is dismantled, they will have nothing to rely upon except dignity and character, which they do not have.

"In the north-east, they know everything about their surroundings and they eat everything. There is no shortage of food. They know how to survive in famine because they know which leaves to eat, which fruits to eat. They can eat dogs, they can eat rats, and they have very good cuisine. They don't overdo anything. And here these Hindu-type people: they can't eat this, they can't eat that. They are the ones really living in famine, if you ask me.

"If a natural catastrophe comes to this city, all hell will break loose. I see that coming. I see this city going into ruins, just tumbling into the dust. When an earthquake hits, when the water runs out, Delhi people will not help each other. They will slaughter each other."

Jaswant is quite merry as he says all this.

"The other day I was sitting in my car, in the market, listening to some music. Three police cars were parked next to me and the policemen were playing cards. I got out and asked them what they were up to. They said they were protecting the son of a cabinet minister. 'He's come to spend some money, he's an irresponsible, useless fellow, all he does is chase women and get drunk. We are his security team, three police cars.'

"That is the society we live in. Our policemen are not supposed to do anything for society. All they're supposed to do is protect rapacious elites from it. But the people who are protecting them have total contempt for them. One day, if things continue like this, they will shoot them dead."

Fifteen

Everyone wants their house to be done up in the style of a Russian oligarch.

– Interior designer to the Delhi rich

Rajiv Gandhi's assassination in 1991, purportedly at the hands of the Liberation Tigers of Tamil Eelam, against whom the Indian army had conducted operations in Sri Lanka, took place in the midst of the largest financial scandal the country had ever seen. The 'Bofors' scandal arose from rumours that the Swedish company had contrived to secure a multibillion-dollar arms contract by paying large kickbacks to several members of the Congress Party, including prime minister Rajiv Gandhi himself. The scandal reached to the heart of the Indian polity not only because of the unprecedented size of the bribes involved – which have been estimated at around $40 million[46] – but also the fact that they reached to the summit of government and, indeed, to the Nehru dynasty.

The exact truth of these allegations has never been reliably confirmed. But it seems quaint, in retrospect, to see the shock they provoked. And this is because the liberalisation of the economy, which took place a few months after Rajiv Gandhi's death, greatly expanded both the scale and the frequency of 'big ticket' deal-making of this sort. It introduced, indeed, an entirely new system of financial flows which concentrated enormous money in the hands of a small nexus of dealmakers from the worlds of politics and business. It generated a new Indian oligarchy.

Insofar as public administration was a money-making venture, liberalisation represented, in the short-term, a disaster. The end of the license regime meant that public officials no longer enjoyed their traditional hold over business. Businessmen did not have to approach them for licenses every time they wanted to expand a factory or launch a new product, which meant that, for politicians and bureaucrats, large revenue streams disappeared.

But administration *was* a business, and like other businesses it found ways to innovate in the face of adversity. Politicians and bureaucrats sought out new revenue streams. They began to collect not small sums from large numbers of petitioners but large sums from a few. And they did not make money any more by charging for the removal of obstacles. Instead they 'earned' their money by becoming partners to business and taking over an entire branch of business operations – that branch which required the powers of the state.

This came at a time when big business, for its part, was greatly in need of this manner of partnership. The years after liberalisation saw a large-scale transfer of ownership of basic resources – the so-called 'commanding heights' of the economy, which Nehru had reserved for the state – to private hands. These included mines, oil and gas, and that fuel of the new economy, the mobile telephony spectrum – and, of course, land, the basic resource par excellence. Whoever could secure control of these resources would inevitably make fantastic gains. But there was no precedent for the process of transfer: it was – in India as in the former Soviet Bloc in the same years – a makeshift scramble, and its outcome lay, ultimately, in the hands of the political establishment. The businessmen who came out on top, therefore, were the ones with strong political connections – often those who had already been cultivating those connections since Mrs Gandhi's time. Since the stakes could not have been higher – for whosoever could control the new Indian economy would be propelled to global levels of influence – politicians could also charge handsomely for their preferment. There was suddenly a level of deal-making that made Bofors seem infantile. The early twenty-first-century scandals surrounding corporations' under-payment for the mobile telephony spectrum and for mines mentioned sums in the tens and even hundreds of billions of dollars. India's pool of billionaires expanded rapidly, increasing their wealth from less than 1 per cent of national income in 1996 to 22 per cent in 2008. Sixty per cent of this billionaire wealth was built up from sectors closely controlled by govern-ment: property development, infrastructure, construction, mining, telecoms, cement and media.[47]

It was no wonder that most people in Delhi, where the largest of these deals were done, believed that the very richest people in the city were not those whose wealth was published in corporate accounts, but the ones who travelled around in ancient white Ambassadors and earned a salary of $1,000 per month. Politicians refrained from acquiring valuable assets in their own names, but somehow their brothers and sons seemed suddenly to own fabulous land and property, and to have investments in a fantastic range of ventures. Was it not suspicious how many political families bid for cricket teams in the Indian Premier League auction? Was it not a sign of how valuable political offices were to their incumbents that campaign spending doubled with each general election[48] – which in turn put even more pressure on politicians to turn their situation to profit? There were extraor-dinary rumours about politicians' personal worth. The media tried to guess what level of riches were involved by tracking consumer indulgences – houses, cars, children at expensive

American schools – and there was in those years widespread resentment about the seemingly charmed lifestyle of so-called public servants. But in many ways, this interest in personal property and lifestyle was to miss the point. Because the people playing at the top of this game had long since passed the level where personal enrichment was the objective. They were involved in something far more grandiose than this, and something that enriched their entrepreneur partners more than themselves. That was not the point, however: these people were the power brokers of the new India, and what they were running was a system for privatised commercial development that was its own reward – a system with an entirely different structure to the 'normal' economy in which middle-class people earned money and bought things to improve their lives.

Mayawati, the politician from Uttar Pradesh who presented herself as the champion of dalits like herself, and of the oppressed in general, and who rose to become four-times chief minister of the state, was certainly one of the most ruthlessly extractive of all Indian politicians, and she accumulated an immense private fortune (it was she who purchased the Delhi mansion that had hosted the childhood of Sadia Dehlvi, whom we met earlier). But the paradoxes of Mayawati's career were not merely of the crude – millionaire-politician-says-she-is-friend-of-the-poor – kind. In Indian politics, money-making was no longer proof of insincerity, especially since a woman like Mayawati, who came from the oppressed classes, who presided over a criminalised state and who had many enemies, could not possibly sustain her position without enormous funds for patronage and re-election. And Mayawati did display a bizarre, carnivalesque commitment to her state's oppressed classes, not only giving them hand-outs and goodies, but also dignifying their status with a campaign of symbolic building and public sculpture that placed her in a rare category of Indian politician: perhaps none other since Nehru had demonstrated such interest in the political mission of architecture. At the gateway from Delhi, where the road crosses the border into Noida, the large suburb on the Uttar Pradesh side, she laid out a bewilderingly elaborate park where twenty-four enormous sandstone elephants – symbols of her party – attended statues of fifteen dalit icons, including Mayawati herself. Like many female politicians, in fact, she designed for herself a goddess-cult in which her low caste and her great wealth became positive images of a new order: her birthdays became major ceremonial events at which she displayed herself to her followers draped in thousands of banknotes.

But in tandem with all this symbolism of dalit pride and wealth, she set about an aggressive redevelopment of her state, one whose dynamism depended not only on the size of her own war chest but also on her partnership with rich businessmen, especially a Brahmin engineer-turned-businessman. Her role in this partnership was to use state machinery to seize land from farmers and to provide the political support necessary for developing it. He, in return, supplied financial investment and business know-how, delivered well-executed prestige projects to the state and, presumably, shared his profits with her. Neither partner could have achieved this without the other. What they developed together, in fact, was a fast-track system for economic development which was sternly authoritarian – for state support came with the full arsenal of armed back-up – but which, unlike China's equivalent system, was housed within a democracy. The democratic context certainly added many layers of conflict and uncertainty to the enterprise – Mayawati's continued patronage was dependent on her winning elections, and on the day in 2012 that she was voted out, shares in the company tumbled. But this system, turbulent though it was, was India's answer to China's more explicitly autocratic one. In post-liberalisation India, it was not enough to have capital, for the flow of capital was blocked on every side by legal and bureaucratic constraints:

only when big business entered into partnership with powerful and visionary political players could adequate outlets be opened for investment.

To cross the Uttar Pradesh border from Delhi was to be assailed not only by hagiographic images of its chief minister but also by the ubiquitous logo of her construction company partner. A publicly traded company whose shares were still majority-owned by one family, the company was an established giant before Mayawati came along, owning India's largest private power station and its third-largest cement conglomerate. In 2000, it branched out into real estate, building a ring of golf courses and apartment complexes around Delhi. It had money and expertise, and was perfectly placed to partner with Mayawati when she came to power. It won from her first of all the contract to build an eight-lane highway from Noida to Agra, home of the Taj Mahal, Uttar Pradesh's most famous tourist destination. The contract required the company to put up the money for the highway but allowed it to collect tolls from users for thirty-five years, after which toll income would revert to the state. To sweeten the deal, Mayawati also 'gave' the company the land on either side of the highway, a tract of some 6,000 acres forcibly acquired from farmers at a rate of Rs 580 [$2.60] per square metre, on which it determined to develop several ventures, including private townships and a private international airport, which would over the next twenty years generate a combined estimated income of $27 billion. This boon was in addition to the 2,500 acres that Mayawati bought from farmers for the company to build a private 'sports city', which included India's Formula One racing track. It seems that the financial equation was enhanced in all these deals by the waiving of great tranches of the company's tax bill.

Realising, belatedly, that the land they had surrendered to the state government for essential infrastructure had ended up in the hands of big business, the farmers began to protest, blocking roads, burning company offices and trying to disrupt the inaugural Formula One event. The protests were dealt with brutally – the police fired into one group of protesters, killing three – and ultimately led to nothing. The company's expansion continued unabashed, with new ventures in mining, chemicals, hospitality, hydropower and foods.

As legal entities, organisations like this one were mercurial and opaque. Tens or hundreds of companies were owned by groups within other groups, some of them privately held, others publicly traded. The controlling interest of the founding families was usually distributed among many of their members. It was crucial to their success that they shield large amounts of capital from public scrutiny – not only because they did not like to pay taxes, though that was part of it, but also because their operations required them to generate significant quantities of black money for bribes, land purchases and the like. Many of them raised money for business expansion not from banks but by borrowing, unofficially, from each other, in accordance with a clubbish honour code that predated the corporate era. In the background of all this, holding things together, was usually some kind of financial genius; for it was not just anyone who knew how to move billions of dollars of black and white money efficiently through large and complex corporate systems, while at all times insulating the company from suspicion and investigation.

This system of collusion between politics and big business thrived because it allowed insiders to operate with great speed. But it did not leave room for many players. Part of its success, indeed, was due to the fact that it eliminated competition: international companies in particular found it almost impossible to duplicate the political know-how of entrenched local interests, who deliberately kept them out in just this way. No: the system was controlled by a few political and commercial figures, who concentrated enormous capital in their own hands and undertook among themselves a formidably dynamic transformation of the Indian landscape. They were not the apathetic, self-indulgent people that the press so often imagined the new 'corrupt' elite to be. Conspicuous consumption was part of their style, but this should not detract from the seriousness of their ambition. The reason they had manoeuvred themselves into this position in the first place was so that they could operate at dazzling scale and break-neck speed. They were enormous investors in the Indian economy and generated huge economic effects. Even those politicians who had swept corrupt gains into Swiss bank accounts during the 1970s and '80s, when India's slow-growing economy was no place to keep them, now brought them back to invest in its boom. Much of the foreign direct investment coming into India was not 'foreign' at all, but illicit Indian money funnelled out to companies in Mauritius or the Cayman Islands which then invested it back into India. In 2010, it was estimated that the present value of illicit funds taken out of India since Independence was close to half a trillion dollars.[49] But in the decade after 2000 it was also conspicuous that tiny Mauritius accounted for over 41 per cent of India's foreign direct investment; as a report issued by India's finance minister in 2012 commented, "Mauritius and Singapore with their small economies cannot be the sources of such huge investments, and it is apparent that the investments are routed through these jurisdictions for avoidance of taxes and/or for concealing the identities from the revenue authorities of the ultimate investors, many of whom could actually be Indian residents."[50] Members of the corrupt elite, in this sense, became highly productive agents in the economy. Politicians and their business partners were like feudal venture capitalists, extracting a forcible tax on a particular turf and channelling it quickly into new business ventures.

This is why even people who observed these goings-on from the outside could be enthusiastic about what they saw: it seemed like this back-room path to development, where members of the political class extracted large amounts of capital which they then poured efficiently into fast-moving, dramatic business projects, by-passing all the friction of political approval and official financial procedure, might be the only way for India's chaotic energies to be channelled into meaningful action. When I asked

Raman Roy, the squeaky-clean father of Indian business process outsourcing we met at the beginning of this journey, what his prognosis was for the Indian economy, he found great hope in this grey zone of politics and business, whose uniqueness he appreciated with almost patriotic affection.

"We are lucky in India to have the windfall of political money. That puts huge capital into the system. And there is also enormous ability, enormous vision. While corporations operate from quarter to quarter, politicians have a five- to ten-year perspective. That's why the two can work together so well. Look at all these new deluxe hotels: politicians acquire the land and they work with corporations to produce world-class products. It is a tested model. Right now this vision is directed at the cream, but later it will serve the masses. Because now all black money leads back into corporate activities. Our bureaucrats have immense administrative capability, and the coming together of political wealth, bureaucratic skills and the corporate ability to manage leads to magic."

It should be clear that this system rewarded people with skills conventionally regarded as underhand, and they often aroused intense disdain among so-called sophisticates. Few of the new billionaires came from the old, anglicised elite, to whom the requisite hustle had become alien over the years. Many of them had moved to Delhi, in fact, from surrounding states – such as Uttar Pradesh and Haryana – where they had operated a local political–commercial nexus even before 1991. English was often not their first language, and their tastes were untrained. They put escalators in their houses because they had seen them in five-star hotels, they scattered banknotes around them like feudal overlords, and they paid for Bombay actors and Los Angeles rap stars to perform at their weddings. But perhaps this, now, was 'taste'. It certainly seemed that the contempt in which the old elite held these people was another sign of its obsolescence. The emerging class's embrace of naked money, as a principle and as a style, equipped it very well for success, not only in the new India, but in the rest of the world too, which broadly was following suit.

Earlier in this book we saw how fondly and often India was likened to America. But for the most part, this was pure ideology. India had much more obvious similarities to America's alter ego: Russia. India and Russia had both had systems of state-run capitalism that had foundered by the 1980s, generating a new class of clever, underground entrepreneurs who came into their own after the old systems – almost simultaneously – collapsed. Both countries developed systems, after that point, in which the existence of electoral democracy did not prevent the emergence of a class of oligarchs who used the political system to take control of their countries' essential resources. Both of them had capital cities, Moscow and Delhi, where the majority watched with resentment as a small number of people used the immense power of large-country politics to their commercial advantage.

And yet, perhaps the distinctions between all these places, even with America, were fading away. In the early twenty-first century, it seemed, the question of over-powerful business elites was local news everywhere. There was a convergence in global culture, and it was not in the direction we were trained to expect. Perhaps everything, in fact, tended towards Russia. We had always imagined that Russia was global capitalism's primitive past. Perhaps it was its future.

Mickey Chopra makes a timid entrance into the quiet hotel lounge where he has asked me to meet him. He wears a black turban and suit; he is stocky and muscular and speaks with a faint lisp. He is twenty-eight years old.

He is not talkative. I try to break the ice by telling him that we have a friend in common, and we discuss her for a while. He relaxes.

I ask him about his life.

"Until I was a teenager," he says, "I thought my dad worked for the government. I used to ask, 'Why do we have this big house?' They told me, 'Your grandfather built it, then we lost the money and now your dad works for the government.'"

In truth, Mickey's father ran a large assembly of businesses across the states of Uttar Pradesh, Haryana and Punjab. The mainstay of this empire was liquor retail, a business which, in gangster states like Uttar Pradesh, offered rewards only to the shrewd, charismatic and violent.

"Of course there were goons around – you can't run this kind of business without a strong arm – but my dad always kept them out of our sight. He believed in discipline. He said, 'If you do bad things, like if you get caught for drunk driving, I can't get you off.' A lot of powerful people said to their sons, I can get you off anything. It makes for a different kind of mentality. Of course, later I discovered that there was nothing I could have done that my dad couldn't have got me out of."

Mickey's father is present throughout his conversation as a kind of spiritual touchstone.

"The company was set up by my great-grandfather in 1952. My family were livestock farmers in West Punjab and they lost everything in 1947. They set up in Uttar Pradesh, where they had to fight to make it.

"When my father took it over in the 1980s, the family was in debt. Now the group has an annual turnover of $1 billion. My father's will to succeed is phenomenal. If he sets out to do something, he will get it done. If there's someone I want to become, it's him."

Mickey speaks about the family business in the first-person plural. He has grown up absorbing business ideas and techniques, and they are a natural part of his speech.

"When our liquor business was at its height, we controlled 19 per cent of Indian liquor retail. At that time, the government auctioned liquor outlets to the highest bidder. Later on it introduced a lottery system to prevent monopolies. But we could still grow the business because we had so many employees. In any lottery in our region, out of 100 entrants, 80 were our men."

Mickey was sent to a series of expensive schools, but he was repeatedly expelled, and at the age of sixteen he dropped out for good. He went to London for a year or two to have fun: clubs, parties, and everything else that a teenager with a well-stocked bank account can think up.

When he came back, he was put in charge of one of the family's sugar mills. But his heart was not in it – and the real estate boom was on. In 2001, the family set up a real estate business and Mickey, twenty-one and entirely untrained, was given the task of building the largest shopping mall in northern India.

"When I was in England I spent a lot of time walking around malls, studying how they were made. There's no point re-inventing the wheel. I know more than anyone in India about how you set up a mall, how you arrange your brands. My father had no experience in a professional context, so everything I know about the professional context I've learned myself. I introduced computer systems into the business: I taught myself Oracle programming because the professional contractors were no good. Then I taught myself all about the latest building techniques. My first mall was built with special pre-fabricated steel pillars which had never been used in Indian malls before. Recently, I taught myself finance. I read finance texts online and every time I didn't know a word, I looked it up. Six months ago I didn't know anything and now I can conduct finance meetings with PriceWaterhouse."

Mickey's mall was famous for having Delhi's most luxurious and hi-tech nightclub. It was Mickey's pet project, his personal party zone, with endless champagne for him and his friends – and his nightly arrival there, surrounded by bodyguards, was always a frisson.

"For a time I was the man in Delhi. Loads of people wanted to be my friend. Women wanted to sleep with me. I said to my wife, 'If I hadn't been married, things would have been very different.' A lot of people were very fake."

Like many Delhi rich boys, Mickey was given a big wedding as a way of winding down his wild years. When he was twenty-two, he married his childhood sweetheart; their reception had 6,000 guests and featured dance routines by Bollywood divas. Mickey still loves parties and, as I discover during our conversation, he becomes relaxed and witty with alcohol, but there is no doubt that he has by now grown into a fully fledged partner to his father. He's ready to shut down his club: he doesn't have time to attend to it anymore, and he doesn't want anyone else to run it. He operates five shopping malls across India, and he has another 1,400 acres under development. And that is just the beginning. He is moving on to much bigger plans.

"We've just leased 700,000 acres for seventy-five years; we're opening up food processing, sugar and flower plantations."

He is so matter-of-fact that I'm not sure if I've heard correctly. We have already discussed how laborious it is to acquire land in India, buying from farmers five or ten acres at a time. I can't imagine where he could get hold of land on that scale.

"Where?" I ask.

"Ethiopia. My father has a friend who bought land from the Ethiopian president for a cattle ranch there. The president told him he had other land for sale. My dad said, 'This is it, this is what we've been looking for, let's go for it.' We're going in there with Boris Berezovsky.[51] Africa is amazing. That's where it's at. You're talking about numbers that can't even fit into your mind yet. Reliance, Tata, all the big Indian corporations are setting up there, but we're still ahead of the curve. I'm going to run this thing myself for the next eight years, that's what I've decided. I'm not giving this to any CEO until it meets my vision. It's going to be amazing. You should see this land: lush, green. Black soil, rivers."

Mickey tells me how he has 100 farmers from Punjab ready with their passports to set off for Ethiopia as soon as all the papers are signed.

"Africans can't do this work. Punjabi farmers are good because they're used to farming big plots. They're not scared of farming 5,000 acres. Meanwhile I'll go there and set up polytechnics to train the Africans, so they'll be ready when the sugar mills start up."

Shipping farmers from Punjab to work on African plantations is a plan of imperial proportions. And there's something imperial about the way he says 'Africans'. I'm stunned. I tell him so.

"Thank you," he says.

"What is on that land right now?" I ask, already knowing that his response, too, will be imperial.

"Nothing."

Mickey is excited to be talking about this. His spirits seem to be entirely unaffected by the recession that currently dominates the headlines. He orders another beer, though we have exceeded his time. All of a sudden, I find him charismatic. I can see why he makes things happen: he has made me believe, as he must have made others believe, that he can do anything. I ask him how he learned to think like this.

"I'm only twenty-eight," he says. "Why not?"

He becomes flamboyant.

"We're going to be among the top five food processors in the world. You know the first company I'm going to buy? Heinz."

I'm interested in his "Why not?" Is it on the strength of such throwaway reason that 700,000 acres of Ethiopia are cleared and hundreds of farmers shipped across the world? I wonder what the emotional register of this is for him. It seems as if, somewhere, it's all a bit of a lark.

"I sometimes wonder why I work," he says. "I do ask that question. I don't need to work. But what else am I going to do? You can't sit in beach resorts for 365 days a year. So I think of crazy things. I like it when you think up something, and it's so wild you're messed in the head and you think, 'How can I do this?' – and then you think, 'Why not?'"

I feel like pointing out that life holds more possibilities for someone like him than just sitting on the beach. "Messed in the head" sounds like language that remains from his wild days, as if the whole thing is about getting a high. I ask him how he wants to spend his money.

"Currently I drive a BMW 750i. It's good for long drives to the mall I'm building in Ludhiana. The car I really want is an Aston Martin DBS. But I'll buy it later, when I deserve it more. My father wanted to buy me a nice sports car three years ago but I said, 'Wait.' I set myself certain goals. By the time I'm forty I want a 160-foot boat. I want a nice Gulfstream plane. And I want to be able to run them without it pinching me."

Mickey talks as if he were saving up for a motorbike or a fridge, and it seems strangely banal. This is a man who can dream up earth-bending forms of money-making, but his ideas of spending it are consumerist in the most ordinary of ways. His middle-class vocabulary seems at odds with his multibillion-dollar scale, and I wonder if he is deferring his sports car so as not to run out of future acquisitions too quickly. I wonder if the whole enterprise does not teeter on the edge of senselessness, if he is not in fact still waiting for someone to supply him with a meaning for this money around which his life is organised.

Unprompted, he becomes philosophical.

"I'm not religious. I'm spiritual. My basic principle is: Whatever goes around comes around. It will come back to you, you can be dead sure of that. I live my life in a Vedic way. Disciplined. No idol worship, no stupid acceptance. Also that you don't just let someone hit you and take it from them. You give it back to them."

I'm not sure if this last point flows from the basic principle, but I don't question it. Mickey is deadly serious. He is letting me in on his knowledge. He tells me a story.

"I was at a party recently, and the waiter was handing out drinks and he moved the tray away a little too soon and this guy hadn't got his drink. So the guy shook up a soda bottle and sprayed it in the waiter's face. I went straight to the host, and I had him chucked out of the party. You have to know how to behave. Some people only feel they have money when they can screw someone else. You have to know how to treat normal people. You see, there are two kinds of rich. There are people who've had money for a long time and they don't give a fuck who you are: they'll be nice to you anyway. Like I'm nice to people. You may get bored being around them because all they talk about is how they've just got back from Cannes or St Tropez, but they will always be nice. But the people who've got rich in the last five years, they turn up at a party and the first thing they do is put their car keys down on the table to show they have a Bentley. They don't know how to behave."

Mickey is a little drunk, and he's policing boundaries that are clearer to him than to me. It's not the first time he's said, 'People have to know how to behave.' Once again I feel that his stand against the nihilism of the Delhi rich is all the more fervent because he is assailed by it himself. He is intimate with all the thuggish bad boys who have given people like him such a bad name, and he is impressed by parables of restraint.

"I have a friend who's a multibillionaire," he says, "and I asked him about the best car to buy for your kids, because I've just had kids, and he suggested a Toyota Innova. He could afford to buy a jet for his kids but he doesn't. They have to earn it. He just buys them an Innova. You see, people say there are bad kids but it's all the parents' fault. It's totally the parents. They have fucked up their kids and once that's happened it can never be undone. One day the guy is driving a Maruti 800, the next day he's driving an S Class, and he buys Beamers for his kids when they're ten years old and they just go crazy. The kids get fucked up."

People like Mickey talk about Delhi as a kind of El Dorado, where fortunes pour in overnight, almost without your asking. In this country, at this time, they say, you've got to be an absolute fool to go wrong. But for all the talk of 'new money', most Delhi fortunes are not, strictly speaking, new. They have certainly exploded in the last few years, and small-town powerhouses have indeed turned into metropolitan, and even global, ones. But they rest on influence, assets and connections built over many decades, and in that sense they are wholly traditional. The sudden prominence of a new, provincial elite should not lead one to think that the economy has become somehow democratic. People like Mickey have always had money, and they see the world from that perspective. The gruelling, arid Delhi of so many people's experience is not a city they know.

"Where do you place yourself in the pyramid of Delhi wealth?" I ask. "There can't be many people turning over a billion dollars?"

"You have no idea." He smiles condescendingly. "Most people don't go public with their money. They don't want scrutiny. I would never list my company."

"Who's the most powerful person in Delhi?"

"It all depends on politics. You can have a billion but if you have no connections, it doesn't mean anything. My family has been building connections for two generations and we know everyone. We know people in every political party, we never suffer when the government changes."

"So why do you travel with bodyguards?"

"The Uttar Pradesh police intercepted communications about a plan to kidnap me, and they told my father. People want money and they think of the easiest way, which is to take it from someone who has it. They can't do anything constructive themselves so they think short-term. We need more professionalism in India. More corporate governance. Then we'll show the entire world."

For good reason, Mickey is grateful to India.

"Since I was fourteen I've realised India is the place. I love this place, this is where it's at. Elsewhere you may have as much money as Lakshmi Mittal but you're still a second-class citizen. This is your fucking country. You should do it here."

Mickey tells me about his dislike for America.

"Why should Walmart come in here? I don't mind Gucci and LV – they do nothing to disturb the social fabric. But keep Walmart out of here. We were under slavery for 700 fucking years. We've only been free for sixty. Give us another thirty, and we will buy

Walmart. I tell you, I was at a party the other day and I had my arms round two white people and I suddenly pushed them away and said, 'Why are you here? We don't need you guys anymore.'"

Twenty-eight years old, well travelled and richer than most people on the planet, Mickey's resentment towards white people is unexpectedly intense. I ask him how the world would be different if it were run by Indians.

"It will be more spiritual," he says. But then he thinks for a moment and says,

"No. It will be exactly the same."

I bring our conversation to an end. Mickey pays the bill, and we walk outside to the quiet car park.

"Thanks," he says, shaking my hand. I don't really know why.

His driver opens the back door of his BMW, and Mickey gets in. The gates open, the BMW sweeps out, and behind it an SUV full of bodyguards.

Mickey lives about 200 metres away.

I drive home, thinking over our conversation. I ponder a little detail: during my loo break he took advantage of my absence to send a text message to our common friend. Just checking that I really knew her. Somewhere in Mickey is something alert and intimidating.

I'm still driving when he sends a text message to me, asking me not to quote certain things he has said. I write back:

ok if you answer one more question. what does money mean to you?

He responds straight away:

one of the end products of my hard work, it does mean a lot I respect it, it gives me more hard work and on the side a bit of luxury (:

Like other political strongmen concerned with hygiene and reproductive discipline, Sanjay Gandhi had been consumed by the dream of developing for his country a 'people's car'.

Sanjay loved cars and planes. He had no academic inclinations, and did not attend college; instead he spent three years as an apprentice at Rolls-Royce Motors in England. In 1967 he returned to India, aged twenty-one, and told his mother, India's new prime minister, of his idea for a new car company. He called it Maruti Motors Ltd, 'Maruti' being an epithet for the ultra-mobile monkey god, Hanuman. Using the power of the Congress political machine he also acquired 297 acres of land for a factory in nearby Haryana. The name and the land were his two significant contributions to the company at the time of his death. The subsequent partnership with Suzuki, and the revolution that Maruti brought about in middle-class car ownership in India, were the work of others.

But Sanjay Gandhi's decision to locate Maruti in Gurgaon was, in the long-term, momentous. It came at a time when the city of Delhi was reaching the limits of its commercial real estate. Neither the British nor Nehru had allocated space in the city for the large number of businesses it began to host from the 1970s, and many of them operated out of houses and hotels. The developmental monopoly, the DDA, made one concession to this need: Nehru Place, a warren of now-rotting commercial buildings in the south-east of the city. But to anyone who could look at the city with the perspective of twenty years, it was set to overflow in a massive way.

Such a man was Kushal Pal Singh, the man behind Gurgaon's extraordinary rise. His father-in-law, who was a civil servant and military man from Punjab, set up a real-estate business around the time of Partition, which was instrumental in developing new neighbourhoods for the waves of arriving refugees; this business was however decimated when the DDA was set up. K.P. Singh was charged with reviving the business, later called DLF, and in 1979, unable to operate in Delhi, he began to buy up rural land to the south of the city around Sanjay Gandhi's then-defunct factory. This is how he describes the process:

I did everything it took to persuade these farmers to trust me. I spent weeks and months with their families. I wore kurtas, sat on charpoys, drank fly-infested milk from dirty glasses, attended weddings, visited the sick. To understand why this was important, it is necessary to understand the landholding pattern. The average plot size in Gurgaon was four to five acres, mostly held by Hindu undivided families. Legally, to get clear titles, I needed the consent of every adult member of these families. That could be up to thirty people for one sale deed. Getting the married daughters to sign was often tricky because the male head of the family would refuse to share the proceeds of the sale with them. So I would travel to their homes and pay the daughters in secret. Remarkably, Gurgaon's farmers sold me land on credit. I would pay one farmer and promptly take the money back as a loan and use that to buy more land. The firm's good will made them willing to act as bankers for DLF. But it also meant I had to be extra careful about interest payments. Come rain or shine, the interest would be hand-delivered to each farmer on the third of every month at 10 a. m. We bought 3,500 acres of land in Gurgaon, more than half of it on credit, without one litigation against DLF.[52]

Even allowing for the romantic distortions of this account, Singh's enterprise was remarkable. Even if things went well, it would take decades before his investment was recouped. And at that time, in the late 1970s, it required a great leap of the imagination to even glimpse that future pay-off. Gurgaon was a dry, inaccessible place where very little happened beyond the wanderings of goat-herders on the baked earth. There were about eight cars in the whole village and one had to book a phone call to Delhi an hour in advance. There was one little shop whose owner used to dry his grain on the sidewalk; the only place to go for dinner was the local dhaba. When K.P. Singh first called Delhi building companies to trudge out into the far-off brushland and discuss building apartment complexes for the rich and successful, the contractors thought he was mad. As late as 1994, when an entertainment complex was set up with a disco and a bowling alley, Delhi consumers were so scared of going to the wilds of Gurgaon that the owner had to set up his own road lighting along the tiny road and provide roving security vans to make visitors feel safe. But with the corporate influx of the late 1990s, everything changed. When I first visited Gurgaon in 2001, it was a bizarre and thrilling scene of huge, glinting skyscrapers rising improbably from the dust of the Haryana countryside and being crowned, finally, with the banners of some of the world's largest economic entities: Microsoft, IBM, Ericsson.

It was not just corporations that set up there. DLF proclaimed a better lifestyle, a "new Singapore" of gated communities, golf courses and shopping malls, and before long corporate employees, too, ran from Delhi's dysfunctional infrastructure and political culture to make their homes in Gurgaon. Flush with boom cash, India's banks handed out loans to anyone who asked, and house prices were rising so fast that it made sense for everyone to put their savings into property. Gurgaon quickly became the largest private township in Asia, a dusty, booming expanse of hypertrophic, high-security apartment complexes which looked down on a landscape of pure commerce. In 2007, K.P. Singh listed his company on the Indian stock exchanges, and the 2008 *Forbes* list estimated him to be the world's eighth-richest man, with a white-money fortune of $30 billion.

By that time of course, there were several other real-estate magnates in the capital. The land surrounding Delhi was an amazing commodity, doubling in value every three or four years, and multiplying its value by sixty times by the simple addition of bricks, concrete and a bit of cheap labour – and the 2000s saw a desperate land rush. Hundreds of thousands of acres of agricultural land were sold on to developers. Companies that had previously made their money from car parts or chemicals now realised the bulk of their profits from real estate, and major banks such as Deutsche Bank and Morgan Stanley queued up to fund them. Small-time developers from drab little towns like Ghaziabad became serious property moguls, who sent their sons to US business schools to learn how to run billion-dollar businesses. Delhi became dominated by real-estate wealth, and this was a certain kind of wealth. Real estate was a scramble, and it was nearly impossible to operate at any significant scale without a wide network of paid connections among politicians, bureaucrats and the police. Brute force was often essential. Real-estate mafias grabbed country houses in Haryana and employed the police to silence the owners by filing false criminal charges against them. In Uttar Pradesh, they forced farmers and tribal communities to sell their land under threat of violence, employed the local police to clear the locals off, and sold it on at a large profit. There was a general escalation of criminality and violence, and the people who came through with new fortunes were a formidable breed. They knew how to hijack state power for their own private profit, and they enjoyed the support of the police and of much-feared extortion gangs. Such people had cracked the muscular equation of contemporary India, and they spurned its liberal platitudes as just so much pious cant.

Land provoked in them a remarkable, almost religious fervour, as nothing else could. The centuries-long precariousness we have already described led people from this part of the world to esteem the ownership and control of land above all other values – often above even family relationships, which is why so many families were split by property battles. Both K.P. Singh and Mickey Chopra came from Punjabi families hit by historical losses, and there was something very Punjabi about the excessiveness of their land ambitions. K.P. Singh's piecing together of his Gurgaon empire, bit by bit, over two decades, has an obsession to it that goes beyond simple commercial ambition. It is a personal crusade, a life's work. At first glance it may seem like pure acquisitiveness, but that is only in retrospect, when the work is done and the land has been turned into money. In the act itself there is something glorious and even selfless that returns us to the warrior ethos we have previously observed in north Indian business. So too in Mickey Chopra's scheme to buy three quarters of a million acres of Africa and farm it with Punjabi farmers: it has a commercial logic which should not detract from the fact that it is also a kind of grand chivalric feat. In the early twenty-first century, warriors from north India were riding abroad, and the impact of their vehemence was as turbulent outside the country as it was at home. One of the many reasons Africa was so attractive to Indian land speculators, in fact, was that rural communities often had a more slender claim to the land they lived on there than in India, and they could be much more easily turfed off in the name of total ownership. In such places as Ethiopia, Kenya, Uganda, Ghana, Sudan and Namibia, Indian businessmen scrambled to acquire mines and especially agricultural land under the sponsorship of their country's politicians, who organised business tours of these places and informed their African counterparts that only India, with its experience of the Green Revolution, could bring to their countries the skills and knowledge they lacked. While some of the people who had previously farmed this land were of course employed as wage workers on the new plantations, the majority were not. Many of these lands were highly fertile and had historically supported very dense populations, only a small proportion of which were now given a place there. In the African countryside too, therefore, Indian money helped accelerate the evacuation of the countryside, leading waves of refugees into the cities, and the escalation of slum living.

The techniques exported by warrior businessmen extended not only to land use. It turned out that the political skills they had acquired at home, where they bought up sections of the political establishment as an extension of their business infrastructure, served them extremely well in the new battlegrounds of Africa. Far from being a primitive, dying breed, India's 'robber barons' saw a bright future for themselves in the twenty-first century. In Africa, central Asia and the other key territories of contemporary resource battles, they had a great number of competitive advantages over, say, American corporations. They possessed large amounts of unmonitored capital which could be turned into cash for bribes or unofficial purchases. They knew far better than American CEOs how to navigate the political corridors of post-colonial countries. And they had a warlike sense of mission that almost nothing could contain.

It is no surprise, therefore, that one began to see, in several countries outside India, new and aggressive Indian elites who were feared by local populations and often treated as new imperialists. An example would be that of the Gupta brothers, who left Mickey Chopra's home state of Uttar Pradesh in 1994 to explore business opportunities in South Africa. Their father was a small-town businessman who sent his sons to high school under armed guard; he set up a trading company in Delhi which the three sons went on to run in the 1980s, gaining their business spurs in the Indian capital in the years either side of liberalisation. During that time, they heard it was possible for Indians who had lived under South African apartheid to receive, like blacks, special business privileges. Having never lived under South African apartheid, they were not eligible for 'Black Economic Empowerment' status, but they managed to secure it all the same. As one newspaper commented, speaking of the commercial advantages won in this way by aggressive businesspeople like the Guptas, "Critics of black economic empowerment legislation say it has increasingly served a small elite, creating Russian-style oligarchs who enjoy vast wealth while doing little to serve the plight of the millions of poor."[53]

The brothers' father sent money from Delhi to fund the early development of their business and, on their arrival, they:

> . . . rapidly made contact with rising stars of the new black elite. Today, the Guptas are known for their billionaire lifestyles and open-door access to the highest levels of

government, including the president Jacob Zuma. Living in a 52 million rand [$6.5 million] mansion in Saxonwold, a Johannesburg suburb lined with century-old oak trees [and a $3-million house in Johannesburg, formerly the home of Mark Thatcher] the brothers are alleged to have used close political links for participation in contracts legislation had set aside for blacks . . .

It is unclear just how the brothers made all their wealth, although they do own one of the largest distributors of personal computers in South Africa. What is known is that the Guptas, together with the president's son, Duduzane Zuma, 28, have become increasingly linked to deals that have been lucrative in the extreme.

The three are part of a consortium that will give them a stake in the global steel giant ArcelorMittal worth more than 3 billion rands [$280 million]. The brothers have been linked to plans to build a 350-billion-rand [$45 billion] high-speed railway system using state and Chinese funding.

They are also said to have become involved in the 9.7 billion rand purchase of the V&A Waterfront in Cape Town, the country's most valuable piece of property, from a consortium that included Dubai World. The Waterfront was sold to a local group that included a state-owned pension fund. Somehow, the Guptas and Duduzane Zuma were able to come on board as black partners, a legal requirement in any deal involving a state entity. The three have denied any impropriety in their deals . . .

It has not helped that the Guptas' lifestyle is so at odds with how most South Africans live. An application for a helicopter landing pad at their compound drew wide media coverage last year. Their launching of a daily newspaper, viewed as a counter to the continuing negative publicity they and their ruling party connections have received, has also not helped.

Now it appears that some in the ruling African National

Congress (ANC) have had enough. Allegations that the Guptas have grown so powerful they can summon cabinet ministers to their compound and authorise the appointment of senior officials at state-owned enterprises appear to be the last straw for some. The party's powerful youth league said this week the brothers were "colonising this country". The country's trade union federation, Cosatu, which is part of the ANC's governing alliance, has also said it will launch an investigation into alleged "plundering" of the economy by the Guptas.[54]

The Gupta empire, which they controlled directly and through a series of family-owned investment companies, may have begun with computers, but it quickly moved into other sectors, especially those sectors most controlled and regulated by politics: uranium and coal mining, media, aviation, etc. The business was plagued by scandal but it managed to maintain its position through a business network that included not only South African businessmen and politicians but other members of the global Indian business elite, such as the steel tycoon Lakshmi Mittal (who himself had to face allegations of improper political influence, this time within the UK government of Tony Blair; a year after the Mittal 'cash-for-influence' scandal, the Blair administration had to answer another set questions about the nature of its relationship to the billionaire Hinduja brothers, who appeared to have the power to fast-track their own UK citizenship applications). The dismay caused by public revelations that the Gupta family in summer 2013 made use of a high-security military base, not only to land a jet bringing guests to their family wedding, but also to absolve them of immigration requirements, showed just how much concern there was about the levels of control enjoyed by the family over systems and installations of the state.

While the Gupta family's fortune certainly derived from its interests in Africa, its style – the pious rhetoric of vegetarianism and the extended family, the public extolling of the brothers' saintly father and simple mother, the friendships with Indian film stars and the personal and financial investment in cricket – all came from its north Indian roots. As did the name of their original company, Sahara Holdings, named for Saharanpur in Uttar Pradesh, but which in the African context took on a different meaning. The brothers liked to joke that they turned things into a desert for their competition.[55]

More than a year after my first meeting with Mickey, I meet him for another drink. He and a friend are booked for a massage at a five-star hotel; he arranges to meet me there beforehand.

He seems to have put on perfume just before getting out of the car; it overpowers me as we shake hands. He's thirty now, and he looks more polished than I remember. His suit is beautiful. He carries nothing except an iPad and an iPhone.

His friend sits down with him and absorbs himself in some activity on a big touch screen. Mickey orders a bottle of Krug. The waiter treats him in the way I suppose he is treated in every five-star hotel of the city.

We start talking about Africa.

"The Ethiopia thing fell through," he says. "There was a change of government and the new government wanted ten times the price. We lost $3 million on that. We had to shift the whole project to Guinea. We took more precautions this time: now we have sovereign guarantees. We managed to get our equipment out, though, which was the important thing. Our South African sugar refinery is safe.

"There are loads of Indians in Africa. Many of them are doing roses. Some rice. The Chinese don't understand farming as well as we do, so we have an advantage. I have the sense that the Chinese are not so liked either, because they make big guarantees about the employment they will give but they end up bringing crowds of their own people.

"Over here, our real estate business is growing very fast. We're building two big developments in Noida. One of them has a 240-metre tower, with a swimming pool and restaurant on the sixtieth floor. We've acquired 8,000 acres across the border in Uttar Pradesh where we're building a complete private township. We've got civic authority status and we're going to do everything ourselves. Garbage, sewers. It's going to be a model city and we will train the population how to live in a modern city. How to divide up their garbage, not just throw it out in the streets. We have a system for collecting fees from all residents to pay for all these services."

I already know about this new development because Mickey's company seems to have bought up pretty much every billboard in Delhi to advertise it. Computer-generated images show a sparkling metropolis of skyscrapers and glass. The rumours are that Mickey spent significantly in excess of a billion dollars acquiring the land for his new city. Given the costs of developing that land, and all the other projects he is funding right now, one has a sense of the scale of financial backing he has.

"We're outsourcing our architecture to the US. We couldn't find people in India who could do the work and have now got an architect in North Carolina whose office does all the work for our projects over here."

While he is talking, Mickey surreptitiously dials the phone number of the friend who is sitting next to him. The friend's tablet starts to ring and he puts it to his ear. It is about the size of a hardback book. Mickey bursts out laughing.

"I just love seeing him put that thing to his ear. It's so big he can't even hold it in one hand."

We talk about other things. I ask Mickey what he thinks of the calibre of other Delhi businessmen.

"Most of them are not very impressive. They're not thinking big. You should meet a friend of mine who makes car parts. Rakesh. He's expanding into the Middle East and Europe, he knows how to compete with China – he's the one person I look up to. The story I hear most often is people selling out. Going to live in Europe. They can't deal with it here – it's too difficult – they have to pay people off at every level and get involved in politics and they just want to sell their father's business and go to Europe. I say, 'What are you gonna do there? What are you gonna do with the cash?'

"People are giving up their family business, moving out of their parents' house and losing their values. I think it's shameful. Why do you need to move out of your parents' house? Are you Indian or not?"

Since I last saw Mickey he has moved, with his parents, into the enormous farmhouse he has been building for the last two years. I have never seen this place, but its scale and opulence have created waves of rumours I hear everywhere I go. The golfing carts for navigating the grounds. The underground swimming pool surrounded by bullet-proof glass panels on steel rollers. The interior decor of gold tiling, red velvet and crystal masterminded by a British nightclub designer

"And those people are idiots," he continues, "because the opportunity is now. This is the time that money your family built up in the last generations can really explode. We're approaching a global food crisis. The climate is changing and a lot of established food markets are having major problems. Look at Australia. There is so much scarcity. The next oil is food."

He says it with exaltation, and I remember this feeling from my last conversation with him: that he is a businessman bred for the era of catastrophe, delighted by food shortages, climatic disturbance and turbulence of all sorts. Unlike American elites, who might have come to maturity in an age that believed that the future would be less assailed by catastrophe, Mickey comes to maturity in an age that believes that catastrophe is just beginning.

"Our next big venture in India is poultry. We're looking to deliver 500,000 chickens per day. They'll be properly packed and hygienic. Currently chicken farms are very dirty. The knife they cut with and the base they cut on are so dirty. We just have to tell people the knife they cut with is dirtier than your toilet seat and they'll all abandon the old suppliers. This will be a very important product for us."

He seems to have even more energy than the first time I met him. Any one of the many projects he is managing would defeat most other people I know. I say he must be working hard.

"Of course it's difficult. I don't get to see my kids. My wife goes on at me about it. I see them for half an hour in the morning and maybe two evenings a week. But I tell her – when they're nineteen, at least they'll have money. Imagine if we didn't have money and they were complaining that they couldn't go to good schools or anything. What would I say to them? 'Well, at least I spent time with you'?"

It is time for Mickey's massage.

"It's a great time," he says, rising, "the greatest time ever in Indian history. There's money to be made in every corner. Everywhere you look there's scarcity. It's very corrupt – you have to work very hard – but it's a great scene."

"Would you like it to be less corrupt?" I ask.

"*No!*" He laughs at length, and turns to his friend in mirth.

We walk out through the hotel. He and his friend head towards the spa. We say goodbye and I walk away. He calls out to me.

"And by the way!"

I turn around.

"I still want to buy Heinz!"

Driving past Delhi's sole dealer of Bentleys and Lamborghinis, I stop in on a whim and ask to speak to the manager. He's not around and I'm sent to have coffee with the PR girls. They are appropriately attractive and, judging by their diamonds, from the right kind of family. ("I've driven a million Porsches and Ferraris," says one. "They're nice cars. But when you get into a Lamborghini, it's something else.") For them, Delhi is a place of infinite money-making, and they fall over themselves trying to express this fantastic fecundity.

"When someone comes in here looking to buy a Bentley, we don't ask him what he's driving now. Just because he drives a BMW doesn't mean he can afford a Bentley. We ask if he has a jet or a yacht. We ask if he has an island."

"Are there many people with jets in Delhi?" I ask.

The girls wax apoplectic.

"*Everyone* has one. And not just one – they have two, three, four."

We chat about nice cars and expensive living. A Lamborghini is driven into the showroom: the noise is so deafening that we have to stop talking until it's in place. I ask the philistine's question: what's the point of spending 30 million rupees [$600,000] on a car that can do over 300 kilometres per hour in a city where the traffic doesn't move? They tell me about the car club that meets at night in the diplomatic enclave, where the roads are straight, wide and empty.

"You have to have at least, like, a BMW or a Mercedes to join. They meet at midnight and they race their cars. The prime minister's office is always calling us to complain."

"Why?"

"Because the prime minister can't sleep. These engines make so much noise they keep him awake. So he calls us to complain, but obviously there's nothing we can do."

As I drive away, I cannot help thinking of prime minister Manmohan Singh tossing and turning in bed, his snowy hair unturbaned on the pillow, his dreams interrupted by the rich boys' Ferraris screaming up and down the roads outside. Manmohan Singh is of course the man who, long ago, as finance minister, opened the window to the storm of global capitalism and set the course for a new oligarchic elite.

Sixteen

You like this table? I designed it myself. Brilliant white.
If anyone comes in to the room unexpectedly they'll never
be able to spot the cocaine on it.

– Delhi millionaire

"Parties in Delhi are no fun, dude! In Mumbai, even when
they're doing coke it's fun to be with them. Here it's not like
that. In Delhi people are crazy, and they go to parties to escape
themselves because fundamentally their shit is fucked up. When
you go into it with that mentality, you're heading for some
morose shit. You go to Delhi parties, and you see two sitting in
that corner, three in that corner, four smoking outside. No one's
talking. It's like that here."

I'm speaking to Krish, who, as a retired drug dealer, knows
something about all this.

"I started out dealing in Goa and Manali but I quickly got
connected to the cities. If any party happened in Delhi, I used to
be there. Nothing works without drugs in Delhi, so without me
there was no party. Without me, there was no Fashion Week. When
Fashion Week happened, they called me up to make sure I was
coming, and they booked me a room in the hotel where it was

happening. Any designer who was having a show would call me before to say, 'Dude, you have to be there on that day.' For Fashion Week you needed 100 or 200g easy in one or two days. I used to get everything. I was perfect. People used to trust me because I never messed up. I would just finish my job and walk away.

"Everyone is using, boss! Big politicians, big industrialists, fashion, media – all of them. But in Delhi you don't see it out much: it happens in farmhouses. The people who do so much coke don't go out. The farmhouse area is a fucking junkyard. I don't care to go these days. Delhi used to be fun. Before 2001 we used to have rave parties in farmhouses. And it was fun, people wanted to listen to music, and the parties were outdoors. And yeah, all kinds of stuff used to be around but nobody used to do coke. Ecstasy or MDMA. Not cocaine. People loved each other and there were only a few people in the scene, they didn't give a fuck what other people thought, they just wanted to dance. Now the parties are all shuttered up and no one cares about music. Everyone's got their expensive clothes on, so they need air conditioning. You can't do MDMA in a closed room, you know: you need to be outside dancing. You can't fucking do it in a room and sit there. So coke is more convenient for people nowadays.

"Coke has taken over everything. People want the feeling of cocaine. To catch a girl, to catch people. Rich people who do a party in their farmhouse, they can't have it without that feeling. They are rich but they don't *feel* rich without coke. If people do a farmhouse party they put down 5 lakhs on the coke.

"And coke is good for all these people who have to work. If you do Ecstasy or LSD the whole night, the next day you can't do anything. Coke, you work the next day. I know so many people who have twenty-four-hour lives. Like that fucking politician – he doesn't sleep for two or three days. He just finishes the night, puts some water on his face and a suit on and then he turns up at meetings fucking hyper, you can tell, you know. Coke is good for that. With other drugs you can't. You are shattered next day. So now there's no weekend: now every day is a weekend. People will call, 'Dude, can you hook me up?' and I'm like 'Today is Monday!'

"Go to all the five-star hotels, the toilet's always busy, mate! Even like all these lounge bars, it's the same thing, everybody knows. They know if they tell one person not to do it then ten others won't come. They don't want to lose business. So they tolerate it. You need to have a crowd in your bar, so you can't fuck around with the dope. Otherwise, next time they won't come and they'll tell everyone else too.

"You can get busted. But it doesn't really happen. The cops take money and then they leave. It's mostly just these black guys who get caught, they get really fucked. Most people who use coke are connected. So even when the cops arrest someone, they somehow get a call from somewhere else like, 'Dude, that's my friend, so take care.' So they just say to him, 'Pay us and fuck off.' It's a kind of business for them. Whenever they catch a politician's son, it's a jackpot.

"It's much more in Delhi than other cities because the people who run things in Delhi are the people who already have money. They have property and businesses, and they live off that. So it doesn't matter whether they work or not. No one sits at home doing nothing in Mumbai because you won't find anyone else around you. Everybody else is at work. Even if they're rich, they still work. They do all this shit and all, but the next morning you'll see them in the office. Here in Delhi, it's like more royal style. Delhi people call each other up in the afternoon and say, 'Oh, what are you doing?' – 'Nothing really' – 'Okay, come for a drink love' – and there you go. You go to their house, fucking every evening you will see ten or fifteen people. Mumbai doesn't have time for that kind of stuff.

"The rich here are really fucked up. These people don't even pay their servants and the people who work for them and all. But they can like spend on drugs like easily 50,000 rupees [$1,000] a night. Especially the boys – they spend too much money in Delhi: go to clubs, find a chick, buy a drink, buy coke. Partly because

Delhi has fewer girls out than Mumbai. Guys are going crazy with competition. Girls are more sheltered in Delhi, they mostly live with their parents. In Mumbai they rent their own places like boys.

"I know this guy who lives in a farmhouse. I was in his house just yesterday. He doesn't work. He's all alone. When you enter his gates, you have to drive a kilometre to reach his palace. And he made his house like one of those old houses in London. The cars are fanned out in front. When he buys a car he spends more money than the cost of the car on modifications. Like whatever car he buys, he calls them and he's like, put this shit, put that shit. So he's got this row of Lamborghinis, Ferraris, Maseratis, Range Rovers. Vintage cars too. And all this guy thinks about is, 'Okay, what guy can get me the best coke? Which girls are new in town?' That's all he does. And his friends are like that too. All of them are like that. They don't need to work like a hundred years and they can spend so much money and still it won't go away. He has a big big company and his money is made. So many of them in this city like that. They are fucking smart enough dude! A couple of them studied in Oxford and they've done like super things, but once this thing is in your head, everything is dead, everything.

"I see people lose everything. You lose your friends, you lose your family. You lose yourself. You go nuts. You go fucking nuts. People destroy everything, they don't work, they lose themselves. So many of those dudes have done too much, they're wired all the time, they can't handle people you know, they're fucking shivering and all, they start shouting. Like *Trainspotting* you know, they fucking freak out."

Was this oligarchy happy? Strangely, perhaps, happiness did not seem to be among its more pronounced attributes. In order to understand why, we might ask another question: "How do you know you own what you own?"

In Western societies, where there was a long-standing and widespread capitalist consensus, the question caused less difficulty. Spiritual problems with money and property had been laid to rest long ago: contemporary Europeans could no longer empathise with the spiritual terror with which their Renaissance forbears contemplated the accumulation of profit. And in modern, democratic times, a consensual explanation had arisen for what some people owned and others did not: hard work. Over the previous century, the wealth of America's financial elite, for instance, had derived less and less from inheritance and more and more from corporate salaries and bonuses. The rich could explain their privilege, therefore, through merit: they had excelled at university, they had shown intelligence and originality in the workplace, they had driven themselves to their limits, they had been promoted because of their skills – and it was quite proper that they should be rewarded with property, luxury and mobility. They did not need to ask themselves, as they drove home at night, if their mansion was really 'theirs' – if they were not, in fact, imposters, hucksters or criminals who merely 'squatted' in wealth. Their ownership of property was not just legal and theoretical: it accorded with their own inner sense, and indeed with society's general opinion. It was all legitimate. What was theirs was 'really' theirs.

It was an absurd rationale. If hard work were really recompensed with property, many of the global poor would look out over rolling estates. If talent always found its way, the planet would not resound so deafeningly with the disappointment of wasted skill and ambition. But this was not the point. It was important to the functioning of a society that there be a consensus as to what constituted a legitimate basis for property, even if the whole thing was a delusion.

In the wake of an economic upheaval like India's liberalisation, where enormous fortunes had simply been seized from the mêlée, the rich did not have such an easy time explaining how or why wealth had come to them, for they knew better than anyone else just how arbitrary the whole thing was. Their money had been acquired by a combination of elements – luck and connections, brute force and cunning – that had nothing individual about it at all. Anyone else could have done the same thing. Wealth remained, at some level, external: it did not feel 'mine'. Looking at their houses and jets, they suffered from a profound misrecognition, like the impotent man whose mental image of himself has no penis, even though he can see the thing hanging between his legs. They found it difficult to *feel* rich. They enjoyed physical and legal control over their assets, but this did not translate into a secure inner feeling of ownership. They were fully aware of how unrepresentative they were of their poor country, and that society at large had little conviction that they deserved what they owned. They were regularly called thieves and pillagers, and the fact that they denied it vehemently did not mean that they did not believe it themselves. "Why has this come to me?" they asked themselves and, since the answer took them into places they did not want to go, they were addicted to distraction. But even Delhi's endless drugs and parties could not cut off the anxiety that all this *stuff* might be taken away from them as easily and quickly as it had come. It was a Hindu idea of wealth too: the goddess Lakshmi, she of the gold coins, was always only a visitor. She had to be coaxed into one's house at diwali time and, given the great whimsy of the Hindu cosmos, she could depart at any time. Every morning the Hindu shopkeepers said prayers to her: not today, Mother Lakshmi, do not leave me today.

This is why spiritual advisers were as prominent in the business world as accountants and lawyers. Having acquired their wealth by hacking the political machine, rich people sought to ensure they did not lose it by employing the services of those who could hack the cosmic machine. Gurus told businesspeople what to do to keep the universal flows pointing in their direction: eat these foods, drive a car of this colour, choose a phone number ending in this digit, marry a woman with this name, wear a ring with this stone. There were gurus who specialised in property, gurus who were experts at legal disputes, and gurus who helped with focus and energy. A business class that, despite all the signs to the contrary, suffered from deep fears about its own downfall, turned to gurus to help it preserve itself. Gurus exorcised this class of its many ghosts: they sought to extract from the equation of Indian business the great accumulation of negativity that they felt.

But it was possible to glimpse something else in Delhi businessmen, something more paradoxical than the simple desperation to hang onto what they had. It was possible to see that their urge to acquire and accumulate sat alongside another, precisely opposite, impulse: to rid themselves of everything, to be pure, ascetic and uncorrupted. In this they had more in common, in fact, with European capitalists of the Renaissance era than with their contemporary Western counterparts. The consumer universe offered many kinds of 'choice' but it did not allow rich people to choose nothing – and yet this desire to possess nothing is actually much more powerful in human history than we consumerists commonly remember. In this part of the world, particularly, the urge to give up the material life and wander in search of something else was significant, as was the relationship entertained by the powerful and moneyed with the spiritual and poor. The way that contemporary business warriors registered their success was through the accumulation of money and possessions, but this in some ways dulled the entire enterprise. For warriors have always prized asceticism: the spiritual economy that allows practitioners to rise above the common condition and achieve truly noble feats. Sometimes the ascetic drive was felt powerfully by these men – particularly the men – whose Hinduism constantly warned them of spiritual corruption. Delhi's businessmen turned to gurus not only to help them keep their wealth, therefore, but to help them endure it.

"In 1999, my life changed. I began an affair with a pretty married woman with two kids. She was separated from her husband and I really liked her. And it was in that year that I began trading.

"I went into business with a man who was India's largest wheat exporter. We began trading a lot of different commodities and the returns were so amazing that everyone was putting money into our business. The richest Indians from all over the world put money in: they would give us a crore and six weeks later we gave them 3 crores back. We were getting capital from everyone and everywhere we could. I liquidated property and investments to put money in; all my friends were doing the same.

"You see: liberalisation was a gradual process, and as late as 1999 trade restrictions were still being lifted on imports. My partner and I knew people in the government, so we had inside information about which restrictions would be lifted next. It was just like all the real estate guys who got inside information about where the new highways were being planned, and then bought land there. We bought up stocks of a commodity before anyone else knew it would be derestricted. We had shiploads ready to come into the country as soon as the restrictions were lifted, and we made a pile of money very quickly. Then the big companies would start to import that commodity and we moved onto something else. We made so much money, it was embarrassing.

"Then it all ended. Because we have something in India called jealousy. My business partner had another business partner who reported us to the police, and straight away every investigative agency in the country was up our ass. Asking how we had made so much money so quickly. We also had huge quantities of black money because we had to give out bribes. A shipload of wheat was worth 40 crores [$8 million] and to get it through you would have to hand out bribes of 50 lakhs [$100,000]. So they were suspicious.

"After that all my bank accounts were frozen and my money was inaccessible. I had 500 crores [$100 million] sitting in the bank but I couldn't touch it. So I didn't make anything during the boom while everyone else was putting money in real estate. There were four years of questions. I became very frustrated

– I'd worked to earn the money but couldn't enjoy the fruits of my work.

"At the same time my girlfriend left me and began an affair with one of Delhi's most insane men, the son of a cabinet minister. She knew he was very violent but she also knew he was about to become very rich because her brother was in on the same deal. So she went to be with him."

Now thirty-four years old, Puneet has not worked for more than a decade. He stays at home, mostly, since his friends are all rich and he has no income. Today, in anticipation of my visit, he has put on a shirt, newly pressed trousers and a pair of leather brogues. We sit together in the spacious living room whose walls are hung with hunting scenes and antique engravings of Indian cities as they appeared to English nineteenth-century travellers.

Puneet's improbable windfall was helped along by the fact that he went to one of Delhi's most prestigious schools, the preferred choice of the political and business elite. His school friends were the sons and daughters of the most powerful people in the country, and they revelled in their shared invulnerability. The school provided, essentially, an apprenticeship in power-mongering.

"There was this guy who married into an army family, which enabled him to become a successful arms dealer. His two sons were at school with me. One day we were at the nightclub at the Hyatt and the sons got into a big fight. The bouncers started fighting them and they called their dad. He rushed over there – he's a huge guy himself – and he beat up the bouncers. He picked up big plant pots and threw them at them. Then he got his sons out. After that he planted a fake picture of his sons bandaged up in hospital in the newspapers to get sympathy for them, and filed a lawsuit against the Hyatt.

"That kind of stuff happened all the time. Whenever trouble broke out, boys would be competing with each other over which of their fathers had more power to intervene: *'I'll call my dad. No, I'll call my dad.'*

"One guy was the son of the minister of external affairs. So his father had control over passports. One day my friend gets off a flight into India and he turns up at the immigration desk. His passport was folded in two in his back pocket. He put it on the desk. The immigration guy said, 'You can't treat your passport like that. You're defacing government property.' My friend replied, 'You want to see how I treat my passport?' and he started ripping pages out of his passport and tossing them one by one in the face of the guy behind the desk.

"Another friend wanted to get a driving license. When you're eighteen, everyone is trying to get a driving license. So he walked into the transport authority. He started dropping the name of his uncle, who was the chief of police. As he went around the office, he moved from the lowest rung to the highest rung until he met the guy in charge, who organised for him to have his full license there and then. This was an incredible feat. Usually you have a provisional license first and a full license is only granted later, and at age eighteen a full driving license is the coolest thing you can get. But while this was going on, someone made a call to the police chief's office, found out the guy was bullshitting about who his uncle was and cut up the license in front of him.

"My friends use connections for everything. How else can you function in this place? I was in a car accident some time ago and they confiscated my license. I called a friend's father, who sent policemen to sort out the situation and rough up the other guys. Then I called up a friend in the ministry whose father had an amazing assistant who got my license back for me the same day. Otherwise I would have had to go to court and everything.

"This is why the elites of this country are so crazy. Their high comes from being able to do stuff that no one else can do and they'll fight like anything to protect that. And it's the parenting too. The parents worship power, so the kids do too. That's partly why loss and failure have been such important lessons in my life.

It's only when everything is taken away that you start to see what crazy things you were doing."

That is what, in 2000, Puneet felt had happened to him. And he felt it was not just a chance event. It was a spiritual message.

"Some negative energy was attacking me that I couldn't deal with. I felt I was being told, 'You can't go the way you were going. At least: you have to go another way before you can go that way.' I got deeper into spirituality so I could get my money unblocked. I started going to see gurus who could help me find out what problems in me were keeping this money away.

"I found a guru who was the head of a big bathroom fittings company. I've had many gurus, but when I met this guy there was an insane exchange of energy, and I've been with him now for a long time. So he listened to my story. I explained that the reason my girlfriend left me was that I turned her down when she asked me to marry her, which was all because I felt I should not be distracted from my spiritual path. He told me I should not have turned her down. When a woman asks a man to marry her that proposal comes with the universal female energy and should not be rejected. To the point where he told me my money would only be released when I got married. So basically it seemed that on the day I turned down this woman's marriage request, somebody pressed the fucking pause button on my life.

"He pressed me to get married. And at some level it's easy for a good-looking guy who has 500 crores sitting in the bank which are going to get unblocked soon. There are so many fucking beautiful women I could have had. But the problem with a guy with my depth is that I can read what's on a woman's mind and if I don't see that she's coming with the right attitude I won't fuck her. The one big problem with Delhi society is that if you fuck any woman who's part of that web, you might as well get a webcam and start broadcasting your sexual activities over the internet because it's pretty much fucking in public dude. You have to have the fucking confidence of a fucking pornstar.

"And it's difficult for me and my brother. He's not married

either, even though he went to Yale and he's a successful banker in London. My brother has a voracious sexual appetite. He's fucking fearless in that department. He scares me sometimes. He'll try his luck with any woman anywhere. He's not good-looking at all now. He's like balding and short. But he's a sweet guy. The thing is our mother is an overbearing personality. That's one reason it's difficult for us to get married. Then our money has got stuck, and anyway we weren't so financially secure after my father died. The expansion of wealth that happened in normal families where the father was alive did not happen with us. You have to understand that when one is living in Delhi, whether one likes it or not, one is part of the rat race, and we have not ridden the wave of wealth multiplication which has carried everyone else with it in the last ten years. We're fucking poor compared to everybody else. We used to have another house from which we used to get rental income and a commercial property too, and both have been sold, so now I don't have any unearned income. That's what everyone in Delhi wants, unearned income. But we don't have any. So that's a problem too for prospective brides."

By this point in the conversation, Puneet and I are smoking a cigarette in the garden outside. His mother walks up the drive – she has been attending a wedding party at the house next door, for which every BMW and Mercedes in the city seems to have turned out – and Puneet hastily throws his cigarette over the garden wall. But he is not quick enough. His mother shouts at him for smoking; he denies it, but half-heartedly.

He returns to his meeting with the guru.

"Anyway, the other mistake that guru told me I had made had to do with my uncle. I had taken my uncle to court, and my guru said, since my father was dead, my uncle was the head of the family and you should always keep peace with the head of the family.

"This house was divided between my dad and his brother. My uncle owns the back half and since my father died he has been trying to get the whole thing. His part is painted a different colour from ours: one night he had the roof of the entire building painted his colour to try and indicate that my grandmother had wanted him to have the whole house. Then he used his contacts in the police to intimidate me: they threatened to arrest me if we didn't vacate the property. And then they issued death threats to my mother. You can imagine if someone can go down to the level of fucking sending my mother death threats when I'm sixteen years old. To a widow, you're doing it to a fucking widow. I can't even imagine what goes on.

"My uncle is a very toxic influence in my life. He's got a fucking crazy family. His elder daughter is a very good-looking woman. Foxy fucking hot chick. Tall, very fair, very slim – very arrogant. She had a lot of guys chasing her so her ego got inflated even more. She had one of the biggest industrial families offering her to marry their son to her – an offer she should actually have accepted if she'd been sensible and humble. She got engaged to some guy whose mother is a big socialite – then she broke off her engagement with that guy, he went nuts, he's never been the same since. Then she got married to a leather exporter, sweet guy, moved into his house in Nizamuddin, a year later got out of there, took all the fucking furniture with her, took all his family's diamonds, divorced him.

"She was friendly with a woman who owned this company that became famous for big scams and fraud and shit. At one point that woman and her entire family were in jail for some scam, or they were on the run. She used to live at the Maurya Sheraton because she was making so much money, and she used to have a Rolls-Royce parked outside which became like a landmark for us boys. Anyway when she went to jail that Rolls-Royce was parked outside our house, because my cousin was her best friend and she was doing all the paperwork for the company. While she was working for that woman she met her nephew, fell in love with that asshole, and one day we come home and find that she's getting married to him. That marriage went on for a while and she made that guy's life hell. I believe one of the servants who later left them told us that she physically kicked her husband in front of him one day. Then there was another divorce. Now she's living in the other part of my house. I have very pleasant company around me.

"Anyway so her father, my uncle, sold one of my father's factories without telling me or my mother. Our side of the family were 50 per cent shareholders. I took him to court and eventually used strong-arm tactics to get our share of the money from the sale. But when I went to see my guru, he said that some of my problems stemmed from this. He said that traditionally, in Hinduism, anybody who takes the head of the family to court will be not treated well by the spiritual ancestors.

"There is a period in the Hindu calendar called the 'sharadh'. This is a period when all the souls of your ancestors are supposed to come down to the earthly plane. And you're supposed to win their blessings. Somebody who has the ancestors on his side is supposed to have amazing good fortune. And when you don't have their blessings, when you have annoyed them, the opposite happens. Everything you try to do there'll be an obstacle. So I believe the reason I've faced so many blockages since my father and grandfather died because I've had what in spiritual terms is called the curse of the ancestors, or 'pitra dosh'.

"The philosophy is like this. After they have died, the same father or grandfather who would have loved you in life, if their souls haven't proceeded to the next plane, they will keep fingering you and bothering you, compelling you to do whatever is necessary for them to be released. In India we have two or three holy sites where you're supposed to go to release your ancestors from whatever earthly plane they're stuck at. Only a son can do this ceremony. That's why Indians are so fucking crazy about having a son, because they believe they can't get their salvation or move to the next level until their son actually cremates them and gets this ceremony done for them. So I did this ceremony finally this year to clear my pitra dosh, which is like twenty-two years after my grandfather and my father died, and I definitely do feel a tangible difference. And after that I went to my guru and he said, 'Half your work is now done.' And I can actually feel one of my channels is absolutely completely clear which is exceptional. I mean basically when you're becoming a master all your three channels have to be absolutely clear – that means you have no pitra dosh, you have no ancestral problems, even your ancestors' sins, which accrue to you, you've paid off. In Hinduism the ultimate son is supposed to be a guy who is so auspicious that he actually releases twenty-one generations of his ancestors from a certain plane and grants them salvation. That's the ultimate son that can be born into a family.

"That bathroom-fittings guru has totally broken me down and rebuilt me, which was the only way I could have been saved. And now things are looking up. My lawsuit is near to completion, and the government has forgiven me the tax, which is an acknowledgement that the money is going to come back to me soon. But I've changed totally in the process. Some experiences I cannot even tell because people would think I'm insane. My ego has been broken down. I'm celibate. My rich friends come to me to find peace. They admire me, because part of them wants to be living the spiritual life like I am, dude. People with money are so attracted to me. Sometimes they have problems in their business lives – they make massive money off two deals and then nothing else happens – and I find a quote or a lesson that will unblock them.

"You see during the period of money-making in Delhi everyone lost their way, dude. My best friend's become a coke addict who spends his time fucking hookers. He just sent me a picture of himself in the Ritz in Singapore with these two hookers. All my friends are going through crazy divorces. Money's all they cared about and now they're realising they don't have anything else. So they come to me."

I have asked Puneet to take me to see his guru this evening, and it is now time to leave. We get in the car and set out for Punjabi Bagh, one of the business enclaves of west Delhi, which is where the guru lives. Puneet is light-hearted on the road. He makes observations about the people in the cars around us. We pass two cops on a motorbike, a man in front and a woman behind.

"That woman cop is giving me the eye, man!" Puneet says. "She wants a piece of me."

A white Bentley limousine powers past us, and we watch as it parts the traffic ahead. It crouches low on its massive tyres; the winged "B" on the back looks like a rapper's medallion. Bentleys and Rolls-Royces used to sit upright like pillared country mansions, but those were the days when wealth aspired to the style of the English aristocracy. Now Bentleys and Rolls-Royces are made to look like vehicles for gangsters, because the aesthetic of twenty-first century money is different. The question of what 'taste' is, is no longer clear: from Los Angeles to Beijing, the rich assume a style of criminality.

We arrive at the ashram, which is packed with waiting people. We are informed that the guru is asleep. We decide to wait in the line, which snakes back and forth across the large basement, up the steps, and around the house outside. Volunteers hand out steel plates of rice and daal to the patient congregation. We wait.

"When he is sleeping," says Puneet, "you're not supposed to disturb him because he's actually at a level of consciousness where he's working on somebody's problems."

It's hot where we are sitting, and this spiritual refuge attracts great numbers of mosquitoes. Puneet starts to get frustrated.

"God has been very kind to me," he says. "My guru has been very kind to me. They've saved me from a lot of danger. Perhaps nothing good has happened in the last ten years of my life but I've been saved and brought out of a lot of danger. A lot! I mean you probably don't even comprehend how much. I'm very grateful. But it's been a long time without my money. It's been a long time since I had good times."

"What will you do when you get your money back," I ask.

"I just want to get laid, man. Just leave all this behind. Spent too much time being a hermit. Do you think I don't want the things other people want? I still like the idea of living in a luxurious house and driving a big car. I like nice women with nice asses. I like the concept of having a family and children and all that. I've put in ten years to cleaning up my spiritual account and my money still hasn't come back to me. It's tiring."

I'm sure everyone with a monastic bent has thoughts like this, and I'm not entirely convinced that it is real. Has the last decade of his life been a "state of exception" – or is this perhaps just who he is? If his deepest impulse were to "get laid" would he not have devoted more of this decade to it? – he has not exactly been short of time. If he had wanted to, he could also have found other ways of earning money over these years, rather than opting out of Delhi's boom. I wonder if he really wants his money back at all, or if the money is just one big alibi, if this money in the bank, which he mentions every five minutes, is not just an excuse for him to lead the kind of life he would like to live anyway. The story of his future liberation – when he has his money, and there will be women and parties and pleasure – may be just a fiction. An attempt on the part of a man who does not really like the world of money and struggle to appear 'normal' in this era of obsessive accumulation.

As if he can hear these thoughts, he says,

"But I don't want physical things to ever smother my connection to God. I want both. So I'm a little confused right now. Because maybe God is just putting this money in my way as one more obstacle between me and him. If you're gonna be so audacious to think that you want to be in God's company all the time – that's a very audacious thought. Out of the seven billion on earth only a few people have that ambition – that I want to be with God. Very few guys wake up in the morning and say that's what I have to achieve today, right? So my guru says to me in that case, a person who's thinking like that – in that case, which is your case, he says, God will do everything the fuck he can do in his power to discourage you. And test you. Because he doesn't want sub-standard people in his company. So if I go the wrong way he'll kick me the fuck out."

The whisper goes around that the guru is awake, and, very slowly, the line of cross-legged people begins to move. After a couple of hours we reach the top of the steps outside the guru's room, and we are ushered in.

The room is large, and there are still many people ahead of us. If I expected any great surge of feeling on seeing the guru, I am disappointed. He does seem like the only normal person in the room – everyone else is in a slightly altered state – but I don't feel anything more exceptional than that. He is just back from a day selling bathroom fittings: he still wears his suit, and he is sitting cross-legged on a bed with his socks on.

People kneel in front of him and everyone can hear what is being said: "My daughter is doing badly at school. I am suffering from pains in my knees." One woman gives the guru a letter to read: she is crying. To most of these supplicants, the guru gives a steel cup of drinking water that he has previously blessed by holding it against his forehead. To others he gives cardamom seeds.

A favourite phrase of Delhi businessmen is, "Your bad deeds always come back to you." In the course of accumulating wealth you must pay bribes, steal from the system, intimidate people, make enemies – and generally forget about everything that is not accumulating wealth. If you are making a lot of money it 'proves' that you are a favoured child of the universe: it is on your side, you have nothing to feel bad about. But even very large fortunes can sometimes seem dwarfed by the negativity that has been accumulated in the process. Making this negative surplus disappear is therefore an eternal preoccupation of the business classes. You have to find other beings to take your negativity from you, places where it can be dumped and never return. Giving charity is good: it shifts some of your negativity from you to the person you are giving to. Going on pilgrimages earns you credit that can be offset against this negativity. But the dream of course is a mechanism that can make your negativity simply disappear.

"Those people have come with manifestations of negative return. An aching back, a child failing in school – it's all because of negativity. The cardamom seeds take the negativity away. The guru blesses the person and the negativity is transferred to the cardamom seeds. The seeds are then thrown into the Yamuna river, where the fish eat them."

If there are still any fish in the Yamuna river.

"Fish, because they live in water, are protected from Saturn, so there the cycle of negativity ends."

But there are volumes of negativity that all the cardamom seeds and all the fish in the world cannot absorb, and struggling against them is a full-time occupation.

Puneet asks me, "What are you going to ask him when you see him?"

I have a pang of unease.

"What do you mean?"

"Well you've waited all this time to see him. What are you going to ask? Why are you here?"

Puneet is not one of this guru's ordinary followers. The guru extends special favours to him because, he says, Puneet has spiritual qualities that most people do not have. The $100 million in Puneet's bank account might have something to do with it too; I don't know. The point is that I have somehow imagined all this time that Puneet and I would have a private audience with the guru. A cosy chat among equals. Now I realise I am coming on my knees to him as just one more devotee among many.

The situation triggers a deep fragility in my personality. My thoughts turn to chaos. My head begins to spin. I don't know how to speak for myself in front of this man. In front of all these other people. Everyone will know I am faking it. I am sweating, and not with the heat.

Puneet's turn comes first. The man on the bed puts his hand on his head. Though the two of them spend their weekends watching soccer together, there is no flicker of recognition from the guru, who asks him why he has come. Puneet tells him that his eyes have recently been stinging a lot. The guru requests from his assistants a steel cup of water, which he places against his forehead and hands to Puneet.

I feel myself collapsing inside. This is the role I choose: I am the observer, not the observed. I am in a panic, and I find myself contemptible. I realise that I know nothing. Everyone else in this room knows something very basic about life that I do not. They *live*; I am just an eavesdropper. I spy on life so that I do not have to live it. A non-existent wind is rushing in my ears and, in that moment, I am convinced that I have reached the age I have without ever embarking on anything real. I realise I *need* to speak to this guru. Maybe this has been the whole point, all along. I need a word from him to draw me in from the comfortable void of the outside. I realise I will approach him in utter earnestness.

Puneet is led away by one of the guru's helpers. The man puts his hand on my head. It feels good. I can sense his power. He looks into my eyes.

"What can I do for you?" he says gently.

I look humbly at him.

"Please tell me," I say, "what it is I still have to learn."

He stares for a second.

"What did you say?"

I am embarrassed to repeat it, but I do. He smiles. He says, "Are you making fun of me?"

"No!" And it's true.

He looks at me inquisitively. Then his face breaks into a grin.

"You shouldn't be here," he says.

I cannot believe it. He says, "Go away and lead your life. Stop making fun of me."

He is laughing now.

It is over. He looks at the next person in the line. I get up and wander away.

I am devastated.

What did I do wrong? How did he see through me?

My feet lead me through the door and into the dark night outside. I run into Puneet. He is bent over and weeping copiously. I understand now why these encounters bring out people's weakness. I put my hand sympathetically on his shoulder.

"Are you okay?" I ask.

"Yeah," he says. "They sprayed fucking lemon juice in my eyes, dude."

I laugh, despite myself. He is so serious about his damn eyes. We walk back to the car. He lights two cigarettes and we stand under the trees smoking.

I ask him what went wrong between me and the guru.

"Did he see through me?" I ask. "Did he realise I was a fake?"

"It's difficult," he says. "You don't get to ask a question like that the first time around. It takes a lot of work to get there."

This street is tranquil save for the crowds milling around the guru's house. The electric gates open next to us to let a BMW convertible glide out.

Puneet says, "And anyway it's intimidating at one level. You have to get used to it. It's easy to fuck up because it's not a normal situation. You know he's looking at you, you know he can take you on a spin if he wants to. You don't want to be fucking with that. Even I looked away from him because I just didn't want to get messed up with that energy today. You might have noticed that I blink less than most people. That's because I'm spiritually clean. But today I didn't want to get into that.

"Normally I'm one of the few guys who, when I'm spiritually completely clean, can stare him down. I'm one of the few guys that he knows of. Usually, when he looks a person in the eyes he can completely fuck them up and they have to look away. But not me. There have been times when we've exchanged energy eye to eye for a good five minutes and people are like, 'What the fuck is going on here?' And then he has to tell me, 'Puneet. Look down.'"

Seventeen

And now we move to the rhythm of this restlessness
On these streets many people dead they drive with recklessness
8% growth has some people flex with Lexuses
In South Ex shop for Rolexes and diamond necklaces
Land developers come down hard build power nexuses
They build more malls and shopping complexcesses
State militia vacate villages – next Exodus
So you can cash checks of Sensex indexes.

– Delhi Sultanate, rapper

What did 'ordinary' middle-class people feel in those years?

As we noted at the beginning of this book, middle-class people were still not really, in this context, 'ordinary'. But there were a lot of them nonetheless. In Delhi they numbered in the low millions. And as in any other group of that size there was essentially an infinity of experience. Happy, unhappy. Extraordinary, ordinary.

But the city was a powerful force of its own, and it did supply certain kinds of consistency to middle-class moods. It was possessed of immense energy, and energy is magnetic, whatever its effects: so people were animated and industrious to an unusual degree – until they were claimed by fatigue, which was also prominent in the city. In its protean shifts and transformations, Delhi was also fantastically *interesting*, and people were extremely preoccupied with their own urban condition, discussing the city's moods, developments and events all the time, ad nauseam, for good and for ill. But Delhi was not particularly hospitable to the more carefree moods. It was unusual to find contentment, except in the old. Pure joy was rare, except in the very young. And there was a diminution of spontaneity, too, over the course of the century's first decade, so that these lighter moods became more endangered over time.

During the 1990s, the middle classes had seen a lot of immediate, and mostly gratifying, changes in their lives. Many of them had been relieved to see the end of state controls: they had been stimulated by new jobs, TV channels, products and travel possibilities – and they had reached the year 2000 with a sense of ever-expanding horizons. They felt this was *their moment*, not only in a local but in a global sense. The world's age-old domination by the West was coming to an end, and with it their country's indignity. They looked out with imperial hopes on the rest of the world, and relished every story of Indian corporations buying Western companies.

But the festive atmosphere turned considerably more gloomy and cynical in the second half of the decade. The middle classes continued to make money, and they were the beneficiaries of a substantial re-allocation of resources from the country's poor. But their lives also became more risky and expensive, and their expanded capitalist incomes did not buy as much as they had thought. Wealth and opportunity seemed to have been won at the expense of a parallel escalation of savagery in their city, and they found themselves more fearful and anxious even as they owned better cars. Wondering what kind of society they were creating, they became wistful for things they had resented while they were still around: cows in the streets, and pavement vendors with improbable trades. Their own get-rich-quick ethos came back to sting them, because in this period of astonishing wealth creation rather little care was taken of the future; and when the new economy's 'low-hanging fruit' had all been plucked, it began to seize up for want of long-term planning and investment. After verging on double digits several times during the decade, GDP growth slowed to around 5 per cent in 2012. One of the reasons for this stalling was that the boom had remained too confined to the educated minority, and had offered rather little opportunity to the great numbers of the unskilled – and it had done frustratingly little to alter the situation of the majority of the Indian population. Development indicators for the country as a whole were lower than in much poorer Bangladesh next door – sixty-one children out of every 1,000 born live still died before the age of five (even in Delhi the number was twenty-eight; China had achieved a nationwide fifteen)[56] – a fact which itself went some way to quelling any excessive pride in the nation's economic achievement. But in their own lives, the middle classes found that infrastructure remained terrible, it was almost impossible to secure a world-class education for one's children, bureaucracy choked all entrepreneurial whims – and the middle classes realised that their own continued rise was far less dependable than they had come to believe.

They also came to the unpleasant realisation during this decade that they were not the ones in charge. It dawned on the Delhi middle classes that their emerging urban society was administered, to a great extent, by a shadowy cabal whose interests were very different, and even inimical, to their own. As time went on, this backroom elite seemed to monopolise more and more of the opportunities and resources of their city, for even very modest entrepreneurial ventures – such as opening a café or a bookstore – demanded levels of political connections that were difficult or impossible for ordinary people. The new consumer landscape of designer bars and fashion boutiques, which might have signalled some multifarious capitalist heterogeneity, therefore felt oddly uniform and, indeed, sleazy: just more profits for the same corrupt gang. By the end of the decade, many middle-class people were blaming these unelected managers for the fact that Delhi, despite its influx of wealth, was still so dilapidated and under-resourced. They began to feel that Delhi was being run as a private racket, and with a depressing lack of care for its development. They felt that their own feelings and opinions were entirely irrelevant to Delhi's evolution, and that many of the things they had dreamed of for their city were never going to materialise. They felt that they were living in a kind of fantasy and that reality was else-where, for even their newspapers hardly mentioned the enormous proportion of the economy that operated invisibly to the state and to the financial community because they had no indepen-dently verifiable information about it. The picture one got of Indian business from the press was therefore an entirely corporate one, but this picture said nothing about the great eruptions of new power and money in India, and it therefore failed to explain why life had taken on the bizarre contours it had. This is why society was so awash in rumour and conspiracy theories, which seemed the best way to express the doubts one has about the fiction of reality.

Perhaps it was with the scandals preceding the 2010 Commonwealth Games that middle-class hopes of their society's future became dashed. For many people, these scandals, which blew the lid on a set of mechanisms usually hidden from view, explained much about why their landscape took the particular form that it did. With some sixty countries attending, the Games had been anticipated as a moment of international visibility and prestige. The affluent classes were in general sympathetic to the avowed ambitions of Delhi's political managers, who saw the Games as an opportunity to secure extraordinary budgets and powers for a profound transformation of the city: building much-needed new transport infrastructure, restoring and cleaning up the city, evicting the poor from informal settlements on what was now much-prized land. For many of the poor, it was a catastrophe, but it seemed to the middle classes that if the gains came at a price, the best people to pay it were the ones who were miserable anyway.

But as 2010 approached it became clear that many of these supposed benefits would never materialise. Even the mainstream press, usually so enamoured of power and money, hurled daily abuse and accusations at the power nexus that had thrown itself into the scramble for the Games budget. This budget was large and, as it proved, highly elastic since, having agreed to host a mega-event, administrators could hardly refuse to pay if key contractors suddenly inflated their prices a few months before the opening ceremony. It was estimated that preparations for the Games, including the attendant development projects, ultimately set public finances back by 70,000 crore rupees [$14 billion][57] – forty times the original budget – and it was obvious that much of the increase could be blamed on an immense racket of bureaucrats and their friends in construction and trade, who over-charged (toilet paper was supplied to the organisers, famously, at $80 a roll) and under-delivered. The sturdy, well-equipped city that the middle classes had dreamed of never arrived: instead there arrived a kind of temporary plaster facsimile of such a thing which, in the end, bore no resemblance to the computer-generated images with which the whole decade-long endeavour had been sold.

"When the Athens Olympics were going on," said a foreign official involved with the Games, "there was a lot of corruption, but the objective stayed fixed. Everyone was intent on producing the games to the requisite standards. In Delhi, the administrators were entirely willing to compromise the Games themselves. The objective was not the Games at all, in fact.

"Look at what happened with the catering contract. The tender was put out and won by an American company, which was just about the only company in the world that had the expertise to camp in Delhi and produce 8,000 meals a day to the quality necessary for athletes. But they refused to pay 10 per cent to the chairman of the organising committee.

"He sat on it for a while. When they still didn't pay up he threatened to re-open the tender. His advisers said this would be fatal because months would be lost and the entire Games could be threatened. Without a caterer there are no Games. They also warned that it would inevitably go to the same company, who would then charge a higher price. But he went ahead and issued the tender again, citing some technicality against the American firm.

"Seven months were lost. Eventually, the contract went back to the same company. What's more, the British company that was going to rent the kitchen equipment now retracted their rental offer and said that everything would have to be bought. Not only that, but there was no longer enough time to ship the equipment over so they had to fly it in. They tried a 747 but it was too small, so they had to rent an Antonov, the largest carrier aircraft in the world, to bring it in. You can imagine what kind of cost escalation all that entailed.

"There were four main ways that people made money out of Commonwealth Games contracts. The first involved awarding them to oneself or to one's family members. Even if this happened they would not then stop at the legitimate profits that could be earned on these contracts. They would massively inflate the prices *and* supply only a cardboard cut-out version of what they were supposed to supply – which is why so many roads and buildings were collapsing just before the Games.

"The venues are built to such a pathetic standard that it's all just trash. Usually when you do these events, there are immediate benefits – like tourism and international prestige – and then there are long-term benefits, which consist mainly of the physical legacy. From the Delhi Games there will be no long-term benefits, because the quality of the buildings has been massively compromised. The steel they provided for the frames, for instance, was of very low quality because of money extraction. So the buildings began to buckle. Enormous money then needed to be spent hiring foreign engineering consultants to re-inforce the buildings.

"The second way to make money was to take a percentage of everything in a certain turf. That's why organising committee meetings always felt like an assembly of gangsters, because they were dominated by turf wars. Many stoppages in the process, which appeared incomprehensible to outsiders, were about conflicts over turf. For instance, one person took 10 per cent of all hotel bookings. That person managed to ensure that the accommodation that was supposed to be built for visiting officials was never approved, so that they had to stay in hotels throughout. The entire form of the Games, in fact, was determined by the structure of internal money-making.

"The third way was to accept bribes for awarding contracts. Administrators made a lot of money in this way, which businessmen obviously had to make back either by inflating the cost of what they supplied, or by supplying sub-standard goods.

"And the fourth way to profit from the Games was simply to steal all this equipment which had been bought at such inflated cost. Much of it disappeared afterwards. Some was taken by the Delhi police, who used furniture and computers for their offices. In other cases the police may have been paid by someone else to take it. Flat screen TVs disappeared, world-class gym equipment. This was helped by the fact there was no inventory of anything. So no one could prove afterwards that something was missing. The entire Commonwealth Games was run on individual computers and private email addresses: there was no central server. This was not just incompetence: it was a deliberate strategy to ensure there was no systematic information. Another thing that was stolen was hard drives. People turned up in the morning to find their entire data gone. I believe this was a deliberate attempt to erase the data trail. The budget of the organising committee simply disappeared, for instance, and this could happen because the management systems were deliberately inadequate. Decision-making was completely fudged and money disappeared through the gaps."

There were endless rumours as to where this money went,

but most people imagined that it was being used to strengthen the grip with which the corrupt elite held onto society and its resources. Some would undoubtedly be used to fund politicians' re-election campaigns, some to invest in new business ventures. But a major slice of it the middle classes could detect for themselves, because each time a new tranche of the Commonwealth Games budget was released, it sent Delhi property prices leaping further out of their reach. Delhi's property market, in fact, was not like those of other places. Delhi property was a sink for billions of dollars of corrupt money, which could not be stored in banks, and this was why prices bore so little relationship either to the nature of the building or indeed the buying power of 'ordinary' people. The media reported those moneymakers who set themselves up in $8 million homes during the Commonwealth Games preparations, but this was just the sensational iceberg tip; most of the money was invested in more discreet purchases – a few $500,000 apartments here and there – which brought the financial elite head-to-head with the middle classes, to the increasing disadvantage of the latter.

At the beginning of the decade, it had still been possible for the middle classes to imagine buying property in Delhi. But by the end, the formula had become impenetrable even to very successful corporate employees. Leave aside the mansions selling for $30 million and $40 million: newly built three-bedroom apartments in south Delhi, even relatively ordinary ones, cost half a million dollars, which was out of all proportion to all but the highest salaries. Not only this but, considering the fact that these properties suffered from all the normal Delhi problems – poor-quality construction, power cut-outs and water shortages – this seemed dismal value for money compared to what that money could buy even in London or New York. Much more than this, however, was the fact that in order to buy property in Delhi you had to come up with some 50 per cent of the price in cash. Now, clearly it was not those who worked in the brightly shining corporate economy as PR executives or TV newscasters who could lay their hands on a million dollars in cash. No: the people with the suitcases of cash were, as likely as not, black money businessmen, criminals, or corrupt public servants. These were the people who expanded their hold very substantially over the physical assets of India's capital during the first decade of the twenty-first century, and if there was a shift in the feeling of the city, towards something darker and more lawless, it was in part because of this. It was generally entertaining to ask restaurant owners who their landlords were: for it was a *Who's Who* of India's black money elite, from paid assassins working for the Mumbai mafia to publicly pious politicians. The professional classes, meanwhile, had no choice but to move out to the new suburbs of Gurgaon and Noida, where the corporate ethos meant that the quoted price was pretty close to the real price, and people with salaries could get a loan to cover their purchase. In practice then, the beginning of the twenty-first century saw a substantial hand-over of India's capital from those who had acquired property after 1947 to a new black money elite, and it was this group that increasingly set the tone – aesthetic, commercial and ethical – for everyone else.

The financial gains that the middle classes made distracted many commentators from the increasing dislocation they felt in those years, from the controlling apparatus of their society, and from the lurking discontent that ensued, even among otherwise thriving people. That they lived in a society controlled by oligarchs was itself a significant factor in their quality of life, for this fact troubled their mind and sapped their energy more than one might expect. They did not know anymore what to believe about the place they lived in, and it became bewildering to them, and laced with threat. Everything seemed to be an optical illusion created by Mephistophelian magicians to mask their own dark purposes – but what these might be it was impossible to know. Delhi became a surreal place to live, because as time went by people lost their faith that the purported nature of anything was the true one. They knew their society not through what they could see and read but through what they speculated or dreamt on fevered nights. Middle-class people worked and prospered in this society, but they had no *image* of what, who, how or why it was, and this left them fretful and unmoored. By the end of the decade there had begun a mass movement of protest and petition aimed at breaking the stranglehold of the shadowy elite. Corrupt power became the number one resentment of middle-class people, not only because it sucked money and resources out of their own economy, which it certainly did, but also because it denied them any sense of their own reality: the world they operated in was not the real world and they seemed to flail, *Matrix*-like, in empty space.

But this resentment of the oligarchs alternated, in middle-class life, with their own fantasies of total wealth and power – for it was difficult to believe in any other route to freedom. The middle classes did not generally entertain mild, democratic sentiments. 'Middle-class contentment' was anathema to them too. They were a ravenous class of people, and they read newspaper stories of their neighbours' billion-dollar fortunes not just with resentment but also with jealousy. They repeated tales of astronomical sums of money with a curious kind of relish, and in their imaginings the power of corrupt politicians reached superhuman, diabolical proportions. They did not believe that power and money would ever be equitably distributed in their society. They felt that the middle-class life would always be one of servitude and illusion, and only the super-rich were in a position to really see what this whole story was about. But since money floated free of intelligence and hard work, since there was widespread disbelief that those who had it were more qualified for it than anyone else, it was also possible to believe that it would one day just pour in to one's own life, too, unannounced. The conclusion that many people drew from the distribution of wealth in their society was that fortune, in every sense of that word, was totally random – a conclusion which made hard work seem slightly less meaningful, and which fuelled hopes of low-probability, high-value windfalls. People who earned $400 a month felt it was worthwhile deciding which Mercedes they would buy if things came to that.

My first conversation with Anurag happens in a bar. Afterwards he calls me to say, "I can't talk in bars. If you want to hear what I feel, you have to follow where I go."

We arrange to meet again. He asks me to pick him up by the side of a main road. Despite the nocturnal neon haze, I easily recognise his six-foot form kicking desultorily at the kerb as I approach. I pull up and he gets in. He directs me to where he wants us to go. Within a few minutes, however, he changes his mind.

"Stop the car," he says. "I'll drive."

We change places, he slides back the driver's seat to accommodate his long legs, and he pulls away at enormous speed.

"It will take us all night if you drive," he says.

He parks outside a dilapidated concrete market and we go inside to buy liquor. Some twenty men are jammed together against the counter, waving tattered banknotes in the air. It is already late, the store is about to close, and more men are hastening down the steps. It's winter, so most of them wear woollen hats. The liquor store is the only one still open: long, dirty corridors of shuttered shops stretch away in every direction.

There are used condoms discarded all around. This city has numberless people without homes, and so many more who cannot use the homes they have for sex. I've never been anywhere where the streets are so filled with post-coital detritus.

We emerge with a bottle each of rum and vodka, and stop outside to buy Coke. Anurag then drives us to Nehru Park, a large expanse in the diplomatic enclave which, by this time, is shut. We climb over the fence and follow the paths, which are shadowy and mysterious under the trees and the full moon overhead.

"Before I gave up eating meat," says Anurag, "I used to buy

chicken kebabs and bring them here to eat in the middle of the night. With my vodka."

"On your own?"

"Yes. Sometimes the cops used to come and make problems. But the watchman liked me and he would keep them away."

He leads us to his favourite bench. We lay our bottles and plastic cups out on it. It's freezing cold, and I hug myself as I sit down.

The watchman hears us and comes out of his shack. He looks about seventy years old and walks with a stick. He is blind drunk. He's happy to see Anurag and asks if we need an extra chair. We decline.

"I'll come for a drink later," says the watchman, slurring. He shuffles back to the shack. Anurag pours rum.

"I used to bring whisky and give it to him. He needs drink. He has to patrol the park all night, and if he doesn't have a drink he gets sick. People used to beat him up but I knew someone in the police here and complained. Now it's fine."

The watchman emerges again, struggling with a chair, which he sets down next to us.

"I'm not so crazy about restaurants," Anurag says. "I'm more comfortable out here. There's a beautiful dog here who comes to see me. Black and white. I don't know where he is tonight. Back when I used to have money, I used to come every night and feed him chicken. It used to make me feel better when I had too many problems. Family, money, girlfriend."

Anurag doesn't have much money anymore. He lives to a great extent off his father, who earns rent from a couple of floors of the building where they live. He used to run a small garment factory, but his business partner left and the business fell through. And he's not interested anymore in the drudgery of running a business like that. He is not looking for a permanent job or a business to build. He wants to get very rich all in one go. So he has become one of the many young men in Delhi hustling for a share of political money.

"You have to match high-value black money holders – politicians who have say 50,000 crore rupees [$10 billion] in black money – with legitimate businesses which are authorised by the Reserve Bank of India to absorb very large amounts of cash. The big real-estate companies, the resort developers, the diamond merchants. When the deal is done, the politician transfers his money to those companies. Some is delivered to the bank, some is sunk into property. They can't make bank deposits of more than their cash limit, which for big companies is 700 crores [$140 million] per day.

"When they receive the cash, they have six hours to count it. Then they transfer white money to the black money party. They show this money as an unsecured loan. Whenever the newspapers investigate politicians' accounts, you'll see they are full of unsecured loans from property companies.

"Moving that kind of cash is a big physical operation. It's stored in warehouses and to move it you need a truck. When one of those trucks starts moving through Delhi, everyone knows about it. The police take a cut of the money and they guard it all along the route. They give the truck driver a code, which he can give to any policeman and they will let him pass. Delhi isn't safe because there are always opposition politicians who are trying to expose this money. Mumbai is much safer. I'm not going to do this again. But this is one of those times when I can earn a lot of money in one go, and I have to try it.

"All the politicians are bringing their black money back now. There is a huge conversion of black to white. This is going to be beautiful for India because it will all be invested here and will change everything. In the next ten years, India is going to fuck everywhere. Until now we've been funding Swiss citizens' old age with our money. Now it's going to come home. Billions of dollars will flow into the country and we will reap the benefit of our corrupt politicians. You can say it's God's will. God is recycling this money. People talk about China, but China can never beat India because our politicians have been corrupt for years and years. Their money is building an empire that will rule the world.

"The black money business isn't my only one. I have another business too: I'm working for a company owned by someone in the Gandhi family, who offers big loans to companies so he can bring back the money he has parked in Swiss accounts. Right now I'm working on a loan to a Gujarati businessman. Very big guy. He needs 15 lakh crores to expand his business and I'm trying to organise it for him."

He rifles in his bag and pulls out a folder filled with letters between him and a business conglomerate in Gujarat. He hands them to me for my inspection.

"I'm meeting them soon to get the papers signed."

I like Anurag but he is unpolished and incoherent, and I find it difficult to imagine him being admitted to the inner circle of Indian deal-making. The letters look official but I have no idea what to make of them.

"Are you sure you mean 15 lakh crores?" I ask.

"Look at these people," he says, showing me letterheads listing business subsidiaries. Mining, infrastructure, mass media, airlines, insurance, agriculture. "See how big they are."

"And you're saying the Gandhis are lending this money?"

"Obviously."

I am trying to work out in my head how much this sum is. Anurag takes out his phone but there is no space on it to type that many zeroes. We finally compute it together: $300 billion.

"Don't be ridiculous, Anurag."

He steps back a little from his position.

"It's not all in one go. It's over many years. It's for many different projects. Power, agriculture."

"$300 billion. Come on!"

"It's the Gandhis! You can't imagine how big they are. Just think: any chief minister of Uttar Pradesh will end their five-year term with 50,000 crores [$10 billion] in their pocket. And now think what the Congress must have. This is the Congress man!

They have been ruling since 1947! Do you know how much Indian business belongs to them? You just don't get it. For them this kind of money is nothing."

"The GDP of India is only five times that."

"Black money is much more than the GDP! This is what I was telling you. Politicians are bringing their money back into India. They want to invest in India and they need good partners. Giving big loans to companies who are building the nation and who pay 24 per cent a year for black money is the best way."

At that moment, someone calls him. He has a conversation about providing a loan for several hundred million dollars. Anurag talks confidently about how he will bring in one of India's leading real-estate companies to finance part of this loan. His commission will be 1.5 per cent.

It feels like a planted call. I feel I am in a fictional world of his making.

Anurag's call ends. He says,

"This is how it works. The biggest businessmen don't go to banks for funding. This Gujarati company has a lot of projects, they need 15 lakh crores, and they know the only place they can get it is from the Congress Party. They went to Ambani [Mukesh Ambani, India's richest businessman], but Ambani can't give that kind of money. So they came to us.

"The Congress has so much money they have to invest it. And it's excellent for the country. They are growing India now. And soon I'll make money for myself and I can do something for the country too. If I make 1 per cent or 2 per cent on any of my deals, I can really start out. I need 1,000 crores [$200 million] for myself, and if my deals start happening it won't be difficult. I have a friend who made 320 crores [$64 million] on a black money deal recently. He bought himself a Bugatti. I wouldn't do that. I would do up my house really nice. But I need money for other things."

In Anurag's stories, the membrane separating reality and fantasy is exquisitely permeable. One never knows how to tell the two apart. It is not clear that he does, either. In fact what I find interesting about him is that he finds society so extreme that there is almost nothing that cannot plausibly be asserted. His Delhi is a bewildering place, full of vast monsters whose species and scale are indiscernible in the spiritual night, and I understand why he is so lost. And why finding himself again can be imagined only in one way: earning loads of money.

"I want to make things better. If only I had 5 crores [$1 million] I would just have a good life and drive a BMW. But then I'd just be living for myself. I wouldn't be able to do anything for my nation. I want to change things. I want to show people how to live. That's why I need 1,000 crores.

"Delhi is a good place but the people are bastards. They're big show-offs. They don't know about life. They have dirty minds and they only think about money. I want to make them feel. Money has killed their feelings. God did not do this. We did it and we can change. If I have the money I will change people's souls."

Delhi is obsessed with money, it is the only language it understands, and to buy myself out of its vulgarity and its money-mindedness, I need lots of money. It is a strange, self-defeating logic which obviously universalises the escalation of that which it hates.

"There was a wedding party in the street where I live, and they put up a marquee outside my house. There was a tree in the way and they cut it down just to put up their marquee. They cut down a tree that took forty years to grow just for one party. They don't understand anything. I went to ask them, '*Why are you fucking this tree?*' But they don't care what I think. I can't fight with them right now. That's why I need money. I want to be strong and when I find people like that, I want to fuck their happiness. You can say there's a fire in me right now."

It's true, it seems, since Anurag, sitting in his shirt, is apparently unaffected by the cold of this February night, while I, wrapped up in a coat, am shivering violently.

The watchman comes back to ask for a drink. Anurag pours him some rum.

"Where have all the good dogs gone?" he asks him.

The watchman spreads his hands in ignorance.

"That black-and-white one was a brilliant dog," Anurag says.

The watchman walks off into the blackness of the park.

"Animals are so pure," says Anurag, "so true to their nature. They don't change. You have no idea how much I love animals. I used to bring food for that black-and-white dog all the time. If I woke up in the night and it was raining I used to drive over here and put up tarpaulin sheets between the trees so he could keep dry. I used to bring a coat for him in the winter.

"People are bastards. I've given up on people. Everyone I have ever trusted has fucked me. I don't have friends anymore. My girlfriend doesn't care about me. My father is a good man, he's worked hard, but he has never believed in me. He has never put his hand on my shoulder and said, *I understand you*. Animals are the only ones who are loyal. Not humans. The simplicity of animals keeps me going. Animals want very few things. They only want money—" He laughs at his own mistake: "I mean they only want *food*. Nothing else."

He shows me pictures on his cell phones of animals being maimed and killed. Hundreds of them. There is a majestic, powerful lizard with its feet broken so it cannot move.

"When I found the guy who had maimed this lizard, I broke his ribs and his jaw. I fucked his happiness. People don't know how to behave. I knew this family who had a Pomeranian that was irritating them and they threw it off their seventh-floor balcony. I would set up a separate animal police to deal with people like that. I would introduce strict laws and have advertising campaigns to educate people about animal rights. I would introduce a 1 per cent tax just to take care of animals."

The watchman circles back to us, making a drunken show of keeping watch, banging his stick exaggeratedly on the ground.

"You see him?" says Anurag. "He's a villager, he's been looking after this place for twenty-five years. He is a real human being. Not like everyone else."

The moon is very high now. The park is silent and the city seems far away. Owls hoot now and again. We are quiet for a while. Anurag is musing.

"I had this idea for a house," he says. "In the front there's the garden and swimming pool. At the back of the house is the car park. There are remote control doors at the front and the back of the house and a wide passageway between them, so you can drive your car right through the house. So in the evening you go out to get your Ferrari, drive it into the house, stop at the bedroom to pick up your girl, and drive away to your party."

He lets the picture form.

"What do you think of the idea?" he asks.

"I'm not sure," I say. "You have a few practical problems. You'd need to get rid of exhaust fumes. And a Ferrari would make a huge noise inside a house."

"It doesn't have to be a Ferrari. It could be a Lamborghini."

"I guess so."

Anurag pours more rum into our plastic cups, and tops them up with Coke. He returns to his rant about "Delhi people" – the same rant that occupies the lives of so many of those same Delhi people too.

"People are not beautiful in Delhi. Look at how they treat women. In Mumbai they don't harass women, but here a woman can't take ten paces without being mistreated. Once I saw this man abusing this girl in public. I knew the man a little bit and I said, 'Why are you abusing her, man? You're abusing her in front of so many people and she's crying. Let it be.' Then I went away and when I came back he was still abusing her. I fucked his happiness. First of all I slapped him. Then he said you have no idea who my dad is. So I said, 'This one is for your dad,' and I broke his rib. And then a big court case happened."

Anurag breathes deeply.

"I just helped her as a human. I'm a human and if I see innocent people suffering I have to help them.

"Another time, I was in Bangkok with my cousin. My cousins

have amazing money. But if I asked to borrow a lakh [$2,000] they would fuck my happiness forever. One day I was out biking on the beach, and I came to the hotel and my cousin had a girl with him. She was naked and he was filming her. She was crying. She was saying she was supposed to get married and now he was telling her he was going to send this video of her all over the world. I said to her, 'He's not going to do that, don't worry.' My cousin was laughing. He said, 'Of course I will. I'll make sure everyone sees it.' I said, 'What the fuck, man? Your business with her is over, now pay her and let her go. What are you trying to prove?' Then he started throwing money at her. 1,000 baht. 1,000 more. And she just threw the money on the floor. I said, 'Not everyone lives for money, man.' I snatched his phone from him, then I changed the phone language into Thai and I let her delete the video. And I shook her hand, and she hugged me and she cried. That was the best part actually."

I feel as if Anurag looks at intimacy through the wrong end of a telescope. It is alluring but far away, its outlines difficult to discern. Other human beings pass close to the soul once in a while, unexpected passings like this woman in the Bangkok hotel, but for the most part they remain hostile and remote. The world of human relations seems completely ravaged for him, in fact. It is sunk in the mire of money, and it is best to treat it as it asks to be treated: as a source merely of connections, advancement, money. For purity, for authentic attachments, one has to look to other species.

His phone has been ringing non-stop.

"It's my girlfriend," he says. "I don't pick up because she thinks I'm in Mumbai."

"But you haven't been in Mumbai for weeks."

"I know. That's why it's awkward. But she's a bitch. She only thinks about money. She doesn't care what kind of person I am. She thinks I'm a loser. She thinks she's higher than me because her family is rich. So why the fuck does she call me if she is more than me?"

She sends a text message.

"Many congratulations on your new relationship."

He reads it out to me.

"You have someone else?" I ask.

"No," he says. "She's trying to provoke me."

He writes back, "Yep. I'm very happy with animals. They don't care how much is in my pocket."

She calls immediately. He answers and puts her on speaker. I wonder if any of this would be happening if there were no audience. She says,

"Can you just drop the attitude and talk to me like a normal person?"

"What do you want from me?" Anurag asks, rolling his eyes at me. "Do you want to be with me or not?"

"I just want to have a normal conversation. I can't say that I want to be with you because I don't feel I know anything about you right now."

"See you're confused right?"

"I'm not confused. I just don't know what's going on."

"What is going on is that you just talk negative about me."

"This negative outlook that I have about you has just been developed by you, it's been created by you. I'm a very positive person. I think it is you who has the negative opinion about yourself."

"What about that wedding you went to? You wouldn't even let me come in with you. Is that how you show your positive opinion of me? I drove you there because I care about you. I sat outside in the car from 10 p.m. till 6 a.m. waiting for you because I didn't want you to go home alone. You didn't come out once to see how I was. Why did you leave me outside? Am I not good enough to be seen with you? Why didn't you take me in?"

"Because I'm not sure about you."

"You seem very sure of me in bed, but you're not sure of me in front of other people?"

"You're disgusting," she says, and the call ends.

Anurag is frustrated and takes a big gulp of his drink.

"She doesn't think I'm good enough for her world. She thinks her world is better than me. So I say to her, 'Then go and be with the world. Why are you hanging around me?' But now she's heard I'm working with the Gandhi family, she's scared I might become a rich guy. That's why she's calling me up. She's from a west Delhi business family and she only understands money. Her dad had seventeen Mercedes and still her mother left him because she couldn't handle these people obsessed with money."

She sends another message.

"Can we have lunch tomorrow?"

He sighs, and with a great effort acquiesces. "OK," he writes back.

"But you won't be in Mumbai tomorrow," I say.

"I know," he says. "I'll cancel it in the morning."

There is a long silence. It's nice out here in the park. The suffocation of the city abates somewhat.

"What was the most beautiful moment in your life?" I ask him.

"When I was seventeen. I gave up my studies to go to Bombay and be a film star. I had a Muslim girlfriend who was perfect. She used to cook me breakfast every day. But then we ran into the Hindu–Muslim problem and now she's married to someone else. Those were beautiful days. I was modelling, I was working out every day, doing martial arts, I looked good. One day I was walking down the street and a big Lexus SUV pulled up next to me. The back window went down and inside was Sanjay Dutt. The movie star. He looked at me and without saying anything he saluted me. For my physique.

"I still want to be an actor but you need money for it. You need a lot of money to get into that business."

It's true that Anurag has an impressive physique. Still not thirty, he is tall and powerful. He has a thick mop of black hair. Were it not for a slight maladjustment he would be a strikingly beautiful man. But there is something bitter in his regard which means that he just misses. He looks shifty and ill at ease.

We've been drinking for a couple of hours, and the Coke is finished. We gather up the bottles; we leave the remaining rum with the watchman. We walk back through the park and climb over the fence, more unsteady than when we arrived. We find my car, which Anurag unlocks proprietarily, and we drive away. A few minutes later, Anurag stops by the side of the road and asks me to wind down the passenger window. He whistles out of it and two dogs immediately come bounding out of the trees. They put their paws on the window ledge and crane their heads into the car. Anurag reaches out to them. The dogs are hyperventilating with excitement. He strokes them and they lick his hand.

"These are two of my favourites," he says.

He tells them he has to go and that he'll visit them soon. As we drive away he is dialling a number.

"I'm trying to call the guy in my company. He's forty-two and he manages money for many Congress politicians. You can speak to him. He works in India but he has a US phone number. Imagine that."

He listens to the phone but there's no response.

"He doesn't always pick up," says Anurag. And, by way of explanation, "He's a little diabetic."

The fact that it is after one in the morning might also have something to do with it.

He pulls up at a roadside kebab place that is still open. There are a few plastic chairs arranged on the sidewalk but Anurag doesn't want to get out of the car because we can't drink there. He summons the waiter by flashing his lights on and off: the horn on my car is broken. The waiter comes over with a menu limp from many late-night hands. Anurag orders paranthas for us and kebabs for some of his canine friends.

"Make them without spices," he says.

He winds up the window, inserts two plastic cups into the car's holder, and pours us both neat vodka. His phone rings: it is his colleague returning his call.

"I wanted to introduce a friend of mine," says Anurag into the phone. "He's British. He needs a big loan for his business."

He thrusts the phone into my hand. The man on the other end speaks well and quickly. He asks me nothing about myself and yet speaks as if the deal is already done.

"We can provide excellent terms in the UK," he says. "Through one other company we can give you funding anywhere else in the world too. So just tell Anurag how much you need and we'll take this forward."

"Okay," I say.

Anurag takes the phone back and speaks into it.

"I have good news," he says. "I bagged a Kolkata company. Their business is grain and they need 1,000 crores [$200 million]. Yeah it's signed."

As the conversation ends, the waiter comes over and Anurag winds down the window. Hot food is passed inside. We begin to eat.

"So you know why I gave you the phone?" Anurag says. "I need your help. You have contacts in London. When I start making big money I will need to expand overseas. I'll need your help to talk to those people. We're going to lend this Indian money all over the world."

I tell him I hope he takes me out when he gets rich. I'd like to see what it looks like. Half of me feels he will spend the rest of his life imagining his future windfall while living off the dwindling rent from his property. Another half believes he may be the kind of nondescript guy who, against all probability, lands something astonishing. It's the kind of thing that can happen here.

We pay up and set off for Anurag's house. As we pull up outside, six dogs come running to greet him. He gets out with the packages of meat, opens up the foil and lays them on the ground. The dogs set to eating, and he strokes them.

"Look at them," he says. "They're so innocent."

I bid him goodbye. He enfolds me in his arms. I get back in the car, jerking the driver's seat forward so I can reach the pedals, and set off for home. I have a vivid dream that night about enormous piles of dead dogs being incinerated in a Gurgaon corporate office.

The next morning, Anurag calls me.

"Did you really like my idea about the house?" he asks. "Or were you just saying that not to hurt me?"

"I don't think it will ever work," I say.

"No," he says. "Maybe not."

Abstract

Delhi has a hacked-off parentage, breeding orphans out of its baked land.

Uprooted from the maternal solace of history and tradition, it has grown to abhor its father figures – politicians, bureaucrats, and all those cynical patriarchs of money and the market – and even real-life parents have grown remote with the jolts and ruptures of break-neck change.

Like an orphanage, the city suffers from a bewilderment of origins and direction. It is shaken by tics and tantrums. It cries out for the relief, on its shoulder, of a tender parental hand.

But once in a while, an orphanage produces beings who are preternaturally free. Never having known the corrosion of parental authority and expectation, such individuals assemble a universe for themselves, and dazzle all around them with their originality, curiosity and wisdom. They do not accept the fossilised judgements of others, and they bring wondrous possibility to the staidest of systems.

In this respect, too, Delhi resembles an orphanage. It can spawn people who seem entirely unconstrained by how a particular problem has been dealt with before, people who can imagine a myriad of ways in which the world might be differently organised. People who transcend the general self-involvement and who see immediately, in the adjacent and particular, the planetary extension. It is in these people that I find Delhi's utopian potential.

One of these resplendent individuals is Anupam Mishra,* with whom I now stand looking out over the Yamuna river.

It is a hot day and we both carry drinking water. I have a litre bottled for me by the Coca-Cola Company and purchased just now from a roadside stall. Anupam has brought a flask from home, which hangs on a strap around his neck. Seventy years old, with a shock of grey hair, he wears a brown kurta, which hangs loosely around his slender frame; on his feet are leather sandals.

We are on the stretch of land where there was, until its demolition before the Commonwealth Games, a large and vibrant township, home to a few hundred thousand people, among them the residents of Bhalswa Colony whom we met earlier. The area is dominated, now, by two enormous sports stadia – and by the new Delhi Secretariat building, which houses the city's government. This building is in two wedge-shaped halves standing at an angle to each other, whose shining surfaces look out over the river like two glass eyes – and indeed the entire complex could not be more blind to the river estuary that sweeps before it. A few metres away, where the Yamuna's flood plain begins, there is a hint of Delhi's primordial landscape: tufted grasses line the water, some three metres high, and cormorants spread wet wings in the sun – but it is as if this suggestion of nature is abhorrent to those who have seized this land for their modern-day forts. High walls surround every building, and the enormous area has been paved with concrete paving bricks, as if someone were worried about some vegetable invasion; these bricks store so much heat on a day like this that pavement dwellers must pour bottled water on them just so they can sit.

The land between these showcase installations and the

* Real name.

waterfront is an uncannily dead zone which the city's managers seem to have designated as a dumping ground. Behind the Secretariat building is a graveyard for retired ambulances, which are piled unceremoniously by the side of the road. There is a huge amount of masonry waste: unused paving slabs, sections of concrete pipe, and entire walls removed from the destroyed township, which are lent against each other like files on a shelf. A few hundred rusting steel chairs have been piled up on one patch of ground, a couple of storeys high.

We are very close to the centre of the city but it as if its consciousness ends just short of the river. Delhi has its back to the water and only the roving underclass seems to come here, whose signs are everywhere: bedding in the bushes, discarded plastic bottles, human excrement, and the charred circles of cooking fires.

"The previous cities of Delhi were built so that rulers could look at the river," says Anupam. "The Mughals loved the Yamuna, and built their Red Fort on its banks. A few hundred miles downstream they built more grand buildings looking over it: the Taj Mahal and the Agra Fort. But the British did not like to look at this river, and when they came they turned away from it. I think it's because they found it unnerving. European rivers flow from gradual glacial melt, and they are the same all year round. You can build walls to contain them and put buildings right on the riverfront. But this is a monsoon river. You have to leave an enormous flood plain on both sides to accommodate the river's expansion during the monsoon, and for the rest of the year this flood plain is muddy and empty. I think the British found it ugly. They found such a volatile river intimidating."

I tell Anupam about an old woman I met in Civil Lines who remembered how the river ran along the end of her garden in the 1920s. There was a mud wall keeping the water out: every month the gardener would make a hole in the wall, the river would flow in, irrigating the garden, and the children would chase the enormous silver fish that flapped about on the lawn.

She and her siblings learned to swim by jumping off the end of the lawn into the river.

"Civil Lines was the first British encampment," Anupam says, "outside the walls of the existing Mughal city. But when they came to build their own city they moved away from the river, and for the first time the city had no aesthetic relationship to the Yamuna. It's more important than it sounds. Looking at a river, swimming in a river – these are the first stages of cherishing it. The Seine can never be ruined as the Yamuna has been, because the whole of Paris is built for people to look at it. In Delhi, there used to be a great amount of life around the river – swimming, religious festivals, water games – but it has all come to an end. Think of religious immersion: it is not just superstition. It is a practice of water preservation. If our prime minister had to immerse himself in the Yamuna every year, it would be a lot cleaner than it is now. But everyone has turned their backs on the river in obedience to the modern city, and so it is filthy and forgotten."

We walk down to the river's edge. The water is black and chemically alive: it heaves muddily with bubbles erupting from its depths. Looking across its expanse, however, one can only see the mirror of the sky, and there is a satisfying feeling of riverine peace. Some twenty metres from the bank is a large statue of Shiva, submerged up to its shoulders. Egrets flit over the surface.

Over our heads is one of the river's road bridges. A young couple have parked their car on the bridge and are now clambering down to the water. It is not easy. The concrete slopes are steep and fifteen metres high. The husband is carrying some kind of package; the wife wears a sari and sandals. Eventually they make it down to where we are standing. The package, it turns out, is a framed photograph of a dead male ancestor – a father, perhaps – decked in flowers. They throw it into the viscous water, watch it sink, and begin to climb back up to the highway above.

The edge of the water is choked with other similar offerings.

Flower garlands, broken coconuts, photographs of Sai Baba, mats of shaved baby hair – and all the plastic bags in which these things have been brought – hug the lapping edge in a broad floating carpet.

"I don't think I would place a photograph of my father in this water," I say.

"No one is looking at the water," says Anupam. "They are acting automatically, without looking."

We begin to walk upstream. We pass the grave of a Muslim saint, around which is a spotless clearing furnished with elegant shelters made of sheaves of long river grasses. We cross stinking canals flowing into the river. No one is around: one would think we were far from any city even though we are now walking parallel to the new overhead highway that runs along the Yamuna bank.

We have set ourselves a long walk, but we have started in the hottest part of the day, and before long we withdraw under the shadow of this highway. The road is like a giant awning overhead, and it is cool here and curiously quiet. Hundreds of cycle rickshaws are parked in rows, and boys are working on repairs. Men go down to the river to wash their hands; they return to eat lunch next to us. Laundry is slung over rickshaws. Birds sing. Pylons carry cables across the river from the power station just a little upstream.

"Why do you think people have always built cities in this place?" Anupam says as we look at the flowing water. "It is because this stretch of the west Yamuna bank has the richest groundwater for hundreds of miles around. Delhi marks the point where the Yamuna comes closest to the Aravalli Hills, which end just to the south-west of us. Seventeen streams used to flow over this plain from the Aravallis into the Yamuna, making the ground abundant in clean water. For the first thousand years of Delhi's history, every city drew its water from this rich underground supply. Every large house had a well in the courtyard. Each locality had fifty or so wells. Large communal wells were built for people to gather water and also to socialise in the presence of water.

"There were always new invasions and new cities. But those dynasties all came from the plains, and though they had different visions of religion and government, they had the same vision of water. Each conqueror inherited the infrastructure of the last and added to it, so that for 1,000 years Delhi evolved a continuous and sophisticated water system. The philosophy was simple: if you take, you must put back. Whenever they sank new wells they also built new tanks. These tanks captured monsoon rain so that it did not run off into the river, and they allowed this water to gradually seep down and recharge the water table. By the Mughal period, Delhi had 800 of these water bodies. Some were small, some as big as lakes. Many of them had religious and spiritual associations, because it is with the sacred that people protect their water systems. Today, people call these systems 'traditional' but this word is condescending, and implies that they are obsolete. They are not. In the entire history of technology nothing has improved on them, and they will still be around in many centuries when electric pumps and dams have long run dry.

"The Mughals were the first to use the river to supplement groundwater supplies. Their metropolis had greater water needs than anything previously built here so they needed to take from the Yamuna. But the river flowed under the walls of their city: there was no way to lift it to the city level. So they went 125 kilometres upstream to where the river was flowing at a higher altitude than their city, and they built a canal from that point which brought water into Shahjahanabad by gravity."

This was the same canal we saw a few chapters ago, in Shalimar Bagh, where Jimmy's mastiff ran so exuberantly along its banks.

"The elegance of their system was that the canal entered the walled city from the west and travelled through it to the Red Fort in the east. Ordinary citizens therefore got water from this canal first and the king got it last. Even in democratic societies the president is not usually on the tail end of essential resources. But these people understood the politics of water. Their system guaranteed that water would be clean all along its course because the king was the final user: no one could pollute the water that he would drink. It does not matter that this was not a democracy: they built their system around an understanding of water, and the needs of water are democratic needs. Only if you are democratic in your heart can you sanction this kind of water system. Otherwise you will reject it."

We begin to walk again. The river bends away from us, and between us and it are the flats of the floodplain where crops are grown at this time of the year. The terrain is difficult and we decide to take the road. We climb on our hands and knees up the steep incline leading up to the highway, holding onto each other for stability. The concrete is burning hot. Finally we get up to the level of the highway, whose black surface is like a radiator. We climb over the barrier and cross eight lanes in front of the speeding traffic.

On the other side is a human-sized road with sidewalks. It leads through another zone of industrial refuse. There are abandoned buildings with broken windows. Any people here are foragers, collecting bits of plastic and cardboard for sale. There is the most enormous pile of shoes caught up in some twisted barbed wire. An old water tower overgrown with vines; the banisters have fallen away from the staircase that once spiralled up around its stem, and the steps jut out like rusty teeth. We pass a waterworks outside which hangs a banner saying, "Water is life". The trees along the road are dead and desiccated. Here and there are rusty observation towers with broken spotlights. They look as if they have been lifted from a labour camp: I can't imagine what they were here for.

"It was the British who ultimately broke with Delhi's 1,000 years of water knowledge. Their rule was different from that of previous kingdoms, which had ruled without interfering in how people lived. The British wanted total rule, which would extend to education, morality, everything. And of course water too. But they had no experience of this landscape and they could not understand its water system. So though they did not set out to destroy it, destroy it they did.

"The British took no notice of the groundwater, which was the reason there had been cities in this place for 1,000 years. They were only interested in the river. They imported modern water practices from Europe, damming the Yamuna to the north of the city, in a place called Wazirabad, and running pipelines into the city from which they delivered water directly into houses. Sewage was then collected in drains which let it out into the river downstream. This is why it is ironic that the British chose not to look at the river. Previous kingdoms had not used the river, but they loved to look at it. The British lived off the river, but they could not bear to look at it.

"The British were used to getting water from taps and that is the system they wished to implement here. They also liked how this monopolistic system boosted their imperial hold on the place: they could make people dependent on them, and they could choose to deliver water to one social group and not another. But it was a total break with local water customs, and many in this city resisted water from taps. It was never considered auspicious. There is an old song which says something like, 'Do anything to us, do whatever kind of harm you want to us, but don't put taps in our houses. Keep your tapped water for your bungalows. Don't bring it to where we live.' Delhi people did not like the smell of piped water: they were used to taking water directly from wells. Before drawing water they would clean their utensils and rope, and then they would dip their vessels directly into the water source, which they could see and maintain for themselves. With piped water they could not see the source. It was far away, they did not know who was supplying it, how clean it was, or what kind of chemicals they were putting in. Even today you hear rumours of poison in the water system: people have not forgotten the paranoia unleashed when the British brought piped water.

"But gradually the British system extended everywhere. People opened a faucet and water came out and the water issue seemed to be 'solved'. Delhi residents no longer had to think about a water 'system'. And gradually the age-old system broke apart. There was no longer any need to maintain the channels and reservoirs. People demolished them because now the population of the city was growing: water tanks were taking up land which could be used as real estate. It did not hurt people to demolish them because they had forgotten what their function was, so they accorded them no prestige. It is the prestige of a system that directs you to conserve it and honour it; if that prestige disappears people cease to care. Of the seventeen rivers and 800 water bodies we had when the British came, hardly any are left."

We are walking through strangely idyllic scenery, with trees and cultivated flats on both sides. In this city of 20 million people, there is no one around. The sun is on our heads, and we drink frequently.

"We still use the British system, which by now has turned into a disaster. It is a disaster because it has been taken out of the hands of people, who have therefore lost all their sense of water as a *system*. Now people think that water is just a wet substance that comes out of a tap, and if you need more you just turn on more taps. Which is why we now have such enormous problems. Delhi has water, it has lots of water. That is why the city came to be here in the first place. But water needs a system. And whereas Delhi once had an intelligent, scientific system, it now has no system at all.

"It is funny that we think 'democracy' is about voting. We are a democracy in the sense that we vote, but everything else, everything that constitutes our actual lives, has moved in the opposite direction. Water systems used to be entirely democratic: knowledge of the system was distributed to everyone, and everyone played their part in taking care of it. Now water provision is centralised, only a few people know how it works, and for everyone else there is only a vague sense of valves and pipes.

And even the people who are running it have no deep knowledge of how water functions in this place.

"As soon as the water tanks were lost, Delhi began to have severe flooding. In our own time, everything that could once absorb monsoon water has disappeared. The tanks have gone and so has all of Delhi's agricultural land. But the monsoon is still with us. The entire city is now one hard surface so there is nowhere for this sudden rush of water to go. Delhi is submerged every year by floods. This is an entirely modern phenomenon.

"But we also began to have severe water shortages. This place that drew conquerors from all over the continent because of the richness of its water is now in a water crisis. The river rapidly ceased to be adequate for the city's water needs: Delhi's population is fifty times larger now than when the British built their system, while the Yamuna is the same size. So Delhi began to take water from other places. Now we have pipelines bringing water from the Ganges and Bhagirathi rivers and from the Renuka lake. We can do this because compared to our predecessors we have acquired some small quantum of technological power. But it is a completely immature solution. First of all because we are close to exhausting these supplies too, and there is no other water we can use that we can bring to Delhi with gravity. Can you imagine if we had to use electricity to raise water to the city? And secondly because it pays no attention at all to the wider economy of water. Thousands of farmers have protested against Delhi taking their water, they have tried to smash the dams that stop their rivers' traditional flow – but so what? Delhi wants water, and Delhi is powerful. Delhi is drying out the country for hundreds of kilometres around, which creates more refugees from the land, who come to Delhi, who require more water, so Delhi takes even more – and so it goes on.

"Not only this, but we do not have the capacity to treat such large quantities of sewage. Our sewage systems were built to treat one river. Now three times this volume is coming into the system. This is why our sewage plants treat a smaller and smaller proportion every year. Most sewage now flows directly into the river. It is a poisonous brew, full of industrial effluent, and Delhi produces it on a monumental scale. And what happens when you pour all this into a single river basin? Look how high the Yamuna is now. It is summer: we are a month away from the monsoon. The Yamuna is a seasonal river, and at this time of year it used to be a trickle. But what you see flowing there is not only the Yamuna. It is also the Ganges and the Bhagirathi and the Renuka lake. We take from all those places but when we have used it we pour it all into one river basin. That is why the river is running so high, and that is why we will at some point soon have a disastrous flood. The river will break its banks."

We interrupt our northwards march to have some lunch. Anupam has brought some daal, roti and cooked vegetables, and we sit under a tree to eat. The landscape is uplifting, and birds sing on every side. Anupam continues.

"Now do you think our middle classes wish to pay the price of our present water shortage? Of course not. They wish to live free of any environmental context. That is the reward they expect from capitalism! They want to turn on their taps at any time and have water. The municipal supply, however, is heavily rationed, and provides water only for a few hours a day. So what do the middle classes do? They remember – they are good at history when they need to be! – that there is a rich supply of water under their feet. Over the last thirty years they have all dug private wells so they can pump out as much as they need. Every middle-class house has such a well, even though it is illegal. This water is completely unmonitored so of course the city's water authorities now have no idea how much sewage they need to build capacity for. And all this additional water also floods out into the Yamuna, raising the level still further.

"But of course by now no one remembers the basic knowledge that governed Delhi's water management for a millennium: if you take water from the ground you have to replenish it. People are pumping water out of the ground for their baths and washing machines and swimming pools but they have not built a single water tank to recharge the ground supply. So Delhi's groundwater is also running dry. But let them not think about it! While it still comes out of the tap, let them pump away!

"As a result of this, many areas of Delhi are now completely dry. Whole sectors of the city have run out of groundwater and are supplied only by water trucks. There is a new five-star hotel that has no water: its water needs – baths, laundry, swimming pool, sauna – are all supplied by trucks which come at night in lines of a hundred or more. But while there is a way to spend oneself out of a problem, this city is curiously indifferent to that problem. Real-estate prices continue to rise even in areas where there is no water.

"Where does this trucked water come from? It comes from water entrepreneurs who buy a plot of land and pump out the water to distribute around the city. According to the law, owning a piece of land also means that you own the water beneath it. But water is a liquid! If you put a pump in a piece of land and start extracting water, you do not simply take it from your own land. You take water from everywhere. Even if your land is the size of a handkerchief you can pump out water for miles around, and the water table falls for everyone. So these trucks are not a magic solution. And even those entrepreneurs are running out of water, so they have to move further and further from the city to find it. How much are people willing to pay for water? If we run out of oil, we can adjust our lifestyles accordingly. But if we run out of water there is no life.

"You have seen these new water parks they have built in Gurgaon and Noida? Where thousands of litres are pumped out of the rock so families can splash around in swimming pools and water slides? I like this phrase, 'water park', but I use it in a different sense. I use it like a 'car park'. Every time I meet a politician I say, 'You can allocate land for people to park their cars. If you want your city to have any future you also need to allocate land for us to park water. Every great ruler of Delhi has been remembered for the water tanks and lakes they built to capture the rain and recharge the groundwater. You could be a great ruler too.' But they don't know what I am talking about, because they have forgotten where Delhi's water comes from. They have forgotten that Delhi's history is full of cities that have been evacuated because they have run out of water.

"We often think that recent centuries have produced a lot of new knowledge. But this is because we are no longer equipped to recognise the knowledge of the past. I see modern times as one long history of forgetting. Even the kings are ignorant now of what every person who used to live in this place once knew."

It may seem surprising, in this place much concerned with physical security and survival, that water, that most essential of material resources, might be so neglected. Anupam's picture of a failed government system bypassed by a middle class which builds private micro-systems of its own and thereby pushes the system much faster towards collapse, seems apocalyptic – and it is. It produces a fatally short-term, marauding mentality: when water is running out and no one is doing anything to replenish it, the rational strategy is just to take as much as you can possibly get before everyone else does.

For some, it might prompt the question: when will Delhi 'grow up'? When will politics finally subjugate these anti-social, insubordinate energies and channel them into an objective system that works in the long-term interests of all?

That this is a tourist's question, which very few people in Delhi ask, says something about the difference between the history of the Western city and the future of 'emerging' cities such as this. For the question derives not from any sense of developments in this city, but from an imported memory of how other cities have evolved. This memory is rapidly changing, however, in our time, from universal to parochial.

It is most excellently exemplified by the case of New York, icon of the century past. We still remember, somehow, the titanic struggles between order and chaos out of which that city emerged; images flicker in our heads of the scheming robber barons of the rising years, the gangs, the corrupt politicians, the slums filled with the gaunt and dispossessed. Great fists descend from the sky: the dogged mayors who took on these rogue forces, strangling gangsterism, breaking up the comfortable cartels of politicians and tycoons, securing the condition of the poor, and building the most ambitious urban infrastructure ever conceived. The battle theme turns lyric as centralised authority looks out over a city subjugated, as it grasps the reins of its varied energies and channels them into that single, glorious urban achievement that all of us know because it is our shared global mythology.

Nor have we forgotten the immense quantity of destruction that happened along the way. We know what once lay beneath: how neighbourhoods were ripped down for highways and parks, how languages sank without trace, how so much life was buried: the spontaneous energies of the street, the animals, the folk variety, the languor, the vice. At every point along the way, New York was in some sense *less*, and there were always New Yorkers who lamented the loss of mystery, the shrinking of horizons, the rationalisation of life. The great film-poets such as Scorsese and Coppola, through whom so many people around the world became citizens of New York without ever going there, created elegies to the older, more shadowy metropolis that was spot-lit into oblivion. The *Godfather* movies, for instance, brought to life this quintessential back-and-forth of New York feeling: the dark grandeur of the lost worlds that produced the modern city, but also, and essentially, the necessity of their passing. They were films about the inexorability of twentieth-century process: the loss of human grandeur and variety in the name of the serene and productive metropolis. The tale of the modern city was that of the absolute inevitability of the victory of unified, centralised administrative power over everything else. The accompanying fear – that all vitality would eventually be lost and human beings would no longer know or love anything except the mechanisms of their own control – was never sufficient to put the brakes on this unidirectional expansion.

Such histories instruct many Westerners, and not just them, that the future of today's 'immature' cities will follow the Western past. *We were just like them,* goes the logic, *before we became like us. And* – since modernity moves inexorably, inevitably in one well-known direction – *they will become like us too.* It is only a matter of time. But as investment advisers are fond of pointing out, the past is no guide to the future. And there are many reasons to doubt that Delhi will follow a course mapped out by other cities in different eras and far away. It is more likely that the emerging places of the world will follow quite different paths and produce different realities. It is probable, in such places, that the formal will never defeat or even rival the informal. Large portions of their cities will continue to be self-administered by communities who are little known to authorities or to each other. They will continue to build architectural and social systems that are both ingenious and unknown. In the grip of 'globalisation' they will remain quite foreign and untamed.

Even the idea of the centralised authority that produced Paris and New York seems difficult to imagine in the place where I write. It must be remembered that this authority had already been in preparation for centuries in the West before it was acti- vated as a political principle, because everything it was imagined to be – benign, omnipotent, omniscient and, above all, singular – was borrowed from the Judeo-Christian idea of God. This model of government was therefore already familiar to Christian societies before it existed: it was a secular translation of widely held spiritual assumptions, and no metaphysical U-turn was required to embrace an authority of that sort. This is not the case where I am: many even of the most Westernised of my co-citizens find the singular eye of the Western state excessively pedantic and tiring, and find relief in India's more paradoxical multitude of authorities.

But perhaps these theological concerns are insignificant beside the much more basic fact that Delhi enters the zone of Western globalisation at a moment when the era of state authority is on the wane everywhere, even in the West. The rise of New York coincided with the intensification of centralised authority in all rich countries. But now there are signs that this is over. Impoverished Western administrations increasingly fail to collect revenues from corporations and financial elites, which can easily out-manoeuvre them in this transnational age. They surrender more and more of their earlier functions and they ride increasingly off the investments made in their days of greater authority and surplus. This is the tenor of the day. And indeed, in Delhi, things seem to be moving in the same direction. The story of contemporary Delhi is one of the gradual *breaking away* of various groups from their historical relationships with centralised authority. Hardly anyone, from any stratum of society, lives as if they believed that governments will solve their problems. The poor have the most direct and necessary relationship with the state, but in the cities many of them have been battling with administrators for many years, and want nothing from them except to be left alone to build their own streets and houses and communities. The middle classes have little taste for what the state does: they do not wish to give to it and they do not wish to receive from it. Ideally they would seal themselves off from the broad currents of this country and exist in as privatised a way as possible; so they run to 'corporate cities' where they pay corporations to provide them with roads, parks and physical security. Many of the very rich, meanwhile, have taken control of politicians and political processes for their own ends, not the other way round. They have engineered a commercial system whose speed and efficiency derives from bypassing and subduing the state's mastery and independence.

What of these rich, some will ask? Can they not use their extraordinary influence to build institutions and infrastructure to organise Delhi's tumultuous energies that they might better nourish the future? In these oligarchic times, indeed, many have begun to feel that only the super-rich possess requisite the power and dynamism, anymore, to build anything of enduring significance. But somewhere in the back of this question, too, is twentieth-century New York. People remember the concert halls, libraries, museums, universities, public housing and all the rest built by the members of New York's gilded-age elite, and wonder when their upstart Delhi peers will take on this role. But that surprising impulse on the part of heedless capitalists to nurture their city and society is unlikely to be reproduced by the Delhi rich. And this is in part because they constitute – like the rich everywhere today – a deterritorialised elite. If the barons of early twentieth-century New York built libraries and opera houses with their own money because it was essential to their idea of success that their city resemble and surpass the great cities of Europe. New York was not only where they derived their income: it was the theatre of their lives and the signature of their arrival. They would create a 'New World' that would better the old: they would not send their sons to study on the other side of the world, in musty Oxford and Cambridge, they would build new, superior, American institutions. They were preoccupied by 'backwardness' in their local infrastructure and population because it was a slight on their own selves. But today's global elite is much less invested in local and even national spaces than the American elite of a century ago. Delhi does not hold the overwhelming significance for its super-rich that New York did for those earlier masters: it is just the place where they accumulate income, and they have rather little inclination to turn it into an urban masterpiece. They have no personal need of such an enterprise because they have become used to seeing the world's existing resources as their own: they do not need to build great universities for themselves because they have already been built for them – in the United States.

Such a feeling is not confined to Delhi. It applies to elites everywhere. Members of the Delhi elite are identical to their peers from Paris, Moscow or São Paulo – in that they possess houses in London, educate their children in the United States, holiday in St Tropez, use clinics in Lausanne, and keep their money – offshore, nowhere. That circumstance in which great quantities of private wealth were ploughed back into the needs and concerns of one place, which was 'our place', no longer pertains. Not here, not elsewhere.

Perhaps, too, we can talk of changes in the sense not only of space but of time. To build great works requires supreme confidence in future time, and this has everywhere diminished. Though capitalism's cycles of investment and return have always clamped down on eternity, somehow its very cruellest phase – during American slavery, for instance, or European imperialism – was able to sustain a more generous sense of the future, delivering to the world schools, hospitals, museums, libraries, universities, parks, public spaces and vital systems which continue to shape our existence today. But then in Europe and America it is difficult to find institutions of culture or learning built now that are imagined to last till, say, the year 2500. Contemporary Delhi, in this respect again, falls in with the general case.

In places where historical ruptures have been few or lenient, and where institutions have been allowed to flourish for many centuries, those institutions have often risen to global significance, in part because the expanse of time they hold within has become so exquisitely rare. Even in aggressively contemporary places like Delhi, people with resources and ambition send their children to universities that have often taken four centuries (Harvard) or even eight centuries (Oxford and Cambridge) to evolve. This is not just about 'brand names': it derives from an understanding that there are aspects of the development of an individual that require him or her to be immersed in much greater currents of time than are available in most of contemporary life. Learning is one of those areas: we understand, intuitively, that it is not possible to build up overnight what ancient institutions of learning possess. But we also know this about our own time: that we are able to use what our predecessors built far better than we are able to build for those to come. In this sense the short-termism of Delhi, the hyper-accelerated existence where everyone is trying to draw out whatever they can get before the whole resource is exhausted, is not just Delhi's problem. It is true that the ramifications of the problem are revealed most starkly in places like Delhi, whose own pre-modern institutions were laid bare, and so cannot block the view of twenty-first-century landscapes. But it is a problem of the global system, and one that may only be avoided if we can recover our sense of eternity – in disobedience to all accepted processes of contemporary thought and feeling.

If the city of Delhi is globally interesting, it is not because it is an example of a city on its way to maturity. It is interesting because it is *already mature*, and its maturity looks nothing like what we were led to expect, in times past, that mature global cities looked like. This city, with its broken public space, with its densely packed poor living close to some of the most sweeping, most sparsely populated areas of any big city anywhere in the world, with its aspiring classes desperately trying to lift themselves out of the pathetic condition of the city into a more dependable and self-sufficient world of private electricity supplies and private security – this is not some backward stage of world history. It is the world's future.

To look at contemporary Delhi is to look at the symptoms of the global twenty-first century in their most glaring and advanced form. We understand here, as we cannot in the centres of nineteenth- and twentieth-century capitalism, which will continue for some time with their old momentum, what a strange and disquieting reality it is, this one we are all heading towards.

The river along whose banks we walk, Anupam and I, is epic. Rising in the Himalayas, near the roof of the world, it flows south-east for more than 1,000 kilometres, passing Delhi and Agra, before pouring into its parallel sister, that other great Himalayan river, the Ganges, which carries its waters the rest of the way across the sub-continent to flood out, finally, into the Bay of Bengal.

The fertile alluvial plain between these two rivers nurtured the ancient Vedic culture which produced such achievements as the *Mahabharata*; the battle of Kurukshetra at the centre of this epic is said to have taken place on the Yamuna banks a couple of hundred kilometres north of Delhi. The place where the two rivers meet, just outside Allahabad, is a place of affecting natural grandeur: the Yamuna's dark waters run up against the light waters of the Ganges, and for kilometres they flow alongside each other in the basin, two unmixed strands, until finally their shades become one. Every twelve years, tens of millions of people gather at this site for the Kumbh Mela, the world's largest religious gathering, whose centrepiece consists of spiritual purification through immersion in the waters of the two sacred rivers.

Of the two, it is the Yamuna that has the more delicate and beautiful mythology. The name 'Yamuna' is a cognate of 'Yami'; Yama and Yami were, according to the Rig Veda, the first mortals: twins born of the sun god. Yami was filled with desire for her brother and tried to convince him that they should produce children together for the population of the earth; Yama was filled with horror and chose to die rather than to commit incest. Lacking offspring, he could never be freed from the realm of the dead. He became the god of death, keeping account of the life-time of all mortals. In some accounts he is a terrible, vengeful figure; in others a tragic one, weeping eternally over his painful duty of cutting beings from their lives.

Yami wept too: for the brother who had spurned her and whom she now would never see — and it was from these sisterly tears that the Yamuna river flowed. Born of grief, these waters had the power to absorb the sin and sorrow of the world, and gods and mortals alike swam in them to cleanse themselves of ill: this is how they turned so much darker than the cheerful Ganges. And Yamuna's sadness continued, for she fell in love with

Krishna, who was born by her side, who played in her waters as a child, whose love affairs unfolded on her wooded banks, and whose great philosophic discourse – recounted in the *Bhagavad Gita* – was delivered by her side; but Krishna left her behind and continued his dance elsewhere. So the Yamuna speaks of feminine melancholy: of the frustrated desire for love, fulfilment and male perfection.

Anupam and I have walked a long way, and the heat of the day has subsided. We have taken the route of the highway, and the river disappears from view for long periods at a time. Over our head a flyover is being constructed: cranes lift immense concrete sections into place.

"Now we are north of the city," says Anupam, "and you will see Wazirabad, where the British dammed the river."

We climb over the barrier at the side of the road and walk towards the river. There's a small shanty town on the banks and some strips of farmland. We come to the edge of a large, stinking channel.

"This is the largest sewage drain flowing into the river. All the sewage from north Delhi comes through here. This channel carries enormous volume. I would say it is six or seven metres deep."

The waters of this channel are like fast-flowing tar. Where they meet the banks, the earth is scorched of vegetation. Anupam and I are both coughing with the fumes. The smell is particular: it is not simply that of human excrement, though this is the base. It has also a vegetable richness, and notes of chemical pique.

"Do you want to hear something about this drain? The canal the Mughals built now empties into here. That canal, which brings crystal clear water from more than 100 kilometres away, which the Mughal emperor used to drink in his palace – the modern water administrators could not think what to do with it. So they just dumped that water into this drain so it could flow back into the Yamuna. Recently I was at a meeting with the Water Board and I told them this, and the head of the Water Board said, 'It is impossible.' I insisted, and he asked his staff to check, and they came back to him and said, 'It's true, Sir.' This is madness, because we are starved here not for water but for *clean* water. And the clean water we have, we mix with effluent without anyone ever using it."

I remember a line from the eighteenth-century poet, Mir: "My weeping eyes are like a canal, my ruined heart like the city of Delhi."

We climb up on a wall to look down at the sewage flowing into the river. The two water streams are of equal size just like, downriver, where the dark Yamuna meets the light Ganges, they are wary of each other for a while. Here it is the Yamuna that is light and the city's effluent that is dark: the two colours flow next to each other beneath us.

"Over there, on the other side, you can see the dam. Upstream from here. You can see all the pipelines taking clean water into the city, where it will be treated and distributed. Sewage comes out of the city back into the river, mostly untreated. This is the first sewage channel – as you can see it's just a couple of hundred metres south of the dam. There are many more such channels feeding into the river as you go southwards. There is a lot of solid waste in this sewage, which is another reason why the water level is constantly rising. The river is getting silted up."

It is difficult to breathe here, and we head back to the road.

"Now you understand why the river looks as it does," he says, climbing back over the fence. We have been walking for hours, and he is as strong and nimble as when we set out. "This is the mess that Delhi sends into the river, and this is what the river looks like to all the cities south of here. Mathura, where Krishna was born and where everyone goes to bathe in the river as he did, is foul. Agra too, where the Taj Mahal was built on the banks of this river. Only after Agra, where the Chambal river flows into the Yamuna, does the water get clean again. The Chambal is another huge river, and flushes out all this effluent from Delhi."

Anupam can see that I am shocked by what we have just seen, and he begins to laugh.

"You should not get depressed," he says. "Human beings have been on the planet for a very short time. Not more than 100,000 years. They have only been in this place for a few thousand years. Their own lives are extremely short. It is true that with technology we have gathered the power to damage this river very quickly. It hurts that it has been done in our lifetime. It should not have been done. But this damage will not last for long. The city is fighting a battle with the river, but the river is millions of years old and Delhi cannot win this battle. When there is no more Delhi the Yamuna will still flow, and it will be clean once more. It hurts to see this damage of course, but it never depresses me. It will be taken care of later. Of course that will not happen in my lifetime, but I do not have the ego to imagine that everything must happen during the short period I am on the earth. It will happen, and that is good enough. History is very long, and we are only a small part of it."

For the greater part of the world's population, the twentieth century was a period of immiseration and lost direction, and it supplies rather few sources of strength or inspiration for their condition today. The reason many of them have seized hold of the twenty-first century with such staggering energy is precisely because they are projected into it with ballistic force by their woeful experience of the twentieth, which, unlike in Europe and America, produces rather little nostalgia. Global capitalism is today stormed by warriors from many places, people for whom the past is cut off and who must therefore, in order to find a home, conquer the future.

The story we have told in this book, in which a place of dazzling wealth and cultural sophistication was taken over by a colonial power, in which that wealth and culture were shaken up and overturned, where a titanic power struggle led to a genocidal catastrophe, and where a post-colonial government undertook a massive project of economic engineering that ultimately exhausted itself and gave way to an energetic free-market backlash – this is, with some variations, the recent history of very much of the world. Of today's two hundred-odd independent nations, roughly one hundred and forty came into being after 1900; most emanated after the Second World War from Western European empires – as India did – or, after 1989, from the agglomeration of the Soviet Union – and most would find something of their own history in these pages. Mine is a local story, but it is also the story of the global majority. It is not extraordinary. It is the normal story of our age.

Until recently, the fully fledged market society continued to exist mainly in those regions – America and Western Europe – that had played the greatest role in inventing modern capitalism in the first place, and over the centuries these regions had been able to come to some sort of truce between society and their volatile progeny. They had overcome their moral repugnance towards its promotion of materialism and greed, and they had developed a philosophical infrastructure which brought to the market society some sense of right and meaningful existence. They had built extra-market social mechanisms to mitigate some of its more terrible human ravages, and they had set up limits to the market's dominion – to ensure the well-being of the poor and sick, for instance, or to maintain the integrity of leisure time and culture. Though they all went through enormous social violence and suffering as the waves of capitalist development passed through their peoples – Victor Hugo and Charles Dickens provide enduring parables of these trials – these societies continued to 'own' capitalism, to believe in its benign potential, and to feel that it could always be turned to new and better ends.

The billions who were abruptly ushered into global capitalism towards the end of the twentieth century had never reached this historical accommodation with it. Most of them, in fact, had spent the better part of the twentieth century being told that global capitalism was the source of all evil and that they should never succumb to it. It was not their system to shape or direct: it was built by foreigners who were traditionally thought of as heartless, spiritless imperialists – and they had a completely different sense of what it was, how it should be used and what it could do for them. They entered it, often, with enormous exhilaration and fervour, certainly, but also with great anxieties: that it would bring only unhappiness, that it would destroy too much, that it would make them resemble those Westerners whose greed and lack of values used to be such an important moral reassurance. The fact that, in the face of capitalism, they chose both to give and to deny themselves more totally than Westerners, the fact that they came to it with very different religious and philosophical histories, made it impossible to read their future out of the Western past. It was clear that they would find very different ways of accommodating capitalism into their social fabric, and that in so doing they would change the nature of the capitalist system itself.

In addition to all this, many of these places brought to the global table the legacy of immense historical traumas which had not been much processed in their societies. Since many of these traumas had had a profound effect on *economic* identities – on trust and suspicion with regard to strangers and contracts, on notions of wealth and poverty, private and common property – there was every reason to believe that this legacy would flood out into the functioning of the global system. We have become used to accepting the global force of the Jewish holocaust, which began to shape world politics, economy and culture from the moment it happened; but many of these other events, such as the partition of India, were 'global' events too, even if for a long time their effects were mostly confined to the place where they happened, and their inner contours remained obscure to the rest of the world. There was not only India's Partition: there were also the mass famines of Stalin's Soviet Union; Mao's Cultural Revolution; the destruction of rural life in Brazil under the military dictatorship, and the accompanying shock urbanisation. Who could tell what residue remained of the 1950s famine that killed tens of millions of Chinese under Mao's Great Leap Forward? – for even its most basic facts were still so unclear that it was impossible to tell how it might shape those survivors and their descendants who were now engaging with capitalism's very different economy of scarcity and abundance. As these old events detonated belatedly into global space they would become part of universal history. Like the holocaust they would be taught in schools everywhere as 'our' history. The entire world would inherit their shock.

The dramatic expansion of the reach of global capitalism would change it profoundly. It was clear that things would get a lot wilder. Many new centres entered global capitalism ready to wage not peace but war. Many of them had had their faith in the idea of 'society' badly damaged, and, at a time when many of the world's most pressing problems required the action of a collective global society, it was uncertain what role these warriors would play. It was clear that the creation of this 'global society' would require enormous empathy between world peoples and cultures. Only so could the vast bulk of newcomers feel any sense of investment in the system itself, or any faith that it was anything but a winner-take-all racket, in which the only reasonable objective was to belong to the small class of exploiters rather than the much larger mass of the exploited.

But it was clear also that the system's experiential and philosophical base would be greatly broadened with the advent of these new members, who had not lost their sense of capitalism's strangeness. It was certain that that this alone would produce radical new insights and visions. It was possible indeed that it might lead to an epochal efflorescence of world civilisation – the creativity and sophistication of which were the preconditions, anyway, for the system to realise its utopian, and not its apocalyptic, potential.

There is one last spot that Anupam wants to show me on the river. We have walked on, upstream from the dam at Wazirabad, and we have lost sight of the water. Anupam asks people how to get to the spot he is looking for; everyone gives contradictory directions. It is bizarre just how difficult it is to find this great river.

"I have not been here for twenty years," he says, "and everything has changed. None of this was built last time I was here."

We start walking down a busy road that is supposed to lead where he wants to go. The potholed road is being re-laid. A water truck pours water into a cement mixer; like all water trucks it is also leaking from every corner, so that the road is flooded. We get to the end of the road and climb over a wall. A boy is burning a foam mattress in order to retrieve the steel from the springs inside; the foam burns with a fierce flame which fills the place with toxic black smoke. Anupam covers his mouth with his handkerchief.

We are in a sort of wasteland where a row of brick houses is being built. Construction work seems to have been abandoned for months, and three-metre-tall golden grasses grow rapturously out of the unfinished brick rectangles. Washing lines are slung between trees, and the ground is covered with unused bricks.

"This entire area is in the flood plain," says Anupam. "All these houses will be flooded in the monsoon. That is why no one built here until now. But land has become so valuable that people will even build in places that are not habitable for part of the year."

We can see the river in the distance. We cross the hard soil. Bits of ancient pillars are lying half buried in the ground. We reach a cluster of small temples. And then, before us, is the Yamuna: blue, tranquil, magnificent.

I gasp with the sight of it.

"Yes," says Anupam sympathetically. "One can never believe that the river can be like this."

This is not the black, sludgy channel we have been following all day. This is the primordial river, clear and fecund.

We are in every sense, 'before' Delhi. Before the river meets the city. Before the city was ever here.

Boys paddle gleefully in the water. Families of moorhens glide across its surface. Rowing boats are moored at the river's edge, where you can see two metres to the bottom. In the middle of the river is a belt of golden reeds; the opposite bank must be a couple of kilometres away. Bright blue kingfishers chirp shrilly in the trees, which lean desirously over the water. A woman collects river water in a plastic canister.

We sit down on the steps to look at the river. Nearby a group of men is playing cards under a peepul tree. One of them is a naked sadhu.

"I don't know why they have to put up these temples," says Anupam. "This is pure encroachment: some businessman who thinks he needs a shrine to himself next to the Yamuna and pays some bureaucrat to let him build here. I would be surprised if God would feel like visiting such ugly things."

And he adds, "But they too will pass away. The river will do the work."

We are in that altered soundscape of a river estuary, the sounds clear over the surface of the water. Birds call out across large distances.

The horizon is open, and it is a relief. I realise how consumed my being has become by the internal drama of my dense adopted city. I have forgotten expansiveness. This megalopolis, where everything is vast, somehow offers little opportunity to see further than across the street. Everything is blocked off. Your eyes forget how to focus on the infinite.

"I'm glad you could see this," says Anupam. "Now you realise why Delhi is here. It is one of the beautiful places of the earth."

Acknowledgements

The conversations I had with the individuals who appear in this book were one of the great privileges of my life. Since I have concealed their identities in order to protect their privacy, my gratitude, too, must remain anonymous; but I thank each one of them devoutly, nonetheless, for the candour and enthusiasm with which they gave of their experiences.

I thank also my parents, not so much for sharing their stories with me, as for the courage with which they lived them in the first place.

Capital owes much to discussions with inspiring friends and acquaintances, of whom the following is surely an incomplete list: Moushmi Basu, Gautam Bhan, Gautam Bhatia, Shalini Bhutani, Arani Bose, Eisha Chopra, Taru Dalmia, William Dalrymple, Puru Das, Veena Das, Sapna Desai, Ashish Dhawan, Raseel Gujral, Satish Gujral, Pankaj Vir Gupta, Deepti Kapoor, Raghu Karnad, Bharti Kher, Martand Khosla, Romi Khosla, Nadine Kreisberger, Siddhartha Lokanandi, Diya Mehra, Pratap Bhanu Mehta, Anurag Mishra, Rajat Mitra, Geetika Narang, Reena Nath, Nandan Nilekani, Ritesh Pandey, Basharat Peer, Gary Reid, Pradip Saha, Vivek Sahni, Aditi Saraf, Chiki Sarkar, Jonathan Shainin, Abhishek Sharan, Sher Singh, Ayesha Sood, Jyoti Thottam, Madhu Trehan and Ashutosh Varshney.

During those interviews that took place in Hindi, Mihir Pandya was much more than an able interpreter. Deepak Mehta and Ashis Nandy were wise and inspiring mentors. I gained enormously from the visionary suggestions and generous contributions of Ashish Mahajan, Kanta Murali, Ayesha Punvani and Anand Vivek Taneja, to whom I am especially grateful.

The companionship, intellectual and otherwise, of Bhrigupati Singh and Prerna Singh was foundational, as always.

Without my amazing daughter, Amália, I would not have been capable of writing *Capital* at all. Thank you, thank you, my love.

NOTES

1. Vivek Narayanan, 'In the Early Days of the Delhi Metro', 2005, in Sudeep Sen (ed), *The HarperCollins Book of English Poetry* (HarperCollins India, 2012), p. 528

2. Mike Davis, *Late Victorian Holocausts: El Niño Famines and the Making of the Third World* (Verso, 2002), pp. 9–21

3. Jawarharlal Nehru, *Soviet Russia: Some Random Sketches and Impressions* (1928), p. 3

4. *New York Times*, 29 June 1991

5. Indeed $10 million *was* loose change to Gary Wendt, who was one of America's highest-paid executives. The year after his meeting with Raman Roy, he paid $20 million to his ex-wife, Lorna, as a divorce settlement. In 2000 he became one of the small group of American executives to earn over $100 million a year when he became chairman and CEO of the financial services giant Conseco. One of the first things he did when he joined the new company was to outsource all Conseco's back-office operations to India.

6. Some months after this interview it was announced that Manish Arora and Paco Rabanne were parting ways for undisclosed mutual reasons.

7. See *The Hindu*, 12 April 2011

8. Akash Kapur, 'How India Became America', *New York Times*, 9 March 2012

9. Quoted in 'Clinton Urges Indian High-Tech Leaders to Help Poor', *Washington Post*, 25 March 2000

10. 'Obama's Passage to India: What He Needs to Do', *Time*, 2 November 2010

11. 'The Prize is India', *Newsweek*, 20 November 2009

12. See for instance the 1966 novel *Mitro Marjani* (translated from Hindi into English as *To Hell With You Mitro*) by Krishna Sobti, which portrays a sensual young woman whose greed for experience causes many disruptions in her husband's household; it is her mother-in-law who stands by her and defends her, in a kind of female solidarity, from the aggression of the family's men, including her own son.

13. Partha Chatterjee, 'The Nationalist Resolution of the Women's Question', in Kumkum Sangari and Sudesh Vaid (eds), *Recasting Women: Essays in Indian Colonial History* (Rutgers University Press, 1990), pp. 237–9

14. My thanks to Anand Vivek Taneja for this translation.

15. Compiled from Emma Roberts' parallel accounts of Delhi in *Scenes and Characteristics of Hindostan with Sketches of Anglo-Indian Society* (1835) and *Views in India, China and on the Shores of the Red Sea* (1835); spellings modernised.

16. Thanks to Basharat Peer for both introducing me to and translating this poem.

17. Letter from 1857 quoted in Ralph Russell and Khurshidul Islam (eds), *Ghalib 1797–1869: Life and Letters* (Oxford University Press India, 1997), p. 148

18. Letter from 1861 quoted in Russell & Islam, *Ghalib*, p. 252

19. Quoted in Malvika Singh and Rudrangshu Mukherjee, *New Delhi: Making of a Capital* (Lustre Press, 2009), p. 22.

20. Guido Gozzano, *Journey Toward the Cradle of Mankind*, translated by David Marinelli, 1913 (reprinted Marlboro Press, 1996), pp. 124–30.

21. Quoted in Singh & Mukherjee, *New Delhi*, p. 22

22. Khushwant Singh, 'My Father the Builder' in Maya Dayal (ed), *Celebrating Delhi* (Penguin, 2010), pp. 2–11

23. My thanks to Basharat Peer for this English translation of Colonel Oberoi's poem.

24. Urvashi Butalia, *The Other Side of Silence* (Penguin, 1998), p. 3; I am indebted to this book, too, for the historical summary which follows.

25. See Pavan K. Varma, *Krishna: The Playful Divine* (Penguin India, 1995), pp. 61, 206 and note 19

26. Veena Das, *Life and Words: Violence and the Descent into the Ordinary* (University of California Press, 2007), p. 23

27. Das, *Life and Words*, p. 29

28. 'What Makes Delhiites Kill?', *Hindustan Times*, 10 January 2010

29. 'Confession of Vikas Before Cops', *Times of India*, 29 May 2008

30. In the interests of protecting identities, this section is compiled from two separate interviews.

31. Quoted in Marshall Berman, *All That is Solid Melts into Air: The Experience of Modernity* (Verso, 1983), p. 88

32. The fortunes of the Indian Coffee House declined with the advent of corporate café chains, and in 2011 it was announced that it was unable to cover its rental payments to the city, and would shut down. The *Hindustan Times* understated the institution's age by more than a decade in its report, 'After 42 Years, Sun to Finally Set on Indian Coffee House', *Hindustan Times*, 14 July 2011.

33. Philip Bowring, 'Maoists Who Menace India', *New York Times*, 17 April 2006

34. *Delhi Human Development Report*, Oxford University Press New Delhi, 2006

35. 'Parents of Nithari Kids Claim to Have Seen Dr Amit Kumar at the Infamous D-5 House of Pandher', *Midday*, 11 February 2008

36. Dr N. Rangarajan, quoted in teesutalk.blogspot.in

37. Quoted in 'Inside Nithari Killer's Mind: "Would Watch Girls Come In, Even I Felt the Urge"', *The Indian Express*, 12 October 2009

38. Quoted in 'Nithari Murder: SC Upholds Death Sentence for Koli', *The Indian Express*, 16 February 2011

39. 'Portrait of Evil', *India Today*, 22 January 2007; I owe to this article the majority of my detail about the Nithari crimes.

40. Quoted in 'Portrait of Evil', *India Today*, 22 January 2007

41. I am grateful to Raghu Karnad for this anecdote.

42. S. Mulgaokar, 'The Grimmest Situation in 19 Years', *Hindustan Times*, 3 November 1966, quoted in Ramachandra Guha, *India After Gandhi: The History of the World's Largest Democracy* (Pan Macmillan Delhi, 2008), p. 415

43. Guha, *India After Gandhi*, p. 569

44. Das, *Life and Words*, pp. 113–4

45. Das, *Life and Words*, p. 168

46. 'Key Players in Bofors Scandal', *India Today*, 28 April 2009

47. Michael Walton and Aditi Gandhi, 'Where Do India's Billionaires Get Their Wealth?', *Economic and Political Weekly*, 6 October 2012, pp. 10–14

48. 'Lok Sabha Polls to Cost More than US Presidential Election', *Mint*, 1 March 2009

49. Dev Kar, 'The Drivers and Dynamics of Illicit Financial Flows from India: 1948–2008' (Global Financial Integrity, Washington DC, 2010)

50. Pranab Mukherjee, 'Black Money: White Paper' (Ministry of Finance, New Delhi, 2012)

51. This conversation took place in 2010, when Russian oligarch Boris Berezovsky was living in exile in England. In March 2013, he was discovered dead in his Berkshire home following his probable suicide.

52. From an account given on the DLF corporate website (2010).

53. 'Guptas in Spotlight over South African Dealings', *The National*, 19 March 2011

54. 'Guptas', *The National*

55. 'The Gupta Interview: A Peek Behind the Sahara Curtain into the "Gupta Desert"', *Business Day*, 4 March 2011

56. 'The State of the World's Children' (United Nations Children's Fund, 2013); and 'Delhi Development Report' (Planning Commission, Government of India, 2013)

57. 'Sprinting to Disaster', *India Today*, 25 September 2010

PERMISSIONS

Every effort has been made to trace copyright holders and obtain their permission for the use of copyright material. The publisher apologises for any errors or omissions and would be grateful to be notified of any corrections that should be incorporated in future reprints or editions of this book.

Epigraph from *The Rise and Fall of the City of Mahagonny* © Kurt Weill & Bertolt Brecht, Bloomsbury Methuen Drama. Extract from "My Father the Builder" by Khushwant Singh, reproduced from the title *Celebrating Delhi* with due permission from the publisher, Penguin Books India and the Editor, Mala Dayal. Extract from *The Other Side of Silence* by Urvashi Butalia, reproduced with due permission from the publisher, Penguin Books India and the Editor, Mala Dayal. Extract from *Life and Words: Violence and the Descent into the Ordinary* by Veena Das, © 2007 by the Regents of the University of California. Published by the University of California Press. Extract from *India After Gandhi* by Ramachandra Guha, Copyright © 2007 by Ramachandra Guha, reprinted by permission of HarperCollins Publishers. Chapter Seventeen epigraph, quoted from and reproduced by kind permission of Delhi Sultanate, rapper.

Index